THE NEGRO PEASANT TURNS CITYWARD

Effects of Recent Migrations to Northern Centers

BY

LOUISE VENABLE KENNEDY, Ph.D.

McGrath Publishing Company
College Park, Maryland

Reprint McGrath Publishing Company 1969
Library of Congress Catalog Card Number: 75-84099

Manufactured in the United States of America
by Arno Press, Inc., New York

FOREWORD

THE present volume is the first of several which are to appear as a result of research conducted during the last four years under subsidy by the Social Science Research Council and the Columbia University Council for Research in the Social Sciences. Grants were made for the specific study of *Negro* population movements. Financial support had been solicited for what seemed to be a relatively small part of the general field of internal migration, which had assumed great importance in the light of the immigration quota laws of 1921 and 1924.

During the entire period of freedom, Negroes have voluntarily moved from the South to the North and West. At times the migration has been large-scale and far-flung. At others it has been a slow-moving and narrow current. Conditions in the North and South during the World War produced an unprecedented flood. From 1915 until 1920 thousands daily left southern farms and plantations at the call of industry in the North and in the Central West. There are indications that since the latter date the channels opened by the war-time demand have continued to carry strong currents. In many northern centers the complexion of the city has been greatly altered and new and emergent social situations created.

Much has been written regarding Negro migration. The first requisite, therefore, has been careful scrutiny of the vast amount of material already in print on the subject. During the years 1926 to 1929 Miss Kennedy has devoted herself to careful and exhaustive work on an annotated bibliography. In this quest, the entire literature on the subject

5

from 1890 to date has been combed, and most of the material prior to 1890 has been covered.

Modern sociologists, welcoming the seeming precision that the statistical method affords, have tended to begin their attack on a field of research by gathering detailed information for large numbers of individuals or by applying mathematical methods to published numerical series. All too often the result is mere demonstration of the obvious or reiteration of what has already long been accepted.

It is an open question whether vast volumes of statistics can throw any greater light on many topics of sociological import than can the carefully weighed opinions of a considerable number of individuals so placed as to have had adequate opportunity for large-scale investigation and with the necessary mental qualifications to arrive at sound generalizations from their experience. This is probable particularly when the opinions are expressed after elaborate survey by statistical and other approaches. Throughout the country there have been many well-trained individuals who have been careful students of Negro population trends. Furthermore, situations have developed in many localities, particularly in the North, which have necessitated elaborate and painstaking investigation. Until now no one has synthesized these scattered opinions and survey results to discover wherein there is practically universal agreement and wherein there is confusion.

The Negro Peasant Turns Cityward—while containing a brief background description of the migration of Negroes and the causes which produced these movements—is concerned primarily with the effects of migration upon the Negro migrants themselves, on the northern Negro group, on members of other races resident in the North, and upon the institutions in the centers in which the newcomers have settled. The period covered is that since 1915, and the scene is laid in various cities throughout the North; these are the years

during which movement has been maximum, and these the
goals of the vast bulk of those who moved. Further, it is
in northern cities during the past fifteen years that the most
thorough studies and the most careful observations have been
made.

The volume is decidedly unusual in method of treatment.
In the several chapters various significant aspects have been
discussed. The author has in each instance placed first such
generalizations as legitimately could be drawn from the mass
of information. Interlarded between these are summariza-
tions and specific citations which substantiate. The reader
finds it easy to make a quick survey of the entire field and
wherever his interest is most keen, to go into fuller detail.
The carefully prepared bibliography in the Appendix is referred to in the footnote references by number, page designa-
tions being usually given. Supplementing and elaborating
these, the second part of the Appendix comprehends an exhaustive topical arrangement of the bibliographical material,
much more full than the footnote references, and making it
possible for the student of a particular phase to reach the
available literature in the very shortest time. Many citations
which constitute mere re-wording of previously published
material are not included, however.

The usefulness of the volume will be extensive. No finer
introduction to the study of modern municipal conditions in
the North is available today. Research workers dealing with
the effects of migration will find it indispensable, and as a
source book for those interested in race problems it is of
highest value.

Frank Alexander Ross

PREFACE

NEGRO migration is by no means a new phenomenon in the United States, for it has been present ever since the first introduction of colored slaves. During the pre-Civil War days these movements, of course, were not voluntary but depended on the sale of slaves to plantation owners. As new lands were opened up in the far South and in the Southwest, planters took with them the colored laborers who were necessary for the operation of their farms. After Emancipation Negroes continued to move from one section of the South to another; sometimes spontaneously in the effort to find unoccupied land, sometimes at the instigation of outside agencies (such as the Freedman's Bureau or colored leaders who at various times stirred up a regular exodus of Negroes), and in other instances, at the command of plantation owners to whom they were bound by financial obligations. Until the World War the major trend of these movements of Negroes had been South and West, for it was only in this direction that agricultural workers were needed and the colored people have always been predominantly farm laborers.

Throughout our history the Negroes have constituted a peasant element in our population, for as a mass, they have been restrained in the rural areas of the South. During the days of slavery their principal occupation was that of tilling the land and they had no chance to escape from the plantations. Since the Civil War they have continued to be bound to the soil because they have lacked money and experience with which to break into other fields. Many of them, too, have been subjected to practical peonage, since in some of the southern states a tenant farmer is required to stay with his land owner as long as he is in debt to him. By seeing to it that the colored tenant has not been able to secure enough profit from his year's work to pay off his obligations, the owners have frequently succeeded in keeping Negroes on the land even against their will.

In recent decades there has been a movement to southern cities where colored workers have found positions in common labor, and domestic and personal service. During the World War period the demand for laborers in northern industries provided an opportunity for Negroes to turn from the cultivation of the land to the urban life of the North. The years since 1915 have witnessed an enormous increase in the Negro population of northern cities. Whether these colored workers have come directly from the farms or from a short sojourn in southern cities, their migration is linked with the trend from the open country, which has been characteristic of all peoples in recent decades. At last the Negro is ceasing to be simply a tiller of the soil, and is entering a wider range of economic activities.

The present study is concerned only with the effects of colored migration to northern centers in the last fifteen years. The author realizes full well that it covers only a small field and omits many ramifications which are significant and important. This northward trend of southern Negroes has inevitably affected the white people of the South and the colored who have remained behind. Furthermore, the effects of recent movements are closely linked with the economic and social conditions in the South and with situations resulting from previous migrations to cities of the North. The whole subject of Negro migration is so vast that it has been necessary in this monograph to make such a temporal and geographical selection.

The shift to the North since about 1915 is especially important (1) because a large number of individuals have been involved; (2) because those migrating have entered a totally new environment; and (3) because the whites have been obliged to adapt themselves to a sudden tremendous increase in a single population group. Factors such as these constitute one of the most vitally important subjects for sociological investigation.

The rapid increase of Negroes in northern cities has led to numerous studies of the resulting conditions, for it was clearly evident that this alteration in the numerical composition of a distinct ethnic element must inevitably affect the social processes of the groups within which they settled. It has naturally been impossible for the same person or committee to make a careful study of conditions in all sections and cities of the North, and unfortunately, there has been a general tendency among writers on race problems to take the findings of one or two investigations and apply these conclusions to the entire North.

Attempt is here made to summarize the conclusions of leading students of race problems who from long experience are familiar with conditions throughout the North, and to check these by synthesis of various special surveys and by governmental statistics, particularly those of the Census Bureau. The method, which is applicable to many fields of study, is that of amassing opinions and comparing them with available factual material. Such comparisons enable us to check up current conflicting opinions and beliefs in the light of actuality. In some cases we can arrive at definite conclusions, and in others point the way to further needed investigations.

The source material which has been used in this study does not cover all the literature dealing with the effects of Negro movements to northern cities. A full bibliography on the subject will be published elsewhere. The present study deals only with those sources which are considered most significant

and valuable and which are, for the most part, available for
other readers and hence are likely to play a part in the
thinking of the layman on this subject of Negro migration
and race problems.   In all more than a thousand titles were
carefully examined, and from these there was compiled the
present bibliography consisting of 247 specific references.
These constitute the bulk of the significant and relevant
documents.

A brief description of the principal characteristics of recent
movements is found in Chapter 1.   No attempt has been made
to give a complete picture of Negro migration.   The extent
and nature of the population shifts which have occurred during the last fifteen years are dealt with only at sufficient
length to furnish a background for the rest of the study.
Likewise, the discussion in Chapter II of the causes of migration is limited to a consideration of only the principal and
outstanding factors which have motivated the recent influx
of Negroes to the North.   Few specific references to source
material are given in these background chapters; in each case
the discussion is the result of a synthesis of the sources listed
in the classified bibliography.   Chapter III contains in Table
8 the information found in leading surveys of specific cities,
so that knowledge of the material concerning a particular city
or subject is at once available.   Table 9, in the same chapter,
indicates the subjects covered by certain investigators or
committees in various sections of the North.   Consequently,
if a student is interested in a particular city, he should supplement Table 8 by referring to the descriptions appended
to Table 9, wherein will be found the specific cities covered
by the surveys listed in that Table.

Chapters IV to XII deal with major economic and social
effects of this rapid growth of Negro groups in northern
cities.   Although Washington, D. C., and Baltimore are
border cities and do not strictly belong in this survey, refer-

ences to conditions in these two places are occasionally included, both because Negroes consider themselves as getting into the North when they migrate to either of these localities, and because conditions in these centers provide a control situation with which to compare typically northern cities.

In these chapters the method of presenting the general conclusions which have been derived from a comparison and synthesis of reports and discussions on the several subjects is different from that usually followed. It consists, first, in the author's generalizations, followed by substantiating summaries and quotations from the source material. These latter have been segregated from the former by indentation in order to make a sharp distinction between the author's deductions and the basic data. Footnote references, giving specific page citation, refer by number to the alphabetically arranged bibliography in the Appendix. Chapter XIII summarizes the major conclusions and the recommendations which have developed out of the critical analysis.

Undoubtedly some of the reports here used are partial and far from being as comprehensive as might be desired. Further, there is certainly considerable difference in the reliability of the several studies. However, they furnish material for comparison and checking with each other, and in combination with more elaborate studies and with opinions of leading students, indicate significant trends and phases in the interrelations of whites and Negroes in northern cities, and in the adjustment of the migrants to their new environment.

The Appendix contains a general bibliography, which constitutes an amplification of the footnote citations in the various chapters. (Part A.) It does not include every reference to the subject. Those that have been omitted are mere repetitions of earlier discussions by the same or another author, and those which have been found to make no new contributions. In Part B the references have been classified by subject matter so that a student interested in a particular topic, such as the causes of migration, or the health or educational situation among Negroes in the North, can easily find the available published material which is relevant.

Summarizing as it does the theories and factual data published to date (early 1930) on the subject of the effects of Negro migration to northern cities, this study enables students of race problems in the North readily to grasp the material already at hand on the subject. It also indicates those phases which so far have been most fully investigated, and points the way to further research.

The author is grateful to the Harlem Library, in which the extensive collection of material proved very useful, and to the National Urban League and its official publication, *Opportunity,* and finally to those individuals and groups, who, faced with practical exigencies calling for prompt solution, have pushed through the surveys which constitute the basis of this study. She also wishes to express her indebtedness to Professor Frank A. Ross for his invaluable assistance and encouragement during the carrying out of this study, and to thank Professors Robert M. MacIver, Robert E. Chaddock, and Alvan A. Tenney for the criticisms and suggestions which they have offered. Grateful acknowledgment is given to Dorothy R. Ross for her help in editing the manuscript and correcting the proof.

L. V. K.

COLUMBIA UNIVERSITY, APRIL, 1930.

CONTENTS

CHAPTER XII

MIGRATION AND SOCIAL CONTACTS

SECTION III

CONCLUSION

CHAPTER XIII

SUMMARY AND RECOMMENDATIONS

APPENDIX

LIST OF TABLES

SECTION I

INTRODUCTORY

CHAPTER I

Characteristics of Recent Negro Migrations

MIGRATION of people from one section of the country to another has at all times been a conspicuous phenomenon in the history of the United States. From the days of the first colonization of the Atlantic seacoast there has been a continuous, general flow of population. The movements of colored people have constituted an important phase of this perpetual flux of inhabitants, for migration of Negroes is likewise no new phenomenon. At the close of every census period statistics of the birth-place and residence of Negroes have indicated a steady movement of colored people from one section to another within the South, from rural areas to urban centers, and from the South to the North and West, or from the latter to the South. The movements which were apparent during the inter-census period 1910 to 1920 were especially significant because they revealed a decided increase in the volume of migration and a peculiar change in the major direction and the length of the moves which were made.

According to the 1920 census the proportion of Negroes who had moved from one state to another was larger than it had ever been in previous decades. (See Table I.)

The major part of the increased volume of migration among colored people took the form of a movement out of the South, and during these ten years the North and West showed a net gain of over 330,000 Negroes. Although this number is considerably less than was generally estimated at the time the migration was at its height, yet it is sufficiently large to involve important economic and social consequences, particularly since there was a distinct trend toward those states and sections of the country where the Negroes had previously been almost inconspicuous because of their small

TABLE I.—NEGROES BORN IN THE UNITED STATES AND LIVING IN STATE OTHER THAN THAT OF BIRTH

(Source: *Fourteenth Census,* 1920, vol. ii, p. 623; and Bureau of the Census, *Negro Population in the United States, 1790-1915,* p. 71.)

Year	Number	Per cent
1920	2,054,242	19.9
1910	1,616,608	16.6
1900	1,373,996	15.6

numbers.   A relatively large increase in such communities connotes more noticeable results than would the same aggregate increase in a community where Negroes formed a larger proportion of the total population and where race relations were already established on the basis of large numbers.

This rapid addition to the number of colored people in the North was also significant because, for the most part, it was crowded into the latter half of the decade and particularly the years 1916 to 1918, when the flow of Negroes to the North became so noticeable that much excitement and discussion were aroused both in the North and South and among white and colored groups.

In considering the increase in Negro population by finer divisions, rather than by general sections of the country, it is evident that during this decade the largest proportionate gains were in the northern states.   In the states of the Middle Atlantic and East and West North Central divisions there were very large numerical, as well as proportionate, gains. It was into the cities of these areas that the Negroes thronged. In the southern divisions, the South Atlantic and East and

PER CENT CHANGE OF NEGRO POPULATION,* 1910-1920

(Source: *Fourteenth Census*, 1920, vol. ii, pp. 38-46)

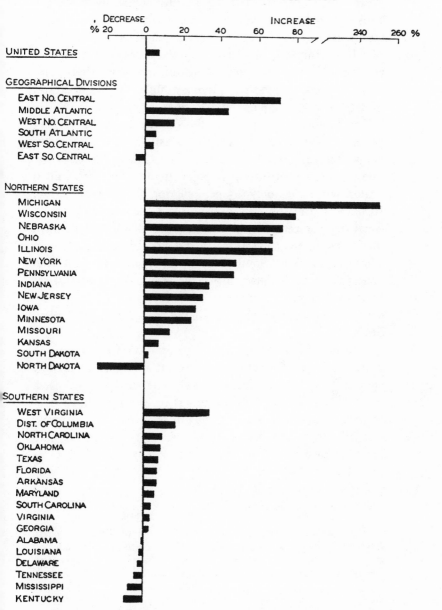

* New England, Mountain and Pacific States are omitted because the absolute numbers involved are very small.

West South Central, there were either actual numerical decreases or gains so small that when compared with gains in
earlier decades they must be interpreted as actual decreases.
The New England, Mountain and Pacific regions contained
very few Negroes in 1910.   Consequently, small drifts into
these sections resulted in extremely high rates of increase,
which, however, were not significant.[1]

The Middle Atlantic states showed an increase of over 43
per cent among Negroes, while the East North Central states
had an increase of 71 per cent.   This is far in excess of the
rate of increase for the Negro population of the entire United
States, which was only 6.5 per cent for the ten-year period.
In none of the southern divisions did the rate of increase
equal 6.5 per cent and in the East South Central division
there was an actual decrease in the colored population.   In
addition, the West South Central division, which had been
one of the conspicuous goals of the previous migrations, reveals an insignificant increase when its rate of gain is compared to the average gain of all the Negroes in the United
States.

Further indication of a large migration from South to
North is seen in a comparison of the increases in specific
states of the two sections.   It is clear from the chart that a
percentage increase of 47.9 per cent for New York, of 67.1
for Illinois, of 251.0 for Michigan is in startling contrast
to such a rate of increase as 2.8 per cent in Virginia, and
to a decrease of 7.4 in Mississippi.   Not only were large
numbers of Negroes flocking to those states which had
previously received the major part of the migrations from
the South, such as New York, Pennsylvania and Ohio, but

---

[1] For absolute numbers the reader is referred to Table 6, vol. ii,
Fourteenth Census. Great caution should always be used in drawing
conclusions from percentage changes where the base is very small. This
situation does not prevail in the other divisions.

at the same time they were moving to some of the more northern states (e. g. Michigan and Wisconsin) which before 1910 had shown little attraction for colored people. On the other hand, few of the southern states showed gains to any extent in excess of the average rate of increase for all Negroes and were losing rather than attracting colored people. West Virginia, as usual, was a striking exception, as the mining interests in that state continued to draw colored laborers. Florida and Arkansas, which in previous decades had been the chief points of attraction, did little more than keep up with the average gain of the Negroes in the entire country, while all of the West South Central states showed decreases in their colored population.

The migration which began during the World War is significant because of the direction of the movement as well as because of its extent. Whereas the major trend of previous movements had been south and west with a continuous but comparatively slight drift to the North, this latest migration was characterized by an entirely unprecedented shift to the North and East.

Within any given decade Negroes have migrated in all directions, but the major trend or net result of such movements is indicated by the " center of the Negro population " as it has been computed after each census enumeration.[1] Such an estimated point, of course, gives no definite information concerning the volume of the shift during a decade, since counter currents of migration would tend to neutralize each other. Yet it does suggest the dominant direction in which Negroes have moved within a given period.

[1] For a discussion of "center of population" see *Fourteenth Census,* 1920, vol. i, p. 32; and W. C. Eells, "A Mistaken Conception of the Center of Population," *Journal of the American Statistical Association,* vol. xxv, pp. 33-41, March 1930.

TABLE 2.—CENTER OF THE NEGRO POPULATION, 1790, 1880-1920

(Source: Bureau of the Census, *Negro Population in the United States 1790-1915*, p. 41; *Negro Year Book 1925-26*, p. 441.)

Census Year	Approximate Location of Center by Important Towns	Decennial Movement in Miles
1790	25 miles west-southwest of Petersburg, Dinwiddie County, Virginia	
1880	10.4 miles east of Lafayette, Walker County, Georgia	443 miles southwest
1890	15.7 miles southwest of Lafayette, Walker County, Georgia	20.5 miles southwest
1900	10.7 miles northeast of Fort Payne, Dekalb County, Alabama	9.5 miles southwest
1910	5.4 miles north-northeast of Fort Payne, Dekalb County, Alabama	5.8 miles west-southwest
1920	1.8 miles north-northeast of Rising Fawn, Georgia	21.5 miles northeast

According to the 1920 Census, all of the states in the far South showed a decrease in the number of Negroes born in the border states. Moreover, such states as Florida, Alabama, Mississippi, Louisiana, Arkansas and Texas, which had previously registered a large number of Negroes coming from other southern divisions, showed a decrease in immigration from practically every state hitherto acting as an important feeder for these newer regions. For example, by 1910 Arkansas and Texas had drawn large numbers of migrants from Tennessee, Kentucky, Alabama, Georgia and other more northern and eastern states. In 1920, however, the only important sources of immigration were found to be Louisiana and Mississippi; there was a decided loss in the number of migrants from the remaining states.

In contrast to this decrease in the number of Negroes migrating to southern states, the chief industrial sections of the North received a significant increase in the number of colored people born in the South.   New York, for instance, revealed the following contrasts in 1910 and 1920.[1]

Negroes Living in		Born in		
New York	N. Car.	S. Car.	Ga.	
1920	13,326	13,102	8,650	
1910	10,283	6,698	3,792	

Pennsylvania in 1920 also showed a gain in the number of southern-born Negroes.

Negroes Living in			Born in			
Pennsylvania	Va.	N. Car.	S. Car.	Ga.	Fla.	Ala.
1920......	60,843	16,664	11,624	16,196	5,370	9,994
1910......	48,995	9,735	2,113	1,578	393	545

Similar increases of colored immigrants were found in the East North Central region, of which Illinois and Ohio are the most important industrial states.

Negroes Living in			Born in			
Illinois	Ky.	Tenn.	Miss.	Ala.	Ga.	La.
1920......	16,470	23,995	19,485	13,668	10,185	8,078
1910......	13,314	15,303	4,612	3,208	2,874	1,609
Ohio						
1920......	24,595	12,088	3,346	17,588	13,387	990
1910......	18,835	3,481	475	781	1,549	233

States along the Atlantic Coast tended to attract migrants from those southern states which are on the eastern coast, while the North Central division drew newcomers along the route of the Mississippi River.[2]

In yet another way this recent migration tended to differ in its general characteristics from previous movements.

---

[1] *Fourteenth Census*, 1920, vol. ii, p. 637; *Negro Population in the United States 1790-1915*, pp. 75-76. States mentioned in the following illustrations are those which are the most significant sources of immigration in each case.

[2] See Bibliography, reference 57 (n), p. 321.

Whereas before 1910 the colored people had shown a strong tendency to move short distances to nearby states either within the South or across the Mason and Dixon line, the latest migrations were frequently long-distance moves from the far South. Negroes from Florida and Georgia migrated straight through to Pennsylvania and New York; many from Alabama, Mississippi and Louisiana went to Illinois and even Michigan. The earlier emigration had been almost wholly from such border states as Maryland, Virginia and Kentucky.

This whole contrast in the source of migration before and after 1910 is well summarized by J. A. Hill, of the United States Census Bureau: [1]

> The northward migration of Negroes in the last decade has been to a much larger extent than ever before a migration from the far South. The earlier northward migration was, as already noted, mostly from the more northern States of the South. Even as recently as 1910, 48 per cent, or nearly one-half, of the southern-born Negroes living in northern States came from two States—Virginia and Kentucky. The migration between 1910 and 1920 reduced the proportion born in these two States to 31.6 per cent. On the other hand, the proportion of northern Negroes coming from the States farther south, or from what we may term the cotton-belt States, including in this class South Carolina, Georgia, Florida, Alabama, Mississippi, Arkansas, Louisiana, and Texas, increased from 18.2 per cent of the total number of southern-born Negroes living in the North in 1910 to 40.5 per cent of the total in 1920. The absolute number of Negroes in the North who were natives of these States increased from 75,517 in 1910 to 298,739 in 1920, so that there were nearly four times as many in 1920 as there were in 1910.

[1] Reference 47 (a), pp. 479-80.

Table 3, cited from the same source, paints the picture clearly, though due to the presence of secondary migrations, probably conservatively.

TABLE 3.—NUMBER OF SOUTHERN-BORN NEGROES LIVING IN THE NORTH *
IN 1910 AND 1920, AND NUMBER AND PER CENT OF INCREASE
FROM 1910 TO 1920, BY STATE OF BIRTH

State of birth	Number of southern-born Negroes in the North		Increase from 1910 to 1920	
	1910	1920	Number	Per cent
South Atlantic States				
Delaware	8,729	9,144	415	4.8
Maryland	33,970	39,636	5,666	16.7
District of Columbia..	8,058	9,728	1,670	20.7
Virginia	130,048	148,303	18,255	14.0
West Virginia	6,186	7,887	1,701	27.5
North Carolina	39,019	55,211	16,192	41.5
South Carolina	16,229	42,952	26,723	164.7
Georgia	15,266	73,898	58,632	384.1
Florida	3,096	16,800	13,704	442.6
Total..........	260,601	403,559	142,958	54.9
East South-Central States				
Kentucky	69,487	84,684	15,197	21.9
Tennessee	42,076	76,509	34,433	81.8
Alabama	10,730	65,128	54,398	507.0
Mississippi	12,716	49,292	36,576	287.6
Total..........	135,009	275,613	140,604	104.1
West South-Central States				
Arkansas	6,343	16,280	9,937	156.7
Louisiana	5,262	17,741	12,479	237.2
Oklahoma	2,443	7,582	5,139	210.4
Texas	5,875	16,648	10,773	183.4
Total..........	19,923	58,251	38,328	192.4
TOTAL NORTHERN NEGROES *	415,533	737,423	321,890	77.5

* Includes all Negroes resident in the New England, Middle Atlantic, and East and West North-Central divisions.

Another significant feature of Negro movements has been the tendency to concentrate in urban centers. Like the white population, the colored has for decades shown a steadily mounting proportion of city dwellers as compared with rural. Yet, while it is true that this urban trend among Negroes is no new phenomenon, it has latterly assumed unusual prominence. Practically all of the migrants to the North went to cities rather than to rural communities. The predominance of the urban element among the Negroes of the North and the increase in this urban trend is seen from Table 4.

TABLE 4.—PER CENT URBAN AMONG NEGROES IN THE NORTH

By Divisions

(Source: *Fourteenth Census,* 1920, vol. ii, p. 79.)

	Per cent Urban	
	1920	*1910*
United States	34.0	27.3
New England	90.3	85.1
Middle Atlantic	86.2	81.2
East North-Central	87.2	76.6
West North-Central	76.3	67.7

There is also a tendency to concentrate in the largest cities, as is seen from the fact that in Illinois 60 per cent of the Negro population of the state were living in Chicago; 68 per cent of the colored people of Michigan were in Detroit; and more than 75 per cent of the New York Negroes concentrated in New York City.[1] Furthermore, eight cities, Chicago, Detroit, New York, Cleveland, Cincinnati, Columbus, Philadelphia and Pittsburgh, contained 38 per cent of the entire colored population of the North, in contrast to only 20 per cent of the total northern population.

In the South the Negroes have shown a similar tendency to drift away from the rural districts into the cities. With one exception (Kentucky) even those states which revealed in

[1] Reference 47 (a), pp. 481-2.

1920 an actual decrease in Negroes had at the same time an increase of urban colored population. In considering the southern states which had a percentage increase for 1910-1920 less than the average rate for the colored population of the whole country, it is clear that all of them had experienced a relatively large gain in the urban districts. The rural districts must, therefore, have been the heaviest losers from migration during the decade, for even the migrants who stayed within the South drifted towards the cities. Movements in the South as well as northward have had a distinctly urban aspect.

Table 5 indicates the significant increase of Negro population in large cities during the decade 1910 to 1920. It is evident that in the South the increase of colored population in these largest centers was usually greater than the average rate of increase for the Negroes in the United States. At the same time, this extra increase, which was probably due chiefly to immigration, tended throughout the South to be less than the increase of the white population of these cities, indicating that the whites were moving into these urban centers more rapidly than the Negroes. In the North, however, the large industrial districts saw a tremendous addition to their colored population during this decade. Moreover, the Negroes increased much more rapidly than did the white population. Many other northern cities with smaller aggregate colored populations had similar startling rates of increase, and throughout the North this influx of Negroes into urban centers was a particularly noticeable phase of the migration.

Since 1920 the removal of southern Negroes to northern regions has continued practically without cessation, although with variation from year to year in the volume of influx. It is impossible to make any accurate statements concerning the number of Negroes who have migrated in the last ten years,

TABLE 5.—NEGRO POPULATION, AND PER CENT INCREASE BY RACE,
1910 AND 1920, FOR CITIES HAVING 25,000 OR
MORE NEGROES IN 1920

(Source: Computed from *Fourteenth Census,* 1920,
vol. ii, tables 13, 14 and 17.)

City	Negro Population		Per cent Increase Negro, 1910-1920	Per cent Increase White, 1910-1920
NORTHERN				
	1920	1910		
Detroit, Mich.	40,838	5,741	611.3	107.0
Cleveland, O.	34,451	8,448	307.8	38.1
Chicago, Ill.	109,458	44,103	148.2	21.0
New York City	152,467	91,709	66.3	16.9
Manhattan	*109,133*	*60,534*	*80.3*	*—4.3*
Brooklyn	*31,912*	*22,708*	*40.5*	*23.3*
Indianapolis, Ind.	34,678	21,816	59.0	31.9
Philadelphia, Pa.	134,229	84,459	58.9	15.4
St. Louis, Mo.	69,854	43,960	58.9	9.4
Cincinnati, O.	30,079	19,639	53.2	7.9
Pittsburgh, Pa.	37,725	25,623	47.2	8.3
Kansas City, Mo.	30,719	23,566	30.4	30.6
SOUTHERN				
Norfolk, Va.	43,392	25,039	73.3	70.5
Houston, Tex.	33,960	23,929	41.9	90.2
Jacksonville, Fla.	41,520	29,293	41.7	76.4
Birmingham, Ala.	70,230	52,305	34.3	35.1
Baltimore, Md.	108,322	84,749	27.8	32.1
Atlanta, Ga.	62,796	51,902	21.0	34.0
Savannah, Ga.	39,179	33,246	17.8	38.5
Memphis, Tenn.	61,181	52,441	16.7	28.7
Washington, D. C.	109,966	94,446	16.4	38.4
Richmond, Va.	54,041	46,733	15.6	45.4
New Orleans, La.	100,930	89,262	13.1	14.6
Charleston, S. C.	32,326	31,056	4.1	28.2
Louisville, Ky.	40,087	40,522	—1.1	6.2
Nashville, Tenn.	35,633	36,523	—2.4	12.0

for no such comprehensive figures as the census enumeration
are as yet available. The United States Department of
Labor has, however, attempted to keep in touch with recent
movements, and other organizations, such as the National

Urban League, have also tried to obtain information as to the extent and direction of present-day migrations among colored people. From the material which is available, it seems evident that there was a decrease during the industrial depression of 1920, but with the renewed activity of northern industries in 1922 there came an accompanying renewal of Negro migration. These latest movements appear to possess much the same characteristics as to direction and source that were observed from 1916 to 1920. Various estimates have been made concerning the extent of these latest migrations but they are, after all, approximations which may possibly be as inaccurate as were the numerous estimates made before the 1920 Census. One of the most detailed statements concerning this latest trend is a press release given out by the United States Department of Labor on October 24, 1923. Its accuracy is not guaranteed but on the basis of such information as was available, the situation in that year is summarized as follows: [1]

> It is announced by the Secretary of Labor, through Phil H. Brown, Commissioner of Conciliation, specially detailed to observe the present movement of migratory Negro labor, that 478,700 or nearly half a million Negro migrants forsook their abodes and occupations in 13 southern states during the year September 1, 1922, to August 31, 1923.
>
> An analysis of the 478,700 total reveals the fact that of Negro migrants for the year noted, Alabama yielded 90,000; Arkansas 5,000; Florida 90,000; Georgia 120,600; Kentucky 2,500; Louisiana 15,000; Mississippi 82,600; North Carolina 25,000; Oklahoma 1,000; South Carolina 25,000; Tennessee 10,000; Texas 2,000; Virginia 100,000. From the above it will be noted that Georgia yielded the highest, and Oklahoma the smallest quota of Negro migrants.

[1] Reference 145 (f).

Surveys which have been made in northern cities in the last ten years furnish additional support to the belief that the flow of Negroes to the North has been steadily and quietly continuing since 1920.[1] In such cities as Philadelphia and Pittsburgh, Detroit and Columbus, it has been found that the colored group has received a large number of migrants from the South since the last census figures were taken. We must await the 1930 census material before there is any valid ground for estimating the net gain of the North in Negro population during the last ten years. It is probable, however, that when those statistics are at hand, we shall find that the migration of Negroes has been at least over half as extensive as it was during the decade 1910-1920, which included the abnormal war period. The movement of colored people into northern cities thus continues to be an important phenomenon at the present time.

Migration of Negroes within the United States has been a continuous, not a sporadic phenomenon, for, like the white population, the colored people have constantly sought new homes. Moreover, this tendency to change of location has been steadily increasing as means of communication and travel have permeated even the most rural sections of the country and as the knowledge of other opportunities has become more widespread among the Negroes of the South.

Ever since the close of the Civil War the greater part of Negro migrations have been within the South. In spite of the fact that there has been a constant and increasing trend of Negroes to the North, the vast majority of colored people are still living within the South. There has, however, been a ceaseless shift from one southern state to another; in addition to the interdivisional and interstate migrations, there has been an ever present flux from one county to another

[1] E. g. references 110 (a), pp. 6-7; 22 (a), sec. ii; 81 (a), pp. 33-4.

and from rural to urban districts. Undoubtedly there have also been many movements for which no census statistics are available; for example, the 1920 records do not include the number of those who may have migrated and died within the ten-year period or who may have migrated and returned to their native homes within a census decade; or seasonal workers who may migrate constantly but retain the same legal residence. Yet when only the more obvious movements are considered, it is evident that there has been a considerable redistribution of Negro population in every division in the country. The net gain or loss of each division for the last two census periods suggests the extent of such migrations. (The figures of Table 6 are obtained by finding for each division the difference between the number of those born in the specified division but living in other divisions and the number of those living in the specified but born in other divisions.)

TABLE 6.—GAIN OR LOSS OF NEGRO POPULATION THROUGH INTERDIVISIONAL MIGRATION

(Source: *Fourteenth Census, 1920*, vol. ii, p. 616; *Negro Population in the United States 1790-1915*, p. 69.)

Division	Gain or Loss (—) through Interdivisional Migration	
	1920	1910
New England	21,325	20,310
Middle Atlantic	296,664	186,384
East North-Central	296,111	119,649
West North-Central	68,222	40,497
South Atlantic	—455,410	—392,827
East South-Central	—405,511	—200,876
West South-Central	127,350	194,658
Mountain	20,085	13,229
Pacific	31,164	18,976

Hill has strikingly illustrated the effect of Negro migration upon southern states by comparing in a single state,

Mississippi, the records of migration to and from that particular state. In 1870 the colored population of Mississippi included 124,377 Negroes who had been born in other states, principally Virginia, Tennessee, North and South Carolina, Georgia and Alabama. At the same time 57,433 Negroes who have been born in Mississippi were living in other states, a majority in Louisiana and Texas. Thus in 1870 the number of immigrants to Mississippi exceeded the number of emigrants by 66,944. This figure represented the net gain to the population of the state through the interstate migration of Negroes. In 1880 this gain had increased to 68,245 but from that time it fell off at every decade until in 1920, there was a deficit of 139,178 as compared with a surplus of 66,944 in 1870. This deficit means that if all the Negroes who were born in Mississippi and have gone to other states were to return and, at the same time, all Negroes who have come into Mississippi from other states were to leave, the number returning would exceed the number departing by 139,178, and the result would be an increase of 15 per cent in the total Negro population of the state, and an increase of nearly 8 per cent in the total population, white and colored.[1]

In addition to these movements within the South, there have been continual migrations from the South to the North and from the North to the South, the volume of the former having at all times been greater than that of the latter, so that the number of Negroes in the North has constantly increased through migration. As the Census Bureau carefully points out, " the increase in the number of migrants shown for each decade should not be confused with the volume of migration as between the North and West, and the South." The increase for the decade 1910-1920, for instance, of 340,260 in the number of southern-born Negroes

1 Reference 47 (a), pp. 476-7.

living in the North and West is the excess of 1920 over 1910 in the number of such migrants reported. During that decade migration must also have been sufficient to cover (1) mortality during the decade among migrants living in these sections of the country in 1910 (and mortality among migrants of this particular decade), and (2) returns of migrants to the South.[1]

TABLE 7.—NATIVE NEGRO POPULATION BY SECTION OF
BIRTH AND RESIDENCE

(Source: *Negro Population in the United States 1790-1915,* p. 65;
Fourteenth Census, 1920, vol. ii, pp. 636 *et seq.*)

	Born in the South and Living in North and West		Born in North and West and Living in South		Net Gain of North and West and Loss of the South	
	Number	Increase	Number	Increase	Number	Increase
1920......	780,794	340,260	47,223	5,734	733,571	334,526
1910......	440,534	90,883	41,489	11,092	399,045	79,791
1900......	349,651	107,796	30,397	7,129	319,254	200,667
1890......	241,855	43,826	23,268	1,229	118,587	—57,403
1880......	198,029	48,929	22,039	6,456	175,990	42,473
1870......	149,100		15,583		133,517	

The migrations of southern-born Negroes are of particular interest because they involve by far the greatest mass of movements of colored people. Thus any consideration of the causes and results of such migrations would deal with conditions affecting the majority of colored migrants. Of especial significance are the movements from the South to the North. Whereas northern-born Negroes moving South go to regions where economic and social conditions are already adjusted to the presence of masses of colored people and where they are practically lost in the large number of their own race, the southern-born Negroes who migrate to the North enter communities where, because of fewer

[1] Reference 141 (b), pp. 65-6.

numbers, their influx is more conspicuous and where racial relations are more subject to change in the presence of a growing colored population. Furthermore, when southern Negroes migrate to the North, they tend to concentrate in large cities, thus necessitating frequently a double adjustment from life in the South to life in the North and from rural conditions to those prevalent in a highly organized urban center. The migration of southern Negroes to northern cities has consequently raised many serious economic and social problems.

CHAPTER II

The Causes of Migration [1]

Fundamentally, behind Negro movements, as behind those of any people, there must be a dissatisfaction with conditions in the present location and the promise of improvement in some other region. The statement [2] that the causes of migration may be grouped under those which are " driving " and those which are " beckoning " is clarifying in that it brings out the necessity of present discontent and hope of future satisfaction. In the case of recent Negro migrations the " push " which has been of dominant influence has been the inability to make a satisfactory living in the black belt, while the principal " pull " has been the prospect of greater economic opportunities in northern industries. In spite of the general predominance of this economic motive, the influence of social conditions should not be overlooked, for the discriminations and disadvantages which have burdened the southern Negroes have resulted in a feeling of discontent and restlessness which, in turn, have tended to a ready belief in promises of better conditions. Once started, the migration has been strengthened by discussions, letters, newspaper propaganda, the desire to join relatives and friends and, at first, the suggestion resulting from a mass movement.

These factors have not only acted as a direct stimulus to further shifts but have also increased the motivating power of economic and social conditions by bringing these into

[1] References supporting this discussion of the causes of migration will be found in the appendix, classified by major causes. This treatment of the subject is a synthesis of the conclusions of many students, since no writer has so far fully discussed the simultaneous action of all of these motives.

[2] See Bibliography, reference 125 (a), p. 1040.

greater prominence and by investing them with a stronger
emotional appeal through the crystallization of public opinion.
The degree in which each of these forces has operated in
producing the determination to move North has undoubtedly
varied with different individuals and in different years; probably in no two cases has the exact combination of motives
been the same.   At the present time the transfer of Negroes
from South to North proceeds persistently but quietly; there
are masses of Negroes now living in northern cities to absorb
the newcomers and so prevent as much wild rumor and discussion as prevailed at first.   This, in turn, is reflected by
the lessened excitement in the South, which is further diminished as Negroes become more familiar with the phenomenon
of migration.   Thus the factors of hysteria and mass suggestion have become less prominent.   Other causes, however,
continue to operate; for example, the economic and social
situation in the South and the influence of letters and increased knowledge of the thrills and pleasures of urban life.
None of the factors works alone but in varied combinations
with a few or with many of the others.

ECONOMIC CAUSES

The chief factor in producing recent mass movements of
southern Negroes to northern cities has been the general economic situation in the North, which furnished an unexpected
and irresistible opportunity for colored laborers.   Previous
to the World War immigrant workmen from Europe
had kept pace with the demand for labor in the various industries.   Northern Negroes had been largely confined to
the fields of domestic and personal service, only a small proportion being found in the manufacturing and mechanical
industries.   With the beginning of the World War there
came an extraordinary expansion of industry in the United
States due to European demands for war materials and
supplies.   The entrance of our own country into the war

resulted in further increased industrial activity; new factories sprang up and old ones enlarged their facilities; labor was needed in the shipyards, in the mines, in transportation, and in all the varied industrial pursuits directly or indirectly affected by a state of war.

Along with this increased call for labor of all kinds, there came a marked decrease in the supply of available workers. One of the first effects of the war was the cutting off of immigration from Europe, as is shown by the following table: [1]

Year	Volume of Immigration	Year	Volume of Immigration
1913	1,197,892	1916	298,826
1914	1,218,480	1917	295,403
1915	326,700	1918	110,618

At the same time, some of the foreign laborers returned to Europe to join the armies of their native country. Upon the entrance of the United States into the war this shortage of laborers was further intensified by the withdrawal of men from industrial pursuits into military and naval service. Immediately, the workmen who remained had an opportunity to go into the higher paid and more skilled positions, thus creating a particularly urgent demand for unskilled labor. Even after the close of the war and the return of the soldiers to peaceful pursuits, the need for colored laborers continued to exist due to the passage of the 1921 immigration law and particularly to the law of 1924, which permitted an annual immigration quota of only two per cent of each national group as it existed numerically in this country in 1890.[2] By reducing the supply of immigrant labor this whole situation diminished the strength of the group which had so successfully excluded the Negro from industry and

[1] Annual Reports of the Commissioner General of Immigration.

[2] Exceptions were made, in that countries situated in either North or South America were not subjected to the quota principle.

furnished him with an unprecedented opportunity in the northern labor market, an opportunity which involved an increase in the amount of employment available and in the variety of occupations open to him.

Higher wages also formed part of this irresistible call to northern industry, for wages in general throughout the North were materially greater than in the South. To the poorly-paid southern farm hands the wages paid by northern industries—and paid in cold cash by the week or month instead of in store credit once a year—seemed fabulous sums promising speedy wealth and success. In the majority of cases they were too ignorant to comprehend that these unheard-of money wages might be largely offset by increased cost of living; consequently, they responded to the difference as if the northern wage scale represented an actual rather than, perhaps, a nominal increase in real wages. As it happened, they were frequently justified in this attitude, for so great was the wage increase that, in many cases, even the exceedingly higher cost of rent, food and clothing did not prevent some improvement in their general economic condition.

This unprecedented economic opportunity in the North exerted the " pull " upon southern Negroes. At the same time, the agricultural situation and prevailing low wages in the South acted as a " push " that made response to the " pull " inevitable. The share-tenancy mode of farming characteristic of the South usually involves crop liens and an unsound credit system which have often prevented the Negro tenants from making an economic profit from a year's work.

The characteristic feature of share tenancy is that the owner furnishes not only the land but also part, or all, of the necessary capital and equipment, receiving in return a portion of the crop commensurate with the amount of capital he has expended. The Negro tenant, on the other hand, provides the necessary labor and, at times, part of the equipment, obtaining his compensation in the form of a share of the product at the final crop settlement. The form of share-tenancy varies not only in the relative proportions of the crop received by the owner and tenant and the extent to which the landlord furnishes the tools, work animals, fertilizer, seed, etc., but also in the amount of supervision exerted by the owner over the tenant. This ranges from the absolute dependence of the tenant who provides only his labor and is practically a wage earner working under closest supervision and direction, to the one who furnishes most of his equipment and works largely on his own initiative. The rent form of tenancy also shows variations, having, in particular, different modes of payment; the tenant may agree to pay a cash rent or a stipulated amount of cotton per acre, or part cash and part produce.

Since Negro tenants usually have little or no capital with which to pay rent and provide the necessities of life while they wait for the maturing, harvesting and selling of their crop—which is usually the single crop, cotton—a system has developed whereby the colored farmers obtain their food, clothing and other essentials by long-time payments, either directly from the landlord, or in cases where the planter is unable or does not wish to furnish these necessities, from the local merchants, the owner securing a lien on the crop for the rent and whatever supplies he advances and the merchant securing another lien to cover his investments. One of the results of this crop-lien system has been the tendency of many planters or store keepers to charge exorbitant prices for the supplies, which the Negro tenant obtains on time instead of with cash. The creditor, whether merchant or landowner, takes considerable risk in investing large sums of capital on the security only of a cotton crop, and necessarily feels justified in protecting himself by charging more than the current

cash prices. This whole system of tenancy with its concomitant evils of long-time credit and crop liens has provided splendid opportunities for unscrupulous planters and
store keepers to exploit the ignorant and illiterate Negroes.
In many cases the white men have taken advantage of these
opportunities and have seen to it that the colored farmer
has little to show for his year's work, though there are, of
course, innumerable instances of white owners who have
dealt honestly and kindly with their tenants and have tried
to encourage them in habits of thrift and industry.   However, the tenancy system has frequently resulted in much
dissatisfaction with the final crop settlements, at which time
the crop is shared between tenant and owner, and from the
tenant's portion is deducted the payment for all advances.
The Negroes complain that they are often cheated out of
their share of the crop, are charged unfair prices, and are
obliged to pay for articles they never bought. As Woofter
points out,[1] " Some of these complaints are justified and
some arise from the fact that the tenants are illiterate and
keep no accurate accounts, and hence are uninformed as to
their true financial status at the end of the crop year."   As
a further consequence of these mortgages and high prices,
the Negro often finds himself in debt year after year and
has little prospect of ever getting on his feet financially.

In recent decades the troubles inherent in the tenancy
system have been intensified by the ravages of the boll weevil,
which had appeared in the southwest corner of the southern
states long before the war period, and had been persistently
spreading north and east. By 1915 and 1916 the pest had
reached Georgia and South Carolina, so that crop failures
and agricultural depression were widespread throughout the
cotton belt of the South.   The economic demoralization
which resulted from this spread of the boll weevil was further

[1] Reference 157 (a), p. 48.

aggravated in 1916 by a series of heavy rainfalls and floods,
which in themselves did a great deal of damage and at the
same time made more difficult the fight against the boll
weevil, which thrives in rainy seasons.

Southern plantation owners have tended to produce only
one principal crop, and in the sections where cotton is the chief
interest this constant shortage or complete failure in cotton
production was, and is, disastrous. Discouraged by the
weevil invasion, many planters have given up the struggle
and turned to other crops, such as corn, oats, sweet potatoes,
peanuts and various food products, and have also frequently
introduced new farm machinery to plant and cultivate them.
For the most part, these new crops have required fewer
laborers than did the production of cotton, and many Negro
farm hands have been thrown out of work as a result of this
change in agricultural products and methods of farming.
Furthermore, since the farming experience of these colored
workers has been practically confined to the raising of cotton,
their ignorance and lack of training have handicapped the
Negroes in their ability to cope with the changing agricultural
situation.

Moreover, the plantation owners have often found it difficult to obtain loans from the banks during periods of agricultural depression and in many cases have been without
means of making the customary advances of supplies, being
obliged by their financial losses to cut down their labor force
and their farming operations. This, of course, has increased both the deplorable financial condition of the Negroes
and the amount of unemployment that had already been
aggravated by the boll weevil and changing farming methods.

The factor of low wages has also been a serious phase of
the Negro's economic situation in the South, for throughout
the southern states wages for all classes have been lower than
in the North. The earnings of farm laborers, particularly,

have frequently not been sufficient to provide an adequate living.

At the time when southern Negroes were first widely afforded opportunity of employment in northern industries they were struggling in the South with the tenancy system, crop failures, the invasion of the boll weevil, changing methods of farming and low wages. All of these factors combined to form an economic situation from which they were glad to escape. Since those days the economic factors in both North and South have continued to operate as motives of migration but in a less striking and more stable form. There is not the acute demand for colored labor in northern industries that there was at the time of the war but Negroes continue to find positions which promise more economic success than can be attained on southern farms with their low wages and frequently unsatisfactory tenancy system. The boll weevil persists in spreading disaster and confusion in the agricultural life of the South, with the result that colored tenants move on to newer lands in the southwest and to the cities of the South and North.

SOCIAL CAUSES

While economic conditions, North and South, have been largely responsible for the mass movements of Negroes which have occurred since the beginning of the war, at the same time certain social factors in the South contributed to the restlessness and dissatisfaction of the Negroes and to their eagerness to leave when the opportunity arose. Southern colored people have constantly listed among their reasons for migrating the discrimination and injustice to which they were subjected in the South.

One of the complaints of the Negroes is that they have been denied participation in the political life of southern states and have been practically disfranchised by such state legislative action as the " Grandfather clauses," educational tests, and property or poll taxes, or by the functioning of the direct primary, from which Negroes are excluded in some states and which is usually equivalent to an election. To some Negroes the right to vote is a coveted privilege, any curtailment of which is considered an injustice, and among migrants who have flocked into the northern cities during the last fifteen years the inability to vote has frequently been given as one of the reasons for leaving the South.

Further, the Negro complains of his widespread insecurity of life and property in the South, which results in his social and economic as well as political intimidation. Although the number of lynchings of Negroes has decreased encouragingly in the last decade, yet the fact that in 1928 ten Negroes [1] were murdered by mobs shows that there is still a basis for those complaints of insecurity which are raised by the colored people. However, recent statistical analyses of the relation between lynching and migration reveal the necessity of caution in attributing too much importance to mob violence as a motivating factor in recent Negro movements. It has been shown, for instance, that: (1) The number of Negroes actually increased in some counties in which lynchings occurred; (2) counties in which Negro population decreased show a similar decrease in white population; and (3) it even happens that a county with several lynchings in its history may show an increase of Negroes but a decrease of whites.[2] In regard to both political discrimination and mob violence it it well to realize.[3]

> That lynching for the past twenty-five years has been slowly but surely decreasing and disfranchisement is no new thing but has been an accomplished fact for more than forty years, . . . (so) that whatever grievance of this

[1] Reference 159 (a), p. 402; *cf.* 74 (a).
[2] References 57 (d), p. 403; 57 (c), pp. 272-4.
[3] Reference 125 (a), p. 1041.

nature the Negro may have against the South, he has at least no new complaint and therefore no stronger reason for migrating on this account in 1917 than he has had for several decades.

While it is undoubtedly true that in numerous instances lynching and other forms of outrage have prompted Negroes to move, yet rationalization of motives is a peculiar tendency of human nature and such a widely discussed evil as lynching might easily be accepted and given as a primary cause in cases where other factors were more fundamental. It seems probable that, like political discrimination, mob violence has exerted an influence upon Negro migration but has acted as an occasional strengthening and accompanying cause rather than as a fundamental and generally prevalent motive.

Racial discrimination in the carrying out of civic laws is another form of injustice of which Negroes complain perhaps even more than they decry mob violence, since this phase of inequality occurs more widely and constantly. Aspects of legal discrimination which are most generally alleged to be motivating factors in the Negroes' discontent are included in such contentions as that laws are unequally enforced, that discrimination is shown by officers of the law in making arrests, and that injustice is practiced in court procedure. Colored people in the South maintain that as a result of these tendencies, they are subject to hasty arrests without sufficient evidence, they are more easily convicted and are given longer and more severe sentences, and their value as witnesses and jurymen is not considered equal to that of the white man.

Lack of adequate educational facilities in the South forms one of the most generally listed reasons for those feelings of discrimination and discontent which have led many Negroes to change their place of residence. The basis of the southern educational situation is to be found in the double school system required by state constitutions and statutes, whereby the two races are segregated in separate schools. The injustice of which the Negroes complain is not so much the fact of separation as it is the discrimination shown in the provisions made for the education of Negro children in these separate buildings. Negro schools do not receive their proportionate share of state school funds, so that the physical equipment which can be provided, such as buildings, seating arrangements, blackboards, maps, etc., is far from adequate, and the salaries are so low that only teachers with meager training and ability can be secured. Furthermore, the lack of funds frequently necessitates a school year of only three or five months instead of the customary nine. In every way Negro children in the South are handicapped by the meager educational facilities which are available for them.

Another form of social discrimination which affects Negroes of any age or walk in life is the practice, found throughout the South, of separating the two races in residential sections, public conveyances and public gatherings. The chief complaint of the Negroes in this regard is that the provisions for their accommodation under this policy of segregation are invariably inferior to those made for white people. Residential areas allotted to the colored population in towns and cities are generally in the most undesirable sections and are frequently without such necessities and civic improvements as pavements, sewers, lighting and sanitary provisions. In traveling, too, Negroes are often given poor and inadequate accommodations even though they pay the same prices as do the whites. On railroad trains they are forced to ride in coaches set apart for their use and are usually unable to obtain places in sleeping or dining cars. As a general rule, the coaches given over to Negroes are crowded and unsanitary. On street cars, in theaters, in stores and in places of public gatherings of all sorts, the separate accommodations provided for them are likely to be inferior and

unpleasant.   At times, too, Negroes assert that in the general
contacts between the two races they are subjected to embarrassments, humiliations and insults which are degrading
to their self-respect and are subversive of their rights as
citizens.

Thus the colored people of the South have complained of
political disfranchisement, of the constant menace of mob
violence and lynching, of inadequate educational facilities for
their children, of legal discriminations, of " Jim Crow "
segregation in transportation and public places, and of humiliations and embarrassments suffered in their contacts with
white people.   The extent to which this social situation has
contributed to actual removal from the South varies with
different individuals but in many cases it has been an influential factor in producing a determination to migrate.
However, during the migrations of the last decade and a
half, social conditions have tended to act as secondary and
contributing causes of the movements rather than as a primary influence.   When an appraisal and examination of their
economic status had once been started, so that the feeling of
unrest and discontent became more conscious and verbal,
social factors readily furnished additional reasons for dissatisfaction and strengthened the desire to take advantage of
the economic opportunities that were opening up in northern
cities.

SOCIO-PSYCHOLOGICAL CAUSES

Other factors have also played a part in producing these
movements.   The Negro's knowledge of the possibilities of
migration and his attitude toward it are inevitably influenced
by his personal relations with others and by the activities of
the social group of which he is a member.   Conversations
with those already moving North, published discussions and
appeals, and the general atmosphere of unrest which existed
in many parts of the South, all exerted an effect upon the

phenomenon of migration. During the first year or two of
the European War the direct appeal of labor agents from the
North was responsible for the migration of numbers of
colored laborers, but the activities of these agents were soon
limited, as many southern states attempted by legislative
action to prevent them from soliciting labor for northern industries. However, this did not mean a cessation in appeals
to migrate, for around 1916 to 1918 the Negro press was
constantly urging colored people to leave the land of oppression and discrimination and fly to the freedom and equality
which awaited them in the North. Probably the most influential of the Negro newspapers was the Chicago *Defender,*
published in the North yet read widely in the South. This
paper is said to have increased its circulation from 10,000 to
93,000 during the years of the war migration. By the use
of glaring headlines and sensational articles it carried on a
definite propaganda of migration which had an incalculable
effect upon southern Negroes. It not only printed direct
appeals to them to come North but gave much space to news
items, anecdotes and poems which created the impression of
a general mass movement and effort to escape from a life of
bondage and oppression in the South. By constantly making
the Negroes conscious of their " wrongs " and holding up
before them the golden opportunities of the North and the
example of their fellowmen, this newspaper and others like it
crystallized the more underlying economic and social causes
of discontent into immediate motives for migration.

After the migration had once started, one of the strongest
incentives to its spread was the pressure exerted by the return
of migrants for visits, by letters from migrants already established in the North, and by the general public opinion which
prevailed in the South. When Negroes came back to visit
their former homes, their tales of financial success and social
freedom and their display of clothes and money as proof of

their prosperity tended to encourage others to follow. Furthermore, as soon as a Negro had received employment in some northern city, he usually wrote to friends and relatives who remained behind, and urged them to join him. Like the Negro press and the return visits of migrants, these letters served to make southern Negroes aware of northern opportunities and conscious of their social and economic deprivations in the South, thus increasing their restlessness and discontent until the point of actual migration was reached. The extent to which such letters augmented migration cannot be estimated accurately but various investigations furnish ground for believing that this factor was highly important.

When the movement of colored people had once assumed noticeable proportions in any community, in itself it served as a cause of further migration. Throughout the South the departure of Negroes, newspaper propaganda, offers made by labor agents and letters from migrants, all started a wave of discussion. The economic and social conditions surrounding Negroes in the South and the opportunities in other regions became the absorbing topic of conversation in the churches, on the streets, in the stores and social gatherings, and wherever groups of colored people congregated. This constant discussion of migration fanned the smoldering restlessness into general awareness of the discriminations endured by southern Negroes and into acute discontent with the existing situation. Likewise, it induced a social pressure which stimulated further movements by suggestion and imitation, until in some communities the departure of colored people from the South assumed the appearance of an hysterical stampede. Credulity was rife, caution and reason were thrown to the winds, and many Negroes sold or gave away their household goods, left their work and homes and followed their friends and neighbors, sometimes not even knowing where or why they were going. The wildest sort of rumors sprang from nowhere apparently and were given full credence, causing migrants to follow the crowd on the flimsiest pretexts. A type of rumor most frequently circulated and believed was the report that on certain dates excursions would be made up to go North; and this setting of a definite date for " The Great Northern Drive " proved an irresistible attraction to many Negroes. Stimulated by discussion, by the suggestions of those around them, by the fear of being left alone and by rumors and alluring tales, many of the migrants were caught up in the wave of enthusiasm and could not resist the impulse to leave.

On the whole, however, such socio-psychological causes of migration tended to be immediate rather than underlying, fundamental motives and were more effective after the movement had begun. Some of these have died out during the last fifteen years and no longer serve as potent causal factors. After the first excitement subsided and the fact of migration became a matter of course, there was less hysteria, wild rumor, and emotional discussion of the subject. On the other hand, such factors as letters of migrants probably increased in effectiveness when the Negroes became adjusted to northern living and working conditions and had opportunity to find jobs and shelter for their friends and relatives. Since that first mass movement to the North, the emotional element has diminished, so that there has been a practical disappearance of some of the motivating forces and a quiet and less spectacular persistence of others.

MISCELLANEOUS CAUSES

In some cases, of course, Negroes have migrated merely in order to remain with members of the family who have already made the move. The influence of these family relationships is, naturally, particularly important in accounting for the migration of children and old people, yet it has also played a part in the motivation of other migrants. Similarly,

colored doctors, lawyers, ministers, storekeepers and various
professional and business men frequently lost most of the
clientele upon which their living depended; migration for
them was induced by the necessity of remaining with the
group.   Furthermore, many Negroes were probably influenced by modern improvements in means of communication and travel.   The development of newspapers, telephone
and postal service, and the automobile, good roads and improved railway service have all tended to increase mobility.
They have also brought home to the colored people of the
rural South a knowledge of the excitement and the pleasures
of city life.   The Negroes have now glimpsed what the city
may give in the way of a thrill and joy in being part of the
crowd and of relief from the lonely monotonous life of the
farm.   Who can say how great a part the " lure of Harlem "
has played in the migration of southern Negroes?   Modern
improvements in means of communication and travel have
served to bring the mass of rural Negroes in close touch with
the attractions and opportunities of other places and have
made migration not only a conscious possibility but an easy
performance.

Consideration of the motives which have prompted movements of colored people inevitably brings the realization that
these causes are by no means unique and peculiar to the
migrations of Negroes.   In the first place, a striking feature
of the shift of colored population has been its participation
in the general urban trend of past decades.   The Negroes
have been attracted to the cities by the same inducements as
those which have drawn the white portion of the population.
Like the whites, the colored people have above all responded
to the demand for labor which resulted from an increasingly
complex and extensive industrial organization.   Like them
too, the Negroes have sought in the cities better educational
advantages, opportunities for a higher standard of living, for

amusements and for the satisfaction of artistic, intellectual and social interests. Similarly, the movements of Negroes have been actuated by much the same reasons as those which have caused the enormous volume of foreign immigration to the United States, for both European immigrants and Negroes have been influenced by the difficulty of making a living at home and by the prospect of an improved economic status in other regions.

C. S. Johnson has made some interesting and suggestive comparisons between colored movements and the trends of European immigration.[1] Basing his comparisons on Professor Jerome's study of migration and business cycles, Johnson shows that, like immigration, Negro movements follow the fluctuations of industrial demands. Among other points he indicates that just as emigration from Europe tends to be large in depressive years and low in boom years, so the high spots of Negro movements occurred in 1878 and 1879, 1916-1918, and 1923, during which years there were floods and crop failures in the South coincident with boom periods and aggravated demands for workers in other regions. He states too, that Jerome's conclusion, that unskilled labor is marked by the greatest fluctuations, is exemplified by the Negro migrants, who are usually unskilled laborers and show the fluctuations characteristic of such workers.

Furthermore, it must not be overlooked that the fundamental causes of Negro migrations are of the same nature as those which throughout the ages have induced men to seek new homes. An increasing struggle in the effort to obtain an adequate food supply, and dissatisfaction with living conditions have at all times been underlying motives for migration. The Negro is but following the tendency of all men and moves in response to factors to which human nature itself is sensitive, and does not migrate merely as the result of some trait peculiar to his race.

[1] Reference 57 (p), pp. 555-6; cf. 125 (a), p. 1035.

CHAPTER III

Nature of the Material

It has been seen that, due to a variety of factors, large numbers of southern Negroes have moved into northern cities during the last fifteen years. The question at once arises: What has happened in these urban centers since the composition of their population has been altered by the rapidly increasing proportion of those who belong to a distinct ethnic group? Various aspects of this query have aroused the interest of different individuals and research organizations, with the result that the last decade and a half has witnessed numerous surveys and the publication of their reports and discussions concerning the results of Negro migration to northern cities. Leading students of race problems have closely watched the movement of colored people from the South and have based their conclusions as to its effects on a wide range of experience and on numerous sources of information. In addition, many investigations have been made of special phases of the economic and social conditions existing among particular groups of colored people in the North.

For the background and extent of the movements and for the discussions of occupational and demographic effects of the migration, governmental sources, primarily the publications of the Census Bureau, have been drawn upon. They constitute the major sources of reliable material for the country as a whole and its main subdivisions. The opinions expressed by the large number of authors cited in the bibliography have been synthesized, and generalizations from

58

them scrutinized, in the light of the specific and detailed surveys.

Table 8 summarizes the nature of numerous reports which have been published as a result of isolated surveys made since 1917 in single localities.[1] They contain information concerning social and economic situations which have arisen in particular places since the influx of southern Negroes. Table 9 presents the nature of investigations which have been carried on by the same person or committee in several cities and sections of the North. The topics covered by these surveys are not uniform; some of the investigations have been concerned with the nature of the occupations into which Negroes have gone, others have been interested only in crime or housing or recreation, while a few have attempted to cover the chief phases of both economic and social conditions. The surveys which are here grouped together also vary in date of investigation and agency by which conducted. A few of the reports, such as those of George Haynes in Detroit and Abraham Epstein in Pittsburgh, were carried on immediately after the first noticeable inrush of southern Negroes. Caution is necessary, therefore, in combining conclusions from such investigations with those derived from studies conducted as late as 1928. It has been felt, however, that there was great value in basing this study on surveys for different years in order to derive a continuous picture of what has happened since Negroes first began to come North in considerable numbers, and in order to determine whether conditions have remained similar throughout the years since the first studies were made. In regard to the auspices under which the investigations were conducted it should be noted that some of them have been carried on by independent individuals, and others by social agencies or by officially appointed commissions.

[1] Those interested in a single city must, in addition to consulting Table 8, refer to descriptive material supplementary to Table 9.

TABLE 8.—NATURE OF PUBLISHED REPORTS OF SURVEYS MADE IN SPECIFIC LOCALITIES IN THE NORTH SHOWING EFFECTS OF RECENT NEGRO MIGRATIONS

(x indicates subjects covered)

Topics Considered in Report / Period Covered	(1) Albany, N.Y. 1928	(2) Baltimore, Md. 1923	(3) Boston, Mass. 1928	(4) Buffalo, N.Y. 1925–26	(5a) Chicago, Ill. *1919–20	(5b) Chicago 1919–20	(6) Cincinnati, O. 1917	(7a) Cleveland, O. *1924	(7b) Cleveland *1926	(8) Columbus, O. 1924–25	(9a) Detroit, Mich. *1917–18	(9b) Detroit 1926	(10) Grand Rapids, Mich. 1928	(11) Los Angeles, Cal. 1926	(12) Michigan *1927	(13a) Minneapolis, Minn. 1925–26	(13b) Minneapolis 1923–25	(14a) New York City 1925–26	(14b) New York City 1924–26	(15a) Philadelphia, Pa. 1919	(15b) Philadelphia 1924	(16a) Pittsburgh, Pa. 1917	(16b) Pittsburgh *1917	(17a) Washington, D.C. 1925–27	(17b) Washington 1926–28	(18) Waterbury, Conn. 1922
1. Increase of Negroes by Migration	x	x		x	x		x	x	x	x	x	x	x	x	x	x		x	x			x	x			x
2. Industrial Conditions.																										
(1) Nature of Occupations	x	x		x	x	x	x	x	x	x	x	x	x	x	x	x		x	x			x	x			x
(2) Business and Professions	x		x		x	x					x	x			x			x								
(3) Wages	x		x		x						x	x	x	x		x		x	x	x		x				x
(4) Unions	x	x			x						x			x		x		x		x		x				x
(5) Relation with White Workers					x	x					x	x		x		x		x		x						
(6) Success					x	x	x	x			x	x		x		x										x
(7) Negro Women Workers			x		x						x	x				x		x								x
3. Composition of Negro Population					x		x			x	x	x		x		x						x				x
4. Housing.																										
(1) Segregation					x					x	x	x										x			x	
(2) Congestion					x					x	x	x										x	x	x		
(3) Conditions	x			x	x	x	x			x	x	x	x			x		x	x			x	x	x		x
(4) Rents			x		x					x	x	x						x	x			x	x	x		x
(5) Lodgers			x		x						x	x						x	x			x	x	x		
(6) Deterioration of Property					x	x				x	x														x	
(7) Ownership	x				x					x	x			x		x		x						x	x	x
5. Health	x						x				x			x		x		x				x		x		x
6. Social Maladjustment.																										
(1) Crime	x				x	x					x	x		x	x				x			x	x			x
(2) Juvenile Delinquency	x				x						x	x						x				x				

TABLE 8—*Continued*

Period Covered	(1) Albany, N.Y. 1928	(2) Baltimore, Md. 1923	(3) Boston, Mass. 1928	(4) Buffalo, N.Y. 1925–26	(5) Chicago, Ill. (a)1919–20 (b)*1919–20	(6) Cincinnati, O. 1917	(7) Cleveland, O. (a)*1924 (b)*1926	(8) Columbus, O. 1924–25	(9) Detroit, Mich. (a)*1917–18 (b)1926	(10) Grand Rapids, Mich. 1928	(11) Los Angeles, Cal. 1926	(12) Michigan *1927	(13) Minneapolis, Minn. (a)1925–26 (b)1923–25	(14) New York City 1925–26	(15) Pennsylvania 1924–26	(16) Philadelphia, Pa. (a)1919 (b)1924	(17) Pittsburgh, Pa. (a)1917 (b)*1917	(18) Washington, D.C. (a)1925–27 (b)1926–28	(19) Waterbury, Conn. 1923
7. Education	x				x			x	x x		x			x					x
8. Political Situation					x													x	
9. Church					x			x	x x	x									
10. Recreation	x				x			x	x x									x	x
11. Race Relations. (1) Contacts	x				x				x		x					x x			
(2) Discrimination					x x				x							x			
(3) Friction					x														
12. Attitude of Northern Negroes									x x							x x			
13. Work of Organizations.					x					x						x x			

3. Composition—includes age, sex and marital condition of Negro population.

5. Health—includes vital statistics and causes of illness.

6. Crime—includes number of arrests and nature of offenses.

7. Education—includes number of Negro children and retardation.

9. Church—includes number of churches and work among Negroes.

10. Recreation—includes provisions for and discrimination in.

(For supplementary material concerning a specific city see explanation accompanying Table 9.)

* Dates marked with asterisk are approximate.

DESCRIPTION OF SURVEYS TO ACCOMPANY TABLE 8

1. Albany City Club: *Survey of Albany's Negro Population*, Albany City Club Bulletin 9, No. 5, March 1929. 15 pp.
   Conducted under direction of National Urban League.

2. Charles S. Johnson: "Negroes at Work in Baltimore," *Opportunity* 1, pp. 12-9, June 1923.
   Conducted under auspices of National Urban League. Limited to economic phases.

3. Eolyn C. Klugh: " Colored Girls at Work in Boston," *Opportunity* 1, pp. 295-9, October 1928.

> (Master's essay at Simmons College.) Brief study of occupations of Negro girls in Boston.

4. Niles Carpenter: *Nationality, Color and Economic Opportunity in Buffalo*, New York, The Inquiry. 100 pp.

> (Assisted by graduate students in sociology in the University of Buffalo. Chapter on " Study of Negro Worker " was Carpenter's Master's essay.) Emphasis is on economic status of Negro. Only brief mention of other topics.

5. (a) Chicago Race Commission: *Negro in Chicago*, University of Chicago Press, 1922. 672 pp.

> Report of a survey made by Commission appointed by Governor Lowden to investigate conditions after Chicago Riot of 1919. Includes report of the riot, causes of migration and extent of migration to Chicago, extensive material on formation of public opinion and race relations. One of the most valuable surveys.

(b) H. R. Gold and B. K. Armstrong: *Preliminary Study of Interracial Conditions in Chicago*, New York, Home Missions Council, 1920.

> Made under direction of Survey Division, Industrial Relations Department, Interchurch World Movement. Of little value except for comparative purposes. Is brief and explicitly only a preliminary study.

6. James H. Robinson. " Cincinnati Negro Survey," *Proceedings, National Conference of Social Work 1919*, pp. 524-7.

> Report of survey undertaken by Council of Social Agencies. Robinson was Secretary of Negro Civic Welfare Committee of this Council.

7. (a) John B. Abell: "Southern Negro in Northern Industry," *Economic World* 27, pp. 620-2, May 3, 1924.

> Survey conducted among 75 of the largest industries in Cleveland. First published in *Trade Winds*, journal of Union Trust Company.

(b) H. L. Rockwood (M.D.) : " Effect of Negro Migration on Community Health in Cleveland," *Proceedings, National Conference of Social Work 1926*, pp. 238-44.

> Based largely on city's health statistics.

8. Mary Louise Mark: *Negroes in Columbus, Ohio*, Columbus, Ohio State University Press, 1928. 63 pp.

> A suggestive but not exhaustive study of Negroes in Columbus.

Survey by graduate students in Sociology at Ohio State University. One of the few studies to distinguish between migrant and Northern Negroes in age and occupation.

9. (a) George E. Haynes: *Negro Newcomers in Detroit*, New York, Home Missions Council, 1918. 42 pp.

Survey made by Home Missions Council to formulate program for churches' activity. Was conducted during early years of migration so must be used with caution in comparison with later surveys.

9. (b) Detroit Bureau of Governmental Research: *Negro in Detroit*. Prepared for the Mayor's Interracial Committee by a special survey staff under supervision of Forrester B. Washington. 12 sections mimeographed, 1926.

Includes discussion of causes of migration. One of the most comprehensive and valuable studies.

10. R. Maurice Moss: "American Cities — Grand Rapids, Michigan," *Opportunity* 7, pp. 12-15, January 1929.

Survey made by the National Urban League in 1928.

11. Charles S. Johnson: "Negro Workers in Los Angeles Industries," *Opportunity* 6, pp. 234-40, August 1928.

Survey made by National Urban League. Emphasizes industrial status of the Negro. Report based on 104 of the most important establishments included in a study of 456 industrial plants.

12. Harold A. Lett: "Migration Difficulties in Michigan," *Southern Workman* 56, pp. 231-6, 1927.

Results of a study of migrants by the Division of Negro Welfare and Statistics. Sketchy but suggestive report of situation observed by the Division of Negro Welfare.

13. (a) Abram Harris: *Negro Population in Minneapolis*, Minneapolis, Minnesota, Urban League, 1926. 77 pp.

Sponsored by National Urban League.

(b) Maurine Boie: "Analysis of Negro Crime Statistics for Minneapolis," *Opportunity* 6, pp. 171-3, 1928.

Used records of the Municipal Court in order to check figures of official publications for years 1923-1925.

14. Joint Committee on Negro Child Study in New York: *Study of Delinquent and Neglected Negro Children before the New York City Children's Court*, published by The Committee, 1927. 48 pp.

Studies the proportion of Negro children brought before the court in 1925, and nature of offenses.

15. Commonwealth of Pennsylvania: *Negro Survey*, 1927. Survey under-taken by State Department of Welfare, directed by Forrester B. Washington, with two paid field workers and many volunteer assistants.

One of the more comprehensive surveys covering both economic and social situations.

16. (a) Sadie T. Mossell: " Standard of Living Among 100 Migrant Families in Philadelphia," *Annals* 98, November 1921.

Primarily concerned with problem of standard of living as shown by analysis of family budgets. Includes study of causes and extent of migration. One of the early surveys.

(b) Anna J. Thompson: " Survey of Crime Among Negroes in Philadelphia," *Opportunity* 4, pp. 217-9, 251-4, 285-6, 1926.

Used records of Detective Bureau and Police Courts. In-tensive study of nature of offenses and criminal statistics among Negroes.

17. (a) A. Epstein: *Negro Migrant in Pittsburgh*, Pittsburgh, Pennsyl-vania, 1918. 74 pp.

A study in social economy published under the supervision of the School of Economics, University of Pittsburgh. Conducted when migrants first came and pictures extreme conditions of that time.

(b) Pittsburgh Council of Churches: *New Negro Population*, Pitts-burgh, Pennsylvania, February 1918. (Pamphlet.)
Useful for comparison with other surveys.

18. (a) William Henry Jones: *Housing of Negroes in Washington, D. C.*, Washington, D. C., Howard University Press, 1929. 191 pp.

Sponsored by the Washington Interracial Committee. Con-ducted by Professor Jones of Howard University with help of students of the University. An exhaustive study of housing situation in Washington.

(b) William Henry Jones: *Recreation and Amusement Among Negroes in Washington, D. C.*, Washington, D. C., Howard University Press, 1927. 216 pp.

19. Charles S. Johnson. " Negro Population of Waterbury, Connecticut," *Opportunity* 1, pp. 298-302, 338-42, October and November, 1923.

Survey by National Urban League. Particularly interesting for its picture of what is going on among smaller Negro groups in the North.

TABLE 9.—NATURE OF PUBLISHED REPORTS OF SURVEYS MADE THROUGHOUT THE NORTH SHOWING EFFECTS OF RECENT NEGRO MIGRATIONS

(x indicates subjects covered)

Investigator / Period Covered	(1) E. J. Scott *1917–1919	(2) U. S. Dept. of Labor (a) 1916–17	(b) *1920	(c) 1920	(3) F. B. Washington *1928	(4) T. J. Woofter (a) 1917–20	(b) 1925–26
Topics Considered in Report:							
1. Increase of Negroes by Migration	x	x				x	x
2. Industrial Conditions.							
(1) Nature of Occupations	x	x	x			x	
(2) Business and Professions.							
(3) Wages	x		x				
(4) Unions....................	x	x	x			x	
(5) Relation with White Workers.	x	x	x			x	
(6) Success	x		x			x	
(7) Negro Women Workers			x	x			
3. Composition of Negro Population						x	
4. Housing.							
(1) Segregation.................	x						x
(2) Congestion							x
(3) Conditions			x				x
(4) Rents	x						x
(5) Lodgers...................	x						x
(6) Deterioration of Property....							x
(7) Ownership							x
5. Health		x				x	
6. Social Maladjustment.							
(1) Crime		x				x	
(2) Juvenile Delinquency							x
7. Education							x
8. Political Situation.............							
9. Church......................							
10. Recreation					x		x
11. Race Relations.							
(1) Contacts...................							
(2) Discrimination							x
(3) Friction							
12. Attitude of Northern Negroes....	x						
13. Work of Organizations..........	x						

* Dates marked with asterisk are approximate.

DESCRIPTION OF SURVEYS TO ACCOMPANY TABLE 9

1. E. J. Scott: *Negro Migration*, Oxford University Press, 1920. 189 pp.
Deals with conditions in St. Louis, Chicago and its environs, Milwaukee, Pittsburgh, Cleveland, Cincinnati, Columbus and several smaller Ohio cities, Detroit, Philadelphia, Newark and Hartford. Based on reports of three investigators, M. N. Work, C. S. Johnson and T. T. Fortune. Deals with causes of migration, stimulation and spread of movement, effects in the South, and public opinion concerning migration. Conducted during war period and valuable for picture of early days of the war migration.

2. (a) United States Department of Labor: *Negro Migration in 1916-1917*, Government Printing Office, 1919. 158 pp.
Northern cities specifically included are: Philadelphia and environs, New York City, Newark, Jersey City, Detroit, Pittsburgh, Cincinnati, Cleveland and Chicago. Report of four investigators (three white, one Negro). Includes discussion of causes of migration and results in South and North. Only brief discussion of effects in North.

   (b) *Negro at Work During the World War and Reconstruction*, Government Printing Office, 1921. 144 pp.
Covers principal cities in New York, New Jersey, Pennsylvania, Ohio, Indiana, Illinois, Michigan. Report of the work done by the Division of Negro Economics. Emphasis is on economic status of Negro during war period.

   (c) United States Department of Labor, Women's Bureau: *Bulletin No. 20*, 1922. Government Printing Office. 65 pp.
Included cities in New York, Ohio, Pennsylvania, Illinois, Michigan and Indiana. Investigation made by Emma L. Shields in conjunction with Division of Negro Economics. Study of Negro women in 150 selected plants in 17 localities in 9 states (North and South). Studies nature of occupations, wages and hours, success and contact with white workers. Only general conclusions can be derived from this, since it does not deal specifically with Negro women in northern industries and makes no distinction between migrants and non-migrants.

3. Forrester B. Washington. "Recreational Facilities for the Negro," *Annals* 140, pp. 272-82, November 1928.
The principal northern cities included by Washington and in surveys listed in Tables 8 and 9 are: Buffalo, Cincinnati, Cleveland, Detroit, Indianapolis, Milwaukee, Minneapolis, Newark, New York, Philadelphia, Pittsburgh, St. Louis and Toledo. Based on his work with the Detroit Urban League and on questionnaires sent to fifty-seven cities. Includes conditions in the South.

4. (a) T. J. Woofter, Jr.: *Negro Migration, Changes in Rural Organization and Population of the Cotton Belt*, New York, W. D. Gray, 1920. 195 pp.

> Deals with North in general, not with specific cities. Based on census material and trip South in 1917, North in 1920. Deals primarily with conditions in the South, only briefly with North.

(b) *Negro Problems in Cities*, New York, Doubleday Doran and Company, 1928. 284 pp.

> Northern cities included are: Philadelphia, New York, Buffalo, Indianapolis, Chicago, Gary, Dayton. Study by a staff of four people; also includes some southern cities. Limited to subjects of neighborhoods, housing, education and recreation. Needs to be supplemented by more intensive surveys.

In view of these variations no attempt is made to rank the studies in order of importance or reliability but from an examination of Table 8 and the more detailed description immediately following it, a few conclusions are obvious. The surveys carried on by the Chicago Race Commission, the Detroit Bureau and the Commonwealth of Pennsylvania are the most comprehensive and among the most useful. Each of these was conducted by several individuals and enlisted the cooperation of both white and colored people. The investigations sponsored by the National Urban League are more uniform in method and scope than are the other studies, and are especially valuable for their material on the economic aspects of the Negro's presence in northern cities; these surveys have tended to emphasize this phase of the Negro's problems but some of them have also included suggestive studies of social conditions.

It is true that these surveys have not been carried on by uniform methods and under similar circumstances and, in consequence, show marked variation. However, by comparing and checking them with each other it is possible to derive general conclusions as to what has been occurring in the North as a whole during these last fifteen years. Such generalizations are strengthened by checking with the opinions of

leading students who have carefully followed the characteristics and effects of the northern urbanization of Negroes,
and who have based their views on an extensive knowledge
of race problems. When the conclusions of such leaders
are combined with the findings of specific investigations it is
evident that certain general trends have appeared in the
economic and social life of northern cities since the intensification of Negro migration to the North. Utilizing this
comparative method, the following chapters examine the
more apparent and important trends.

SECTION II

ECONOMIC AND SOCIAL EFFECTS
OF MIGRATION

CHAPTER IV

Occupations, Wages and Hours of Labor

As has been pointed out in earlier chapters, the spectacular movement of southern Negroes to northern cities was fundamentally a response to the demand for labor which arose from the lessened immigration of European workmen and a concomitant increase in industrial activity occasioned by the manufacture of war products. The situation provided an unexpected economic opportunity for the only laborers available—the Negro workmen, who before this period had been given practically no chance to enter the northern industrial field. Under such circumstances the economic effects of the migration were conspicuous and important.

LABORERS AND THEIR JOBS

The movement of colored laborers from the rural districts of the South to the industrial centers of the North not only fulfilled the demand for labor and increased the number of Negro wage earners in northern cities but at the same time altered the distribution of Negroes in the various general classes of occupations. Previous to the war period the largest numbers of southern colored workers were found in agriculture, and of northern, in domestic and personal service; in fact, in 1910 over three-fourths of all Negroes gainfully employed were classified in these two occupations. The migration of farm laborers to northern cities resulted in a disturbance of these proportions, for the 1920 figures revealed a marked decrease in the proportion of Negroes employed in agricultural lines and an increase in the per-

71

centage found in other types of work, particularly in manufacturing and mechanical industries. Although 58 per cent
of the Negro males were engaged in agriculture in 1910, by
1920 only 48 per cent were so employed, whereas the proportion of those in manufacturing and mechanical industries
had risen from less than one-fifth to almost a fourth. The
decade 1910-1920 witnessed an increase in the proportion of
male Negroes in every class of occupation except those of
agriculture and domestic and personal service.[1]

TABLE 10.—PER CENT DISTRIBUTION BY GENERAL DIVISION OF
OCCUPATION OF NEGRO GAINFUL WORKERS TEN YEARS
OF AGE AND OVER, 1920 AND 1910

(Source: *Fourteenth Census,* 1920, vol. iv, p. 340.)

Occupation	Per cent Negro Gainful Workers Ten Years and Over					
	All Negro		Males		Females	
	1920	1910	1920	1910	1920	1910
All Occupations	100.0	100.0	100.0	100.0	100.0	100.0
Agriculture, Forestry and Animal Husbandry	45.2	55.7	48.2	58.0	39.0	52.2
Extraction of Minerals	1.5	1.2	2.2	1.9	*	*
Manufacturing and Mechanical Pursuits	18.4	12.2	24.0	17.7	6.7	3.4
Transportation	6.5	4.9	9.5	8.0	0.2	0.1
Trade	2.9	2.3	4.0	3.5	0.7	0.3
Public Service	1.0	0.4	1.5	0.7	0.1	*
Professional Service	1.7	1.3	1.3	1.2	2.5	1.5
Domestic and Personal Service	22.1	21.6	8.4	8.5	50.3	42.4
Clerical	0.8	0.4	0.9	0.5	0.5	0.2

* Less than one-tenth of one per cent.

A study of the occupational distribution of all colored
workers in the United States reveals the shift from agri-

[1] For an exhaustive treatment of occupational distribution, see the
companion volume by O. D. Dutcher, *The Negro in Modern Industrial
Society,* soon to be printed.

culture to other classes of labor, but the exact nature of the occupations into which Negroes were flocking in the North is more clearly indicated by an examination of the distribution of Negro male workers in several leading cities of the North. Table 11 indicates the numerical increase of colored males in northern centers and the noticeable trend toward the occupations of manufacturing and mechanical industries. Previous to this period Negro males in the North tended to show a decided concentration in the field of domestic and personal service. That this decade witnessed a shift from this type of labor in the North just as it saw a transfer from agriculture in the South, is evident from a study of the proportions in the chief occupations. (See Table 12.) There was a decrease in the per cent of male workers in domestic and personal service and a concomitant increase of those in manufacturing and mechanical industries. This was true even in New York City, which has no such specialized industry as has Pittsburgh, Detroit or Chicago. Whereas nearly half of the workers in New York were in domestic and personal service in 1910, the proportion found in this field in 1920 was nearer one-third. The middle western cities revealed a decided increase in manufacturing and mechanical industries; in Detroit, for example, the percentage of males in this field rose from 17.0 in 1910 to 70.1 in 1920. Whether Negroes have continued this advance into industry since 1920 or have even retained the positions they secured during the War, remains to be seen after the 1930 census figures are available. Surveys which have been made in the last ten years indicate that colored workers are still far more numerous in northern industries than they were in 1910 but that they have lost a little of the ground they held in 1920.[1]

[1] See Bibliography, reference 110 (a), ch. 3.

TABLE II.—NUMBER OF MALE NEGRO WORKERS TEN YEARS OF AGE AND OVER
BY GENERAL DIVISION OF OCCUPATION FOR CERTAIN
NORTHERN CITIES, 1920 AND 1910

(Compiled from *Fourteenth Census*, 1920, vol. iv, pp. 1049 *et seq.*;
Thirteenth Census, 1910, vol. iii, table viii.)

	Number of Male Workers in					
	New York City		Philadelphia		Chicago	
	1920	1910	1920	1910	1920	1910
Total Male Workers	56,516	33,110	50,809	29,561	45,123	18,437
Agriculture	158	249	310	259	41	22
Extraction of Minerals	14	....	27	80	31	48
Manufacturing and Mechanical..	12,067	4,504	22,702	7,407	16,307	3,073
Transportation	12,235	5,197	10,103	5,676	3,441	1,849
Trade	3,919	3,072	4,342	3,393	8,461	1,505
Public Service	1,749	486	1,686	674	959	224
Professional	1,571	1,040	870	538	1,191	640
Domestic and Personal	21,144	16,224	9,378	8,509	12,666	9,426
Clerical	3,659	1,528	1,391	929	2,026	771

	Detroit		Pittsburgh		Cleveland		Cincinnati	
	1920	1910	1920	1910	1920	1910	1920	1910
Total Male Workers	19,808	2,350	15,071	9,940	15,010	3,495	11,605	7,755
Agriculture	25	....	31	....	39	....	64	21
Extraction of Minerals ...	13	....	79	....	19	....	26	....
Manufacturing and Mechanical	13,892	409	7,971	2,859	9,493	755	5,849	1,913
Transportation	1,426	182	1,862	1,232	1,561	414	2,068	1,609
Trade	841	108	873	814	883	290	765	547
Public Service	166	29	286	193	235	57	150	146
Professional	337	75	227	134	212	50	240	116
Domestic and Personal ...	2,791	785	3,343	3,023	2,261	1,150	2,238	1,830
Clerical	317	64	399	224	307	106	205	121

Such a comparison of the proportion of Negro males in
the two occupational divisions of domestic and personal
service, and manufacturing and mechanical industries for the
periods 1910 and 1920 apparently justifies the conclusion that
colored laborers who have come to northern cities in recent
years have found unprecedented economic opportunities and

TABLE 12.—PER CENT DISTRIBUTION BY CHIEF OCCUPATIONS OF NEGRO MALE
WORKERS IN CERTAIN NORTHERN CITIES, 1920 AND 1910

(Sources: Same as Table 11, from which this was computed.)

Per cent of Negro Male Workers in

City	Manufacturing and Mechanical		Transportation		Trade		Domestic and Personal	
	1920	1910	1920	1910	1920	1910	1920	1910
New York City	21.4	13.6	21.6	15.7	6.9	9.3	37.4	49.0
Philadelphia	44.7	25.1	19.9	19.2	8.5	11.5	18.5	28.8
Chicago	36.1	16.7	7.6	10.0	18.8	8.2	28.1	51.1
Detroit	70.1	17.4	7.2	7.7	4.2	4.6	14.1	33.4
Pittsburgh	52.9	28.8	12.4	12.4	5.8	8.2	22.2	30.4
Cleveland	63.2	21.6	10.4	11.8	5.9	8.3	15.1	32.9
Cincinnati	50.4	24.7	17.8	20.7	6.6	7.1	19.3	23.6

for the first time have had a chance to break away from the limited fields of agriculture and of domestic and personal service. Unfortunately, however, this entrance of Negroes into industry is not so complete and encouraging as these general figures indicate. When attention is directed to the particular type of work in which Negroes are chiefly engaged within the general fields of trade, transportation and manufacturing, it is seen that although colored workers have gained a foothold in northern industry yet they are still largely confined to unskilled labor and positions which are closely allied to domestic and personal service. In practically every northern city Negroes who are listed as being employed in manufacturing and mechanical pursuits are found in largest numbers in the various " laborers " categories. In the division, transportation, the largest single groups of Negroes are chauffeurs, and draymen or teamsters. In some cities, such as New York, the number of longshoremen is also large. Of Negroes listed as engaged in trade, the majority are " laborers, porters and helpers in stores," while in the division, public service, the greatest number are classified as

laborers.   There is, therefore, among Negroes a decided predominance of the manual and service type of occupation even
in the industrial field.

The limitation of Negroes to processes calling for unskilled
manual labor is strikingly apparent in such industries as
iron and steel mills, slaughter houses and stockyards, automobile, chemical and textile factories.   In these establishments
and others like them the majority of Negro employees are
unskilled laborers and seldom advance beyond this status.
Yet it must not be overlooked that the presence of Negroes in
even these unskilled positions marks a real improvement in
their economic standing—for until the war period they were
practically negligible in such occupations—and constitutes a
necessary initial step toward further possible industrial progress.   In Detroit, for example, the number of Negroes
employed as laborers in the automobile factories was only
17 in 1910 but had jumped to 3,870 in 1920.   The blast
furnaces and rolling mills of Pittsburgh reported only 507
Negroes in 1910, but a decade later the number had risen to
4,350.   Similar increases occurred in the number of colored
men employed in the stockyards and slaughter houses of
Chicago, and various other industrial occupations in northern
cities have received an unprecedented number of colored
workers.

The surveys substantiate the situation disclosed by the
1920 Census and indicate a continuation of the trend.

In New York City the majority of Negroes are engaged
as personal and domestic servants, elevator operators,
porters and laundry workers.   Although the number of
colored males in domestic and personal service is still large,
the concentration in that field is being broken and many
men have entered the industries of the city.   They are,
however, largely confined to the unskilled occupations in

such industries as have opened up to them.[1] Surveys of economic conditions in Buffalo (about 1925) have shown that the vast majority of Negroes in that city are employed as unskilled laborers or in domestic and personal service. Although the latter field still claimed the largest number of Negroes, most of whom were newcomers, yet colored laborers were entering industrial pursuits, particularly the blast furnaces and rolling mills.[2] Epstein's study of the migrants in Pittsburgh during 1917 showed that, on the whole, Negroes were still limited to domestic service and common labor, 95 per cent of them being employed in unskilled labor " in the steel mills, the building trades, on the railroads or acting as servants, porters, janitors, cooks and cleaners." While there had been a decided increase in the number of colored industrial employees, they were held in the lowest stages of the work, particularly in the larger plants, where almost 100 per cent of the Negroes were doing unskilled work. It should be pointed out that many of the Negroes were in the steel mills, which by their very nature necessitated a large force of unskilled labor.[3]

According to the report of the survey sponsored by the Commonwealth of Pennsylvania (1925) the industrial opportunities open to Negroes are much more numerous in the western than in the eastern part of the state. However, in Pennsylvania as a whole, the number of colored workers has shown a marked increase since 1910 and an interesting redistribution of Negroes in the general classes of occupations. " Ten years ago the Negro was almost an unknown factor in productive industry in (Pennsylvania) . . . Throughout the Commonwealth previous to 1915 the Negro was engaged as a mass in domestic and personal service occupations." In 1920 there was a de-

[1] References 57 (a), pp. 641-3; 96 (a), p. 69.
[2] References 16 (a), p. 162; 57 (n), pp. 323-4.
[3] References 32 (a), pp. 22, 30-3; 151 (a), p. 295; 124 (a), p. 122; 145 (d), pp. 125-6.

crease of 23.3 per cent in the number of Negroes employed
in domestic and personal service, whereas there was an increase of 151.1 per cent in the number employed in manufacturing and mechanical industries. " It was the first time
that the number of Negroes engaged in domestic and personal service had decreased between two census years. . .
and for the first time in the 300 odd years that Negroes had
lived in Pennsylvania there were more Negroes in the
manufacturing and mechanical industries than there were
in domestic and personal service. . . . During the five
years between 1915 and 1920 almost a miracle took place
in the industrial status of the Pennsylvania Negro. From
a hewer of wood and a drawer of water, from an unimportant menial employee . . . he suddenly became an industrial producing unit." During the next five-year period,
1920 to 1925, the number of Negroes decreased in all
classes of occupations except domestic and personal service,
and agriculture; there was a shrinkage of 10 per cent in the
number employed in manufacturing and mechanical industries. However, in spite of this setback, colored laborers in 1925 showed a great advance over their pre-war
situation. And " in some sections of the Commonwealth
the number of Negroes working in certain industries is even
higher than it was during the peak of the War period." [1]

Of all the investigations of the Negro's place in the industrial life of northern cities, that made by the Chicago
Race Commission in 1920 is one of the most extensive.
Between 1910 and 1920 Chicago's colored population increased over 148 per cent, and there was an accompanying
addition to the number of colored workers in some of
Chicago's occupations. This gain was apparently greater
in the manufacturing field than in that of domestic and
personal service, for the proportion of Negroes employed
in the latter class decidedly decreased while the proportion
in the former class of occupation showed an increase. The

[1] Reference 110 (a), pp. 14-8.

Chicago Commission concluded that there had been " a remarkable increase since 1915 in the number of Negro workers employed in manufacturing, in clerical occupations, and in laundries. As was to be expected, the number of Negroes in personal service (hotels, dining cars and parlor cars) also increased, but the increase was negligible in comparison with the gain in the other fields mentioned." Particularly significant advances were reported for such manufacturing establishments as box making, clothing, food products, iron and steel, and tanneries. Furthermore, this report of the Race Commission reveals the tendency of Chicago's colored workers to follow the Negro's usual concentration in the ranks of unskilled labor, since most of the Negro workers were reported as being in this class.[1]

Very similar situations are disclosed in surveys which have been made in Cincinnati, Cleveland, Columbus, and other industrial centers.[2] In all of these places, there has been since 1915 a noticeable increase in the number of colored industrial laborers, but the vast majority of them are employed in the lowest classes of unskilled work. On the basis of the surveys of the Negro in Detroit made by Haynes (1918) and the Detroit Bureau of Governmental Research (1926), it is evident that here, too, colored workers have found an unprecedented industrial opportunity but are still largely confined to common, unskilled labor. Both the Bureau of Research and Haynes point out the enormous increase that has taken place in the number of Negroes living and working in Detroit and report that the majority of Negroes are doing unskilled work. The few colored wage earners in Detroit in 1910 were almost entirely limited to domestic and personal service but in 1926 the Detroit Bureau of Research estimated that between

[1] Reference 17 (a), pp. 362, 166, 358-72, 382, 391-3, 623-6.

[2] References 120 (a), pp. 524-5; 1 (a), pp. 620-2; 81 (a), p. 41; 44 (b), p. 25; 124 (a), pp. 112-4; 57 (g), pp. 301-2.

25,000 and 30,000 Negroes were employed in Detroit's industrial establishments, most of them in the field of unskilled labor. 1

Comparing these reports of numerous specific investigations with the census material and with the opinions of leading students of the Negro's economic status, it is evident that throughout the North there has been a tremendous increase in the number of colored wage earners employed in various industries. It is known that many of the new industrial positions have been filled by migrants from the South. More investigation is needed to determine whether those who still remain in the field of domestic and personal service are northern Negroes who already held the positions or are newcomers taking the places left vacant by northern colored men when they entered the industrial realm. Negroes are still largely limited to the lowest types of work but they have found a wider range of occupations open to them and they have been able to gain at least a footing in the complicated industrial life of northern cities.

THE TREND TO SKILLED AND SEMI-SKILLED POSITIONS

The Negro has attained the lowest rung of the industrial ladder, and has also succeeded in taking a few tentative steps toward the better-paid skilled positions. During the last fifteen years in most northern cities there has been an increase in the number of Negroes employed in semi-skilled and skilled occupations, although the industrial centers show variation in the extent to which such positions have been opened to colored workmen. In the cities of the Middle West, such as Chicago and Detroit, there is apparently a

---

[1] References 46 (f), pp. 15-6, 19; 22 (a), sec. iii. *Cf.* references 145 (c), p. 89; 93 (a), pp. 175, 181, 185; 145 (d), p. 128; 2 (a), p. 11; 57 (i), pp. 14-6; 140 (a), p. 28; 57 (j), pp. 235-7; 46 (j), pp. 30-1; 57 (a), pp. 642-3; 57 (n), pp. 322-4.

stronger trend toward the inclusion of Negroes in skilled work than exists in many eastern cities like New York and Philadelphia. The number of skilled Negroes is affected by the nature of the industry and the extent of its organization by labor unions; the automobile factories of Detroit need a larger proportion of skilled workers than do the steel mills of Pittsburgh and hence offer more opportunity for Negroes to work up to positions requiring skill and training. Moreover, in contrast to the relatively highly specialized industries of a place like Detroit, the predominance of trade over industry in New York City offers proportionately fewer opportunities for skilled work. The attitude of the labor unions is another exceedingly important factor in determining the extent to which colored skilled workers are successful in finding positions. Many of the unions do not encourage the inclusion of Negroes and where an industry is highly organized in locals possessing this attitude, the Negroes have little chance of entering. Unfortunately for the colored man, most of the industries which need a noticeable proportion of trained workers are organized. Where there are numerous skilled positions, the unions bar the way to the Negro; where industries are likely to be open-shop, the majority of positions are in unskilled work. In spite of these handicaps Negroes have made steady progress in the number of their race employed in such occupations in northern cities.

Semi-skilled and skilled positions and trades in New York City include a much larger number of Negro employees than they did in 1910 but in view of the tremendous influx of colored people into this center during the last decade and a half, there is reason for believing that this type of economic opportunity has not opened up for the Negro in New York to the extent that it has in some other northern cities. Students of this phase of the Negro's economic status in New York tend to agree that the colored

worker is still prevented from freely entering highly
skilled trades, such as those of brick masons, painters,
plasterers and plumbers.[1] Negroes in Buffalo have advanced a little, since in 1920 the proportion of colored
laborers in several semi-skilled and skilled positions exceeded the proportion of Negroes in the total population;
this was particularly true in semi-skilled tasks in rolling
mills and in the skilled work of cranemen and derrick men.
However, the vast majority of Negroes in Buffalo were
limited to unskilled and domestic labor and Carpenter concluded from his survey (1926) that colored wage earners
could only rarely find an opening in skilled occupations and
could never expect to be " rated as a high skilled worker,
foreman, or office worker." [2] The Pennsylvania Survey
Committee felt that Negroes in the western part of the state
had greater opportunities for advancement into skilled
trades than they did in and around Philadelphia. But the
number of skilled workers among the colored people is not
large in any section of Pennsylvania.[3]

In the industrial centers of the Middle West the colored
wage earners were apparently a little more successful in
entering semi-skilled and skilled occupations, for the surveys of conditions in Chicago, Cleveland, Milwaukee and
Detroit all speak more optimistically of the advance made
by Negroes in these lines.[4] According to the Chicago Race
Commission, migrants who had been skilled workers in the
South had difficulty in securing similar positions when they
first came to Chicago but on the whole, the proportion of
skilled workers among Negro laborers was increasing in
that city.[5] In comparing the various reports of the status

[1] References 145 (c), p. 95; 57 (a), p. 518.

[2] References 16 (a), p. 139; *cf.* 57 (b), p. 132.

[3] References 110 (a), ch. 3; 145 (d), pp. 125-8; 32 (a), pp. 20-1;
124 (a), p. 122.

[4] References 124 (a), p. 113; 151 (a), p. 298.

[5] References 17 (a), pp. 166, 364; *cf.* 57 (a), p. 718; 145 (d), p. 128.

of colored skilled laborers, it seems evident that Detroit is conspicuous for its opportunities in this line, as the automobile establishments are employing Negroes in semi-skilled and skilled positions as well as in the field of common labor. While only eight Negroes were listed as semi-skilled laborers in the automobile factories at the time of the 1910 census, 809 colored workers were so classified in 1920. The Detroit Bureau of Research concluded that almost a third of the Negroes employed in the firms covered by their survey could be classed as semi-skilled or skilled, about half of these being in the automobile factories.[1]

After an extensive analysis of labor conditions, Wesley maintains that throughout the North the Negro has made a real advance in skilled occupations, and as an illustration of this progress he quotes a press release of the United States Department of Labor showing the increase of skilled and unskilled workers for the year 1922-1923. The following extracts from that table indicate the trend of Negro labor.[2]

INCREASE OF SKILLED AND UNSKILLED NEGRO WORKERS
APRIL 1922 – APRIL 1923

	Per cent Increase	
State	Skilled	Unskilled
Michigan	70.7	62.5
Ohio	68.0	71.2
Pennsylvania	43.7	77.5
Illinois	39.9	46.7
New York	30.0	39.8

On the other hand, in spite of this advance in the number of colored skilled workers in the North, the proportion of Negroes employed in semi-skilled and skilled positions is still extremely small compared to the proportion of colored people

[1] References 22 (a), sec. iii; *cf.* 46 (f), p. 19; 124 (a), p. 129.

[2] References 151 (a), p. 300; *cf.* 57 (g), p. 302; 57 (i), p. 14; 57 (n), p. 323.

in unskilled labor and in domestic and personal service, or compared to the percentage of white wage earners engaged in skilled occupations. There are, of course, a variety of factors back of this situation. The policy of the unions has already been mentioned. Students of the subject contend that the attitude of organized labor is one of the most persistent and effective checks to the Negro's advancement in skilled work. When trades and occupations are almost completely controlled by unions the Negroes are usually prevented from even gaining an entrance, even though they may have practiced these trades in the South. Moreover, employers often refuse to advance Negroes to positions which would place them on an equal plane with white skilled workers or in authority over white unskilled employees. Then, too, the majority of Negroes have previously had no experience save in the field of agriculture and are totally untrained and unfitted to fill the skilled positions which might be available in northern industries. This handicap is frequently intensified by the inability of Negroes to secure from employers and unions a chance to acquire this necessary training.[1]

The surveys indicate that the years since the beginning of the World War have witnessed an increase in the number of Negro workmen employed in the semi-skilled and skilled occupations in northern industries. Final confirmation of the post-war trend must wait upon publication of the results of the 1930 Census, some years hence.

NEGROES IN BUSINESS AND PROFESSIONS

There is little reliable information concerning the effect of migration upon the status of the Negro in the business and professional life of northern cities. However, there are indications of increased activity along both lines, for the crowd-

[1] References 57 (n), p. 326; 57 (a), p. 643; 16 (a), pp. 116, 139.

ing of migrants into the " Negro areas " of the principal urban centers naturally increased the need for stores, restaurants, amusement places, and similar establishments, and for such professional men as doctors, dentists and clergymen. Judging from the brief surveys which have been made of the Negro's business activities, it seems evident that colored men have at least begun to take advantage of these increasing opportunities and to open up business establishments of their own. So far reports indicate that the majority of these Negro proprietors and owners are migrants from the South, as northern Negroes have shown less initiative in this direction. Most of the Negro business establishments are barber shops, hair-dressing parlors, tailor shops, restaurants, cabarets, dance halls, pool rooms and similar concerns. This predominance of the " decorative," refreshment and amusement types of projects is accounted for to a large extent by the fact that these are the lines in which colored people meet most forcefully and conspicuously the race prejudice of their white neighbors. With the rising tide of discrimination and segregation which has appeared in many northern cities since the noticeable increase in colored populations, there has been a greater demand among Negroes for amusement and refreshment places of their own. Furthermore, business establishments of these types tend to require less capital and training at the start than do many other projects, and Negroes, as a rule, have little of either.

Both the Negro business concerns and professional men tend to serve a clientele almost entirely confined to the colored population. Previous to the migrations of the last decade and a half most of the colored professional men who desired to work up a large practice were obliged to go South, but the rapid growth of the northern Negro population has apparently increased their opportunities. The increase in the number of colored clergymen has been particularly evident, although other professions have been augmented, too.   The 1920 census figures for a few of the more important centers indicate the possible widening of professional fields for Negroes in the North.   Probably the forthcoming census

TABLE 13.—NUMBER OF NEGRO MALES IN CERTAIN PROFESSIONS
IN DESIGNATED CITIES, 1910 AND 1920

(Sources: Same as Table 11.)

Number of Negro Males in

	New York		*Philadelphia*		*Chicago*	
	1920	1910	1920	1910	1920	1910
Clergymen	176	120	278	169	215	76
Dentists	96	42	47	16	68	14
Lawyers	50	50	13	13	95	44
Musicians	554	318	178	143	254	216
Physicians	94	57	90	78	195	109

Number of Negro Males in

	Detroit		*Pittsburgh*		*Cleveland*		*Cincinnati*	
	1920	1910	1920	1910	1920	1910	1920	1910
Clergymen	82	—	96	63	73	—	91	50
Dentists	24	—	15	—	13	—	10	—
Lawyers	32	11	8	5	10	11	8	4
Musicians	106	58	22	37	28	30	47	43
Physicians	28	6	27	27	27	8	16	14

figures will show more decided increases, for it is natural to suppose that the growth in the number of professional men would begin only after the opportunity was clearly established and thus would lag behind the increase in colored population. The Negro interested in starting a professional career is confronted with the serious problems of competition from white men, difficulty in obtaining the necessary training, and the time required for such training.   There is also an unfortunate tendency among Negroes to prefer white doctors or lawyers, or the stores owned by white proprietors to those of their own race.   Consequently colored men frequently find it up-hill work to start a business or professional practice among their people. Many Negroes, lacking capital to finance their own businesses, are found as managers or superior employees of concerns owned by whites and serving a colored clientele. In spite of these handicaps the number of Negro business establishments and of Negro professional men in the North has shown a tendency to increase in recent years.[1]

Although up-to-date comparable figures showing the growth of Negro business and professions in northern centers will not be available until the 1930 census material is at hand, in the meantime, reports of various surveys indicate the trend of this phase of the Negro's economic activities in specific cities. In Minneapolis (1926) the survey of the Negro group disclosed several thriving business enterprises, chiefly restaurants, that were trying to meet the needs of the growing colored population.[2] The Chicago Race Commission mentions the increase in Negro business concerns that had occurred in the two years preceding the survey and estimated that the number of commercial and industrial establishments conducted in Chicago by Negroes had increased nearly 25 per cent in the one year 1919 to 1920. A large proportion of such establishments were barber shops, grocery stores, hair dressing parlors and restaurants.[3] The Detroit survey (1926) also found that Negro business establishments had increased and that most of them might be classified as decorative concerns, including under this title barber shops, beauty parlors and tailor shops; or amusement places, such as dance halls, pool rooms and cabarets.[4] The Pennsylvania Commission (1925) reported that nearly two-thirds of the

[1] In the past few weeks (February, 1930) Harlem Hospital, New York City, has been put on a half-white, half-Negro basis as regards its entire staff.

[2] References 44 (b), p. 18; cf. 16 (a), p. 168.

[3] Reference 17 (a), pp. 140-1.

[4] Reference 22 (a), sec. iv.

Negro business enterprises in Pennsylvania were conducted by men who had come from the South and that the majority of these concerns were " beauty culturists, barber shops, restaurants and undertakers." The report concludes that " while the number of businesses conducted by Negroes is still comparatively small, the advance that has been made in recent years in numbers and variety is much more rapid than formerly was the case. . . . Much of the Negro's progress in business has been due to the migrant, who, coming from the South where he had been discriminated against by white merchants, learned to patronize those of his own race. . . . The migrant . . . had a much greater inclination to patronize Negro business than the Pennsylvania-born Negro, and he was more apt to go into business for himself. . . . Negro professional men are increasing in numbers and becoming more prosperous for the same reason that Negro business has prospered." [1]   Such well known leaders of the race as George E. Haynes and Ernest K. Jones, who have kept in close touch with Negro problems throughout the North, also believe that recent years have seen a real improvement in the Negro's status in business and professions.[2]

OCCUPATIONS OF NEGRO WOMEN

The vast majority of colored women gainfully employed in northern cities are still in the field of domestic and personal service just as they have been in previous decades. However, the acute labor shortage of the war period created some openings elsewhere. Before 1915 the number of colored women employed in northern industries was so small as to be practically negligible; almost four-fifths of the Negro women workers in the North were limited to the one field of domestic and personal service. Since that date they have appeared more frequently in such positions as the unskilled processes

[1] Reference 110 (a), pp. 27-9, 90.

[2] References 46 (d), p. 72; 62 (b), pp. 971-2.

connected with garment trades, paper box factories and meat packing houses, and to some extent in clerical occupations connected with mail-order houses.

An investigation in New York City found that colored women were being employed in larger numbers than ever before in a variety of establishments, principally in the garment trades, but also to some extent in paper box factories, leather products and similar work.[1] In Philadelphia industrial openings had increased for these wage earners in garment trades, munition factories, textile, paper, tobacco and other establishments.[2] The report of the Chicago Race Commission shows an increase in the employment of Negro women in such work as sewing machine operators, slaughtering and packing house workers, box making, tannery processes and clerical occupations. It has been pointed out, however, that colored women have made little progress in entering skilled work in Chicago, most of them being kept in those phases of industry which are more closely allied to domestic service.[3] In Detroit this group has apparently had a slightly greater chance to enter the better paid, skilled or semi-skilled occupations, for Negro women are found in these positions in the automobile plants. They are also at work in the garment and meat packing establishments, but the number so employed is not so great as in such non-industrial enterprises as laundries, hotels and restaurants.[4] In other cities, for example Buffalo, Waterbury, Albany and Columbus, investigators of this subject have concluded that Negro women have practically failed to enter industry and are still almost entirely employed as servants or in allied occupations.[5]

[1] References 19 (a); 145 (g), p. 7; 46 (a), p. 307.

[2] Reference 145 (g), p. 7.

[3] References 17 (a), pp. 367, 378-85, 402, 625; 145 (g), p. 7.

[4] References 22 (a), sec. iii; 145 (g), pp. 7-8.

[5] References 16 (a), pp. 139, 166-7; 57 (g), pp. 301, 338; 2 (a), p. 11; 81 (a), p. 41; *cf.* 67 (a), pp. 295-9.

Even in the largest centers such as New York, Philadelphia and Chicago, where Negro women have gained at least an entrance into industry, the majority of colored females gainfully employed still remain in the ranks of domestic and personal service.   In fact, the proportion so occupied constitutes in practically all northern cities, about three-fourths of the group of those gainfully employed.

TABLE 14.—PERCENTAGE OF COLORED FEMALES GAINFULLY EMPLOYED
BY TWO OCCUPATIONAL CLASSES FOR CERTAIN CITIES,
1920 AND 1910

(Computed from sources used in Table 11.)

	Percentage of Colored Females Gainfully Employed in			
City	*Manufacturing and Mechanical Industries*		*Domestic and Personal Service*	
	1920	1910	1920	1910
New York	22.6	9.2	71.5	86.0
Philadelphia	11.5	5.7	84.0	89.9
Chicago	21.5	11.2	63.8	78.4
Detroit	12.3	7.7	79.1	78.0
Pittsburgh	6.7	6.0	87.3	88.3
Cleveland	14.1	10.0	77.8	81.1
Cincinnati	12.0	7.3	83.2	86.6

Like Negro men, they are, as a class, in the most poorly paid and the least desirable kinds of work.   Even those who have secured a high school or business training find it difficult to obtain work other than that of servants, waitresses or elevator tenders.[1]   Confronted by low wages, little chance for advancement or improvement and poor working conditions, it is no wonder that Negro women often feel that their chances for economic success or even a living wage are hopeless, and fill the ranks of prostitutes or floating domestics.   Moreover, most of the northern employers who have been interviewed have stated frankly that they hired Negro

[1] Reference 67 (a).

women only because of the acute labor shortage at the time of the war, and many concerns are still reluctant to engage them if other workers are available. It would seem, therefore, that industrial openings for women are not yet firmly established. Further studies are needed before we can know whether Negro women are being retained in or further drawn into northern industries during periods of retrenchment when workers other than Negro women are at hand.

> In his recent volume on the occupations of women, J. A. Hill has shown that the number of Negro women employed as laborers and as semi-skilled operatives in factories increased between 1910 and 1920, but adds—" We shall need the statistics of at least one more census to determine whether the large increase from 1910 to 1920 marks the beginning of a more general employment of Negro women in factories, or whether, being an increase due to the great temporary demand for factory workers which came with the World War, it will not outlast the exceptional conditions which caused it. Much depends, perhaps, upon whether—with continued restricted immigration—there will be a sufficient supply of white workers." [1]

The various investigations which have been made of the employment of Negro women in northern cities are not sufficiently comprehensive and comparable to justify more than a tentative conclusion as to their present status in industry. Yet these surveys indicate that there has been a real increase during recent years in the industrial openings for Negro women, since they have become a more important factor in meat packing, in the tobacco industry, in power laundries, in textile and garment factories, in munition plants and in clerical positions. In various cities there has been a tendency for the proportion of colored females in domestic

[1] Reference 47 (b), p. 117.

service to diminish while there was an increase in the proportion listed under manufacturing and mechanical industries.   It should not be forgotten, however, that in cases
where they have won a place in industry, Negro women have
usually been kept in the least desirable phases of the work
and have lacked even the meager economic opportunities that
were opening up for Negro men.   They " were the marginal
workers and had to fill the gap, either in domestic or industrial openings, wherever they were needed," for on the
whole " industry was not ready to receive the large numbers
of Negro women who moved North and West." [1]

A LOOK TO THE FUTURE

To some extent at least, Negroes have succeeded in breaking away from agriculture and domestic and personal service,
and have gained an entry into the industrial life of the North.
For the most part, these colored workers have entered the
unskilled occupations of " seven basic industries: iron and
steel mills; automobile manufactures; chemical and allied
factories; foundries and hardware factories; slaughtering
and meat packing; the stone, tile and glass industry; and the
clothing trades." [2]   So far only a small percentage has
entered the semi-skilled and skilled occupations; the great
mass of colored workers who have found a place in northern
industry are confined to its unskilled processes either on
account of their lack of training and ability, or because of
the prejudice of their white associates and the opposition of
organized labor.   On every side the colored worker is confronted by barriers which handicap his economic advancement, barriers which are comprised of his own lack of industrial experience, his inability to receive training in many
trades by the refusal of organized groups to admit him as

[1] Reference 145 (g), pp. 10, 8.
[2] Reference 46 (d), p. 69.

an apprentice, his inability to secure admission to many local unions so that he has an equal chance at unionized jobs, and the prejudice of white employers and a white public which assumes that a Negro is fit only for menial labor and so completely shuts him out from many positions.

The nature of the occupations still practically closed to him is indicated by the following summary: " Where the manufacturing processes demand highly skilled work Negroes are not employed. Where the positions entail authority over white workers they are not employed. Where the work entails association on an equal footing in operations requiring semi-skill and skill they are rarely employed. Where the nature of the work requires that they meet customers in the capacity of agents or representatives they are not employed. Where the work assumes the mastery of a trade, such as brick laying, carpentry, painting, they are rarely and irregularly employed, and wherever employed they are subject to the opposition of labor organizations." [1]

The opinions voiced by Carpenter after his study of the situation in Buffalo serve as an adequate summary of the views of many other investigators and students of the Negro's economic opportunities in northern cities. " There can be no avoiding the conclusion that . . . the Negro suffers from a severe restriction of his economic opportunities; the men being held chiefly within the confines of the unskilled and general labor groups, and having virtually no chance of going beyond skilled labor, whereas the women are unable even to gain a foothold in the humblest occupations in the community's industrial and mercantile establishments, but are forced to limit themselves almost entirely to domestic and personal service, and to hotel and restaurant work. . . . In general, the net impression left by this group of interviews (with Negroes) is not a

---

[1] References **57 (r)**, p. 140; *cf.* **119 (a)**, pp. 240-2.

happy one. There is more of downright discrimination and denial of opportunity, more of bafflement, more of defeat, more of bitterness, less of success in breaking out of the coil of struggling penury in these records than of those for any other ethnic group included in . . . the study. Some progress is indicated, but it appears to be infinitely hard-won." [1]

Negro wage earners have indeed gained a footing in the industrial life of today but they have little more than this footing. Though the number and variety of their occupations have increased, colored laborers are still limited in their economic opportunities and lack the white man's freedom to enter any trade and to be advanced according to worth and ability. Government statistics show, however, that the total number of Negroes employed in domestic and personal service decreased from 1910 to 1920. At the same time, the number in manufacturing and mechanical pursuits, trade and transportation favors the conclusion that opportunities for Negroes have increased even though they are still far from equal to the economic chances of the white man.

The 1930 census figures on occupations are eagerly awaited by students of the Negro's economic status in the North. The last census was taken at a time of prosperity and marked business activity; [2] since then there have been periods of depression in which white men have been looking for work and in which employers have tried to reduce the cost of production at every turn. Are the Negroes losing the opportunities which were opened up to them during the war and are they

[1] References 16 (a), pp. 140, 118; cf. 110 (a), p. 20; 46 (d), p. 69; 57 (a), p. 643; 70 (a), p. 235.

[2] It is highly probable that the figures for the 1930 Census, taken at a different time of year than the 1920 Census (April 1, 1930, contrasted with January 1, 1920) and at a time when unemployment is more extensive than for many years past, may again make difficult, comparisons of the actual situations.

being displaced by other nationality groups? Since they are so concentrated in the field of unskilled labor, are they in danger of replacement by machine processes which might be substituted for common labor during those periods when employers try to find the cheapest mode of production? These are only a few of the questions which have so far received little intensive study and which will be clarified by the coming census. Not until further studies are made along these lines will we have some of the fundamental facts which are necessary for the formation of conclusions as to the present trend of economic opportunities for Negroes in northern cities.

WAGES AND HOURS OF NEGRO WORKERS

Material which is available concerning wages and hours of Negro workers in northern cities is not sufficiently adequate and uniform to justify any detailed comparison of the situation as it exists in the chief urban centers. Some of the reports base their information on wages per hour, some use the daily wage, while others use the weekly or monthly pay check, or piece-rate earnings. Differences in the wage scale of various cities, in the tendency toward periods of unemployment or time off or, on the other hand, toward extratime, and differences in the cost of living, further increase the difficulty of drawing definite conclusions concerning the wages and hours of Negro laborers throughout the North. Practically all of the reports and discussions, however, indicate a few common tendencies which suggest the general trend.

. There is little doubt that wages of colored laborers in the North are higher than in the South. In surveys which included comparisons of wages received by the migrants before and after they moved North it was found that they had materially increased their average income. The actual per cent increase in the amount of money received is, however, no adequate measure of the real financial improvement, since the higher cost of rent, food and clothing diminishes the actual surplus.   But in spite of this increased cost of living most of the migrants report themselves as being better off financially than they had been in the South.

> The survey made under the auspices of the Commonwealth of Pennsylvania (1925) illustrates the effect migration has had upon the wages of Negro laborers.   "The average wage of the Negro in Pennsylvania is 91 per cent higher than it was in those positions of the South from which a typical group of Pennsylvania migrants came. While these figures show a marked increase in money wages, they do not show that there has been a similar increase in real wages.   A budget study of the cost of living of some 500 Negro families was made and from the data obtained it is possible to state that the cost of living for these families was about 23 per cent more than in the South.   It is evident from this adjustment that the increase in real wages is about 70 per cent."   While these exact figures would not hold true for all northern communities, yet they typify the general trend toward an increased real as well as higher nominal income among Negroes who have moved North.[1]

When the attempt is made to compare wages of white and of colored laborers in northern industry, conflicting evidence at once appears.   It is frequently assumed that Negroes are discriminated against in the matter of wages, and many of those interested in this phase of the Negro's economic situation would agree with Scott Nearing that "Among white men . . . equal pay for equal work is accepted as an axiom. This is not so where Negroes and whites work together; on the contrary, there is persistent wage discrimination."[2]

[1] References 110 (a), p. 21; cf. 145 (d), pp. 22-3; 17 (a), p. 168.
[2] Reference 97 (a), p. 101.

However, the situation throughout the North cannot be so simply described, for the existence and extent of such wage differentiations are not uniform in northern cities.

As an illustration of one situation the report of the New York Urban League may be noted, for this organization concluded that " colored workers receive lower wages than white workers in similar occupations, except when both are members of trade unions." [1] On the other hand, the Detroit Bureau of Research and the Chicago Race Commission both found " practically no complaints of discrimination in wages on the same tasks." [2]

Further investigations are needed before definite conclusions can be drawn but on the basis of the material at hand the general situation in the North in regard to wage discrimination seems to be as follows: In nearly all of the cities there is apparently no open or general policy of differentiation, for Negroes tend to receive the same pay as white laborers when they are working together on the same jobs. This is particularly true of larger establishments; inequalities in wages for similar positions is more noticeable among small concerns. On the other hand, there are evidences in every city of more subtle forms of discrimination which result in a lower average wage for the Negro population. In many cases the opposition of the labor unions prevents the Negro from entering the highly skilled trades and positions which pay more desirable wages. If he can gain admittance to these trades and especially if he can join a local union, he generally receives the same level of wage as is given the white man. The difficulty lies in his inability to secure such positions. Furthermore, many employers refuse to advance deserving colored workers to higher, better paid jobs, especially if

[1] Reference 96 (a), p. 69.
[2] References 22 (a), sec. iii, pp. 14-5; 17 (a), p. 365.

these entail authority over white employees. Similarly, in piece-work occupations the tendency of foremen to keep Negro common laborers upon the processes which yield lower returns than those given to white co-workers assists in producing a lower average wage among colored people. Consequently, it is difficult to compare wages of white and colored laborers because, considering each as a group, they are not always working on the same jobs and do not possess the same opportunities for advancement into the better paid positions.

The general situation as it has been found in northern cities when specific investigations of Negro wages have been made finds typical expression in such reports as that of the Detroit Bureau of Research (1926). " Many employers stated accurate comparisons were difficult because Negroes and whites were not working on the same jobs. None of the Negro workers who were interviewed knew of discrimination in pay on the same job. . . . (Yet) the Negro group as a whole is working on the more inferior jobs and therefore earning less proportionately as a group." [1] Similarly, the Chicago Race Commission concluded that " Wages of Negroes in the branches of employment where they were permitted to work were generally the same as for white workers. There were instances, however, of discrimination in placing or keeping Negroes at work on processes in which they could not earn so much as in processes on which white men were engaged. Also there were instances of discrimination in piece-work, the foremen invariably giving Negroes only the job yielding a low rate." [2] The Urban League's survey of the Negroes in Baltimore (1923) reported the same situation: " No important instances of discriminatory rates for whites and Negroes working on the same jobs and performing the same

[1] Reference 22 (a), sec. iii, pp. 14-5.
[2] Reference 17 (a), p. 624.

processes (were observed. But) over 75 per cent of all
the Negroes working were confined to the branches of work
yielding the lowest pay." [1]

Thus, as a rule, Negroes are limited to the poorly paid
positions or to the seasonal or irregular, and hence less desirable, jobs, so that they earn less in dollars and cents than a
group of white workers of the same occupational level. In
addition they tend to earn less in real wages, since they
usually pay higher prices for necessities, particularly for rent.
Practically all of the investigations found that far too large
a proportion of the Negroes gainfully employed were earning
an income below that necessary for the maintenance of
health and decent standards of living. In many cases the
low wage of the men has made it necessary for the women to
seek employment outside of the home in order to supplement the family income. The result of this is seen in the
abnormally high proportion of Negro women who are working. Their wages tend to be even lower than those of Negro
males and, as a consequence, the combined earnings of the
husband and wife are all too frequently insufficient for the
proper support of the family.

In his report of the situation in Minneapolis, Abram
Harris points out the fact that in 1919 the United States
Bureau of Labor Statistics considered a weekly wage of
$43.51 essential to maintain an acceptable standard of liv-
ing for a family of five. In contrast to this, Harris found
(1926) that of the 222 married Negro men with families
whom he interviewed in Minneapolis, only 12 were receiving more than $40.00 a week, 200 were earning between
$15.00 and $30.00 a week, and the median weekly wage of
the 222 men was $22.55.[2] In Philadelphia (1919) over

[1] Reference 57 (i), p. 19.
[2] Reference 44 (b), pp. 28-30.

half of the families investigated by Mossell were receiving incomes from all sources sufficient to maintain a fair standard of living as described in the study, but, on the other hand, in only 41 per cent of the families was the income of the father alone sufficient to maintain this standard.[1]

There is even less material in regard to the number of hours which Negroes work per day or week, but that which is available leads to the tentative conclusion that the migrant common laborer works on the average about the same number of hours as he did in the South, with a tendency toward a lower average length of day in the North. However, exact comparisons are impossible on the basis of present information. In northern cities there seems to be no widespread discrimination between white and colored laborers working together on the same jobs. Nevertheless the occupations with longer and less desirable hours are usually filled by Negroes, so that, as a group, colored workmen tend to have longer hours of labor than do white wage earners. As the Detroit Bureau of Research remarks: " Many of his jobs are tedious, long-hour, poor-hour jobs, but the Negro has to take them because he can get nothing better." [2]

When a comparison is made of occupations, wages and hours of the mass of colored wage earners in a northern city and a corresponding group of white workers, it is evident that the status of the Negroes is lower and more undesirable. There are numerous evidences that many Negroes are not earning an income sufficient to maintain an adequate standard of living, in spite of the fact that their wages are, on the whole, higher than those which could be obtained in the South.

[1] Reference 93 (a), p. 214.
[2] Reference 22 (a), sec. iii, p. 15.

CHAPTER V

RACE CONTACTS INVOLVED IN THE INDUSTRIALIZATION OF THE NEGRO

THE NEGRO AND THE WHITE WORKER

THE influx of large numbers of colored migrants from the South naturally resulted in more frequent and more intimate contacts between black and white workers. Among many employers and others who were interested in the economic situation it was fearfully expected that the mingling of the races in industrial establishments would lead to much friction and open violence. Contrary to this general assumption, surveys of race contacts in specific northern industries have found that, considering the masses of common laborers of both races competing for industrial openings, there have been surprisingly few serious clashes or race disturbances in establishments which employed both white and Negro labor. It is true that in nearly every city there have been instances in which the introduction of Negro labor has been followed by the demand of white employees for segregation and separate working accommodations and by an antagonistic attitude. Generally, however, the actual daily contacts of Negroes and whites in most establishments have been peaceful and have gradually been accepted as a matter of course. There are indications that when northern employers use colored workmen they tend to mass them in certain occupations or in certain plants, and so there may be less actual mingling of the races in industry than might be assumed simply from a consideration of the large increase in the

number of Negro industrial workers.   More information is
needed before conclusions can be drawn as to this tendency
to separate the two by kind of occupation, but if this does
exist to any great extent, the practice would inevitably lessen
the possibility of friction.   At the same time, it would also
tend to limit the industrial opportunities of the Negroes and
to diminish the chances for racial adjustment through intimate daily contacts and the development of understanding
and friendship on the basis of shared work-interests.   Added
investigation along this line would be very valuable.

Furthermore, the development of a hostile or friendly relationship between the workers in an establishment apparently
depends to a great extent upon the circumstances under which
the Negroes are introduced.   When open conflicts have
occurred between white employees and the newcomers, the
hostility has usually been generated by the introduction of
Negroes as strike breakers or by their substitution for white
laborers in a certain industrial process at a lower wage in
order to reduce labor costs.   Under such circumstances the
economic fears and struggles of white wage earners tend to
be linked with the objective fact of racial difference and
hence to intensify race prejudice and hostility.   In cases
where colored men have been brought in during a labor
shortage and have been given equal wages, there has generally
been little opposition on the part of the white workers.

The reaction of the whites has also been influenced by the
manner in which the employer has brought in the Negroes
and by the attitude of the management and of the foremen at
the time of the Negroes' first appearance.   When employers
have made no point of emphasizing race differences but have
assumed or openly stated that the colored man would be
placed on an equal plane with white workers, the latter are
likely to accept the situation with little feeling or comment.
On the other hand, when employers and foremen conspicu-

ously indicate their feeling that the Negro is inferior and begin a strict policy of segregation in all phases of working conditions, such as workrooms, washrooms and eating places, the white employees inevitably reflect this policy of race discrimination.

Moreover, the attitudes and characteristics of the newcomers have influenced the nature of the resulting race contacts; Negroes who have reacted to the new environment of greater economic and social freedom by braggadocio and a tendency to ostentatious " showing off " have naturally aroused more race feeling than those who quietly accepted their industrial chances and sought to prove their worth and to earn the respect of their co-workers.

Then, too, the previous experiences of the white employees with Negro labor have tended to affect their reactions during and since the war; where white workers have known the colored man only as a " scab " and hated competitor, they are likely to resent his appearance even in times of labor shortage. It is evident that the nature of racial contacts in northern industry have been influenced by a multiplicity of factors, which have often been unrealized or ignored by employers, industrial managers and white and black workers.

Two of the most intensive surveys of the racial contacts in industry which resulted from the migration and entrance of Negroes into the industrial field were those carried on by the Detroit Bureau of Research and by the Chicago Race Commission. As a result of their studies, both of these committees reported that industrial contacts as a rule were peaceful. The Detroit Bureau maintained that " Employers were unanimous in stating that they had no more clashes in their plants between Negroes and whites than between groups of white workers of other national groups " although the races were not segregated.[1] The

[1] See Bibliography, reference 22 (a), sec. iii, p. 29.

Chicago Commission also reported that practically none of the Negro laborers who were interviewed (nearly a thousand in number) complained of disagreeable relations with their white co-workers, and among the replies from employers in nearly one hundred and fifty establishments employing over twenty-two thousand Negroes, there were only two reports of disturbing race friction. One of these was due to the prejudice which had been aroused among the white workers by previous employment of Negroes in the plant during a strike and the other was caused chiefly by fear that Negro girls were going to supplant the white workers.[1] Epstein's study of the situation in Pittsburgh indicates a less satisfactory adjustment between the newcomers and the white employees, but the investigator evidently felt that the antagonism was not an inevitable accompaniment of race contacts in industry, for he concluded that although there was " an undesirable hostility to Negroes on the part of a few white workers, the objection (to them was) frequently exaggerated by prejudiced gang bosses." [2] An illustration of serious friction arising from the presence of Negroes is found in the incident of the East St. Louis riot, which expressed an open and violent hostility to the Negro newcomers in that city. By some, this riot was attributed to the activities of the labor unions; by others, to the fierce economic struggle of unorganized white and black labor. The actual causes of the riot were complex and involved many social as well as economic factors, but undoubtedly the new contacts between Negroes and white workers in East St. Louis were provocative of intense racial feeling and antipathy.[3]

The influx of migrants into northern cities and the entry of Negroes into the industrial field have resulted in more

[1] Reference 17 (a), pp. 394-5, 626.

[2] Reference 32 (a), p. 32.

[3] References 57 (a), pp. 718-9; 145 (d), pp. 134-5; 129 (a), p. 339; 103 (a), p. 627; 142 (a).

frequent contacts between white and colored workers, though exactly to what extent such relations have been increased still remains uncertain. The nature of these contacts has varied from establishment to establishment and from city to city. On the whole, however, although there have been cases of open hostility shown by white laborers, the majority of concerns employing both races have not been seriously disturbed by race conflicts, particularly after the first pronounced appearance of Negroes in northern industries.

RELATION TO ORGANIZED LABOR [1]

Before 1915 the vast majority of Negroes in the North were engaged in work of the personal service type, and so few were employed in skilled or organized occupations that Negro laborers were practically ignored by the unions. A new situation was created, however, when thousands of colored workmen moved up from the South and when Negroes began to enter industrial positions which they had previously not occupied at all or only in small numbers. Recent migrations have made the unions more aware of the necessity of recognizing the existence of the Negro, because it soon became evident that this steadily increasing supply of unorganized colored workers could easily furnish a substitute for white laborers during a strike or when employers desired to reduce the cost of labor. It is not surprising, therefore, that during the last fifteen years expressions of interest in Negro workers have occurred much more frequently than ever before in the official records of labor organizations and in published articles and public speeches of union representatives.

[1] For exhaustive treatments of this subject see the forthcoming volume by Sterling Spero and Abram Harris, and also *Negro Membership in American Labor Unions*, now in press, by the Department of Research of the National Urban League, Ira de A. Reid, Director.

This theoretical acceptance of the Negro is, however, far in advance of the actual practice of local unions. In its official utterances the American Federation of Labor has long stood for a policy of no racial discrimination and in the last decade has emphasized the necessity of organizing Negroes, even passing resolutions to organize them under charters from the Federation in cases where internationals persisted in barring them from membership. In reality these activities of the central organization are less important than they seem, for the Federation is unable to compel affiliated internationals and locals to admit colored workers when they do not desire to do so. Among the nationals and internationals few of those affiliated with the American Federation now officially deny membership to Negroes but the four railroad brotherhoods not connected with the Federation still exclude the colored worker by constitutional provision.

Local organizations exhibit widely diverse policies in regard to colored members; some of them frankly refuse to admit Negroes; others practice virtual exclusion through raising the membership fee for colored applicants to an exorbitant price, or by technical rules of admission which Negroes are not allowed to fulfill. Many locals which do include colored workers limit them to membership in segregated organizations, either as subordinate groups completely controlled by the white members or as coordinate organizations. Then there are locals which admit Negroes to full and equal membership; but survey of the situation in the North leads one to the conclusion that unions of this last type tend to be the exception rather than the rule. In spite of the friendly utterances and resolutions of the central organizations, most of the local unions in northern cities are still far from enthusiastically encouraging Negro membership. As Woofter remarks: " Removing this proscription in charters against Negro members and overcoming the prejudice of the membership to such an extent that colored men are actually admitted to the locals are, however, two entirely different matters." [1]

The most noticeable increase of Negro members has been in organizations of less skilled labor, such as among the longshoremen or hod-carriers, in which occupations so many Negroes are now employed that the unions must include them or lose control of the trade. On the other hand, unions of more skilled and more desirable occupations are reluctant to admit the Negro laborer and in many cases manage to exclude him.[2]

Details of the situation vary, of course, from city to city, but the general trend in the organization of colored labor is much the same in all of the large northern cities. In Buffalo, for example, Carpenter found (1926) that there were very few colored members of local unions. When they were admitted, however, they were members of the white organizations, as there were not a sufficient number to warrant the establishment of separate Negro locals. This investigator concluded that " the recent arrival of the Negro workman in the North in increasing numbers has meant the formulation of union policy in local organizations that have never been confronted with the problem before. . . . Informal exclusion is probably practised in more than nine unions. Some are quite frank in admitting that they can easily find some excuse to prevent the admission of Negro workmen. Others have no hard and fast rule, but are generally content to follow a national or traditional policy of practical exclusion." [3] Epstein's study (1917) of the labor status of the Negro in Pitts-

[1] Reference 157 (c), p. 161.

[2] References 151 (a), pp. 266-74; 157 (c), pp. 158-62; 17 (a), pp. 405 et seq.; 110 (a), p. 22; 48 (e), p. 323; 57 (b), p. 135; 57 (i), p. 19; 57 (j), p. 239; 119 (a), pp. 243-4.

[3] Reference 16 (a), p. 113.

burgh reveals a general attitude of hostility on the part of the local organizations. Epstein asserts that the unions did not attempt to organize the Negroes and many of them excluded colored applicants in one way or another. Although two trade organizations did admit Negroes—a local of the Hod Carriers Union and one of the Hoisting Engineers—the other locals investigated apparently discouraged Negro membership.[1]   Harris, in his survey (1926) of the situation in Minneapolis, concluded that the American labor movement was not free from race distinctions and race prejudice. Although some of the locals in Minneapolis were branches of internationals which prohibit the admission of Negroes, yet the majority of the locals were not required by their constitution to discriminate on the basis of race. In spite of this freedom to include the colored workers, very few of the locals had any Negro members.[2] The Chicago Race Commission reported on the basis of its investigation (1920) that in Chicago " the union attitude and policy toward the Negro cannot be summed up by any simple generalization." Some of the unions in Chicago admitted Negroes either freely or in coordinate or subordinate locals, while others excluded them entirely. The Commission found (1) that when Negroes were admitted on an equal basis and given a square deal, the feeling inside the union was nearly always harmonious; (2) that Negroes objected to being organized in separate locals which were subordinated to the affiliated white local but at times seemed to prefer separate coordinate locals; and (3) that there were cases of exclusion of Negroes even by locals which were not compelled to do so by the constitution of their international organization. In spite of such cases of exclusion, however, the Commission concluded that " the proportion of Negro union members to the Negro population in Chicago is almost exactly the same as the propor-

[1] Reference 32 (a), pp. 32 *et seq.*
[2] Reference 44 (b), pp. 37-9.

tion of white members to the white population in Chicago."
The majority of these Negro union members were apparently in unions of the less skilled occupations such as those of stock yard workers, hod carriers and janitors, whereas the more skilled trades, machinists and electricians, for example, tended to excluded colored workers.[1] Similarly, in Pennsylvania (1925) "the bulk of the Negro membership is confined to longshoremen, workers in the building trades, teamsters, soft coal miners and musicians. The Negro has no representation in machine and other skilled and well paid trades."[2] Among students of this problem it is generally felt that in most northern cities the trade unions fail to provide adequate leadership for the Negro. His strength lies in the open shops and in many cases he has made his way against active opposition from unions.[3]

A variety of conditions and attitudes have been given at various times as explanations of this lack of organization among colored workers in cities of the North. The unions contend that Negroes are not found in the skilled trades, which are those most highly organized, because they do not possess the requisite ability or training, or else are unwilling to fulfill the long periods of necessary apprenticeship. In answer to this argument, it is frequently contended by Negroes and students of race problems that colored men coming from the South with experience and training in skilled work are even then not allowed to practice their trades, while, in addition, Negroes are almost never admitted as apprentices in the specialized industries of the North. The unions further allege that it is practically impossible to organize Negroes, as they lack the ability to cooperate, are entirely apathetic or antagonistic in regard to organization, and are

[1] References 17 (a), pp. 628-9, 411 *et seq.; cf.* 40 (a).

[2] Reference 110 (a), p. 22.

[3] References 111 (a), p. 2; *cf.* 57 (a), p. 719.

too timid to oppose employers in demanding better wages and conditions of work; in other words, that Negroes are not good union material.[1]

In opposition to these contentions it is frequently pointed out that where colored workers have been admitted to unions they have proved loyal and desirable members, and refutation of the belief that they are unable to cooperate is seen in the occasional organization of their own unions, such as the national union of colored railway men. It is true that Negroes are often uninterested in joining labor organizations, but this is due partly to their ignorance of the benefits which might be derived from cooperation, and more largely to their previous experiences with unions. These have very often generated the feeling that it would be futile even to think of joining, since many unions deliberately exclude colored men in one way or another, or, if Negroes are admitted, they are not given equal consideration with white members and are likely to pay their initiation fees for nothing. The Negroes complain of exclusion, of not being given employment after they have joined, and of being discriminated against when strike settlements are being made, so that they lose positions they have occupied before they joined the strike. Undoubtedly the colored worker has reason for that feeling of suspicion and dislike which is frequently attributed to him, for there are evidences of his mistreatment by unions.

The unions have frequently shown a tendency to consider the Negro as a sort of natural-born strike breaker and to accuse him of being a " scab." This is resented by the Negroes, who contend that often they are not allowed to join the striking union or that attempts to include them were made only on the eve of the strike, and, too, that many times they did not know they were being employed as strike breakers.

[1] See references in Section 5 (2) of the Classified Bibliography for substantiation of these and the following opinions.

Furthermore, in many cases the Negro owes his industrial opportunity to the employer alone or to the vacancy occasioned by the strike, both of which considerations lead him to sympathize with the employer and not with organized labor.

A study of organized labor's attitude toward the colored worker leads to the conclusion that although the size of colored populations in northern cities has increased by leaps and bounds and although Negroes are entering northern industries in heretofore unparalleled numbers, yet this influx has not been followed by the free acceptance of Negroes into northern labor unions. It is true that the majority of colored workers are in occupations which have not been extensively unionized, but race prejudice still abounds in northern cities to such an extent that Negroes who are engaged in organized trades are prevented from joining the unions of those trades. The situation is not entirely discouraging, for there are evidences of a growing desire on the part of union leaders to organize colored workers, and the entry of Negroes into the industrial field has led to an increase in the number of colored union members.

An illustration of the recency of this inclusion of the Negro in organized labor is found in the report of the Chicago Commission.[1] Of 33 nationals and internationals stating the length of time Negroes had been members of their organizations, 12 had included Negroes only within the last two years and 20 only within the last four years (about 1916 to 1920).

In general, the attitude of the unions seems more favorable to the organization of colored workmen than it has in previous decades and " the policy of excluding Negroes from unions, whether by direct or indirect means, is considered

[1] Reference 17 (a), p. 408.

wrong and shortsighted by the great majority of labor leaders." [1]   What is needed now is the adoption of this attitude
in the actual practices and policies of local unions which deal
directly with the Negroes.   The increase of Negroes in
northern cities and industries has strengthened the official
interest of organized labor in the problem of the colored
worker but the pressure exerted by these new industrial
laborers upon many local unions is, as yet, very slight.

THE INTERRELATIONS OF WORKER AND EMPLOYER

The increase of colored workers in northern cities has
brought the Negro into more frequent contact with white
employers of the North.   The resulting attitude of indus-
trialists has varied according to the needs of the time, the
employers' past experiences with Negroes and their personal
prejudices.   Some consented to hire the Negro because he
spoke English, was cheerful and strong and was not a union
man; others accepted him merely because they needed labor
and could find it nowhere else; others, again, refused even to
give him a trial because they considered him lazy, unreliable,
and incapable of speed, training or skill, or because they felt
their white workers would seriously object to mingling with
colored laborers.   Whatever the basis for these beliefs, the
Negro was dependent upon the resulting policy of the
employers for the chance to gain a foothold in northern industry.   These policies and attitudes have influenced his
entrance into the industrial field, his contacts with white
co-workers and his chances for promotion.   Largely because
of the labor shortage during the war, Negroes were called
North and given an opportunity to try their fortunes in
various occupations.   Their retention in those occupations
depends largely on what the employers think of them, par-

---

[1] References 17 (a), p. 433; *cf.* 119 (a), p. 244; 129 (a), p. 339; 46 (a),
p. 303.

ticularly now that war conditions are not limiting the supply of laborers and a freer choice of employees is possible. Since northern employers are naturally not hiring Negroes from altruistic or philanthropic motives, their opinion as to the desirability of retaining their colored workers or employing new ones will depend upon the extent to which Negroes have been successful in competing with other available labor and in measuring up to the demands of northern industrial standards.

CHAPTER VI

The Negro's Industrial Achievement

Few aspects of the Negro's entry into the industrial field have been the subject of as much biased discussion and unfounded opinion as has the question of the colored laborer's success or failure in his new occupations. For many decades white people have assumed that Negroes are inherently unfitted for industrial work; consequently, when they began to be extensively employed during the war, it was often taken for granted that the experiment was doomed to failure. Many of the employers in the North shared this feeling and at times refused even to give the Negro a trial because they considered his unfitness to be an established fact. Moreover, employers have frequently used their own prejudices or their experiences with a few Negroes in one particular establishment as a basis for generalizing on the characteristics of all colored laborers throughout the North. Both white people and Negroes have tended to view this phase of the Negro's industrial activities only in the light of their personal and often unwarranted prejudices, for this question of his success seems to be exceptionally subject to the influence of individual bias. It is particularly desirable, therefore, to discover how large numbers of employers throughout the North tend to regard Negro labor since they have had a few years of actual and extensive experience with these workers.

ADAPTABILITY OF NEGRO WORKERS

In recent years, investigations have been made in the effort to obtain as reliable an estimate as possible of the

Negro's success in the industrial life of northern cities. From a consideration of these surveys it is evident that no single nor final conclusion can be drawn for the entire North, since in some cases colored workers have been eminently satisfactory; in others, they have been decided failures; and in the majority of instances, they have been classed as falling at various intervals between these two extremes. In regard to the general quality of giving satisfaction, the majority of employers consider the Negro's labor to be as satisfactory as that of the white man, especially as that of the European immigrant whose place he has been taking. In every city there are employers who think the Negro is a failure as an industrial worker but, as a rule, the number of such employers is surpassed by the number who found him satisfactory, and employers of the largest groups of colored workers are found in the class of those who express themselves as satisfied with the work of the newcomers.

Surveys which have been carried on in Cincinnati, Chicago and Detroit exemplify the extent to which Negro labor has given satisfaction in the industrial centers. In Cincinnati (1919) inquiries were made of over 1,700 employers and over three-fourths of these considered Negroes to be satisfactory employees, while less than one-fifth of them held the opposite view.[1] The conclusions of the Chicago Race Commission (1920) are particularly important because a careful attempt was made to cover representative industries employing large numbers of Negroes, so that their findings might be as complete and reliable as possible. Of 137 establishments employing 5 or more Negroes, 118 reported that colored labor had been satisfactory, while 19 said it had not. The predominance of the favorable opinion is more evident when it is seen that the 118 establishments were those employing the largest

[1] See Bibliography, reference 120 (a), p. 526.

groups of Negroes, since the Negro employees who were thus reported as giving satisfaction numbered 21,640 in contrast to 697 colored workers employed by the concerns which were dissatisfied. The Commission concluded from its survey that " Despite occasional statements that the Negro is slow or shiftless, the volume of evidence before the Commission shows that Negroes are satisfactory employees and compare favorably with other racial groups." [1] A diversity of opinions among employers was found in Detroit. The survey made by Haynes (1918) contains a report from the general manager of an association comprising in its membership the leading firms and employers of the city.. This report states that some of the employers were highly pleased and some were not, but Haynes concluded that, on the whole, Negro labor was successful in Detroit. Eight years later the Detroit Bureau of Research found an even more pronounced atmosphere of satisfaction.[2]

Similar conclusions are expressed by several individuals who have made a close study of the Negro's progress in the industrial world. C. S. Johnson states that in a survey carried on by the National Urban League among 600 plants in eight northern cities, " fully two-thirds of these were unqualifiedly satisfied with the quality of the work done by (Negroes). Among the others, some had found them satisfactory only under white leadership; some found differences between northern and southern Negroes; some found them suited only for certain kinds of work; and some could not use them satisfactorily anywhere." [3] Among the most thorough and reliable investigators of this subject, Epstein and Reuter are the two who have voiced the greatest number of reservations in their opinions of

[1] References 17 (a), pp. 378, 373-4; cf. 57 (r), p. 140.

[2] References 46 (f), pp. 17-9; 22 (a), sec. iii, pp. 17-22; cf. 157 (b), p. 420; 124 (a), p. 130.

[3] References 57 (d), pp. 407-8; cf. 157 (a), pp. 51, 108; 145 (d), p. 109; 151 (a), p. 303; 102 (a), p. 9; 46 (j), p. 31.

the Negro's success. The former considered that up to
the time of his survey of conditions in Pittsburgh, the
Negro newcomers had not adjusted themselves to industrial demands in Pittsburgh with complete satisfaction.
He intimated, however, that they might ultimately be successful, as Negroes who had been in the North any length
of time were as efficient as white people.[1] Reuter believes
that the colored laborer has usually proved less satisfactory
than the white man in manufacturing industries, but in the
non-manufacturing establishments the opinion of his success are more favorable.[2]

Most of the opinions and investigations in regard to the
Negro's status in the industrial establishments have been concerned mainly with this question of the employers' views as
to the general satisfaction Negroes have given.   In addition,
a few surveys have sought information on the more specific,
subordinate factors of efficiency, reliability, amount of absenteeism and turnover, which undoubtedly influence an employer's conception of the Negro's success or failure.   Where
the question of efficiency has been mentioned, it has been
found that the majority of employers believed colored
laborers to be as efficient [3] as white workers, although there
were instances of employers who felt that Negroes were less
efficient.   The proportions on each side seem to follow
closely the division of opinion concerning the satisfaction
given by Negro labor.   Little has been done in investigating
the comparative amount of supervision required by white and
black workers and the slight material which is at hand is so
variable that no definite conclusions are possible.   It is gen-

[1] Reference 32 (a), pp. 33-4.

[2] Reference 119 (a), p. 242. For other investigations see references
145 (c), pp. 41-4, 93; 115(a), p. 836; 57 (g), p. 302; 57 (i), p. 19.

[3] The reports do not define their use of the term "efficient" but from
the context it evidently means the ability to work without waste of time
and effort.

erally felt, however, that the right kind of supervision plays an important part in the attitude of the Negro toward his work and in his final output.   Likewise, only a few surveys have been concerned with the regularity or extent of absenteeism among colored employees as compared with white. In the studies which have been made, employers seem to be rather evenly divided in their opinions as to whether Negroes are absent from work more frequently than are white workers, with a slight preponderance in favor of the view that Negroes are no more irregular than other groups.   However, employers of the largest numbers of colored workers tended to feel that they were absent more frequently than white employees and attributed this to the previous work habits of these Negroes in the South, where they had been accustomed to working intermittently; they seemed to feel, too, that the Negro's tendency to be absent from work was lessened with his increased length of residence in the North. On the basis of available material it seems probable that Negroes are subject to a great amount of absenteeism and the almost balanced opinion of employers on this subject leaves a less favorable impression regarding the Negro's regularity than is found in a study of opinions concerning his general satisfaction and efficiency.[1]

Reports from a few of the intensive surveys which have included consideration of these specific factors illustrate the findings of most of the investigators of the subject.   The Detroit Bureau of Research concluded after its investigation that " two-thirds of the employers, hiring 82 per cent of the men, believed that their colored workmen were as

[1] For efficiency, see references 145 (c), p. 117; 151 (a), p. 297; 124 (a), p. 125; 127 (a), pp. 202-3; 44 (b), p. 27; 22 (a), sec. iii, p. 17; 17 (a), pp. 374-5; 57 (r), p. 140; 157 (a), p. 106; 43 (a), p. 733.

For reliability, see references 17 (a), pp. 376-8; 56 (a), p. 1225.

For regularity, see references 1 (a), p. 620; 44 (b), p. 27; 22 (a), sec. iii; 46 (f), p. 18; 17 (a), p. 377; 127 (a), p. 202.

efficient as white workers on the same type of work or were even more so." [1]   The Chicago Race Commission received reports on the efficiency of colored workers from a large proportion of the employers interviewed.   Some of the employers were reluctant to make comparisons between colored and white labor, as they felt that the Negro had so recently entered manufacturing industries that he could not be expected to be as efficient and reliable as the more experienced white worker.   Of those reporting, however, 71 considered the Negro as efficient as the white worker, while 22 had found him less so.   It was noted that "the 71 establishments which reported Negro labor as equally efficient as white labor included all of the large employers of Negro labor, with very few exceptions."   In regard to the comparative reliability of white and colored workers, the number of employers who reported to the Commission that the Negroes did not require more supervision than whites was nearly three times as large as the number of those who felt that he was less reliable.   However, as contrary opinions were expressed by industrial concerns in which conditions seemed very similar, it is impossible to draw definite conclusions from this material.[2]   The information in regard to amount of absenteeism is also so varied and contradictory that deductions from it are hazardous.   For example, in a survey of the largest industrial employers in Cleveland the conclusion was reached that although there was a popular belief that Negroes were inclined to take a holiday every few days, yet when employers had thoroughly investigated the matter by actual check, they found that "the lay-off evil was actually less prevalent among the family Negroes from the South than with immigrants assigned to like work." [3]   At the time Haynes made his survey (1918) of industrial conditions in

[1] Reference 22 (a), sec. iii, p. 17.
[2] Reference 17 (a), pp. 374-8.
[3] Reference 1 (a), p. 620.

Detroit, he found a widespread impression that Negroes were lacking in regularity but the Detroit Bureau of Research (1926) reported that the majority of employers considered the Negroes as regular and in some cases more regular than white workmen on the same job. However, the Bureau also stated that although the employers who considered the Negro less regular were in the minority, yet their establishments contained the greatest number of Negroes and those holding the more skilled and better-paid jobs. The Bureau concluded, therefore, that the Negroes as a group were slightly more inclined to absenteeism than a similar group of white workers.[1]

LABOR TURNOVER

Labor turnover has been one of the most conspicuous problems in connection with colored workers and one of the chief complaints against them. When Negroes first began to be used extensively in northern industries, it was found that they had a strong tendency to move on from one job to another, often before they had worked out the transportation which in some cases had been advanced.

The experience of the railroads during the war period was anything but encouraging; many companies imported thousands of southern Negro laborers but were unable to keep them any length of time, as the migrants soon moved on to more promising fields. The railroads were constantly short of labor, although they were pouring a steady stream of migrants into their camps. The Erie Railroad was considered one of the most successful organizations in handling colored labor but even this concern reported that among 9,000 men brought during a period of six or seven months, a full turnover occurred every eleven days, and only the first 2,000 stayed long enough to work out their

[1] References 46 (f), p. 18; 22 (a), sec. iii.

transportation.[1]   The steel mills and industrial concerns were frequently faced with the same problem.   For example in Pittsburgh, Epstein found there was a prevailing tendency among the migrants to jump from one job to another and gives an instance of one company which had imported a thousand men within a year and at the time of Epstein's visit had only 300 left.[2]

This problem of labor turnover seems to have been particularly acute during those years when Negroes were first moving into northern industries in large numbers.   In recent years, since they have had time to become more adjusted to conditions in the North, there has apparently been a lessened tendency to change jobs, although according to most of the recent surveys Negroes still have a higher rate of turnover than do white workers.   However, numerous investigations indicate that in establishments showing great mobility of colored laborers, this condition is usually due to poor selection of employees, poor housing, and to unsatisfactory conditions of labor. ·

The factor of selection is highly important because the Negro laborers are not a homogeneous group of identical personalities but present the variations of character, training and ability that would be found among a similar group of white workers.   Therefore, the employer needs to know as far as possible what sort of colored workers he wants and is getting.   When employers have hired Negroes on the theory that they are all alike and without reference to their individual characteristics and ability, the result has naturally been a large proportion of misfits, who soon gave up or were forced out.   This factor of selection—or lack of it—was particularly noticeable in the movements during the war, for

[1] Reference 145 (d), pp. 122-4.
[2] Reference 32 (a), pp. 21, 34.

railroads and labor agents were so eager to secure a large
supply of workmen that they did not stop to consider the
characteristics of the laborers they brought North. Agents
often received a commission on the basis of the number of
men they sent, not on the quality or permanence of the
supply, so that they made no attempt to weed out even the
obviously undesirables.

Naturally, the first response to the call for workmen was
made by the young, restless, single men who were able to
accept the offers of immediate free transportation. Many
of them were the idlers and loafers who saw a chance for
easy money and delightful change. The more mature and
reliable—usually married men—could not so easily break
loose and join the rush. As a consequence, the earliest movements contained a large number who had not been economically successful in the South and were even greater failures in
the midst of the complex industrial life of the North. They
simply floated on from one job and one place to the next,
inevitably swelling the turnover rate for colored laborers as
well as arousing the wrath and disgust of employers. When
industrial managers began to exercise more discrimination in
selecting their Negro workers, after the first rush and excitement, the complaints against Negro labor tended to be less
widespread. The survey of the United States Department
of Labor expresses the view of many students when it says:
"The labor problem of the Negro worker is largely one of
selection and supervision. Industries with executives far-
sighted enough to pick the men, to think in terms of the
Negro's human relations, and to provide housing quarters
on a family basis were universally favorable to Negro
workers."[1]

Among the Negro laborers there were also steady, married

[1] References 145 (d), p. 150; *cf. ibid.,* p. 124; 60 (a), p. 384; 1 (a), p.
621; 32 (a), pp. 10, 21.

men who would probably have been permanent workers had not the inability to secure decent living quarters led them to seek other cities where conditions, they hoped, would be better. Employers, as a rule, gave little consideration to the housing problems of their new colored workers, and the deplorable situations in some of the railroad camps and the Negro urban sections caused migrants to move on.

Then, too, labor transients have maintained that they would not remain any longer than necessary in plants where wages were low, or where discrimination was shown in the type of work and the wages given Negroes, or where the working conditions, such as the places of work, the wash-rooms and lunch rooms allotted to them, were unsatisfactory and inferior to those assigned to their white co-workers. In fact, where Negroes have made extraordinarily unfavorable showings in efficiency, turnover, regularity and general satisfaction, a great deal of the difficulty has been due to poor selection of employees and to lack of provision for adequate housing or decent working facilities. It is probably true that where wages, conditions of work and the nature of the job are similar, so that only the factor of race is different, the rate of turnover would be no greater among Negroes than among white workers. More careful, statistical analysis of this phase of the situation is needed.

Specific investigations [1] of colored workers in northern industries contain evidence of the extent of labor turnover among Negroes and of the underlying factors to which it is largely attributable. The Chicago Race Commission reported that the majority of employers who were interviewed considered the rate of turnover to be higher among Negroes than among white employees; in discussing this situation the Commission emphasized the fact that the Negroes shared the white man's desire to better his wages

[1] It is improbable that the exact figures can legitimately be compared.

and conditions of work wherever possible, so that if he were not allowed to advance or if he found himself subject to discrimination, he felt justified in seeking other employment.[1]   In a survey conducted among 75 of the largest industrial employers in Cleveland it was found that the rate of turnover varied considerably in the different firms. " In some instances firms report that where 25 per cent of their workers are Negroes, the turnover among them has sometimes been as high as 75 per cent of the turnover for the entire plant.   On the other hand, an equal number of firms state that the turnover has never . . . been any greater than for other racial groups.   Employment managers . . . state that where the turnover has been out of proportion to the number of Negroes employed, the explanation is not to be found in any fundamental deficiencies of the race, but rather in conditions which are rapidly correcting themselves."   On the whole, this survey concluded that the problem of labor turnover was at that time (1924) little more serious among Negroes than among other groups, although some individual firms did show high rates of turnover.   The report maintains that " in spite of the fact that the Negro in industry is a comparatively new factor in this territory, he is but slightly more responsible for the shifting of jobs than is the native of the district or the foreign born, who on the whole has had a longer time to adapt himself to local conditions." [2]   The effect of working conditions upon the amount of turnover is also indicated by reports of the situation in Detroit.   The general impression derived from surveys there is that, on an average, the rate of turnover is not much higher for Negroes than for white workers and that it varies considerably in different firms.   Wesley maintains that the largest labor turnover among Negroes in Detroit is in plants with the smallest wage scale, while firms paying high wages

[1] References 17 (a), p. 377; 124 (a), p. 117.
[2] Reference 1 (a), pp. 620-1.

are not bothered with a high turnover. For example, it was found during one survey in Detroit that the average monthly turnover of Negro labor in the foundry which employed the largest number of Negroes was only 10 per cent, while the largest turnover reported at all was 70 per cent, which occurred in a small foundry. It was discovered that in the large establishment the Negro worker received 80 cents an hour, which was the same wage as that received by white men used on the same work, whereas in the other case, the Negroes received 53 cents an hour compared with 70 cents an hour given to the white laborers.[1] In the survey report of the American Management Association it is maintained that the disparity in the rate of turnover among white and colored workers would not be great if intelligent methods of employment were used, as experience has shown that careful selection lessens the turnover of Negro employees.[2]

Investigators and students of these problems of turnover, absenteeism and general success of Negro labor do not contend that all Negroes have proved efficient, competent and satisfactory members of the northern industrial community. They recognize the existence of many shiftless, lazy and incompetent failures among them, but they do maintain that the proportion of unsatisfactory laborers is inevitably lessened when the workers are carefully selected, are not discriminated against in wages and working conditions, and are given even a little personal care and attention during the period of their adjustment.

OTHER ASPECTS

In considering the characteristics and success of Negro labor, employers have at times distinguished between workers

[1] References 22 (a), sec. iii, p. 20; 43 (a), p. 735; 151 (a), p. 303.
[2] References 4 (a), p. 25; *cf.* 110 (a), p. 39; 111 (a), p. 2.

who had, recently arrived from the South and the Negroes who had been in the North for a considerable period of time. Where such distinctions have been made, the majority of employers are found to favor the northern Negro, believing him to be more reliable and satisfactory, and contending that the southern Negro is handicapped by his former habits of irregular, haphazard labor. There are, however, a few instances of employers who maintain that the migrant is a more successful industrial worker than the northern Negro, but this view is contrary to that expressed by the majority of those who have considered the subject. The contentions on both sides tend to be mere belief, as the factual basis for these opinions has not been sufficiently investigated to lend much support to either side.

In Abell's report of the Cleveland survey he contends that " employers hold that the Negroes born in the North whose parents lived here before them, are giving the factories more difficulties than the newcomer." [1] Epstein found that Pittsburgh employers believed that the Negro who had lived there any length of time was less docile but more reliable and efficient than the newcomers.[2] Stronger opinions in favor of the northern Negro are found in the reports from Detroit and Chicago. During the investigation carried on by the Detroit Bureau several employers expressed the opinion that the Negroes who had just migrated tended to retain their southern habits of intermittent and indifferent work but as they remained in northern industries they gradually lost these undesirable characteristics.[3] Some of the employers interviewed in Chicago also differentiated between the newly arrived southern Negro and his northern co-worker, contending that the

[1] References 1 (a), p. 621; cf. 35 (a), p. 126.

[2] References 32 (a), p. 34; cf. 124 (a), p. 125; 145 (d), p. 127.

[3] Reference 22 (a), sec. iii, p. 19.

former had more pronounced habits of irregularity and unsteadiness than the latter. The Commission found, however, that it was only the employers of large numbers of Negroes who made a distinction between these two types, as the employers of small groups were likely to judge all Negroes by the recent migrants.[1]

In many cities special agencies and commissions have endeavored to increase the Negro's chances of success in his new occupational field by aiding him in his task of adjustment to northern industrial life. This work has been carried on particularly by the branches of the National League on Urban Conditions Among Negroes, which in many cities have been established or have enlarged their activities in order to help migrants become satisfactory members of their new working groups.

For example, the Urban Leagues in Detroit and Chicago have not only found employment for the newcomers but have sought to aid employers in selecting suitable workers and to instruct the Negroes in modes of dress and work and in the qualities and habits demanded of them in industrial organizations. The Industrial Department of the Chicago branch has found places for migrants, has made industrial investigations, provided lectures for working men and foremen of Negro labor, has investigated complaints of all sorts, and has selected and fitted men for various positions.[2]

The Division of Negro Economics which was established in the United States Department of Labor during the war was another organization of important assistance to the migrant in his process of industrial adjustment. This Division was

[1] Reference 17 (a), pp. 372-3.
[2] References 17 (a), p. 147; 145 (d), pp. 151-3; 150 (d), pp. 334-5; 43 (a), p. 730.

under the direction of George E. Haynes, who was instrumental in establishing numerous Negro Advisory Committees throughout the country. These Committees were organized by states, counties and cities, and sought to provide a meeting place where representatives of employers, white workers and Negro workers could discuss their mutual problems frankly and amicably. The chief aim of these Committees was to bring about a peaceful and satisfactory adjustment of the Negro to his new situation in the industrial world.[1]

EMPLOYERS' ATTITUDES TOWARD NEGRO WOMEN

On account of the scarcity of material it is impossible to form conclusive opinions on the success of Negro women in northern industry. The colored woman has entered the industrial world so recently that further investigations are needed before reliable conclusions can be drawn concerning the satisfaction she has given or in regard to the comparative success of southern and northern Negro women.

Some suggestive indications along this line are to be found in the Chicago Commission's report (1920). Although the statements of industrial employers were by no means unanimous, the Commission concluded that, on the whole, Negro women workers were considered as teachable and efficient as white women after they had received the necessary training; and the report specifically states that " Many of the establishments had employed large numbers of Negro women as an experiment and had found them satisfactory." [2] The report of a survey (1920) carried on under the auspices of the Women's Bureau of the United States Department of Labor indicates that Negro women have, as a rule, been fairly successful.

---

[1] References 145 (c), pp. 12-3, 19-21; 46 (a), p. 302; 46 (h), p. 460.
[2] Reference 17 (a), pp. 380-5, 625.

The statement is made: "Examination of available data shows that the Negro woman was as successful as could reasonably be expected in view of her handicaps, the discrimination against her, and the dearth of industrial incentives." While this investigation included women in some northern states, a large number of the Negroes studied in the survey were working in southern tobacco plants, so that the conclusions do not apply solely to Negro women in northern industries. Specific statements from employers in New York, New Jersey and Illinois, however, leave the impression that a similar conclusion would express the situation in the northern centers.[1]

IN SUMMARY

An analysis of the information which is available concerning the Negro's industrial success shows justification for believing that the colored laborer is not always the slow, irregular, and inefficient workman he is popularly pictured as being. Although many employers are apparently not satisfied with their colored labor, specific investigations of employers' opinions, of actual production and of habits of work among the Negroes throw the weight of evidence in favor of the conclusion that the Negro is a satisfactory industrial worker. While this objective evidence is not so sufficient as it should be, it at least suggests the conclusion that Negroes have certainly not been proved universally less satisfactory than white labor but, on the contrary, have given good indications of comparing favorably with their white co-workers. The success of Negro labor in modern industry has not yet been established beyond question and disagreement. However, in forming an opinion on the subject it is well to keep in mind the caution: " The habit of making generalizations from one or two experiences can do great damage. Whereas among white workers, a poor worker, or ten of

[1] References 145 (g), pp. 9-10; cf. 145 (c), p. 130; 151 (a), p. 303.

them, are regarded as poor individuals, the distinctiveness of the Negroes, and the common disposition to regard them as a group, make it easy to pass judgment on all Negro workers on the basis of a few outstanding unfortunate incidents." [1]

It is desirable to have more intensive studies of the nature of the occupations in which Negroes are reported as being satisfactory and the sort of jobs in which they are unsuccessful. Is there a difference according to the kind of work or does the factor of success depend wholly on selection of employees, conditions of work and living, and attitudes of employers and white co-workers?

RETENTION OF NEGROES IN INDUSTRY

In a consideration of the new economic opportunities for the Negro the question naturally arises as to whether colored laborers have been able to retain the positions which they secured under unusual circumstances. The true test of the Negro's success in northern industry lies in his ability to keep his job in the face of competition and in times of depression when there is a labor surplus and white men are searching for work. The close of the war threw thousands of white laborers back into the industrial field, thus materially increasing the supply of labor. On the other hand, the passage of the immigration acts of 1921 and 1924 curtailed the number of foreign laborers available and strengthened the position of the Negroes as a source of supply for unskilled labor.

The need for a large number of colored workers has varied considerably within the last fifteen years; during periods of depression such as occurred around 1920-1921 and such as exists in the present winter of 1929-1930, the status of the Negro in northern industry is beset with diffi-

[1] Reference 57 (d), p. 408.

culties and dangers. Inevitably at such crises many establishments have curtailed their activities and reduced their labor force, with the result that race prejudices and antagonisms have had numerous opportunities for full expression. Employers who had employed Negroes only because of the scarcity of labor, and those who preferred white men, or who considered colored laborers unsatisfactory, had a chance during these periods of depression to eliminate colored men from their industrial plants. The full extent of the increase in industrial opportunities for the Negro is only evident when his status is observed after he has weathered this increased competition of white labor and the months of decreased industrial activity. We must await the 1930 census figures for comprehensive information concerning the number of Negroes at present employed in the industries of northern cities, although these figures will probably portray an over pessimistic picture. In the meantime the estimates and reports of various students and investigators provide indications of the trend toward the industrial retention or elimination of Negroes.

All of the surveys made since 1920 have found the Negro still a member of the industrial world, even after the close of the war and the depression of the winter of 1920. There are indications, however, that a smaller proportion of Negroes in the North are now in the fields of manufacturing and mechanical industries, trade and transportation, and that numbers of them have gone back into the general field of domestic and personal service, while many of the Negro women who had given up outside employment have been forced to return to work.

For example, in 1925 the Pennsylvania survey found that since 1920 the number of Negroes had decreased 10 per cent in manufacturing and mechanical lines, and agriculture and domestic service were the only two classifications out of the nine showing slight increase over 1920. The report states, however, that " While it is a fact that after 1920 Negroes fell back from their high peak, nevertheless, they gained a foothold much in advance of their pre-war situation. . . . There are still 22.2 per cent fewer Negroes working in ' domestic and personal service ' than in 1910." [1]   It remains to be seen after the 1930 census whether a similar situation prevails throughout the North.

Undoubtedly a period of business depression tends to force many out of the industrial field and at such times Negroes as a group are probably the worst sufferers, although white workers, too, are faced with unemployment and the necessity of accepting more undesirable jobs.   Negroes, however, have the added handicaps of discrimination based on color and more frequent lack of experience and training; furthermore, purely on the grounds of seniority of employment they would be forced out of work before whites who had been on the field for a longer time.   During the winter of 1920-1921 a serious unemployment situation arose in such centers as Chicago and Detroit, and thousands were without work. Surveys which were made of the situation at that time, however, agree fairly well that the Negroes were not much worse off than the white workers and that comparatively few evidences of race discrimination were found in employers' methods of reducing their supply of labor, so that in many industries Negroes tended to retain the proportion of the total workers which they had held before the depression. Although this occasion of enforced reduction gave employers a chance to get rid of colored workers if they were dissatisfied, there seems to have been no widespread and disproportionate dismissal of colored employees, particularly in the largest establishments.

[1] Reference 110 (a), p. 17.

The Chicago Race Commission reported that during the winter of 1920-1921 " common labor was reduced in all the large plants from 20 to 50 per cent. Negroes, mostly common laborers, suffered most from this reduction. At one period there were as many as 15,000 Negros unemployed in Chicago." The Commission concluded, however, that " the reduction of labor was usually carried out by employers with some system, and few instances of gross race discrimination were reported." [1] In a discussion of this same situation, the Chicago Urban League was reported to have placed only 631 men during the six months from January 1 to June 30, 1921. " Prior to this the League placed 1,200 a month, or twice as many monthly as were placed in six months during the period of unemployment. Women returned to domestic service from the factories and their placements were double those of the men for the same period. . . . But the significant development in this matter of unemployment is the fact that Negroes have retained their ratio in all the large factories and industries now opened. . . . If colored workers who occupied positions that were vacated by whites during the war can retain these places now, when many of these same white workers are looking for employment, it is fair to assume that they have made very definite progress toward permanency in industry." [2]

With the revival of industrial production after 1922 and the renewed migration of Negroes from the South, they became more firmly intrenched in northern industries and are still important.[3] Whether the present period of industrial depression (1929-1930) will reduce the Negro to a lower place on the industrial scale than he has yet occupied

[1] References 17 (a), pp. 626-7; *cf. ibid.,* pp. 402-3.

[2] Reference 48 (e), p. 325.

[3] References 110 (a), p. 17; 22 (a), sec. iii, pp. 6-7; 151 (a), pp. 304-5; 62 (b), pp. 970-1; 48(e), pp. 323-6.

since the war is a matter that cannot be settled on the basis of the material now in print. Studies of unemployment now in process, under the auspices of Departments of the Urban League and other agencies, indicate that the per cent unemployed among Negro workers is considerably larger than among other population elements,[1] but that the duration of unemployment tends to be shorter. Though the view is subject to drastic revision after the 1930 census information is at hand, the situation at present seems to be that Negroes have lost some of the gains they made during the peak of the war demand for labor but are still far ahead of their status in 1910 in regard to the number of their race employed in industry. Moreover, they are evidently being retained in the industrial concerns, though to what extent still remains a question.

[1] Reference 104 (b), pp. 11-5.

CHAPTER VII

DEMOGRAPHIC READJUSTMENT OF THE NEGRO POPULATION

THE age, sex and marital status of Negro populations in northern cities directly reflect the economic nature of these recent movements. Since they were primarily a response to new economic opportunities, they inevitably tended to select young adults who were in the best working years. The effect of this tendency is seen in the fact that throughout the North, children under 20 years of age form only about one-third of the total Negro population, whereas a similar age group forms practically one-half of the colored people in the South and over 40 per cent of the group of native whites of native parentage in the North.

AGE

Table 15 indicates similar disproportions in the age group 20 to 44 years, the period in which laborers are especially valuable in unskilled industrial positions. Over half of the Negro population of the North falls within this group, which, on the other hand, forms only a little more than a third of the colored people living in the South. The age distribution of Negroes in northern cities, as shown in the 1920 census, gives further evidence of the selective nature of a migration which is called forth by economic opportunties. For example, 66 per cent of the colored groups in Detroit were between 20 and 44 years of age, with only 22.7 per cent under 20. In New York the young adults comprised 60.9 per cent of that city's total Negro population and in Chicago the same age group formed 59.9 per cent. When these proportions

135

TABLE 15.—AGE DISTRIBUTIONS OF NATIVE BORN, BY RACE
AND BY SECTION, 1920

(Computed from *Fourteenth Census*, 1920, vol. iii, pp. 16, 21 *et seq.*)

	Per cent Under 20 Years	Per cent 20–44 Years	Per cent 45 and Over
Total U. S. Population	40.7	38.4	20.8
Total Native White of Native Parentage	45.2	35.9	18.8
Total Negro Population......	45.2	38.2	16.4
Native White of Native Parentage in North	43.7	36.1	20.1
Negroes in North	29.8	51.4	18.6
Negroes in South	47.9	35.9	16.0

are compared with the age distribution for the Negro population in the entire United States, the influence of this migratory factor is apparent, for in the country as a whole colored children under 20 form 45.2 per cent of the Negroes and only 38.2 per cent of the race fall within the period 20 to 44 years.

Wherever recent surveys of conditions among Negroes in northern cities have included a study of the age composition of the group, they have found that the colored population contained an abnormally large proportion of those in the early adult years.[1]   Such findings are not surprising in cases where the surveys were made during the early years of this rush of Negroes to northern industries, when the presence of many recent migrants inevitably exerted an influence upon the age composition of this group.   Similar conditions, however, were found a decade after the first widespread demand for colored labor,[2] and the disturbing effect of migration upon the age distribution of colored populations in the North has been emphasized both in the reports of investigations of

---

[1] See Bibliography, references 32 (a), pp. 18-9; 57 (g), p. 300; 44 (b), p. 14; 120 (a), p. 525.

[2] References 22 (a), sec. ii, p. 9; 81 (a), pp. 35, 37.

specific cities and by students of conditions in general among northern Negroes.[1]

In Columbus, Ohio, the proportion of young adults among the Negroes was remarkably high and became even more abnormal when the study of age distribution was limited to those who had come to Columbus within the last six years [2] for the ages of more than two-thirds of these recent migrants were between fifteen and fifty years. The report of the Urban League's investigation of the Negroes of Waterbury, Connecticut, contains a typical discussion of the age composition of a group of colored people in a northern industrial center: " The unnatural composition of the Negro group is evident both in the unusually large percentages in the age groups 25 to 34, 35 to 44, and in the unusually small percentage of children. This suggests migration of adults as a strong factor in population increase. Among the Negroes 7.1 per cent of the population was under 5 years of age as compared with 11.4 per cent for the city as a whole. On the other hand, for the age limits 35-44, the proportion for Negroes was 20.0 per cent as compared with 14.6 per cent for the city as a whole, even with the large number of adult immigrants included." [3]

Where careful studies have been made of the age composition of northern Negro populations, there is general agreement concerning the abnormal distribution of the various age groups. Throughout the North there is this apparent tendency for a colored population to show a massing of individuals in the early adult years and a small proportion of children and old people.

[1] References 57 (a), p. 718; 119 (a), pp. 53-6.

[2] Reference 81 (a), pp. 35, 37.

[3] Reference 57 (g), p. 300.

MARITAL CONDITION

Since the 1920 Census little has been done in the way of careful analysis of the marital composition of colored people in northern cities.   Surveys which have been made of specific urban groups in the North during the last ten years have seldom paid much attention to this aspect of Negro life and have done little more than record a few general observations.

Among the studies which have been made, the report from Columbus, Ohio, shows an unusual trend.   The survey undertaken in that city in 1924 reported an abnormally low percentage of single people in the group investigated, only 20.7 per cent of the males and 14.5 per cent of the females being unmarried.   This was admitted to be in " striking contrast to the proportions shown for the whole Negro population (of Columbus) in 1920 or earlier censuses." The census of 1920 disclosed that 35.1 per cent of the males and 19.5 of the females were single.[1]   Epstein (1917) found that over 41 per cent of those whom he interviewed were single,[2] but this was a higher rate than that of the 1920 census, when 35.3 per cent of Negro males over 15 years of age were reported as single and 19.6 per cent of the Negro women.   These rates seem fairly typical of Negro groups in the North, where the percentage of single males tends to be higher and the percentage of single females somewhat lower than in the South or for the Negro population in the country as a whole.

Table 16 presents a comparison of the per cent single among Negro males and females 15 years of age and over in the United States at large, in the four northern and the four southern states containing the largest Negro populations, and in the six northern cities with the greatest number of

[1] Reference 81 (a), p. 39.
[2] Reference 32 (a), p. 19.

TABLE 16.—PER CENT SINGLE 15 YEARS OF AGE AND OVER AMONG
NEGROES IN THE UNITED STATES AT LARGE, IN CERTAIN
NORTHERN AND SOUTHERN STATES, AND IN SEVERAL
NORTHERN CITIES, 1920

(Compiled from *Fourteenth Census*, 1920, vol. ii, ch. iv,
tables 1, 21, 11 and 16.)

	Males	Females
Total Negro Population in U. S.	32.6	24.1
Total Negro Urban	33.3	22.8
Total Negro Rural	32.1	25.0

STATES

Northern	Males	Females	Southern	Males	Females
Pennsylvania	37.2	23.5	Georgia	29.9	23.2
New York	36.6	28.8	Mississippi	28.7	22.9
Ohio	36.2	18.9	Alabama	30.5	24.4
Illinois	34.1	18.3	South Carolina ...	32.4	28.1

NORTHERN CITIES

	Males	Females		Males	Females
New York	36.0	29.0	St. Louis	34.7	19.4
Philadelphia	34.5	24.2	Detroit	38.3	14.5
Chicago	34.4	17.6	Pittsburgh	35.3	19.6

Negroes. The full extent of the discrepancies between the
two sections is somewhat obscured by the fact that both New
York and Pennsylvania contain an unusually high percentage
of single Negro females; most of the other northern states
with smaller colored populations tend to have lower rates of
unmarried women, such as Wisconsin with 19.7 per cent, and
Michigan with 15.2 per cent.

Since the northern colored population tends to concentrate
in the principal cities of each state, the marital condition of
Negroes in specific centers tends to follow that of their respective states. On the whole, the cities show a fairly uniform tendency for a high rate of single males, but greater
variation in the percentage single among colored women.
Such figures also show a distinct difference in the percentage
single found among Negro men and that found among Negro
women in the North. A greater preponderance of single

males is, of course, to be expected under the circumstances, for unmarried men could more easily and quickly respond to sudden economic opportunities than could those having families.   On the other hand, such wide discrepancies between the percentage single for males and females must be viewed with caution, for it is quite likely that many male migrants reported themselves as single after they had shaken off marital responsibilities by the simple process of migration, and unmarried mothers could easily report themselves as married, widowed or divorced.[1]

SEX

The sex distribution among Negroes also tends to vary in different sections of the North.   In New York State in 1920 there were only 92.6 males to every 100 females, whereas in

TABLE 17.—PROPORTION OF NEGRO MALES TO 100 NEGRO FEMALES IN CITIES OF NORTH AND SOUTH WITH LARGEST NEGRO POPULATIONS, 1920

(Compiled from *Fourteenth Census*, 1920, vol. ii, pp. 117 *et seq.*)

Northern Cities		Southern Cities	
New York City	90.3	Richmond	84.2
Philadelphia	100.1	Atlanta	85.8
St. Louis	102.5	New Orleans	86.9
Chicago	104.5	Memphis	89.7
Pittsburgh	111.8	Birmingham	94.7
Detroit	137.0	Norfolk	100.9

Pennsylvania the ratio is 108.8; in Ohio, 116.4; and in Michigan, 132.6.   The colored population of the entire United States shows an excess of females, since there are only 99.2 males to every 100 females.   In the South, such an excess of females is practically uniform; even the southern cities show a preponderance of women.   On the other hand, the principal centers of the North show a general tend-

[1] Reference 81 (a), p. 40.

ency for an abnormally large proportion of Negro men, so that there is a contrasting form of sex-ratio disturbance.

> Reports of surveys which have been made in specific northern cities and general discussions of the sex composition of northern Negroes all emphasize this disturbance of the sex ratio. In New York it occurs in the form of an excess of females but the Middle Western cities, such as Detroit, Pittsburgh, Cleveland, Cincinnati, Youngstown, Toledo, and Milwaukee, show a preponderance of males.[1] The Detroit Bureau stated that the disproportion was not so great in 1925 as it had been in 1920, when the men had come in large numbers to fill the vacant places in Detroit's industries; the disproportion was, however, still much greater among the Negroes than among any other population group.

Among students of this problem it was generally held that the nature of the economic opportunities open to the sexes greatly influenced the extent to which either males or females predominated. For instance, New York City, heterogeneous in the nature of its positions available for Negroes, exerted no such exclusive call for men as was the case in the Middle West, where the more specialized industries demanded large numbers of Negro males to perform the unskilled manual labor formerly done by European immigrants. Although this economic cause is usually given as the general explanation of this abnormal sex composition of northern Negroes, the subject has not yet received sufficient analysis and study to warrant any conclusive statement as to the real cause for this phenomenon. There is, however, little doubt that the northern industrial cities do not show an equal number of colored males and females, and, in general, throughout the cities of the North there tends to be an excess of males.

[1] References 120 (a), p. 525; 57 (a), p. 718; 22 (a), sec. ii, pp. 7-8; 38 (a), pp. 26-9; 63 (a), p. 113.

An examination of the available material concerning the composition of Negro groups in the North reveals a fairly uniform picture of a preponderance of young adults and a comparatively small number of childen and old people, a disproportion of the sexes that in some cases results in a significant excess of men, and a slight tendency for an abnormally high rate of unmarried men, which would be the expected result of a preponderance of males. Hitherto, the surveys which have been made of particular groups have tended to give little detailed attention to this subject of the composition of the Negroes and most of our information has to be based on the 1920 census material. Hence it is impossible to tell as yet whether there has been a decrease in these abnormal conditions as the Negroes have had time to become better adjusted to their new environment. Further careful study along this line and the coming 1930 Census should provide valuable material for checking up the present assumptions concerning the composition of northern Negroes. All of these tendencies toward an abnormal composition are characteristic of a migrant group and should be mitigated as the migrants become adjusted and settle down in a more permanent home life. Since the sex, age and martial status of a group exerts a direct influence on such major social problems as the amount of crime, of immorality, and of instability of family life,[1] where there is a preponderance of single, young, adult males, all of these problems tend to increase. Consequently, the composition of Negro urban groups should receive careful consideration in studies of the social life of Negroes in the North.

[1] References 157 (d), p. 34; 157 (c), pp. 152, 171, 149.

CHAPTER VIII

THE HOUSING OF NORTHERN NEGROES

PROBLEMS connected with the housing of Negroes in northern cities have been the subject of more investigation and discussion than has any other one phase of the social situation created by the influx of colored laborers from the South. Since the industrial centers had made no adequate provision for housing the newcomers, the sudden phenomenal increase of colored people tended throughout the North to create problems of congestion, attempted expansion of Negro residence sections and consequent race friction. Frequently these conditions became so acute as to demand recognition from the community, and the resulting discussions and surveys provide a vivid picture of the effect of Negro migration upon the housing situation.

RESIDENTIAL SEGREGATION

The most fundamental factor in the Negroes' housing troubles has been their segregation in certain sections of the cities. This concentration in particular districts is, of course, not a situation peculiar to the colored population, for many nationality groups tend to congregate in special areas, and every large city has its Jewish section, its China-town or its Italian quarter. In the case of the Negroes, however, the situation is more complex and serious because of the emotional tension involved and the race prejudice of the white people, who discourage attempts of the Negroes to expand or change their customary residential area. Nor is segregation a new phenomenon in the North, as for decades practically every northern city has exhibited to some extent a segregation of the colored residential sections from those of the whites. Although complete and exclusive segregation of Negroes into a district entirely colored was never prevalent, yet, as a general rule, most of the Negro inhabitants lived in a few sections of each city, the remainder being scattered in varying proportions among the white neighborhoods. Thus virtual segregation had been more or less quietly practiced for years, but with the arrival of hordes of Negroes from the South this whole question of segregation assumed new prominence and importance. In industrial centers which received a noticeable increase in the number of colored inhabitants, the migration tended to increase the amount of segregation and to build up more distinctly Negro communities within the cities.

The question of segregation has received consideration in many of the surveys of Negro communities which have been made since the first noticeable movement of colored laborers during the World War. These reports show practical unanimity in contending that there is residential segregation of Negroes in the North and that the migration has tended to increase the concentration of Negroes in certain districts. Segregation on particular streets exclusively or almost entirely inhabited by Negroes was uniformly present, and generally there were also larger, well-defined Negro districts.

> Although the Negroes of Washington, D. C.,[1] are not limited to a few clearly marked districts as is the case in many more northern cities, yet there is a general attitude which requires the residential separation of the two races. " Washington differs from most cities in that the Negro

---

[1] This is really a border city but is treated here because of its peculiar interest.

population is not huddled into one specific geographical area. It is rather loosely and irregularly scattered throughout the various districts of the city. . . . Although there are many streets on which Negroes and white people are intermingled, they still maintain certain residential distances. In many instances, white people were found occupying one side of the street and colored people the other." [1] In Minneapolis and in Columbus, Ohio, the Negroes were scattered throughout the city, yet in spite of the fact that there was no exclusively colored section, they tended to cluster in certain areas.[2] Chicago and Detroit [3] were found to possess well defined Negro districts, which became more densely populated upon the arrival of migrants from the South. In Chicago " the large increase in Negro population did not bring into existence any new large colonies but resulted in the expansion and increased density of areas in which groups of Negroes already existed in 1910." [4] The survey made by the Commonwealth of Pennsylvania found that " while residential segregation of the Negro does not exist in Pennsylvania by law, a very effective residential segregation of Negroes by force of public opinion occurs in many communities in the Commonwealth." [5] In Pittsburgh " before this great influx of Negroes from the South, the Negro population . . . lived in half a dozen sections of the city. Although not absolutely segregated, these districts were distinct. . . . The sections formerly designated as Negro quarters have been long since congested beyond capacity by the influx of newcomers, and a score of new colonies have sprung up in hollows and ravines, on hill-

---

[1] See Bibliography, reference 63 (a), p. 148; also pp. 57-64, 83, 88-9.

[2] References 44 (b), p. 14; 81 (a), pp. 11-27.

[3] References 22 (a), sec. v; 46 (f), pp. 8-10.

[4] Reference 17 (a), pp. 106-7.

[5] Reference 110 (a), p. 31.

slopes and along river banks, on railroad tracks and in mill yards." [1]   In Philadelphia the migrants were practically forced to seek homes in the customary colored sections— " the housing problem was itself a result of the determination on the part of the white people that the migrant should live only in that part of the city in which Negroes had previously lived." [2]   The report of conditions in Waterbury, Connecticut, states that: " As in practically every other city, the Negroes in Waterbury live in rather close contact.   There are not exclusively Negro sections but what amounts practically to the same—there are sections in close proximity in which over 90 per cent of the Negro population lives. . . . The antagonistic sentiment of whites prevents them from moving outside of the narrow limits of a recognized ' Negro Area '." [3]   This policy of residential restriction was not limited to these particular cities in which surveys were made.   According to many students of conditions among northern Negroes, segregation was the typical situation throughout the urban North. [4]

Recent migrations have tended to increase residential separation of the two races both by enlarging the Negro group within the colored districts and, at the same time, by intensifying the opposition of white people whenever the Negroes attempted to enter new neighborhoods.   Frequently the influx of migrants so crowded the former Negro sections that many of the colored people sought homes in other neighborhoods and thereby aroused the antipathy of white residents.   As Burgess points out: " Every residential community offers resistance to the intrusion of a new group of

[1] Reference 32 (a), pp. 7, 16.

[2] Reference 93 (a), p. 177.

[3] Reference 57 (g), pp. 299-300.

[4] References 46 (h), p. 460; 57 (r), p. 140; 157 (d), ch. 3; 14 (a), pp. 105-15.

imputed inferior status whether on the basis of race, economic standing, or cultural difference." [1]   Resentment of Negro " invasion " of white districts was based on all three of these factors and the white people usually showed no desire to welcome the newcomers even when they represented the better class, for distinctions were seldom made on the basis of the type of colored people who were trying to buy or rent homes in decent surroundings.   The opposition ranged all the way from chilly aloofness or the speedy withdrawal of the white residents from the neighborhood, to such violent measures as bombing the houses of the newcomers and other forms of intimidation.   A common expression of dislike was informing colored applicants that the vacant houses were not for rent or sale, or of openly refusing to sell or rent if the prospective buyer or tenant showed traces of Negro blood. Another widespread method was that of getting property owners to sign an agreement or covenant not to sell or rent their property to Negroes for a definite period of time, unless all the signers agreed to the transaction.   In some cities neighborhoods faced with an influx of Negroes also formed associations for the purpose of influencing owners and real estate agents against admitting colored people.   The means used for securing adherents to the " cause " assumed such varied forms as personal interviews with white owners, publication of pamphlets asserting the menace of a Negro invasion and spreading propaganda which would inflame race prejudice, and the sending of letters threatening violence to white people who admitted Negroes, and to Negroes who attempted to enter the neighborhood.

The situation in Washington, D. C., and that in Chicago typify the two extremes of the range of opposition faced by the Negroes when they attempted to enlarge their resi-

[1] Reference 14 (a), p. 112.

dence sections. " In Washington the ' covenant ' seems to
be the most widely employed method for keeping Negroes
out of ' exclusively white ' residential districts. . . . The
Negro has encountered hostile attitudes on the part of white
people, which have at times crystallized into corporate action against him. But it is interesting to note that in the
majority of instances white people have given way to Negro
invasions with little or no struggle to retain their homes.
The conflicts have been more conspicuous than they have
been frequent. At times, however, feeling has become
very intense, but has not eventuated in programs of bombing or incendiarism." [1] The report of the Chicago Race
Commission contains a careful analysis of the resentment
shown by white groups in that city when Negroes settled in
new neighborhoods and of the attempt to restrict the
colored people to regions formerly occupied by the race.
Particularly in the districts of Kenwood and Hyde Park
the opposition was intense and violent. Real estate firms
and white property owners organized to " keep these neighborhoods white " and spread much anti-Negro propaganda
that tended to arouse intense racial feeling. Finally, in
order to drive out the Negroes already in the neighborhoods and frighten away others, the white people resorted
to bombing Negro homes and the property of real estate
men who had sold or rented houses to Negroes.[2]

Opposition to the expansion of Negro residence sections
did not generally assume the violent form of bombing and
incendiarism, but throughout the North there was widespread resentment among white groups whenever Negroes
tried to settle in new neighborhoods. This antipathy tended
to force the migrants to find shelter, if possible, in the
former colored districts, which were thus more densely

[1] Reference 63 (a), pp. 70, 148.
[2] References 17 (a), pp. 114-36; cf. 53 (b), pp. 323-4; 93 (a), p. 177;
152 (b), pp. 125-29.

populated. Due to this increased concentration of Negroes in particular sections of the cities and to the augmented racial antagonism of the white people which resulted from the housing situation, residential separation of the two races has become a more distinct, noticeable and emotionally fraught situation in northern cities.[1]

This policy of residential segregation is usually justified on the ground that the coming of Negroes into a neighborhood brings about a depreciation in property values. In fact, the reason most frequently given by white people for their resentment over a prospective " Negro invasion " is that the exclusion of the colored man is necessary in order to keep up property values and realize anything on real estate investments. The process of Negro habitation of a neighborhood is typically summarized as follows: " When Negro families move in, the whites move out, property values fall, deterioration takes place, and more Negro families move in." [2] The full potentialities of such a belief began to be realized at the time of the housing troubles in Chicago, Detroit, Kansas City, Cleveland and other northern cities. Then it became clear that this fear of economic loss tended to exert an important influence on the housing problems of industrial centers and upon the general status of race relations. Consequently, within the last decade some of the most important surveys of conditions among northern Negroes have made the beginnings of an attempt to discover the basis and justification for such a widespread opinion.

The reports of these surveys [3] are in practical agreement and show the complexity of the factors involved. Upon

[1] *Cf.* references 119 (a), p. 219; 46 (h), p. 460; 156 (a), pp. 179-80; 57 (r), p. 140; 3 (a), p. 532; 65 (a), p. 94.

[2] Reference 119 (a), p. 219.

[3] References 22 (a), sec. v, pp. 25-32; 17 (a), pp. 194-211, 608; 63 (a), pp. 78-80, 65; 110 (a), pp. 39-40; 81 (a), pp. 27-9; 157 (d), pp. 74-5; 14 (a), pp. 113-4.

actual investigation it is found that Negroes tend to move into older, less desirable sections of a city where property values are already depreciating because of the encroachments of business places, garages, railroads, factories or immoral houses. With their low incomes, colored people as a rule find it impossible even to contemplate residence in the new, easily accessible and more desirable districts, and thus seek those neighborhoods where prices are lower. Since these sections are already on the downhill road due to natural and inevitable changes accompanying the expansion of the city, the coming of Negroes is not the sole source of property depreciation. An equally important factor in causing depreciation is the psychological reaction of white people when a Negro first appears in the neighborhood. Because of this current belief in the invariable accompaniment of lowered values and the presence of Negroes, a wave of hysteria tends to sweep over the neighborhood and many white people sell to the first bidder without regard for real property values. Such panics so frequently accompany the appearance of Negroes that shrewd realtors have been known to introduce a Negro family for the express purpose of cleaning up large profits on property deals.

On the other hand, there are numerous cases of actual property appreciation. Particularly since the recent migrations, the Negroes have experienced serious difficulty in securing homes and the result has been keen competition for houses which were available. In such cases a Negro buyer or tenant is often willing to pay a higher price than will a white man and a cool-headed white owner can thus sell out at greater profit. According to the Pennsylvania survey "Rents and selling prices have always been raised when Negroes moved into the houses that formerly were occupied by whites. The increases have averaged all the way from 25 to 50 per cent." [1]

[1] Reference 110 (a), p. 40.

The whole situation has been well summarized by T. J. Woofter as a result of his survey of property values in various cities: " The areas that are usually penetrated by Negroes in their expansion are in neighborhoods that are already depreciating in value. . . . If one of these depreciating sections lies close to a Negro neighborhood, or if it has good transit service to places where Negroes work, the time finally comes when Negroes are willing to pay more for property there than the white occupants are, and the transition begins. It is a perfectly normal operation of real estate supply and demand." [1]   The Chicago Race Commission has so far made the most careful study of the basis and result of this belief in property depreciation, and their report provides a possible summary of the findings of the other investigations. These latter were on a more limited scale but tended to agree with the Chicago Commission on aspects mutually covered. The Chicago report states that in some cases Negro occupancy has resulted in depreciation and deterioration; in other cases, there has been an actual appreciation. It was felt that, on the whole, depreciation did not so much result from colored habitation as that Negroes were impelled by their low economic standing to enter neighborhoods where the buildings had already deteriorated and property had depreciated because of years of occupancy by whites and because of the encroachments of vice, business and factories. Consequently, the Commission contends that it is unfair to hold the colored people entirely responsible for lowered property values, though it admits that " at present, the fact stands that Negro occupancy is an unmistakable symptom of depreciation." Like the Detroit Bureau, the Chicago Commission emphasizes the effect of the psychological factor: " The principal influence of Negroes upon property values in a neighborhood is psychological, due to the deep-seated and general prejudice of whites against Negroes,

[1] Reference **157 (d)**, p. 74.

which begets and sustains the belief that Negroes destroy property values wherever they go." [1]

Furthermore, this belief that Negro penetration of a white neighborhood lowers property values arouses an antagonism which spreads to all other relations and is used as an excuse and reason for any sort of unfriendliness and opposition to the Negroes.[2]   With the coming of large numbers of Negroes from the South, this cause of racial antagonism was greatly augmented by the attempt of the colored people to find adequate housing. We do not yet have enough knowledge of the actual effect of Negro occupancy upon property values.   Recent surveys have at least recognized the importance of this phase of racial relations and have begun a study of the factors involved.   Further investigation is needed to discover what occurs in property values over a period of time sufficiently long to include years of both white and Negro occupancy.   We also need more detailed studies of the psychological forces at work before we understand whether depreciation really does occur, and before we know what are the most effective ways of combating the hysterical fear and race prejudice which operate whenever Negroes move into new neighborhoods.

HOUSING CONDITIONS

This antipathy of white people to any attempted expansion of Negro districts was an important factor in producing the congestion which has been prevalent in northern cities.   As hordes of migrants arrived from the South they tended to crowd into the " Negro areas " already established.   To a great extent this was necessitated by the prejudice of white people which prevented their overflowing into new neighbor-

[1] References 17 (a), pp. 205, 608; *cf.* 22 (a), sec. v, pp. 25-32.
[2] *Cf.* references 17 (a), p. 194; 22 (a), sec. v, pp. 25-7.

hoods. At the same time, the fact must not be overlooked that the newcomers had a natural desire to live among their friends and members of their own race during the period of adjustment to a new social and economic environment. Thus the condition of acute overcrowding that resulted from the migration was both a natural and a forced phenomenon. The latter was, however, the most serious element, for as congestion increased in the old Negro districts, both new and former residents found it extremely difficult to obtain homes in new sections. As a result of these two factors, serious overcrowding and an increased density of inhabitants became a common condition in the Negro districts of northern cities. Students of Negro problems throughout the North and investigators of specific industrial centers have united in calling attention to the abnormal congestion found in Negro neighborhoods.[1] This condition was naturally prominent during the first months of the recent movements before the newcomers had been able to find permanent homes, but reports of overcrowding are not confined to the early years of the migration.

Lack of uniformity in methods used by investigators of congestion, render it impossible to make any comparison of the degree of overcrowding existing in particular cities. Most of the surveys have merely commented upon a general situation of congestion, basing their conclusions on such factors as statistics of the increase of Negro population in the city and the numerical growth of particular districts, and on personal observations during house to house investigations. A few discussions and surveys have included estimations of room overcrowding or land crowd-

[1] References 46 (f), p. 21; 46 (h), p. 460; 17 (a), p. 106; 93 (a), p. 175; 31 (a), p. 557; 145 (d), p. 148; 32 (a), pp. 11-8; 114 (a), p. 3.
Later surveys: references 14 (a), pp. 108-9; 157 (d), ch. 4; 110 (a), p. 31; 81 (a), pp. 51-3; 105 (a), Annual Report for 1923, pp. 19-21; 121 (a), p. 239.

ing, computing the number of persons per room or per acre. Considering any ratio greater than one person per room to signify a condition of overcrowding, Mark found that in Columbus, Ohio, one-third of the Negro households studied fell in that class.[1]   In Cleveland it was found that the area which contained about 90 per cent of the colored people had a population density per acre of 35 or 40, whereas the density for the entire city [2] was only 21. According to E. W. Burgess,[3] in Chicago, Cleveland, Detroit, New York and Pittsburgh, the Negroes showed greater concentration of population than did any other racial group, and Woofter [4] concluded from his survey of several cities that "the density of Negro areas in most cities is much greater than the density of white areas. In some cities it is four times as great."

As a rule, general discussions and specific reports of housing conditions among northern Negroes have pointed out the serious overcrowding of Negro areas which followed the migration. There are, however, a few exceptions, since surveys in Buffalo, Minneapolis and Waterbury, Connecticut, found little or no evidence of overcrowding.[5]

Conflicting reports from Philadelphia suggest the need for more extensive investigation in that city but it seems evident that room crowding has not been so prevalent in the last few years as it was around 1917 and 1918.[6] In Chicago, too, the Race Commission reported a congested Negro neighborhood but, on the whole, less room crowding than prevailed among many foreign families.[7] How-

[1] Reference 81 (a), pp. 51-3.

[2] Reference 121 (a), p. 239.

[3] Reference 14 (a), pp. 108-9.

[4] Reference 157 (d), p. 78.

[5] References 16 (a), p. 175; 44 (b), p. 17; 57 (g), p. 301.

[6] References 46 (d), p. 71; 105 (b), p. 47; 80 (a), p. 11; 93 (a), pp. 175, 194-6, 205, 217.

[7] Reference 17 (a), pp. 106, 156-7.

ever, the present state of our information is not sufficient
to warrant conclusions as to the relative amount of congestion in various cities or concerning the extent to which
overcrowding is decreasing as Negroes become adjusted
to their new environment.

In regard to the whole matter of overcrowding, it is well
to bear in mind the fact that mere statistics concerning the
number of persons per room or acre do not measure the
fundamental significance of congestion.

The seriousness of overcrowding depends largely on
" the sex and age distribution of the members of a household and (on) the relationships which exist between them.
In the household containing but one family, it can be readily
seen that sex and age distribution play a large part in
measuring the seriousness of congestion. Thus a six-
person family consisting of father, mother and four children is less seriously affected by cramped quarters when
the children are all below the adolescent age than after
some of the children have reached their teens. Again, this
family is less seriously affected if the children are all of
one sex or are evenly divided as to sex than if an unequal
division of the sexes necessitates either extreme congestion
in one sleeping room or the sharing of a sleeping room by
persons of opposite sex.

" These complications are of minor importance when
compared with the situation in some of these Negro households, where cramped quarters are shared by two or more
families, or by a family and a number of unattached persons with only an economic relation to the family. The
annoyances, sacrifices and dangers, physical and moral, involved in a large household of this type cannot be shown
by numbers or ratios. They can be imagined only by comparing the condition of one's own life with the conditions
which must surround an individual who is sharing four

rooms with five or more persons of varying age, sex, personal standards and relationships." [1]

In many cities at the beginning of the migration the demand for houses could not possibly be met, particularly as little building was carried on during the war. When the migrants were, therefore, crowded into houses and rooms already occupied by Negro families, the poorly built and frequently dilapidated quarters were taxed beyond the limit and in many sections housing conditions among the Negroes became deplorable. The story is much the same no matter from what part of the North it comes, although here and there an investigator reports that the situation is above the average.

The housing problem was particularly acute during the early months of the movement and in the cities nearest the South which received the first onslaught. Many of the earliest migrants were brought North by the railroads and were housed in camps. Some of these consisted of temporary sheds with large bunk rooms, mess room and sometimes a rest room; others were simply rows of box cars, tents or old two-story houses which had been converted into dormitories. In some cases the camps were well kept; in many, however, there were no adequate sanitary provisions, and the sleeping quarters were filthy and lacking in ventilation, with serious congestion. In one of the better camps, for instance, which was investigated during the Department of Labor survey, a space 20 by 40 feet was filled with 30 cots and there were but three windows. In one of the worst camps visited the rough shacks housed about 400 Negroes who slept in wooden bunks piled close together in tiers of three or four. [2]

---

[1] Reference 81 (a), p. 54.

[2] References 145 (d), pp. 145, 148; *cf.* 106 (a).

These railroad camps had no monopoly on congestion and unsanitary living quarters, however. Throughout the industrial centers of the North the majority of Negro homes are located in sections where transportation facilities are inadequate, or in areas where the expansion of business houses, railroads and factories has rendered the district undesirable for residential purposes, or else in old sections where the paving, lighting, street cleaning and sanitary regulations are neglected. Frequently, the colored people have fallen heir to old, one-family houses which in early days had belonged to the wealthy society folk of the town. These have presumably been turned into apartments for several families, but provisions for sanitation and privacy are usually totally inadequate. As a rule, the percentage of Negro houses without modern conveniences of electricity, hot and cold water, bathrooms, inside toilets, furnaces, etc., is far higher than the same percentage among white families. Many of the houses are in poor condition and the Negro tenants find it extremely difficult to secure necessary repairs from landlords who are loath to spend good money on wornout buildings. There are, of course, many Negro families living in modern, comfortable homes but their proportion is far less than the proportion of decently housed families among white people.

Philadelphia and Pittsburgh are two of the cities which have faced serious housing problems. In Mossell's study (1919) of migrant families in Philadelphia,[1] she found that with only four exceptions the houses investigated were in exceedingly poor physical condition, particularly those single-family houses which had been sublet to various roomers or several families. In such cases, the premises were usually uncared for, the houses were sadly in need of repair, the rooms had not been rebuilt to accommodate

[1] References 93 (a), pp. 175, 194-6, 205, 217; *cf.* 105 (b), pp. 46-7.

the added number of families so that bedrooms were doing double duty as kitchens and sleeping quarters, and the lack of privacy and sanitation was appalling. In some instances ten families were crowded into one three-story house, all using the same bath and toilet. Not only were whole families living in one and two rooms, but there was an accompanying overcrowding of single rooms, sometimes four or more persons occupying the same room. Often every room in the house was turned into a bedroom or apartment and even cellars and attics were called into use. Such conditions in Philadelphia were not simply the temporary result of the migration but persisted after the first influx. Haynes remarks in 1924: " The Philadelphia Housing Association found in a recent survey that only 10.5 per cent of the houses occupied by Negro families were equipped for sanitation, conveniences and comfort, while 28.6 of the houses occupied by whites were so equipped." [1]

Epstein's vivid description of the deplorable conditions in Pittsburgh (1917) is frequently quoted in discussions of the entrance of southern Negroes into Pittsburgh industries. So great was the influx that every available space in the Negro districts was requisitioned to shelter the migrants. " Attics and cellars, store rooms and basements, churches, sheds and warehouses had to be employed for the accommodation of these newcomers. Whenever a Negro had space which he could possibly spare, it was converted into a sleeping place; as many beds as possible were crowded into it, and the maximum number of men per bed were lodged." At times beds were made to do double duty, night workers using them during the day while the other occupants were employed. The lack of ventilation and sanitation was strikingly apparent; Epstein notes some rooms with more than six people sleeping in them at one time and with practically no openings for light or air. Moreover, many of the migrants were forced

[1] Reference 46 (d), p. 71.

to find shelter in old dilapidated buildings that had been abandoned by the white people and in many cases, that had been previously condemned by the City Bureau of Sanitation.[1]

Similar situations were reported throughout Pennsylvania and in many cities which have been subjected to detailed investigations. In one Negro district of Cincinnati, for example, it was found that 54 per cent of the houses were without bathrooms and 85 per cent were fire traps.[2] In Chicago, the Race Commission discovered that the majority of Negro families were living in poor houses which often lacked those ordinary conveniences of bathrooms, furnaces, gas and electricity, considered necessities by most white people. For the most part they were living in old houses which were deteriorating rapidly because the owners refused to make the necessary repairs. Furthermore, the Negro districts were frequently inferior with respect to the cleanliness of the streets and condition of the walks and pavements because the city paid less attention to civic improvements in colored sections. The Commission points out the difficulty of maintaining standards of sanitation and cleanliness under such handicaps and concludes that " None of the houses occupied by Negroes are of as high a standard, generally speaking, as those occupied by whites of a similar economic status." [3]

On the other hand, there are a few instances of northern cities which report that housing conditions among Negroes are not seriously inadequate. Since the standards and methods used in various housing investigations are not uniform, it is impossible to conclude exactly to what extent the

---

[1] Reference 32 (a), pp. 8, 11-8.

[2] Reference 120 (a), p. 526.

[3] References 17 (a), pp. 194, 152-94, 93, 113. *Cf.* 124 (a), pp. 141-2, 121; 145 (c), p. 89; 109 (a), p. 571; 46 (d), p. 71; 22 (a), sec. v; 145 (d), p. 149; 2 (a), pp. 7-9; 81 (a), pp. 46-63; 63 (a), pp. 91-110; 110 (a), pp. 31-6; 57 (g), p. 301.

housing of Negroes in these localities is an improvement over that of other urban centers. However, Baltimore, Buffalo and Minneapolis were found to lack the serious housing conditions of most northern cities.

> Baltimore was reported as having no acute housing problem or the lack of homes which was so evident in other cities.[1] Carpenter concluded that conditions in Buffalo were not bad, but another report in Buffalo stated that about 75 per cent of the colored families lived in a section of the city that contained the poorest houses. It would seem, therefore, that the general status of Negro homes was below that of other groups.[2] Conditions in Minneapolis were also reported as being more satisfactory, for there was no crowding, 97 per cent of the homes investigated had water, 90 per cent had sewer connections, 95 per cent had gas and 74 per cent had electricity.[3]

The housing situation in northern cities has been well summarized by Haynes and by Reuter.[4] Haynes concludes: " In New York, Pittsburgh, Chicago and other cities, while there are many good houses, the majority of the people are overcrowded in houses lacking in facilities for sanitation, convenience and comfort." Reuter says: "The Negro population is generally concentrated in one of a few neglected and undesirable districts to which they have been attracted because of the relatively cheap rents or into which they have been forced by the difficulty of securing living quarters in the better residential areas. The buildings are generally old and frequently dilapidated, the surroundings usually neglected, the sanitation poor, and the health regulations not enforced. Even in the better class of houses occupied by laboring classes the

[1] Reference 100 (a), p. 898.
[2] References 16 (a), p. 179; 46 (d), p. 71.
[3] Reference 44 (b), p. 17.
[4] References 46 (d), p. 71; 119 (a), p. 219.

ordinary conveniences are often lacking; the heating is usually from wood or coal stoves, the lighting is commonly by gas or by oil lamps, and bathrooms are unusual."

From a comparison of these various surveys it would seem that Reuter's statement is a fair description of the general housing situation among the Negroes in northern cities. A few cities such as Buffalo and Minneapolis show a better average but in most of the urban centers the Negroes are faced with a real housing problem which affects their family life, standards of decency and morality, and their tendency to lawlessness and crime.

RENTS

The serious housing shortage which prevailed in nearly all northern cities as soon as the migrants began to arrive in large numbers naturally resulted in high rents for the rooms and dwellings that were available. As a general rule throughout the North the congestion, the limitation of the colored residential area, and the lack of houses tended to compel Negroes (1) to pay excessive rents considering the accommodations they secured, frequently higher than white people paid for similar living quarters; and (2) to spend an abnormally large amount of their income for rent. The problem of increasing rents has also faced the Negroes who have come to northern industrial centers. In many of the largest places rents advanced throughout the city during and after the war, but in most cases these increases were excessively high for colored tenants.

A comparison of actual investigations which have been made of this subject in recent years substantiates the contention of general students of Negro problems that rentals are disproportionately high for colored families.[1] The re-

[1] References 157 (d), ch. 7; 93 (a), pp. 194-7; 105 (b), p. 47; 32 (a), pp. 13, 17; 114 (a), p. 3; 100 (a), p. 898; 57 (r), p. 140; 124 (a), pp. 140,

port of the Commonwealth of Pennsylvania gives a typical picture of the situation throughout the northern states, where the mass of Negroes are concentrated in the leading cities. Conditions reported as existing in Philadelphia and Pittsburgh are similar to those found in such important centers as Cleveland, New York, Chicago, Detroit, Hartford and Gary. " The unskilled workingman who constitutes the mass Negro pays more for his housing in Philadelphia and Pittsburgh than does the white man. This is due, of course, to the fact that landlords take advantage of the great pressure on Negro housing resulting from the large number of Negroes in the two cities. In the rest of the Commonwealth the rentals are either the same for white and Negro workingmen of the same financial condition or slightly higher for the whites. This is due to the fact that there is not quite the pressure in the rest of the Commonwealth for Negro housing as in the cities of Philadelphia and Pittsburgh. However, since over 60 per cent of the Negroes in Pennsylvania live in Philadelphia and Pittsburgh, a proper weighing of the figures shows the average rent for the Commonwealth. The mere fact that Negroes in a few rural districts pay a smaller rent than whites does not change the fact that the great mass of Negroes in the State are paying a much higher rental. The real injustice to Negroes in the matter of rents is in the quality of the housing that the Negro gets for the rents he pays. The Negro who pays the same rent as the white man, or even the Negro who pays more rent than the white, gets much inferior housing for his money." [1]

The most striking exception to the general report of high rentals is found in the border city of Washington, D. C.

142, 105; 145 (c), p. 89; 145 (d), p. 149; 17 (a), pp. 93, 162, 199; 22 (a), sec. v, pp. 1, 8; 46 (f), p. 26; 150 (d), p. 334; 110 (a), pp. 36-7, 41; 81 (a), pp. 47-56; 105 (a), Annual Report for 1922, p. 16, for 1923, pp. 24-5, 29, for 1927, p. 27; 57 (g), pp. 300-1.

[1] Reference 110 (a), pp. 36-7.

As a result of the housing investigation in that city, the conclusion was drawn that: " The question as to whether Negroes in Washington are forced to pay exorbitant rents for the houses which they occupy is one which—in the light of the facts brought out in this survey—must be answered in the negative. There were very few cases which showed that rents were outrageously high. . . . Rather . . . Negroes in Washington pay very normal rentals for their homes. In many cases it was found that the families were having difficulty in raising the money with which to pay their rents, but this was not due to the fact that they were being overcharged as much as it was to the fact that they were financially incapable of providing the price of normal rentals. There were found, however, several instances in which excessive increases accompanied trivial and inexpensive repairs. . . . Many small houses which had been allowed by their owners to become dilapidated and insanitary were exacting as much rental as they would merit only when in good repair." [1]

Even in cities such as Washington where rentals were reported as normal, the colored people evidently pay a "normal" rent for exceedingly poor dwellings. Among most of the students of Negro housing in the North there seems to be a practically unanimous opinion that Negroes are charged high rents and that rent occupies a central place in their expenses, particularly in view of their meager incomes and inadequate houses. " These rents are excessive whether they are measured by the kind of house and equipment, by the relation of rents paid by Negroes and those paid by white people for similar quarters, by the steady increase in rents, by the relation of rent to the value of the property, or by the proportion which rent forms of the family budget." [2]

[1] Reference 63 (a), pp. 131, 133.
[2] Reference 157 (d), p. 121.

LODGERS

Among many of the colored families the combination of these high rents and low wages has necessitated the taking in of lodgers in order to meet expenses. Consequently, the " lodger problem " is conspicuous in many of the urban groups of Negroes. In order to meet the rent or the monthly installments, if the home was being purchased, the colored family added a few lodgers. Moreover, in order to supplement the family income, families in smaller dwellings frequently rented space they could ill afford to spare. Then too, the shortage of rooms and houses was so acute in many cases that colored families felt obliged to shelter newcomers, especially if they were friends or relations who had come North at the solicitation of people already there. In the more specialized industrial centers, such as Detroit, a further important cause of this situation was the presence of large numbers of unattached men who had come to take advantage of the industrial openings and for whom no housing provisions had been made.

This practice of including adult persons who are outside the family group is at all times and everywhere a potential menace to a desirable family life. In small dwellings it prevents any family privacy and weakens the integration and cohesion of the family. Even in large dwellings the situation is fraught with danger and is conducive to immorality and family disorganization, since the houses available for colored habitants are usually not easily adjusted to the presence of outsiders. It is often necessary for the lodgers to come and go, and to live in the midst of the family group, and frequently to share a bedroom with some member of the family. This is particularly undesirable where there are children or young adults of the opposite sex, as the consequent lack of privacy often leads to weakened family discipline or even to vice and immorality. It is true that the lodgers were frequently relatives and friends but even in such cases the resulting situation was likely to be detrimental to the welfare of the children. The Chicago Race Commission, which made one of the most careful investigations of the "lodger problem", found that, fortunately, the proportion of children was smallest in those sections where the percentage of lodgers was largest. However, the children who were placed in such family situations were subjected to most unwholesome surroundings.

Several investigations have attempted to discover to what extent this practice of taking in lodgers prevails among northern Negroes and what are likely to be its causes and consequences. Reports of the situation in such industrial centers as Chicago, Detroit, New York, Philadelphia, Buffalo, Gary and Pittsburgh, show that from one-fourth to over one-half of the Negro families studied included lodgers, with an average for the North of about 35 per cent.[1] The reports almost unanimously agreed that the principal causes for the situation were the scarcity of houses available for Negroes and the high prices charged for those that could be rented or purchased. They further agreed in pointing out the dangers to normal family life which were inherent in this custom of taking lodgers.

As in the case of disproportionate rents, the city of Washington, D. C., provides the chief exception to a situation which seems to prevail throughout the North. According to the Washington survey a comparatively small proportion of homes were keeping lodgers—only 19 per cent. Furthermore, high rents were not given as the chief reason for having lodgers. This is not surprising since rents in Washington are apparently more normal than in most northern cities and since the increase in population was considerably less. The report concludes that "in a large

[1] References 17 (a), pp. 155-65; 22 (a), sec. v, pp. 5-6, 8-10; 157 (d), pp. 86-8; 110 (a), p. 39.

number of the homes where lodgers are kept it is not the result of the necessity of money in addition to the regular family income to meet extremely high rents, but, usually, the attempt to get further ahead financially. The lodger problem expresses more of the desire to enjoy extravagances than it does the necessity of raising money for rent and living expenses, or for payment on homes." However, the report also states that the scarcity of houses available in Washington has induced many Negroes to buy their own homes " and many who do not have incomes sufficient to purchase homes are forced to take lodgers in order to make a success of their financial undertakings." [1] It would seem, then, that even in Washington there is a relation between economic necessity and the practice of taking in lodgers.

From the material available it is apparent that the " lodger problem " is chiefly due to conditions following the migration of numbers of colored laborers from the South. (Woofter, for instance, contrasts the high percentage of lodgers in northern cities containing many migrants with the low percentage in more static southern towns.) [2] The consequent housing shortage and the inability to spread out into new neighborhoods created a demand for rooms. Colored families who had dwellings, partially satisfied this demand by taking in lodgers, being influenced to do so either by their gregariousness and hospitality or by a situation of low incomes and high rents that made lodgers an irresistible solution to the pressing economic problem.

HOME OWNERSHIP

The scarcity of houses, high rents and congestion which followed the migration not only strengthened this practice

[1] Reference 63 (a), p. 112.
[2] Reference 157 (d), p. 86.

of taking in lodgers but at the same time tended to increase
the amount of home ownership among Negroes in northern
cities.   A much larger proportion of Negroes owned homes
in 1920 than in 1910, and the few surveys which have been
made of this situation since 1920 report an even greater
tendency toward ownership.[1]   Higher wages during war
times made it easier for Negroes to purchase homes, and the
prevailing inadequate supply of houses frequently necessitated buying in order to secure shelter.   In several northern
industrial centers the influx of colored laborers has resulted
in the opening up of new real estate divisions in the districts
where Negroes can purchase.

Woofter and the Chicago Race Commission both found
that the migration and consequent scarcity of houses and
high rents had led to a marked increase in home ownership
among Negroes in the North.   Woofter believes that
" since 1920 home ownership among Negroes in northern
cities has about doubled " and gives instances of an increasing tendency to buy in New York City, Chicago and
Philadelphia.[2]   Moreover, there are indications that this
is only one phase of a noticeable progress of the Negroes
in saving money, opening bank accounts and developing
thrift in general.[3]

Ever since 1916 at least, books, magazines and newspapers
have contained frequent references to the housing problems
found by Negroes in the North.   Sensing the seriousness
of the situation, individuals and commissions have investi-

[1] References 157 (d), pp. 106-8, 136-43; 17 (a), pp. 216-20; 46 (d), p.
71; 63 (a), ch. 6; 110 (a), p. 38; 2 (a), p. 7; 22 (a), sec. v. p. 18;
151 (a), p. 294.

[2] Reference 157 (d), p. 138.

[3] References 17 (a), pp. 227-30; 32 (a), p. 24; 151 (a), p. 294; 22 (a),
sec. iv.

gated the housing of colored groups in specific industrial
centers. When these surveys are synchronized and compared, and are checked up with general opinions expressed
by leading students of racial problems, it is apparent that
difficulty in securing adequate homes, or any shelter at all,
is a fairly uniform problem for Negroes throughout the
North, though its seriousness varies from city to city.

In many of its phases the situation is no different from
those housing problems faced by any nationality group which
has migrated in large numbers to one of our big cities. On
the other hand, the Negroes' difficulties are intensified by the
race feeling involved, for more emotional tension is apparently aroused when colored people seek homes in a neighborhood hitherto unoccupied by their group than when such
foreign groups as Italians or Russians begin to " invade " a
new district. This race prejudice of white people was particularly aroused when the arrival of thousands of colored
laborers made the presence of Negroes in northern cities
more noticeable and their contacts with the white inhabitants
more frequent and intimate. As a result, much antagonism
was expressed when Negroes began to seek homes in white
neighborhoods, and in practically all parts of the North there
was an increased attempt to draw lines of residential segregation. The degree of opposition aroused and the manner
of its expression were not uniform among the centers which
received large numbers of Negro migrants, being much more
overt and violent in Chicago and Detroit, for example, than
in New York City. So far no attempt has been made to
study conditions in various cities for the purpose of dis-
covering why some cities were faced with bombings, incendiarism or avalanches of propaganda inflaming race prejudice, while other cities sought to restrict Negro residence
largely by increasing prices and refusing to sell or rent. The
reason usually given everywhere for antagonism to an influx

of Negroes was the belief that property values depreciated as soon as Negroes moved into the neighborhood. The few investigations which have been made of this subject point out the numerous factors which cause depreciation of values and refuse to hold the Negroes even largely responsible.

The practically uniform attempt to restrict the rapidly growing Negro population to former " Negro areas " as a rule led to serious problems of congestion and unsanitary housing conditions. Here and there, however, there seemed to be less crowding and a better type of housing than prevailed in most of the northern cities. In many centers there is a tendency, now, toward less congestion and a less serious scarcity of houses. Apparently Negroes are becoming better adjusted to the urban environment of the North, but even in cities which reported less congestion than prevailed around 1916-1918, the colored people are still crowded into undesirable sections. Inadequate, and often deplorable housing, high rents and an abnormally large number of families with lodgers are found to be fairly uniform factors in the housing situation among northern Negroes.

CHAPTER IX

VITAL STATISTICS AND HEALTH

THE belief has been commonly held among white people that Negroes as a group cannot survive in a northern climate. Whenever colored people have moved in large numbers to northern cities, comments have been freely made concerning the deteriorating effects of such a migration upon the health and rate of increase of the Negro race. Pointing out the low birth rate and high death rate of northern Negroes and the tendency to disease, numerous writers have contended that Negroes are inherently unfitted for a northern environment and cannot maintain their numbers save by continued recruitment from the South. Such comments and discussions were especially rife during the war period, when Negro laborers were swarming into northern cities. The subject is naturally of prime importance to the Negroes, since there will be a steadily decreasing colored population in the United States if the northern group cannot maintain itself and must be constantly replenished by southern Negroes.

Among all people the birth rate of those living in cities is lower than that of the same population group living in rural districts; the Negroes have been no exception and their birth rate in both southern and northern cities has been less than that of rural colored people. During past decades there has also been a tendency for the birth rates of Negroes in northern cities to be lower than those of white people. At times, too, the Negro birth rates have been lower than their death rates in the North, so that any decided increase of northern Negro groups has been due to migration from the

South. For the years immediately following the first mass influx of colored migrants, comparison of Negro birth and death rates in northern industrial centers would seem to justify the contention that the colored population could not be self-sustaining in the North. When the migrants arrived, there was a great deal of sickness and a startling number of deaths in some cities, for the process of adaptation to a different climate and the crowded, unsanitary dwellings of many of the newcomers exacted an enormous toll of lives. The death rate was high and the birth rate was low. Between 1915 and 1925 in most northern cities the number of Negro deaths tended to exceed the number of Negro births. The mortality rate was naturally high during the period of adjustment to a new environment. At the same time, the birth rate felt the disturbing effects of migration, which tends to upset the ratio between the sexes, thus decreasing the marriage rate. It also tends to raise the standard of living, with consequent postponement of marriage, and smaller families.[1]

It is a natural assumption that the death rate should decline and the birth rate increase among northern Negroes as the years pass. Presumably, the gradual adaptation to a northern climate and social environment would lower the mortality rate, while the birth rate should show a trend in the upward direction as newcomers send for their families and as women, in their turn, begin to move North, thus lessening the disproportion between the sexes. In many northern cities this assumption is supported by the facts disclosed in recent surveys, but in other centers the death rate has constantly fluctuated with little real decrease since 1919 and 1920. Compared with the death rate for northern Negroes

---

[1] See Bibliography, references 44 (b), pp. 43-4; 32 (a), pp. 58-9; 16 (a), p. 179; 145 (d), p. 144; 157 (d), pp. 33-5; 157 (a), pp. 41, 52-3; 38 (a), pp. 27-8; 26 (e), p. 44; 49 (a), p. 559; 2 (a), p. 9; 22 (a), sec. vi, pp. 1-3; 146 (a), pp. 16-8.

in 1910 and for the high water marks of 1917 and 1918, the reports since 1920 show a trend toward improvement in Negro mortality throughout the North but, at the same time, there are numerous indications that many cities have witnessed an increase in Negro deaths over the rate which prevailed in 1919 to 1921, so that the mortality rates seem to be rising again.[1]

TABLE 18.—NEGRO DEATHS PER 1,000 POPULATION IN NORTHERN CITIES HAVING 25,000 OR MORE NEGROES IN 1920

(Source: U. S. Bureau of the Census, *Mortality Rates 1910-1920,* and subsequent annual volumes.)

Year	Chicago	New York*	Philadelphia	Cincinnati	Cleveland†	Detroit†	Pittsburgh	Indianapolis	St. Louis	Kansas City, M.
1910....	23.3	23.8	26.6	28.6	...	...	23.3	24.8	25.6	27.2
1915....	15.8	18.9	20.2	25.3	...	...	16.4	19.5	20.7	25.9
1916....	15.1	18.2	20.2	26.4	...	...	20.7	21.9	21.6	25.6
1917....	20.0	18.9	25.7	31.6	...	...	25.8	22.8	25.7	27.3
1918....	24.1	24.7	32.2	35.2	...	...	33.9	24.5	30.1	31.1
1919....	18.1	19.3	19.9	24.1	...	...	19.1	18.5	19.7	22.7
1920....	19.8	19.2	21.2	24.1	21.3	23.9	22.3	20.9	19.9	24.9
1921....	17.2	17.3	17.4	23.7	17.5	17.6	20.3	16.5	17.5	23.8
1922....	17.1	18.1	19.1	23.9	17.8	21.1	20.2	18.1	17.8	24.0
1923....	23.2	18.7	22.1	27.9	21.6	not given	25.6	19.7	21.4	23.9
1924....	24.2	26.3	22.0	26.7	24.3	19.2	28.7	19.0	23.3	24.4
1925....	24.3	30.5	22.5	27.2	23.8	19.7	23.7	18.9	22.8	26.0
1926....	23.5	35.0	23.8	28.4	25.6	21.2	21.1	18.7	22.5	25.2

* New York figures are for Manhattan only, since the Negroes are concentrated in that borough.

† No published separation of colored and white deaths until 1920.

Several surveys of specific sections of the North have revealed an increasing birth rate and a decreasing death rate, although the latter is still higher among Negroes than among white people. Certain industrial centers such as New York, Detroit, Toledo, Cincinnati and Cleveland

[1] The estimates of population on which rates for the later years are based are probably highly inaccurate due to differential migration.

were at times reported as having a Negro death rate lower than that which prevailed at the beginning of the migration.[1] This is usually true only of reports of conditions prior to 1922 and on the basis of official mortality statistics would not be justified in New York, Cincinnati and Cleveland, for example, if such reports were made for the years 1924 to 1926. However, a discussion of birth rates among northern Negroes for 1924 and 1925 concludes that the leading northern states in those years showed more births than deaths among Negroes, although in 1915 all these states, except Massachusetts, had shown an excess of deaths over births.[2]

In Pennsylvania, " the Negro death rate for the State for 1924 was found to be 20.83 per thousand, and the white death rate for the same districts was found to be 14.13. These figures mean that approximately twenty-one Negroes and fourteen white persons died out of every thousand for the same period." This excess of 6.7 in the Negro over the white death rate was shown to be an improvement over the situation a decade earlier when the Negro death rate exceeded that of the whites by 9.5. The darker side of the picture is found, however, in the statement that " in 1919 only 14.3 out of every thousand Negroes died in the districts of Pennsylvania for which we were able to get vital statistics. (This included almost 90 per cent of the Negro inhabitants of Pennsylvania.) This was two per thousand more than the death rate for whites in the same districts, but in 1923 the number of Negro deaths had increased to 19.9 per thousand, while the death rate of the whites remained 12.4. . . . In 1924 the Negro death rate had increased to 20.8 per thousand. . . . In Philadelphia, where in 1921 there were only three more deaths per thousand among Negroes than among whites, in 1924

---

[1] References **62 (e)**, pp. 69-70; **46 (d)**, p. 70; **121 (a)**, p. 241; **22 (a)**, sec. vi.

[2] References **49 (a)**, p. 559. *Cf.* **26 (e)**, p. 44.

there were eight more deaths per thousand." [1]   It would
seem, therefore, that in Pennsylvania the death rate for
Negroes has diminished since 1910-1915 but has shown
an upward tendency in the last decade.   The findings of
the Pennsylvania survey agree with the conclusions derived by Dublin from his intensive study of Negro death
rates and life expectancy among colored policy holders
of the Metropolitan Life Insurance Company.   Since most
of these policy holders are urban dwellers and many of
them are in northern cities, his report may be taken as
indicative of the trend of death rates among Negroes in
northern cities.   The Metropolitan rates are more reliable
than those of the Census Bureau, since the former are
based on known populations, while the latter use population estimates.   From the cases which he covered, Dublin
found that between 1911 and 1927 the death rate of Negro
policy holders, in general, had declined from 17.5 per 1,000
to 14.0 and that the life span had increased.   On the other
hand, he found that there had been significant increases
in mortality in the years preceding 1926, particularly in
several northern cities, and believed that these higher rates
are due, in part at least, to migration of Negroes to these
industrial centers.   In commenting upon the increase in
mortality rates between 1921 and 1926, he maintains:
" There is every reason to believe that when the figures
for the general colored population are available, they will
show the same drift " as the result of this movement from
rural to urban centers and from the South to the North. [2]

The extent to which the mortality rate among Negroes has
declined in northern cities varies considerably from city to
city.   The actual variations are shown in Table 18.

The influx of southern Negroes resulted in a great deal of

[1] Reference 110 (a), pp. 44-5, 33-4.

[2] References 26 (e), pp. 43-4; 26 (a) ; 26 (b), p. 234; 26 (d), pp. 77-82;
26 (f), p. 7.

sickness among the colored people in all urban centers, and vastly increased the health problems of the cities to which they migrated. Philadelphia, Pittsburgh, and Cleveland, for example, were confronted with epidemics of smallpox which were directly traceable to the southern Negroes and which compelled extensive vaccination and quarantine throughout the cities. Infant mortality, tuberculosis, pneumonia, heart and venereal diseases were increased and constituted serious problems, as in all these illnesses the Negroes tended to show higher rates of morbidity and mortality than did the white group.[1]

TABLE 19.—MORTALITY RATES * PER 100,000 POPULATION BY COLOR AND CHIEF CAUSES, 1920

FOR NORTHERN CITIES WITH 25,000 OR MORE NEGROES IN 1920

(Source: U. S. Bureau of the Census, *Mortality Rates 1910-1920*, pp. 258 *et seq.*)

	Pneumonia		Tuberculosis		Heart	
	White	Negro	White	Negro	White	Negro
Chicago	152.3	349.3	77.4	266.5	154.9	238.9
New York	177.7	409.6	105.6	327.2	167.9	167.3
Philadelphia	175.4	393.0	105.3	316.3	181.9	183.8
Cincinnati	111.5	369.1	116.3	424.6	190.7	245.0
Cleveland	144.4	348.8	82.6	362.4	101.1	152.1
Detroit	208.2	776.0	78.4	232.6	106.6	232.6
Pittsburgh	322.8	604.5	86.9	255.8	128.0	186.0
Indianapolis	157.8	344.2	83.9	315.9	163.2	225.7
St. Louis	193.0	399.4	70.0	259.7	149.6	229.0
Kansas City, Mo.	225.2	457.4	72.0	371.0	145.4	339.0

* Rates adjusted for age and sex might show materially less discrepancy between the races.

The addition of large numbers of Negroes, who showed a marked tendency to such an infectious disease as tuberculosis, was of serious import to every city within which they settled.

[1] References 145 (d), pp. 143-4; 22 (a), sec. vi; 121 (a), pp. 241-2; 110 (a), pp. 46-7; 44 (b), pp. 46-51.

The health situation among one population group is not limited in its effects to that group but influences the health of the whole city. Through contacts in transportation, at work, and in public places, the entire population is brought in touch with those who are below standard in their general physical condition; and the city must perforce take into account the health of Negroes whether or not it desires to do so. The situation in every northern city is, to some extent at least, similar to that in Cleveland: " The effect of the Negro migration has been to bring into Cleveland a 360 per cent increase in a population group which, both before and after the migration, shows mortality rates from tuberculosis over 300 per cent greater than similar rates among the entire population. . . . The same increase of health hazards for the entire community arises in connection with any other communicable disease which has a greater incidence among the migratory group." [1]   Furthermore, the southern Negro's general ignorance of the laws of health, of means of preventing illness and of the necessity of quarantine, all added to the problems which confronted the cities when migrants arrived. Table 20 indicates some of the conspicuous increases in health problems faced by those northern cities which were the centers of this influx of colored laborers during the early years of the war-time migration.

Those surveys of specific northern cities which have considered the health problem of the Negroes, unite in stressing the seriousness of the situation. The Detroit Bureau called attention to the high rate of tuberculosis among the Negroes and to the fact that this disease was increasing among the colored group, although decreasing among the whites.[2]   In Minneapolis, the Negro tuberculosis death rate

[1] Reference 121 (a), pp. 240-2.
[2] Reference 22 (a), sec. vi, p. 3.

TABLE 20.—DEATH RATES AMONG NEGROES PER 100,000 POPULATION
FOR YEARS OF MIGRATION AND FOR CHIEF CAUSES, 1920

IN NORTHERN CITIES HAVING 100,000 NEGRO POPULATION
OR MORE IN 1920

(Source: U. S. Bureau of the Census, *Mortality Rates 1910-1920,*
pp. 258 *et seq.*)

	1915	1916	1917	1918	1919	1920
Chicago						
Pneumonia	222.4	191.7	366.5	518.0	263.0	349.3
Tuberculosis	331.1	287.6	335.1	357.7	334.5	266.5
Influenza	7.3	15.8	10.5	209.2	66.9	144.0
New York						
Pneumonia	327.9	287.1	365.7	733.1	335.6	409.6
Tuberculosis	435.9	389.3	387.8	409.6	399.1	327.2
Influenza	11.4	16.7	10.4	188.2	67.4	43.9
Philadelphia						
Pneumonia	263.2	259.4	484.8	800.8	320.2	393.0
Tuberculosis	390.4	389.5	415.5	455.9	347.3	316.3
Influenza	24.9	26.4	22.8	341.7	51.9	74.5

was many times that of the total population and the infant
mortality rate far exceeded that of the white group.[1]   In
Cleveland there had been a marked increase in diseases
which are prevalent among infants and young adults.[2]
The survey of Negroes in Pennsylvania concluded: " As
compared with whites, deaths among Negroes are relatively more numerous for pneumonia, tuberculosis of the
lungs, heart disease, syphilis and cerebral hemorrhage. . . .
Syphilis is most prevalent in the congested industrial centers and the large cities.   Philadelphia shows the highest
rate, 78.6 deaths per 100,000 Negroes.   This is an increase of 527 per cent over the death rate of 12.5 for
Negroes who died from this disease in 1914.   The increased number of deaths from syphilis is probably due to
the presence of large numbers of Negro newcomers in the
congested centers of Negro population and perhaps to the

[1] Reference 44 (b), pp. 46, 51.
[2] Reference 121 (a), pp. 238-44.

increased facilities for diagnosis as well as to more accurate reporting. These people come largely from the rural districts of the South where they possessed neither the facilities nor the knowledge to obtain proper treatment for their ills. As a rule, death from syphilis occurs only after the disease has continued over a long period. It is probable that most of the Negroes dying from the disease in Pennsylvania in the last few years incurred the infection elsewhere." [1]

A disproportionate increase in mortality and amount of illness as a result of the migration was not surprising in view of the decided change in climate and mode of living which the movements involved. The migrants necessarily experienced a period of adjustment to new customs of housing, of food and of clothing and, in consequence, were particularly susceptible to such diseases as pneumonia and tuberculosis. Their ignorance of disease, of sanitation and of means of securing help in a large city in times of illness, and their poverty, all contributed to increase deaths and sickness among colored groups. Unaccustomed to confinement both at home and at work, to lack of ventilation and to the nervous strain of city life, they necessarily showed the effects of these changed conditions in a lessened physical resistance. Furthermore, the unsanitary, congested housing facilities in these centers tended to further both the inception and spread of disease.

Evidence from studies of the Negro's health status points to the conclusion that his high death rate is not entirely a racial trait or merely the effect of climatic change, but to a great extent is due to poor housing, poverty and ignorance. As the Negro's standard of living improves, as he is given a chance to find better homes and as his knowledge of health

[1] References 110 (a), pp. 45-6; *cf.* 57 (g), p. 341.

precautions is increased by campaigns of the Health Department and by social welfare agencies, health conditions among the colored group tend to improve.

Woofter, for instance, has made a correlation of density with death rates from tuberculosis and infant mortality on the basis of which he points out the serious effect of crowding upon the health of the Negro.[1] Likewise the Pennsylvania survey stresses the effect of poor housing and the Negro's ignorance of a suitable mode of living upon the mortality rates and amount of illness within this population group.[2] The effect of ignorance upon the health problem of Negroes is indicated by the results which have been obtained in several cities when Health Departments have carried on systematic campaigns to educate the colored people in matters of sanitation and prevention of illness. In New York such efforts of the Health Department resulted in a decrease of infant mortality among Negroes from 202 per 1,000 births in 1915 to 164 per 1,000 births in 1920. A similar campaign in Newark, New Jersey, reduced the infant death rate from 172 per 1,000 in 1919 to 106 in 1921.[3] After careful analysis of Negro death rates for a long period of years, Dublin concludes that " The problem, then, in my judgment, is largely one of environment. The very diseases and conditions from which the Negro suffers point out clearly that we are not concerned to any serious degree with weaknesses of stock or of stamina. Other races when subjected to similar conditions of housing, hard work, limitations on food, clothing and medical attendance, show mortality rates no better than those for Negroes." [4]

[1] Reference 157 (d), p. 90.
[2] Reference 110 (a), pp. 48-9.
[3] Reference 62 (b), p. 974.
[4] Reference 26 (d), p. 82.

Although the migration brought the Negroes to a more severe climate and to a more strenuous mode of life, it also brought them under the influence of more rigidly enforced sanitary regulations and in touch with publicly-given information concerning the importance of higher health standards. Change of climate has undoubtedly affected the death rate and the amount of sickness, though bad housing and poverty were so prevalent among the migrants that it is difficult to know to what extent the health situation should be attributed to climate and to what extent to living conditions. On the whole, it seems probable that the Negro has the capacity of adapting himself, if he is given a chance to attain a normal standard of living. The death rate among Negroes in northern cities is still far higher than that of the white population, particularly from diseases of the respiratory organs, infant mortality and syphilis. Furthermore, in their fluctuations from year to year the mortality rates of northern colored people are not steadily diminishing. According to Dublin, the tendency toward an increased death rate from 1923 to 1926 is probably only a temporary condition; among the cases which he studied, at least, the 1927 figures for Negroes showed a decrease for both men and women.[1]

Information collected by surveys of specific cities around 1920 to 1924 have optimistically indicated the improved health status of colored people in northern cities.[2] It is probably true that in such specific instances as infant mortality or pneumonia, the death rate and amount of illness have at times been diminished by campaigns of Health Departments and by the Negroes' increasing knowledge and adaptation to northern life. A comparison of Negro mortality rates in northern cities from 1920 to 1926 reveals,

[1] Reference 26 (d), p. 82.

[2] References 62 (e), pp. 69-70; 46 (d), p. 70; 121 (a), p. 241; 22 (a), sec. vi.

however, no firm basis for believing that the Negroes are steadily improving in health conditions. On the other hand, it is true that the majority of the northern states and cities which have received the largest share of migrants have decreased the mortality rates since 1910, and this in spite of the large influx of southern Negroes who had to pass through a period of adjustment necessarily unfavorable to normal health. A comparison of official reports, individual surveys and general discussions leads to the conclusion that, in general, there has been a real improvement in the health status of northern Negroes since 1910. It is apparent, however, that most of the industrial centers did not give adequate attention to the problem of Negro mortality and illness nor to the causes and consequences of the health status of their colored populations.

CHAPTER X

The Social Maladjustment of the Negro

CRIME

Due to the widely held belief that the tendency toward crime is greater among Negroes than among other population groups, many expected the recent migration to result in a tremendous increase in the problems of crime and vice in northern cities. A study of the latest information available leads to the conclusion that this pessimistic prophecy was justified, for practically every important center to which migrants flocked witnessed an increase in the number of Negro cases brought before the police courts. Furthermore, in the North as well as in the South, Negroes undeniably show a larger proportion of arrests and convictions than do white people. Every investigation of court records and criminal statistics in northern cities reported that the Negroes' contribution to the criminal cases was relatively much higher than their share of the total population.[1]

According to the survey made by the Commonwealth of Pennsylvania " There were 15,734 arrests made in the city of Philadelphia during the first six months of 1924. Of this number 3,842 (or 24.4 per cent), or practically one-fourth of the total arrests for this period were Negroes. The 1920 Census showed that the Negroes constituted

[1] See Bibliography, references 110 (a), pp. 69-72; 139 (a); 32 (a), pp. 46-50; 145 (d), pp. 138-41; 114 (a), p. 4; 120 (a), p. 527; 22 (a), sec. ix; 17 (a), pp. 331, ch. 7, pp. 621-3; 119 (a), ch. 14; 46 (j), pp. 37-8; 9 (a), pp. 171-3; 70 (a), p. 235; 57 (g), pp. 341-2.

7.4 per cent of the total population of Philadelphia. Comparing the proportion of Negro arrests with their percentage of the population, they have more than three times as many arrests as might be expected. . . . Seven out of every 1,000 of the white population were arrested during the period of January 1 to June 30, 1924, in comparison with approximately 29 Negroes arrested out of every 1,000 of the Negro population. The investigation in Pittsburgh showed for the same period 3,678 Negro arrests, which amounted to 13.8 per cent of the total arrests. Since Negroes at the 1920 Census constituted 6.4 per cent of the total population of Pittsburgh, they had more than twice as many arrests as one might expect. Negro arrests for this period approximate 97 out of every 1,000 of the Negro population. On the other hand, only 45 white people out of every 1,000 of the white population were arrested." [1] In Cincinnati Negroes comprised 23 per cent of those arrested although they were only 7 per cent of the total population.[2] Investigation of the criminal statistics for the state of Michigan revealed the fact that 18.7 per cent of all the prisoners were colored, whereas only 2.6 per cent of the state population was Negro.[3] Similar situations were reported in Detroit and Waterbury, Conn.[4] The Chicago Race Commission made a careful investigation of the crime situation among Chicago Negroes and concluded that the apparent rate of crime among colored, as this was measured by arrests and convictions, was greater than among whites.[5]

Some sort of upward trend in the number of Negro arrests and convictions was to be expected as an accompaniment of

[1] Reference 110 (a), p. 69.
[2] Reference 120 (a), p. 527.
[3] Reference 70 (a), p. 235.
[4] References 22 (a), sec. ix; 57 (g), p. 341.
[5] Reference 17 (a), p. 331.

the rapid growth of colored population, so that the appearance of more Negroes before the courts did not in itself mean a sudden jump in the criminal tendencies of the race.   There are indications that the amount of crime did not increase so rapidly in the North as did the total Negro population, but there has been so little comparison between increase in Negro crime rates and increase in Negro population for the years before and during migration, that nothing definite can be said on this subject.   However, surveys made by the United States Department of Labor, by the Chicago Race Commission and by the Commonwealth of Pennsylvania all concluded that in the specific localities studied, crime among Negroes had not increased at the same rate as had the total colored population.[1]   The numerical increase which did undoubtedly occur is usually attributed to the newcomers from the South.   Since the migrants contained an abnormally large proportion of adults between the years 20 and 44, during which there is most likely to be conflict with the law, it was natural that they should augment the number of those arrested and convicted.

The conspicious and inevitable effect of the migration on crime increase is further indicated by a study of the nature of offenses for which Negroes were arrested.   The increase in arrests for petty offenses was much greater than the increase for major crimes.   In practically all the cities in which investigations of Negro criminality have been made, the majority of colored prisoners had been arrested on charges of immorality, gambling, drunkenness, being suspicious persons, and violating city ordinances.   Among the major crimes, larceny was the most conspicuous offense.[2]   When distinctions are made between Negro men and women in

[1] References 145 (d), pp. 138-41; 17 (a), p. 331; 110 (a), p. 72.

[2] References 145 (d), pp. 138-43; 110 (a), p. 70; 32 (a), pp. 48-51; 120 (a), p. 527; 2 (a), p. 13; 57 (g), p. 341; 139 (a), pp. 251-4.

studying the causes of arrest, it is found that by far the most important single offense of colored women is that of being inmates of disorderly houses.   So far, insufficient attention has been paid by investigators to the subject of the causes and significance of the high rate of prostitution among Negroes in northern cities.   Thus the existence of a migrant group which has not yet become adjusted to a new economic and social environment is revealed in the nature of the Negroes' offenses.   Furthermore, where relative proportions of northern and southern Negro criminals have been obtained, it is evident that the newcomers contributed a large share to these cases.[1]

A study of criminal statistics obtained from the court records of northern cities would thus seemingly substantiate the belief that Negroes are naturally more criminal in their tendencies than are white people, and that the influx of southern laborers must necessarily augment the problem of law observance in these industrial centers by increasing the danger from potential criminals.   However, the fallacies involved in this sort of conclusion must not be overlooked.   In the first place, criminal statistics in northern cities are by no means infallible and must be used with caution.   Even the enumeration of arrests may be unreliable, as is seen in the case of data on arrests in Minneapolis.

> The Municipal Court of Minneapolis reported the number of arrests of Negroes for 1923 as 470, for 1924 as 930, and for 1925 as 890.   When these figures were carefully checked with police court records by Miss Boie, working under the auspices of the Urban League, it was found that the totals should have been 517, 389 and 478 for each of the three years respectively.[2]

[1] References 70 (a), p. 235; 145 (d), pp. 138-9.

[2] Reference 9 (a), pp. 171-3. For other examples of unreliability of criminal statistics see 128 (a), p. 54.

Furthermore, comparisons of criminal tendencies inherent in Negroes and white people are usually made on the basis of the number of arrests and convictions, but these do not furnish an adequate measure of the amount of actual crime. The number of arrests and convictions furnish particularly inaccurate estimates of criminal proclivities among colored people because Negroes are handicapped by the tendency of authorities to arrest them more freely, " to book them on more serious charges, to convict them more readily and to give them longer sentences." [1]   Frequently police officers do not hesitate to arrest Negroes on insufficient evidence because their inferior economic and social status renders it unlikely that there will be disagreeable results if the arrests should prove unwarranted.   As a matter of fact, a large number of Negro cases are discharged without trial because of the lack of any excuse for their arrest.

" Of the Negroes arrested in Philadelphia . . . 31.1 per cent were discharged. . . . In Pittsburgh, of the total number of Negroes arrested . . . 36.7 were discharged." [2]   " The very high rate of discharges of Negroes for certain offenses as compared with arrests is undoubtedly in a very large measure the result of unwarranted arrests." [3]

This tendency toward the hasty and wholesale arrest of Negroes on insufficient basis is augmented by the general inclination of white people to regard a Negro with suspicion and to consider him guilty until he is proved innocent—and sometimes even then.   Police officers share this wide prejudice and in case of a violation of the law are likely to arrest a Negro if he is within hailing distance of the crime.   The

[1] References 17 (a), pp. 329, 345.   *Cf.* 128 (a), pp. 54-6; 119 (a), pp. 355-7; 157 (a), pp. 53, 127-8, 138.

[2] Reference 110 (a), p. 70.

[3] Reference 128 (a), p. 56.

policy of the white press further intensifies this attitude of suspicion, for whenever a Negro is connected with a crime, falsely or not, the factor of his race is made prominent in headlines and write-up, so that white readers inevitably and unconsciously associate the word criminal with that of Negro. Reuter has summarized this phase of the situation: " The press thus caters to the general belief and the general belief is in turn reinforced by the stories in the press. There is, in consequence, a vicious circle; a tradition of Negro crime, the deliberate or unintentional selection of news, the confirmation of the popular belief." [1] With this subtle but powerful background of race prejudice and suspicion, it is natural, perhaps, that policemen, lawyers and judges should tend to apprehend and convict a Negro suspect on less objective grounds than would be required in the case of a white man. The situation is also aggravated by the fact that colored people are often too ignorant and poor to secure intelligent and capable lawyers for their defense.

Other factors likewise serve to invalidate the common opinion that high rates of crime among northern Negroes are due to inherent racial criminality. Their low economic status frequently prevents them from paying fines, so that they are forced to the alternative sentence of imprisonment. This naturally adds to the number of colored cases in prisons. Poverty and the restricted opportunity of securing employment which the Negro faces in northern cities contribute their share to the cases of larceny and robbery. Likewise, the inability to secure employment except in poorly-paid servants' work has contributed to the high rate of prostitution which prevails among Negro women.

The very composition of the northern Negro groups is an important factor in their crime rate, for, as has been shown, colored populations in these industrial centers contain high

[1] Reference 119 (a), p. 356.

percentages of those age groups, 20 to 44, which constitute the highest proportion of criminal offenders among any people.   Furthermore, migration brought in hordes of southern Negroes who were ignorant of the rules which govern living in northern cities.   Such factors naturally increased the number of colored people who were arrested for such offenses as drunkenness, immorality, being suspicious persons and violating city ordinances.   Newcomers from the South were frequently left stranded without friends and hung around the streets in the congested districts while they solved the difficult problems of finding work and shelter; thus they were easily apprehended as suspicious persons, loafers or vagrants.   Many of them were illiterate and ignorant of city regulations, seeing no reason why they should observe sanitary requirements or why they should not carry weapons or settle their family and personal difficulties by brawls and fights, if they wished to do so.   The tendency toward drunkenness and immorality was not surprising in view of the fact that a large number of the migrants were young men with no family ties in the North who were often forced into the streets and saloons by the housing situation.   Congestion in poor dwellings led to close contact of both sexes and to a lack of privacy that increased the prevalence of quarrels, assaults and sexual crimes.   Lack of proper recreational facilities also played a part in increasing crime, for in many northern cities colored people are discouraged from entering amusement places with white people and are forced to spend their leisure time in saloons and cheap recreational centers where drunkenness, gambling and immorality are prevalent.   The high crime rate among northern Negroes is the effect of poor environment and lack of economic and educational opportunities rather than of ineradicable racial traits.

JUVENILE DELINQUENCY

Intensive studies of the problem of juvenile delinquency among colored children in northern cities are not numerous but on the basis of the information which is available it is evident that delinquency among Negro children in the North is usually higher than among white children.[1] Wherever actual figures have been obtained in northern cities, Negroes have contributed a proportion of delinquents larger than their proportion in the total population. Much of this high rate was due to the recent migration from the South. The colored children were frequently without adequate home care and supervision because both parents were working. Due to their low economic status, Negroes show an abnormally high percentage of married women engaged in gainful occupations, and the outside employment of mothers has a direct effect upon the amount of juvenile delinquency. Furthermore, colored children are likely to be influenced by undesirable home surroundings resulting from congestion, poor sanitation, and the presence of lodgers who may be a menace to the morals of adolescents and to the privacy and integration of the whole family. Most northern cities have failed to provide adequate recreational facilities for the children and this, coupled with lack of home care, leads to a misdirected use of spare time and energy that may easily result in detected offenses.

Conditions in the schools have aggravated the situation by producing restlessness, a sense of defeat and rebellion in children who have been handicapped by poor schools in the South and are consequently placed with younger children in northern schools. Many of the little newcomers were thrown into a strange environment with practically no assist-

[1] References 61 (a); 17 (a), pp. 333-5, 341; 22 (a), sec. ix, pp. 44-7, 55; 120 (a), p. 527; 70 (a), p. 235; 157 (d), pp. 227-9.

ance in making the necessary adjustment; hence, they frequently failed in the process and ended in the juvenile courts. Surroundings and not innate tendencies would seem to be largely accountable for the high rate of delinquency among Negro children in northern cities.

The Joint Committee on Negro Child Study in New York City investigated the cases brought before the children's court in 1925 and found that the percentage of Negroes among juvenile delinquents was nearly three times as high as the proportion of Negroes in the total population. However, disorderly conduct was the most frequent charge against Negroes, whereas among white children stealing was the most common offense. It was felt that recent migrations had decidedly augmented problems of delinquency because of the consequent lack of adjustment of Negro families to northern city life. The high rate of delinquency among colored children was attributed chiefly to this maladjustment, to the lack of parental control which was increased by the absence of mothers who were working, to retardation in school and to lack of proper recreation.[1] In Chicago and Detroit the proportion of colored children among juvenile delinquents far outdistanced the percentage of Negroes in the total population, and in both cities the chief factors in producing the high rate were connected with problems resulting from the recent influx.[2] The Pennsylvania survey concluded that there had been " an apparent increase in juvenile delinquency. This, however, is to be expected as the result of the presence of a large number of families in the community, the heads of which are unacquainted with the institutions of the city, and who do not know how to properly direct their children into the desirable avenues. In addition, the economic status of Negroes in Philadelphia is

[1] Reference 61 (a).

[2] References 22 (a), sec. ix; 17 (a), pp. 333-5, 341.

still such that many Negro women have to go outside of the home to work to increase the family budget. Another cause of juvenile delinquency among Negro children . . . is that contributed by over-aged Negro children in the public schools. These children have come from sections of the country where they have had very little schooling. They are placed in classes with white children much younger and much smaller than themselves. Consequently, they feel out of harmony in their school relationships, and are unhappy with the inevitable ' inferiority complex '; and frequently ' become the ' incorrigibles '; then truants; and finally, juvenile delinquents." [1]

DEFECTIVES AND DEPENDENTS

There is so little adequate information concerning the effect of recent Negro movements upon the problems of caring for colored defectives and dependents in northern cities that no conclusions or opinions can be stated. There is some evidence pointing to a high rate of insanity among Negroes who have migrated, which may be due to the strain of urban life and lack of adjustment to a totally different environment. It also seems probable that, especially in times of business depression and consequent unemployment, the problems of dependency and poverty have been increased in northern cities by the addition of southern Negroes.[2] Further investigations are needed, however, before definite statements can be made on these subjects.

[1] Reference 110 (a), p. 72.

[2] References 157 (a), p. 53; 22 (a), sec. xii; 120 (a), p. 527; 16 (b); 110 (a), p. 84; 70 (a), p. 235.

CHAPTER XI

The Negro and Northern Institutions

EDUCATION

In spite of the fact that the southern migrants contained an abnormally small proportion of children, the number brought North was sufficiently large to create serious problems in the northern city school systems. These have been further complicated by the addition of children born since the parents came North, and who have reached school age. In 1923 it was estimated that the number of colored children in northern schools had increased over fifty per cent since the beginning of the migrations,[1] and specific surveys in various cities have united in emphasizing the enlarged enrollment of Negro children in the public schools of industrial centers.[2] Even mere increase in numbers has inevitably affected the problems and expenditures of northern school boards, for it has been necessary to provide teachers, space and equipment for these new pupils. At the same time, other problems have arisen and have complicated the educational situation.

Legally, northern states do not require the segregation of colored children in separate schools, but since the rapid increase of Negro population, in several northern cities there has been an increasingly apparent tendency to bring about some degree of separation. Inevitably, as a district becomes more completely Negro, the neighborhood school shows less

[1] See Bibliography, references 43 (a), p. 731; *cf.* 157 (d), pp. 173-5; 111 (a), p. 1.

[2] References 32 (a), p. 71; 110 (a), p. 57; 157 (d), ch. x; 22 (a), sec. viii; 117 (a), p. 537; 17 (a), p. 93; 145 (d), pp. 10-1; 93 (a), p. 177; 81 (a), pp. 42-4; 2 (a), p. 13.

and less mingling of white and colored children, and in some cities where the schools are mixed, such as New York and Buffalo, the predominance of one race or another tends to be determined by the character of the neighborhood. However, all cases of segregation of Negro children in northern schools cannot be explained by such natural forces. It is not unusual for colored children to be transferred, or enrolled at the beginning, in a school which is predominantly Negro, even though another school may be nearer to their homes. Likewise white children living in or near a neighborhood largely colored are sometimes sent to more distant schools in order to avoid mingling the races. Even in cities where schools are mixed, there may still be signs of segration in the form of seating arrangements, separate classes or separate rooms. There are also evidences that in some northern cities no attitude of discrimination was apparent as long as there were only a few colored children, but when large numbers arrived, the tendency toward forced segregation became more noticeable.

Specific surveys illustrate the divergent policies of various northern cities and show the manner in which segregation in schools is frequently accomplished. " Some northern cities not only have schools attended by both white and colored pupils, but also separate schools, or separate rooms, for colored pupils. The distribution of the colored pupils between separate schools and mixed schools is not wholly determined by the number of colored pupils in a given area. It was found that some of the Negro areas of greatest density are served by mixed schools; while some of the separate schools for colored pupils are more accessible to white pupils than to colored pupils. Of the northern cities included in this survey, Philadelphia, Indianapolis, Gary and Dayton have some form of separate accommodation for Negro pupils. (This survey also reported a growing tendency toward segregation in the last three cities.)   New York, Chicago and Buffalo have no separate schools or separate rooms within schools." [1]   In spite of no general policy of segregation in Chicago, the Chicago Race Commission reported instances in which colored children were sent to particular schools which were largely Negro or were discouraged from enrolling in schools which contained a large majority of white pupils.   However, where distinctions between Negro and white children do occur in Chicago, they seem to be due to the attitude of individual principals and teachers, since the Chicago School Board makes no such differentiation and does not make a practice of maintaining separate schools. [2]   " There are 42 separate public schools for Negroes in Pennsylvania.   This separation is frankly carried out in some quarters and subtly in others.   For instance in Philadelphia, there are 12 schools which have 100 per cent Negro attendance.   All the teachers are Negroes, including the principal.   Negro children living in school districts bordering on the districts of these 12 schools are sent out of their district to the school having all Negro pupils and teachers, and white children living in the district of the schools having all Negro pupils and teachers are sent out of their district to schools which have 100 per cent white attendance. . . .   In many of the smaller cities and towns the school authorities have been quite frank in their segregation of the races.   Such towns as Coatesville and Chester have separate schools for all Negro children up to and including the junior high school grade. . . .   Even in communities where it was financially difficult to establish separate school buildings for Negroes, the authorities have developed what have been called ' Union Rooms '.   In these ' Union Rooms ' are placed all the Negro children in the school, irrespective of grades. The resulting situation is that while the white children of the school are distributed in grades, usually one grade to

[1] References 157 (d), p. 177.   Cf. ibid., ch. x.
[2] Reference 17 (a), pp. 238, 242, 253.

a room . . . the Negro children of varying ages are grouped together regardless of school grade." [1] In New Jersey " there will be found . . . types of schools varying from those completely mixed, with Negro teachers placed without strict regard to the preponderance of Negro pupils, in the northern part of the state, to types in which segregation is carried to the point of dividing a building so that white and Negro children are completely separated, with white teachers for the white and Negro teachers for the Negro students, and a heavy wire screen dividing the playground. . . . The situation in New Jersey is by no means atypical, and represents in general the method of bringing about segregation artificially in cases where natural means do not turn the trick." [2] On the other hand, Negro children in Minneapolis seem to be scattered in various schools and the survey of that city contains no record of any general policy of segregation of school children.[3]

Further evidence of divergent policies in regard to separation is seen in the report that even in mixed schools " Seating arrangements . . . differ widely; and often depend on the attitude of the teachers. . . . Colored pupils sometimes occupy only the front seats or the back seats; in some schools or rooms they are grouped on one side, or occupy alternate rows; sometimes they are seated without regard to race; or they share seats with white pupils, a method used regularly by one teacher for punishing white pupils. In one room a colored pupil is literally forced to take the back seat, in another room he is president of his class and in another the editor of the paper, in another in charge of the tool room, while in another he is expected to do more than his share of menial tasks." [4]

[1] Reference 110 (a), pp. 58-9.

[2] Reference 108 (a), p. 227.

[3] Reference 44 (b), pp. 19-21.

[4] Reference 157 (d), p. 183. For similar reports see references 111 (a), p. 3; 93 (a), p. 177; 120 (a), p. 526; 22 (a), sec. viii; 117 (a), p. 538; 94 (a), p. 690; 126 (a).

Principals, teachers and school boards have at times maintained that separation of school children on the basis of race is a necessity because of the high rate of retardation among Negro children, for the presence of a number of slow, overage pupils is likely to hinder the progress of other members of the class.   There is no doubt that retardation among Negroes in northern schools is more prevalent than among white children, and that the problem of handling these overage pupils presents serious difficulties to northern school authorities.   Not only is the proportion of retarded children higher among colored than among white children, but also the degree or number of years of retardation is highest among colored pupils, since many are from two to five years behind their normal grades.[1]

Specific surveys of school conditions in Pittsburgh, Philadelphia, Chicago, Detroit and other northern cities emphasize the seriousness of this problem of retardation among Negroes.   The Chicago Race Commission reported that " Over-age or retarded children are found in all the lower grades, special classes, and ungraded rooms, and are noticeable all the way to the eighth grade, where seventeen- and nineteen-year-old children are sometimes found." The Commission selected " three groups of schools to be studied for comparative retardation.   The group comprised six schools having the largest percentage of Negro children, six attended mainly by whites in neighborhoods where the family income might be comparable, and twelve attended mainly by children of immigrants. . . . (The results showed) the much greater amount of retardation among schools attended by Negroes than in schools attended by white Americans or by children of immigrants." In the group of schools attended largely by Negroes 74

[1] References **17 (a)**, pp. 256-61; **108 (a)**, pp. 228-9; **2 (a)**, p. 13; **81 (a)**, pp. 42-4; **22 (a)**, sec. viii; **157 (d)**, pp. 184-6; **32 (a)**, p. 72; **57 (g)**, p. 340; **110 (a)**, p. 57.

per cent of the children were retarded as compared with 49 per cent in each of the other two groups. The degree of retardation was also higher among the colored children. " The largest single groups of backward white American and foreign children are retarded less than one year—42 per cent of the white American and 39 per cent of the foreign group. . . . In the case of the Negroes 19 per cent are retarded less than one year . . . and many more children are retarded two, three, four, five years and more." [1] Likewise, in Pennsylvania " the age-grade standing of Negro pupils is somewhat lower than that of the children as a whole of the Commonwealth, according to the figures of those cities which keep separate records of Negro children. . . . In Philadelphia the percentage of white pupils over-age is 1½ per cent while the percentage of Negro pupils over-age was 3 per cent." [2]

The conspicuous prevalence of retardation among Negro children is often accepted as conclusive evidence of their inferior mental ability, for it is assumed that there would not be so many over-age pupils among Negroes if their native intelligence were equal to that of white children. Careful investigations of the problem among colored pupils in such cities as Chicago, Detroit and Philadelphia indicate, however, that there are many other factors which have influenced the extent of retardation among Negroes. Fundamentally, this whole problem was closely linked with migration, for many of those retarded had recently come from the South. When distinctions were made between northern and southern Negroes it was found in comparing them with white pupils that there was usually no great discrepancy between northern Negro and white students in this respect.

For example, the Chicago Race Commission contended

[1] Reference 17 (a), pp. 239, 256, 258.

[2] Reference 110 (a), p. 57.

that "The Negro child born in the North is not found to an unusual extent among the retarded children. He has been able to enter school on time and to attend the full term of nine months; his teachers compare favorably with those in white American and foreign neighborhoods, and his parents as a rule have a better background. Many teachers say that the progress of the northern-born Negroes compares very favorably with that of whites." [1]

In fact, all of the surveys which investigated the causes of retardation among Negroes emphasized migration from the South as one of the chief factors in producing this situation. Children who had transferred from southern schools had been seriously handicapped by the poor educational facilities there, by the short terms and by the inadequate compulsory school laws. A large proportion of the children had been over-age when they entered school and others who had been in their normal age-grades in the South had been demoted in the North because they had not received sufficient training to keep up with the northern classes.

Another common cause was found to be poor home conditions; many of the parents were migrants who needed the economic help of the children and put them to work if possible, or else were unacquainted with northern school systems and did not voluntarily observe the school attendance laws. Furthermore, many of the mothers were at work away from home all day and consequently were unable to see to it that their children went to school regularly and stayed there during school hours. However, irregular attendance did not seem to play so large a part in producing the higher rate of retardation among Negro children as did an inferior quality of previous education. Undoubtedly economic and social causes have been highly important factors contributing to the backwardness of Negro children.

[1] References 17 (a), p. 241 *cf.* 108 (a), pp. 228-9.

The Detroit Bureau of Governmental Research concluded that " The chief causes of retardation among the colored children are (1) inferiority of the schools which they attended in the South; (2) the higher average median age at entrance of the colored children in the Detroit schools; (3) poor home conditions; (4) lack of familiarity with the Detroit system." The Bureau also pointed out the difference in the per cent of retardation among Negro children born in the North and those born in the South. For example, only 4.7 per cent of the colored children born in Michigan were among those retarded, while over 21 per cent of those from Georgia and North Carolina, and 25 per cent of those from Mississippi were over-age.[1] The Chicago Race Commission reported that " The majority of retarded Negro children are southerners, and their retardation can be readily understood when the gross inadequacies of southern schools for Negroes are considered. . . . The predominating cause of retardation among Negroes is late entrance. . . . This is generally explained by the fact that the family came from the South, where there was no school near enough for the child to attend, or the school was overcrowded, or the family was uneducated and indifferent. . . . The next most important cause . . . is family difficulties. The fathers are often kept away from home weeks at a time by their work. A large number of the mothers are working, and the parents' lack of education is frequently the cause of a home life that is below standard, physically and morally." Other factors listed as causing retardation were lack of adjustment to urban life, demotion because of the short terms and inferior standards in southern schools and the sensitiveness of some children about over-age and larger size.[2]

Similar opinions are expressed by students of the general status of colored children in the North. For instance,

[1] Reference 22 (a), sec. viii, pp. 9, 4.
[2] Reference 17 (a), pp. 615, 258-66.

it is pointed out that "many (of the colored pupils) are from southern schools with poor standards, and . . . the early education of many was neglected entirely. The low educational background of their families, economic necessity which makes it necessary for both parents to work, frequent moving, and other factors handicap many of the Negro pupils." [1] Payne also concludes that "retardation is immediately connected with the character of the previous education, regularity of school attendance, and the character of the schools and teaching, and not to difference in learning capacity and ' native intelligence '." [2]

There is sufficient evidence to warrant the conclusion that recent movements of southern Negroes have seriously added to the educational problems of northern cities. A larger number of Negro children had to be provided for and in many cities the question of segregation arose for the first time, or was intensified. In addition, the prevalence of retardation among colored children coming from southern schools has increased the burdens and complexities of northern school systems. Retardation has also rendered more difficult the adjustment of these over-age pupils to their new environment, for when grouped with younger, smaller children, many of them grow discouraged and hopeless.

On the other hand, the migration has resulted in marked improvement in the educational opportunities of colored children. Even where the influx of migrants has led to increased segregation, the schools of the North have been far superior to those attended by the children in the South. One of the greatest gains of the migration has been the increase of educational opportunities for colored children.

[1] Reference 157 (d), p. 184.
[2] References 108 (a), pp. 228-9. *Cf.* 110 (a), p. 57.

MIGRATION AND POLITICS

The effect of the migration upon the political situation in the North has yet to be adequately investigated. So little is known concerning the extent and manner in which the increase of colored population has influenced either the political problems of northern cities or the Negro's attitude toward politics that only a few general opinions can be given. These are by no means established facts but merely suggest the possible reaction of migration upon politics and indicate the need for further study.

Since northern states do not legally deprive the Negro of the franchise, the colored laborer who moved north naturally obtained the right to vote which had been denied him in the South. In so far as the migrant desired franchisement and gained it by settling in a northern city, the migration was a distinct advantage to him. At the same time, there have been concomitant dangers due to the migrant's inexperience in matters of city government and his consequent susceptibility to the influence of corrupt politicians. There is at present little factual basis for determining whether the increased Negro vote in northern cities has been beneficial or harmful. Undoubtedly there are instances of both results even in the same city but lack of sufficient evidence prevents any conclusion as to which predominates. Cases have been found of the exploitation of Negro voters by northern politicians, with the result that the colored vote was a detriment to the community.[1] On the other hand, the Detroit Bureau concluded from its survey that "the newly arrived migrants have exercised the use of the ballot in a commendable fashion when one considers their lack of experience in politics and the fact that they have been so completely exposed to the activities of political demagogues."[2] The extent to

[1] References 17 (a), p. 3; 59 (a), p. 406; 114 (a), p. 4; 136 (a), p. 692; 22 (a), sec. xi, p. 7; 25 (a), ch. 6.

[2] Reference 22 (a), sec. xi, p. 7.

which the new colored voters are to be considered either a benefit or menace depends, in part, upon their numerical strength and significance in a particular city. Several students have maintained that the vast increase in Negro votes has at times made the Negro an influential factor in municipal elections.[1] However, there is not sufficient information on this point to make comparisons between various cities or to draw conclusions for the North.

> The limited studies which have been made of the political situation among northern Negroes since the migration tend to report such conclusions as the following: " In Pittsburgh the Negro is politically, at least, as free as the whites of the same class. Coming from places where the vote is denied him, he is naturally very glad to have his right of suffrage restored. It is a well-known fact to Pittsburghers that the Negro vote may be a deciding factor in the results of municipal elections." [2]

The migration has resulted in the enfranchisement of thousands of colored voters. However, on the basis of the material at hand conclusions cannot be drawn as to whether the increased political power of Negroes throughout the North is potential or actual, advantageous or harmful.

THE CHURCH AND THE MIGRANT

Since colored people possess an unusually strong interest in religious activities and since a large proportion of them are members of some religious organization, the churches of the North were immediately affected by the movements of Negro laborers and their families. As soon as a crowd of migrants arrived, most of them sought at once to transfer their membership to some local body. The churches already

---

[1] References 17 (a), p. 3; 62 (b), p. 973; 32 (a), p. 30; 145 (d), pp. 124-5; 110 (a), p. 90; 13 (a), pp. 370-3.

[2] References 145 (d), p. 124. *Cf.* 32 (a), p. 30; 13 (a), pp. 370-3.

established in northern cities were soon faced with serious problems of accommodating these newcomers. Many were so overtaxed that they were compelled to hold double services in order to care for those who desired to attend.[1] This congestion was further increased by the strong tendency toward racial separation which is characteristic of northern religious organizations. Colored people in the North usually have their own institutions instead of uniting with white people. Consequently, in many of the cities there has been a decided increase in the number of Negro churches.

In Chicago during the five year period, 1910 to 1915, twelve Negro churches were organized but in the following five year period, 1915 to 1920, which covered the years of heavy migration, thirty-four churches were organized and fifteen of these in the year 1918 alone.[2] In Detroit there were thirty-eight colored churches in 1919 as contrasted with nine in 1914, and the Detroit Bureau of Research believed this marked increase to be a direct result of the migration. The large proportion of church members was also attributed to the recent influx of Negroes; more than 55 per cent of the colored people in Detroit were affiliated with some religious organization, and 85 per cent of these members had joined Detroit churches since 1915. As a result, many of the Negro churches could not seat their full memberships.[3] In Pennsylvania 38 per cent of the Negroes were reported as enrolled in some church and in ten years the number of Negro churches had increased about 30 per cent.[4]

Among colored groups the church is frequently the center of the social as well as of the religious life, and this double

---

[1] Reference 124 (a), p. 144.

[2] Reference 17 (a), p. 145.

[3] Reference 22 (a), sec. x, pp. 1-5.

[4] References 110 (a), pp. 62-3. *Cf.* 81 (a), p. 45.

hold has probably been important in the development of the Negroes' keen interest in religion. It has also strengthened their tendency and desire for organizations of their own. The importance of the social function is particularly evident in southern rural churches, but it retains a prominent place in the activities in the North. When migrants began to arrive in large numbers, many northern churches established employment bureaus, recreation centers and welfare agencies in order to meet the complex needs of the colored people in their new environment.[1] The Negro church has been described as " 75 per cent a social center and 25 per cent a religious institution " [2] and there is no doubt that even in the North it has been called upon to help satisfy the colored man's desire for social relationships and recreation. Negroes are so frequently prohibited from mingling with white people in public amusement and recreational centers, or are so subject to the possibility of embarrassment if they do enter places frequented by white people, that many of them prefer to find recreation in the activities of their churches.

> The Detroit Bureau has summarized a situation which is found in many northern cities: " The Negro has been humiliated in so many public and privately owned institutions and amusement places that he has resorted to the church as a place in which he can be sure of peacefully spending his leisure time. To a large extent it takes the place of the theater, the dance halls, and similar amusement places, and fills the vacancy created by the failure of the public and commercial places of recreation and amusement to give him a cordial welcome. Consequently, the average Negro church in Detroit keeps its doors open constantly for the use of the community. Numerous suppers, lec-

[1] References 22 (a), sec. x; 17 (a), pp. 142-6; 110 (a), ch. ix; 46 (k), pp. 266-7; 119 (a), pp. 332-3.
[2] Reference 110 (a), p. 62.

tures, recitals, debates, plays and the like are given by clubs and individuals from within and without the congregation." [1]

In spite of these social and religious activities, it is possible that the migration has tended to loosen the hold of the church upon some of the Negroes at least, since they have settled in an environment which has a multiplicity of agencies to fulfill the functions of amusement, education and social relations which in the rural South were satisfied mainly by the religious group. This is a mere hypothesis, however, that awaits further investigation. It seems plausible that young people particularly, and those who came North without a close circle of friends and relatives, might tend to drift to commercial amusements and the recreational centers which are open to Negroes, thus breaking away from controls exercised by the church group.

> Reuter contends that in general among Negroes, the church is "losing ground. This is to some extent a part of the general decline of religion resulting from the development of science and the spread of knowledge; the Negroes are being influenced to some extent by the spread of modern ideas. But there are other and more important reasons, chief of which is the development of new avenues of expression and amusement. In the larger towns the churches no longer have a monopoly on social resources. There are other meeting places and other means of amusement. . . . Places of amusement are developing and with them the church cannot compete. . . . There is a growing tendency to restrict the sphere of (the ministers' influence) to religious affairs and so reduce the power of the church in racial life." [2]

[1] References 22 (a), sec. x, p. 9. *Cf.* 17 (a), p. 143; 110 (a), p. 62.
[2] References 119 (a), p. 333. *Cf.* 57 (a), p. 642; 63 (b), p. 65.

However true it may be that the church has lost its strong grip on many Negroes, it still plays an important part in the social and religious life of northern, as well as southern, Negroes. The increase of colored groups in northern cities has resulted both in the rapid building of new churches and in the enlargement of the social and welfare activities of these religious organizations.

RECREATIONAL FACILITIES

Problems connected with the recreation and amusements of northern Negroes have assumed serious importance since recent migrations have augmented the size of colored groups in various cities of the North. In many cases the Negroes now have a shorter working day than they had in the South or in previous occupations in the North, and with this increased leisure the necessity for wholesome recreation becomes more prominent. This is particularly true among the migrants, who are often unaccustomed to the temptations of commercialized amusements which they find in the city, and are more easily swept away by the excitement and gayety, the tension and thrill of city life. With many of them, too, the pressure of social control is decidedly weakened by this move to a new environment, where intimate face-to-face contacts are less frequent and forceful and where it is possible to live without the close observation and criticism of neighbors and relatives. Consequently, there are fewer forces tending to prevent them from resorting to questionable amusements if such are the chief forms of recreation available. Furthermore, the part which recreation may play in the development of hostile or friendly race relations and in the assimilation and cultural advancement of the newcomers renders this question of proper recreational facilities of vital importance in urban centers where the number of colored inhabitants has rapidly grown.

The few students and investigators who have broken the path in considering this phase of the Negro's urban life unite in pointing out its importance and seriousness. The report of one careful survey of recreational facilities for colored people contends: " Probably no greater problem arises in connection with the Negro's adjustment to urban life than that of how to achieve an effective organization and control of his leisure time activities in the face of race prejudice and other barriers which limit his contacts and frustrate his wishes. . . . In the city, the routinized life, along with the mechanical and impersonal relationships, produce a great deal of social unrest and stress. Hence the problem of relaxation and release from mental strain resulting from intense psychic and muscular application is presented." [1] Similarly, another student of this subject believes: " The use which the Negro has made and has been able to make of his leisure time both in the past and at present must have considerable effect upon his status as a race. The present situation is somewhat more important than the past because of the part which the migration of the Negro to the cities is playing in it. He is coming to the cities now in larger numbers than ever before motivated by the desire to have a good time. . . . It has been proven that there is a connection between the improper use of leisure time and ill health and crime. . . . Consequently, it must be obvious that the way in which the Negro spends his leisure time is almost as important to the community as a whole as it is to the Negro." [2]

In several cities, such as New York, Chicago, Detroit and Cleveland, the National Urban League, various social agencies and the churches are at least making an effort to deal

[1] Reference 63 (b), pp. 25, 193.

[2] References 150 (c), pp. 272, 282. *Cf.* 157 (d), part iv; 150 (d), p. 334; 17 (a), pp. 271-95, 616-19; 110 (a), ch. 7; 22 (a), sec. vii; 46 (f), p. 24; 57 (g), p. 301.

with this problem of recreation. It has been shown in the preceding section that one effect of the migration was an increase in the social activities of northern churches; many of them established recreational rooms and clubs, and held numerous suppers and parties in the endeavor to provide wholesome recreation for the newcomers. Branches of the Urban League in many cities have obtained the use of public school buildings for dances, games and social gatherings.[1] However, these efforts on the part of private organizations are entirely incapable of meeting the situation. Most of the churches do not have sufficient funds to carry on any extensive recreational programs, and even then their more restricted and supervised entertainments can seldom compete with public and commercialized amusement places. Such organizations as the National Urban League frequently lack resources and time to add recreational activities to their crowded schedules. Private and semi-private undertakings cannot satisfactorily supply that lack of public provision for the Negro's recreation which is so evident in practically every northern city. Throughout the North it is almost universally true that public facilities such as playgrounds, recreation centers, parks and bathing beaches, have not been instituted or increased in Negro areas in order to furnish means of recreation for the rapidly mounting numbers of colored inhabitants. As a consequence, few northern cities provide proper resources for the recreation of Negroes.[2]

This inadequacy of facilities for colored people is further intensified by the growing tendency of northern whites to exclude Negroes from many of the sources of amusement which do exist. In all parts of the North there are evidences

[1] References 157 (d), ch. xvi; 145 (d), pp. 154-5; 17 (a), pp. 143-4, 147, 341.

[2] References 17 (a), pp. 296, 616; 63 (b), p. 37 et seq.; 150 (c), pp. 272-82; 157 (d), ch. xv.

of increasing discrimination against Negroes in such public places as parks, beaches, theaters, dance halls and Y.M.C.A.'s. Where separation of the races had not already occurred, it tended to appear either openly or indirectly as soon as the Negro population began to show a conspicuous increase in numbers. In cities nearer the border, such as Baltimore and Washington, there is practically complete segregation of blacks from whites. In other cities Negroes are freely admitted to libraries, public parks, zoological gardens and museums but are prevented from mingling with white people on beaches or in playgrounds and theaters. Frequently, segregation is only partial; colored people are allowed to enter but are restricted to certain sections of the playgrounds or theaters. In settlements, Y.M.C.A.'s, Y.W.C.A.'s, swimming pools and playgrounds certain evenings or days, or separate classes, are set aside for Negroes, so that they do not mingle with the white visitors or members. In theaters, moving picture and vaudeville houses with mixed audiences, colored people are frequently limited to seats in the balcony or the least desirable places in the house. Naturally such restrictions serve to discourage the Negroes from taking advantage of public recreational facilities which are at hand, so that they are limited more than ever in their chances for wholesome amusement and well regulated entertainment. It is small wonder that many of them are thrown back on the cheap, vulgar, commercialized places in which alone they are given a hearty welcome. Unfortunately, this limitation of recreational facilities through discrimination and exclusion seems to be increasing in many northern cities. Hence, the problem of recreation among northern Negroes has become steadily more serious.[1]

---

[1] References 157 (d), part iv; 150 (c), pp. 275-8; 110 (a), ch. vii; 22 (a), sec. vii; 17 (a), pp. 277, 310, 317-20; 63 (b), chap. ix.

After an extensive study of forty northern cities, Washington writes: " It is obvious that segregation in theaters, including moving picture houses, picture-vaudeville houses and legitimate theaters, is extending throughout the country. It is forcing many of the cultured Negroes in the North to practice the same boycott of the theater that many of them have practiced in the South for years, which consists of remaining away from the theater altogether or attending only the ' all-colored ' theaters in cities where such institutions happen to exist. . . . The effect on the culture of the Negro of this self-denial is obvious." [1]   The situation which is described as existing in Pennsylvania is similar to that in many northern states: " One of the most dangerous tendencies that is developing in the State is that of the gradual restriction of leisure time opportunities for Negroes.   Not only is the newcomer unhappy and dissatisfied in not finding the opportunities for a more abundant life, but a psychological reaction is taking place in the native born Negro who finds himself suddenly shut out of the opportunities for pleasure and recreation that previously he had been privileged to enjoy before the migration increased the density of the minority group. . . . The investigation of leisure time activities among Negroes indicates a deplorable situation.   The institutions of wholesome recreation in the community are beginning to close their doors to Negroes when the need is most dire. It is impossible economically for Negroes to duplicate the several institutions of wholesome recreation available to whites, and as a result the Negro is being thrown back more and more on the limited facilities of the Negro community for his leisure time entertainment." [2]

So far there have been few intensive studies of this problem of recreation among northern colored groups, but those

[1] Reference   150 (c), p. 277.
[2] Reference   110 (a), pp. 53, 55.

surveys which have been made, indicate that cities in the North do not provide adequate facilities for the recreation of their Negro citizens. Furthermore, in most urban centers an increase in the number of colored people seems to result in a growing tendency toward discrimination against them in public amusement places, so that their leisure-time activities are even more limited than appears on the surface. Migration of southern Negroes has tended to increase the problem of recreation in northern cities both by adding to the numbers of those for whom provision should be made and by arousing race prejudice to the point of causing a restriction in the number of amusement places freely open to Negroes.

CHAPTER XII

Migration and Social Contacts

RACE RELATIONS

THE effect of the conspicuous increase in colored population upon race relations forms the most serious and vitally important result of recent migrations. The influx of colored laborers has brought white inhabitants of northern cities into more frequent contacts with Negroes, and has drawn public notice to their presence as they have become increasingly numerous and evident on the streets, in transportation, in stores, parks and libraries, and in the schools and residential districts. The whole question of race relations and attitudes has become of more conscious and immediate importance to northern white people than ever before. In many cases the reaction of whites has been the emotional one of strengthened prejudice and antipathy, and, in general, throughout the North there has been an increase of race feeling and discrimination against the Negroes as a result of this growth in their numbers. Various cities which formerly made no distinctions on the basis of race now furnish numerous instances of a desire to separate the Negroes, or at least to make a differentiation in the sort of treatment accorded them. Instead of leading to a stronger personal interest in each other and to greater friendliness and understanding, these more numerous contacts in northern cities have tended to increase the distance between the races.

In some cities, such as Columbus, Ohio, this increased feeling is slight and has apparently not resulted in pronounced antagonism.[1] Yet, in the majority of cases, students of Negro problems find that " With the migration of a large number of Negroes to northern cities, there have been tendencies indicating that wherever Negroes are numerous enough to impress themselves upon the community, disturbing race prejudice develops." [2] Similarly, Johnson concludes that " With few exceptions, the increased proportion of Negroes in the total population of cities of the North tends to increase adverse sentiment," [3] and Woofter likewise states "In areas gaining by migration, prejudice seems, at least temporarily, to assume its most aggravated form." [4] Both the Chicago Commission and the Detroit Bureau of Research found that in each city the attitude of whites had changed toward the entire Negro group, both former inhabitants and newcomers, as a result of the growth of Negro population during the migration.[5] The Pennsylvania survey reported: " In dealing with her increased Negro population, Pennsylvania does not seem to have profited by the failure of the South to solve the race problem, but rather seems inclined to copy the ' accommodation ' methods of the South and is beginning to introduce segregation and discrimination in various forms in public life." [6] In Michigan "With each inroad made by the Negro into the industries, into residential districts, and their more noticeable presence in public places, distaste, resentment, and bitterness, each in turn, became reflected in the utterances and actions of the hitherto agreeably passive white man." [7]

[1] See Bibliography, reference 81 (a), pp. 26-7.

[2] Reference 156 (b), p. 538.

[3] Reference 57 (f), p. 325.

[4] Reference 157 (c), p. 167.

[5] References 17 (a), p. 273 and section on housing; 22 (a), sec. ii, p. 20.

[6] Reference 110 (a), p. 85.

[7] References 70 (a), p. 232. *Cf.* 93 (a), p. 177; 111 (a); 46 (d), p. 73; 124 (a), pp. 136, 107-8; 120 (a), p. 527; 29 (a), pp. 63-9.

This increasing tendency toward discrimination is not, however, associated with all phases of relations between whites and blacks, since northern cities do not—yet, at least —maintain the strict racial separation which prevails in the South.   The extent to which the growth of colored population has tended to generate prejudice and antagonism varies according to the nature of the contacts involved.   In such public places as libraries the North makes practically no distinctions on the basis of color, and there the relationships are usually matter-of-fact and unattended by friction.   Most of the contacts which have been free from growing prejudice are those in which relations are impersonal and casual.   More frequent mingling of the races in transportation has often crystallized individual feelings of prejudice and dislike but, in general, has produced few serious clashes.   This type of mixing is particularly important because the two groups are inevitably thrown together (since there is neither legal nor physical provision for race separation on northern transportation systems).   Also, it is sometimes only under such circumstances that the whites and blacks come near each other, so that many whites tend to judge the Negroes entirely on the basis of these chance encounters.

Previous chapters have pointed out the trend toward increased race feeling and discrimination which has appeared in the housing situation, in industrial contacts, in the schools and recreational centers of northern cities.   Thus, throughout the North Negroes mingle with whites more freely than they do in the South; in the more impersonal relations there are practically no distinctions but other forms of association have frequently aroused ill feeling and hostility.

> Both white and colored students of conditions among northern Negroes and individual investigators of specific cities unite in pointing out the increase in race prejudice and discrimination which has resulted in the North from

the more frequent contacts between the races since the migration. In discussing the effects of these northward movements, George E. Haynes remarks that " the reaction of public opinion seems to have become one of our foremost problems. For instance, anyone would have been considered an alarmist twenty years ago had he predicted that public opinion would allow 58 Negro homes in Chicago to be bombed with impunity as increasing numbers forced Negro residents to spread beyond the areas where they had formerly lived. Race riots and outrages in East St. Louis, Omaha, Chicago and Washington paralyzed these cities for days and shocked the nation." [1] Similar conclusions are found in the statement that " the movement has increased prejudice in the North, strengthened the tendency to draw the color line and the tendency on the part of colored leaders to resent discrimination. This has in some instances culminated in riots." [2] Surveys of the situation in Philadelphia, Cincinnati, Dayton, Chicago and the states of Pennsylvania and Michigan report this tendency toward increased segregation and differentiation. For example, it has been maintained that in Dayton, Ohio, " the colored people before the migration could go unquestioned into any place of amusement and be served to any usual public accommodation. But when five Negroes came instead of one, the erstwhile liberal-minded people began to make the natural mistake of trying to get rid of a problem instead of facing and solving it." [3] In a study which was made of recreational facilities in northern cities it was found that " in the 40 northern cities (studied) . . . there is some form of segregation practiced in connection with the Negro and public recreation in at least two-thirds of their number. . . . (In regard to private recreation) in only 5 of the 40 northern cities have Negroes been admitted to settlements

[1] Reference 46 (d), p. 73.
[2] Reference 111 (a), p. 1.
[3] Reference 113 (a), p. 603.

with representatives of other racial groups.   Even in these
cities the handling of the Negro patrons has been considered somewhat of a problem. . . . Of the 40 cities, 33
had some segregation in connection with movie theaters—
24 in connection with picture-vaudeville houses, 19 in connection with amusement parks, and 26 in connection with
legitimate theaters." [1]

The Chicago Race Commission has made a careful study
of the nature and results of the increased contacts which followed the rush of southern Negroes to Chicago.   Since this
report presents the most exhaustive analysis of the subject
that has so far been made, it is used here as the principal
illustration of the effect of migration upon race relations.
The situation in Chicago may be taken as indicative of the
condition of interracial contacts in most northern cities which
received large numbers of migrants, for though no other
survey has made such a comprehensive study of this situation as did the Chicago Commission, the brief studies which
have been made indicate similar trends.   Were similar reports available for other northern cities, it would be valuable
and interesting to compare conditions in various localities;
in the absence of such material the Chicago study presents a
significant picture of what has probably occurred, in greater
or less degree, throughout the North since the recent influx
of colored laborers.

Many neighborhoods in Chicago revealed a strong determination to exclude the Negroes and draw the color line
by streets or districts.   In the industrial field Negroes were
still discriminated against in promotions, occupations and
ability to become union members.   Legally and openly,
Chicago provided for no segregation in the public schools
but actually and indirectly there were at least occasional

[1] References 150 (c) pp. 275-7.   *Cf.* 157 (d), part iv; 110 (a), pp. 53-6,
89; 22 (a), sec. ii, sec. vii.

evidences of discrimination in regard to enrolling pupils, transfers and in the equipment and physical condition of school buildings largely given over to colored children. In sections of the city containing large numbers of Negroes the theaters, restaurants, stores, barber shops and public service places accommodated both Negroes and whites, but the Commission found a very decided discrimination against the Negroes in parts of the city where whites predominated. Negroes who investigated the situation for the Commission reported their inability to secure service in many white restaurants and lunch rooms; the various humiliations and annoyances to which they were subjected revealed the proprietors' determination to exclude colored patrons. It was discovered that theaters and moving picture houses tried to seat colored people in certain sections, principally in the balcony, and did not always accord them the same treatment as that given white people. Most of the stores apparently served the Negroes courteously and without prejudice, although there were instances of discrimination and opposition in this field. Segregation of the races in public parks and beaches was usually unofficial but an actual fact in many cases. The young children tended to mingle without distinction or friction but in places used by older children and adults the Negroes were often given to understand that they were not wanted. Sometimes they were terrorized by gangs of boys and, as a result, did not make use of public recreational facilities or merely used the meager provisions allotted to colored people. In transportation and in cultural institutions there were no evident discriminations. The Commission concluded from its intensive survey that " Negroes in Illinois are legally entitled to all the rights and privileges of other citizens. Actually, however, their participation in public benefits in practically every field is limited by some circumvention of the law." [1]

[1] Reference 17 (a), p. 614; (Housing, pp. 115-116, 108; Industry, p. 391; Schools, pp. 614, 242-4; Public Places, pp. 309-311, 318, 320; Recreation, pp. 277, 296-7; Transportation, p. 299).

Antagonism between the races has at times become sufficiently strong to break out in overt acts of hostility and violence. Many of these open expressions of intense dislike
have resulted from housing troubles, as was shown in
Chapter VIII, and have taken the form of intimidating letters and bombing of Negro houses.[1]

In several northern cities the contacts between colored and
white people became so hostile that actual race riots occurred.
Most of the riots have grown out of similar underlying situations, although, of course, the immediate inciting causes have
varied. At times the riot has been due almost entirely to
the resentment of white workers over the introduction of
Negroes as strike breakers. Friction has frequently started
over the attempted residential expansion of the colored
people. In addition, Negroes have usually been limited to
the poorest districts where they have come into contact with
the lowest class of white inhabitants, among whom open acts
of violence more quickly occur. Once started, these riots
have been characterized by a rapidly mounting flame of race
hatred which swept away all reason, tolerance and human
feeling. During the progress of these conflicts the every-
day business of the cities was stopped, property was destroyed
and many lives lost, while the resulting intensification of race
prejudice tended to widen the gulf between the races.

The situations which arose in East St. Louis and Chicago
illustrate the growth and outbreak of race prejudice which
occasionally followed the increase of Negro population in
the North. The riot in the former city has already been
mentioned in Chapter V. That which raged in Chicago
from July 27 to August 2, 1919, was a particularly serious
outbreak of race friction. Since the beginning of the
migration during the war, Chicago had been one of the

[1] References 53 (b); 17 (a), pp. 122-3, 134; 93 (a), p. 177; 152 (b);
157 (d), p. 73; 57 (d), p. 409.

chief points of attraction to southern Negroes and had received a vast number of the migrants. It has already been shown that the rapid increase of the colored population led to more frequent and more emotionally fraught contacts between the Negroes and whites. Colored and white laborers were thrown into closer relationships in the industrial world and came into keener competition for employment. On the whole, however, the industrial contacts of the two races in Chicago did not result in serious hostility. The housing situation furnished more dangerous potentialities of race friction. As the migrants poured into Chicago, the growing colored population could not possibly find living space in the districts which had been occupied by Negroes before 1915. Inevitably they overflowed into adjoining white neighborhoods, thereby arousing the intense opposition of the white inhabitants. A great deal of friction resulted from this housing situation, leading to various forms of intimidation of the Negroes and even to numerous bombings. The political situation added further difficulties, as the colored vote had been an important factor in the recent election and had caused much resentment and bitterness among the whites. Moreover, the activities of gangs of hoodlums had done much to increase the tension between the races. Members of these gangs had frequently assaulted Negroes in public parks and playgrounds, at bathing beaches and even on the streets. Various near riots had occurred when Negroes had been murdered or seriously injured as they were going to or from work. Such occurrences were played up by the press of both races and sensational propaganda in the white and colored newspapers had heightened the opposition and ill feeling. In the weeks preceding the riot, trouble between Negroes and whites had been frequent in public places of recreation, and five weeks earlier, two Negroes had been assaulted without provocation and murdered by some of the gangs. Thus there was a general background of tension, bitterness and hostility in the racial contacts before the riot.

The trouble started on Sunday afternoon, July 27th, when a Negro boy who was swimming at one of the beaches was stoned by white men, and drowned. This beach was used by both races and tension was already high that afternoon as the result of various minor clashes between the Negroes and the whites. The Negroes immediately assumed that the boy had drowned as a result of being hit by stones and charged a certain white man with the crime. They also demanded that he be arrested by a white policeman who was present. The policeman's refusal aroused much resentment among the Negroes and feeling on both sides became intense. That evening reports and rumors circulated rapidly, crowds gathered at various places and much violence was perpetrated against the Negroes. The next afternoon as the colored laborers were returning from work, they were attacked and pulled from street cars, beaten, stabbed and shot. Negro districts were raided by men who rode through the streets in automobiles and shot at random. A reign of terror prevailed, in which the "Athletic Clubs" and gangs figured prominently; the Race Commission later reported that the mobs were composed largely of boys between fifteen and twenty-two years of age. On Wednesday, the militia was called in and by Friday, the trouble had ceased. As a result of the riot, thirty-eight persons, fifteen white and twenty-three Negroes, were killed, 537 injured and about 1,000 rendered homeless and destitute.[1]

Other northern cities have had outbreaks which were more or less similar. It is sometimes held that race riots are merely forms of a labor struggle but complex factors usually underlie such friction. Rapid growth of the colored group causes a sudden and unaccustomed increase in the contacts

[1] Reference 17 (a), chs. i, ii.

between the races. Problems of housing, industry, politics and social relations result and an emotional tension is soon aroused. Then some inciting cause occurs at the psychological moment and the riot is on. As Reuter says: " With the proper background of prejudice and sentiment, any incident may precipitate a racial war." [2]

Most northern cities have not experienced such open and violent conflicts as occurred in East St. Louis and Chicago. It has been several years since the last instance of marked violence and it is possible that the two races are becoming more adapted to each other. However, one wonders what may result if the present period of unemployment with its increased economic competition should continue for any length of time. The growth of colored population through migration has already tended to strengthen indirect forms of discrimination against Negroes and to increase race feeling and antipathy among many northern white people. In view of the extent of the migration to northern cities which previously had had comparatively few Negro inhabitants, the number of violent outbreaks of race antagonism are not numerous, but such riots as have occurred call attention to the seriousness of those tensions, misunderstandings and prejudices which underlie seemingly casual and unimportant contacts and which are apparently increasing among northerners as a result of the influx of Negroes.

MIGRANT AND NORTHERN NEGROES

The preceding section has shown that the arrival of large numbers of southern Negroes tended to increase the race prejudice of whites in northern cities and, consequently, to strengthen policies of segregation and discrimination. As a rule, white people are prone to class all Negroes together instead of reacting to them on the basis of their individual

[1] Reference 119 (a), p. 419.

merits; hence the northern Negroes were subjected to the same racial distinctions that confronted the newly arrived migrants.   In many northern cities the native colored inhabitants had been accustomed to a large measure of freedom and equality in participating in the public and educational life of the town.   With the coming of the migrants, these northern Negroes found themselves being differentiated from other inhabitants on account of their color and felt the barriers of dislike and prejudice strengthening against them. Inevitably many of them were inclined to hold the migrants responsible for these increasing social restrictions and tended to resent the influx of other blacks, many of whom were inferior in education and culture to the northern Negroes and most of whom were unaccustomed to northern standards of living and modes of conduct.   There are various indications that numbers of northern Negroes did not eagerly welcome the migrants but, instead, sought to keep aloof from them. In many instances the resentment was probably only a temporary first reaction; so few facts are known concerning the extent and permanence of this feeling, that no statements as to its duration can be made.

Several students of the migration have been impressed by the problems created for northern Negroes by the arrival of the migrants.   The Pennsylvania survey concluded that " the Negro natives of the State . . . have lost a number of social privileges as a result of the migration of thousands of their color into Pennsylvania " and that " the migrant is not always welcomed by his more fortunate fellows." [1]   For example, Philadelphia " had long possessed a relatively small population of Negroes of culture, education and some financial means.   They had always enjoyed the same social and educational facilities as the whites and courteous treatment from them.   But, with

[1] Reference 110 (a), pp. 89, 88.

the increase in population by a group of generally uneducated and untrained persons, these privileges were withdrawn. . . . The old colored citizens of Philadelphia resented this, placed the blame at the migrant's door and stood aloof from him. Negro preachers invited the new arrivals into the church but many of the congregation made him know that he was not wanted. In some cases the church split over the matter, the migrants and their sympathizers withdrawing and forming a church for themselves." [1] In Milwaukee, also, there were, at first, indications of aloofness and a separation of the two classes of colored people. [2] Investigators of the situation in Detroit reported that the " old Detroiters " held the migrants responsible for their altered status in that city, for the whites had tended to increase the discriminations against all Negroes since the influx of southern colored people. Negroes who had been in Detroit for generations had frequently been servants in the homes of white people and had developed friendly contacts with them. Also, they were much better educated and adjusted to northern ways than were the newcomers. On the basis of these factors, a class line tended to develop between the old and new Detroiters, especially as many of the latter resented the attitude of the older inhabitants. The investigators felt, however, that more friendly contacts had been established as the migrants became permanently settled in the city and adjusted to urban life. The various colored classes based on cultural and professional interests have apparently accepted without restriction those who had similar interests and training. [3]

It must not be assumed that northern Negroes were

[1] References 93 (a), p. 177. *Cf.* 124 (a), p. 136.

[2] Reference 124 (a), p. 112.

[3] References 22 (a), sec. ii, pp. 19-20. *Cf.* 46 (f), p. 10; 117 (a), p. 539; 81 (a), p. 10.

actively hostile to the migrants or universally resentful of their presence. As would have occurred in any group, individual members of the older colored population reacted to the influx in a variety of ways. Many of them were earnestly desirous of aiding the newcomers in their task of adjustment to a new environment and were glad to see them coming to new industrial opportunities and to greater social freedom. Negro churches were active in assisting the migrants and various Negro organizations were formed among the older residents for the purpose of looking after the southern Negroes.[1] Thus, contrasting attitudes of resentment and friendly cooperation were evident among the northern Negro groups.

It is also possible that class distinctions have been increased among the colored people in the North because of the rapid growth of the Negro population and the consequent increasing complexity of their economic, educational and cultural life. Economic groups have probably differentiated to some extent in conformity to the differing occupations of common laborer, domestic, skilled worker, business or professional men, and social distinctions have arisen from differences of education, wealth and standards of living. However, this is largely supposition because intensive surveys of class distinctions among Negroes in the North are still non-existent.

A few suggestions as to the probable trend toward greater class differences are seen in one or two reports of investigations. The Detroit Bureau found evidence of tentative class lines being drawn on the basis of residence, culture and professions.[2] The Pennsylvania survey reported " no great dividing line in Negro social classes based on income " but indications of a great deal of difference in culture with a concomitant feeling of superiority among

[1] References 124 (a), p. 164; 93 (a), p. 176.
[2] Reference 22 (a), sec. ii, pp. 19-20.

the group of better-educated northern Negroes.[1] Careful investigation of this problem in various northern cities would be valuable.

One of the best known leaders of the race has well summarized the entire situation of the northern Negroes :

> " The position of this group is not strong economically or socially. Its security depends largely upon the non-agitation of the race problem. If racial differences are not emphasized by newspapers or by new facts the northern Negro becomes gradually a citizen judged by his individual deserts and abilities. If, however, there comes a sudden new migration, the level of intelligence and efficiency in these newcomers is almost inevitably below that of the Negro already established in the North. Public opinion lumps the new with the old without discrimination. New racial irritation, hatreds and segregation arise. . . . The northern Negro, therefore, faces a peculiar dilemma. He knows that his southern brother will and must migrate just as he himself migrated either in this generation or the last. He feels more or less acutely his own duty to help the newcomer. . . . But, on the other hand, the black northerner knows what this migration costs." [2]

The Negro in the North may sympathetically understand and even welcome the arrival of the southern colored laborers but at the same time, he realizes that their coming means increased economic competition for the limited positions open to Negroes, increased discriminations and segregation, and a lowering of the average culture and education of the Negro group. The migration has thus not only increased the frequency and complexity of the contacts between Negroes and whites in northern cities but has likewise affected relationships within the Negro group itself. However, further

[1] Reference 110 (a), pp. 10-11.
[2] References 27 (a), p. 540. *Cf.* 156 (a), pp. 186-7.

studies are needed before any reliable opinions can be expressed concerning the full extent and permanency of the effect of migration upon northern Negroes.

WELFARE ORGANIZATIONS

Many of the social and welfare agencies, religious organizations and civic federations of these cities have enlarged their activities in order to assist the southern migrants in making a satisfactory adjustment to their new environment. In some cases, special committees and agencies were organized for the express purpose of meeting the needs of the growing colored population, and in various cities, social, civic and religious associations have united to carry on welfare work among the migrants. As was earlier shown, many of the northern Negro churches increased their extra-religious activities by establishing employment agencies and various committees to help the newcomers with their financial, housing, and other personal problems. In some cities, too, white and colored representatives of churches, clubs and social agencies formed interracial committees to further friendly cooperation and understanding between the white and colored residents. Local branches of the National Association for the Advancement of Colored People and of the Interracial Commission have been particularly active in matters of race adjustment. Thus, in all sorts of ways the activities of many social and welfare organizations in the North were influenced by the migration of southern Negroes.[1]

For example, in Chicago neighborhood associations were formed in some districts to secure better cooperation between the colored and white inhabitants, or to improve sanitary and moral conditions.[2] In Philadelphia several

[1] References 17 (a), pp. 146-7, 192-4; 110 (a), chs. xi, xii; 46 (d), pp. 72-5; 48 (e), p. 322; 150 (d), pp. 334-5.

[2] Reference 17 (a), pp. 192-3.

organizations united in helping the migrants find work and suitable homes; representatives of the Philadelphia Housing Association, the Armstrong Association, The Travelers Aid, the Philadelphia Academy of Medicine and other agencies all joined in trying to ease the newcomers' difficult task of adjustment to a northern urban environment, by giving them information concerning residential districts, industrial opportunities and health requirements, and by financially aiding those who needed such help.[1] The Welfare Federation of Cleveland has supervised the organization of committees which deal with problems of housing, labor, health, and general welfare among migrants. Cincinnati, Pittsburgh and Detroit have similar agencies which have either originated as a result of the migration, or have enlarged the scope of their activities in order to care for the migrants.[2]

The National League on Urban Conditions Among Negroes has been one of the most active agencies in meeting the problems created by the migration, and its work illustrates the type of activities that were called forth by the influx of Negroes. In many cities, such as New York, Philadelphia, Chicago, and Detroit, the League has had committees to improve the housing situation. Investigations of colored housing problems have been made, civic authorities and large industrial establishments have been approached in the effort to provide better living conditions for the colored group, and the migrants have been assisted in finding the best possible dwellings. Another important line of work carried on by the League has been the campaigns of assimilation. Committees have met the migrants at the stations, assisted them in finding homes and employment and given them instruction concerning clothing, food and standards of conduct expected of them in the North.

[1] References 93 (a), p. 177; 124 (a), pp. 137-8.

[2] References 46 (d), p. 73; 145 (d), pp. 152-3; 124 (a), pp. 103, 121, 137-8, 164.

Other workers have visited the homes of the migrants in order to educate the newcomers in the health and living requirements of a northern urban existence, and have encouraged them in keeping their houses and neighborhoods clean and respectable, in sending their children to school, and in maintaining an inconspicuous deportment in public places.[1]

In various ways and in varying degrees many of the social, religious and welfare organizations in northern cities responded to the problems which resulted from the northward movement of colored people by increasing the nature and extent of their activities.   Likewise, new organizations were created to meet the needs of Negroes who were not being cared for by existing agencies, either because such needs were outside the scope of established organizations or because Negroes were not served by the white groups or because the growth of the colored population necessitated separate agencies.   It is true that much remained to be done in the way of meeting the problems created by the migration, and by no means all of the social organizations made any attempt to cope with the effects of this influx.   In spite of these facts, however, many of the northern welfare agencies were profoundly influenced by the arrival of southern Negroes.

[1] References 124 (a), p. 104; 17 (a), pp. 193-4, 146-7; 145 (d), pp. 23, 152-5; 32 (a), p. 68; 151 (a), p. 288; 150 (d), p. 334; 10 (b), p. 348.

SECTION III

CONCLUSION

CHAPTER XIII

SUMMARY AND RECOMMENDATIONS

THE movements of Negroes within the United States have been only one phase of the perpetual ebb and flow of human kind. In the days of slavery colored workers were shifted from one state or county to another, wherever they were most useful; since the close of the Civil War there has continued to be a constant flux of the Negro population, with the tide turning most strongly in the direction of the greatest demand for their labor. It has been shown in previous chapters that this call for colored workers came with unusual insistency from the cities of the North during the World War period, and as a direct response, hordes of southern Negroes began to flock to those northern centers. Instead of being held on the land by lack of economic opportunity in other directions, colored wage earners were able to leave the rural districts and join the present-day urban trend.

The desire to leave the southern farms was all the stronger because this demand for industrial workers in the North came at a time of agricultural depression, when the Negroes' chief occupation, raising cotton, was beset with hardships and threatened with extinction by the spread of the boll weevil. Apprehension over their economic difficulties was accompanied by an increasing discussion of the social restrictions which surround Negroes in the South, and when these factors were strengthened by reports of opportunities in the North, the scene was set for a northward trek of southern Negroes of unprecedented proportions. Consequently, they forsook the farms and cities of the South in order to take the industrial jobs formerly filled by foreign immigrant labor. Inevitably the economic and social life of the northern cities was distinctly affected by this rapid increase of a population group which heretofore had played an inconspicuous part in their urban activities.

The arrival of colored laborers from the South enabled northern industries to carry on production at unslackened rate during the war and afterwards. At the same time, these movements required the conversion of Negro agriculturalists into industrial workers. Negroes are still mainly confined to the unskilled and more poorly paid positions, but at least the variety of occupations open to them has been decidedly increased, and there has been a significant addition to the number performing skilled and semi-skilled tasks. The growth in the size of colored groups in northern cities has also opened up new opportunities for Negro business and professional men, who are thus enabled to secure adequate clienteles among their own race. Colored women have shared to some extent in these new industrial openings, but their status is still uncertain and their advance out of domestic service into industry has seldom equalled the transference of colored males into the industrial field.

In many establishments colored employees have been partially segregated in particular occupations instead of being scattered among the white workers, yet colored and white laborers have been brought into closer contact by the migration and have worked together with comparatively little serious friction. Northern unions, too, have been forced to take more cognizance of the colored wage earners; occasionally they have included the newcomers in their membership and have sought to organize them, but to date, as a rule, the locals have shown a spirit of opposition rather than of welcome. The gulf between organized labor and the Negro workers has become more apparent and serious, for northern locals continue to discriminate against colored men in spite of the fact that their more conspicuous presence increases the possibility of their being used as substitutes for white workers in times of labor difficulties. Notwithstanding the handicaps involved in the opposition of unions and in the Negroes' industrial inexperience, as a group they have apparently given satisfaction in their new work, especially after they have had reasonable time in which to make the adjustment from simple agricultural processes to the complex operations of modern industry.

Compared with other groups, the Negro is still handicapped by limitation of economic opportunities and discrimination in the matter of employment and advancement. In general, however, migration from the South has resulted in real improvement in the colored laborer's economic situation, for he has a wider choice of occupations and usually secures higher wages than he did in the South. Unlike previous movements to the North, those since 1915 have occurred in response to a definite demand for labor, and on account of this unprecedented economic opportunity, Negroes have made their first real entrance into the industrial world of the North.

This influx of southern Negroes has also created serious problems of housing, health, crime, education, politics and race contacts. The whole social structure of northern cities has been in some degree affected by the migration, for with every increase in the size of the colored groups, the social conditions existing among them have tended to exert more and more influence upon the corresponding conditions among the white people. Thus, as the congestion in Negro areas has increased, the white inhabitants of the city have felt the results both in a strengthened race prejudice, which followed attempts of colored people to find homes in other neighborhoods, and also in the extent of crime, juvenile delinquency and immorality, which have inevitably accompanied such unwholesome and overcrowded living conditions.

On the other hand, the migrants have faced the problem of finding suitable homes and of adjusting themselves to urban life in the North, a process of adaptation which has involved learning to maintain health standards in crowded cities, becoming acquainted with urban laws and regulations, fitting their children into northern school systems, and finding satisfactory provisions for amusement and recreation. One of the most serious effects of these increased race contacts has been a noticeable tendency on the part of whites toward discrimination against Negroes and toward segregation in schools, amusement centers and public places. This mounting prejudice with its emotional barriers of suspicion and antagonism has been applied to Negroes who had long been established in the North as well as to the migrants, so that the former have frequently felt an augmented restriction in their social activities. At the same time it has lessened the ability of white northerners to think clearly and impartially on race problems.

Although Negroes in northern cities are not accorded the full measure of freedom and opportunity of the whites, yet it must not be overlooked that migration has tended to improve the social, as well as the economic, status of the newcomers. They have found decidedly better schools than they had ever been accustomed to; they have gained the right to vote and to feel themselves a part of the community; they have free access to libraries, museums and, in some degree, to public parks and recreational centers; they have been brought under the influence of organized health programs and sanitary inspection, and in many cases, even, they have found homes which are at least a little better than those they left in the South. In spite of the higher cost of living and the difficulties of adaptation to a totally new environment, there seems to have been, as a rule, a real advance in the migrant's standard of living.

The foregoing are some of the important economic and social situations in the North which have been affected by the arrival of large numbers of southern Negroes. This movement to northern cities was not confined to the abnormal war period, but has continued during the last decade, and undoubtedly will persist for years to come. Comprehensive and reliable figures concerning the extent of these movements of the last few years will not be available until the 1930 census statistics are at hand, but it is certain that the period from 1920 to 1930 has witnessed a decided increase in the number of Negroes living in northern cities. The forthcoming Census is also awaited for general information concerning occupations and for population figures on which to estimate vital statistics among Negroes. On the basis of past experience, it is probable that there will be a lag of from two to four years in the availability of this material, so that discussions of the Negro's economic and social status in the North must continue to be based on assumptions of estimated trends and on a synthesis of isolated surveys.

It is probable that the next Census will show not only large numbers of migrants but also a change in the Negro's industrial status, compared to that of 1920, for recent investigations indicate that there has been a shift of colored workers from industry back to domestic and personal service. It is unlikely, however, that they have returned to their occupational status of 1910, and much of the industrial loss which will probably be indicated may be due in great part to the present business depression, which provides a situation as abnormal as was the very active business period at the time the 1920 Census was taken. The rate of population increase among Negroes in the North should show an upward trend, since the migrants have become more adjusted to urban health conditions, and since the proportion of the sexes has had time to become equalized. As women begin to follow the men and a more normal family life is established, we should expect an increased birth rate.

These are only two of the trends which may be apparent from the 1930 census figures. Others in connection with such problems as the age, sex and marital status, and the educational situation among the colored inhabitants, will also be available. However, a complete understanding of the economic and social situation of Negroes in the North can never be obtained simply from census statistics, but must be supplemented by investigations of particular groups and cities. It is to be hoped that further surveys will base their studies on an examination of what has already been done, and will strive to fill up many apparent gaps. It is unfortunate that, so far, surveys of Negro groups in northern cities have done little in the way of securing a " control " study by investigating conditions among the whites or by specifically and intensively comparing conditions in the North with those which the migrants had experienced in their previous southern homes. Much remains to be done along both of these lines.

The problem of housing conditions has already received extensive treatment, and future studies would do well to emphasize either particular phases of the housing situation or other, less well-known conditions. It is agreed that Negroes in the North live in the less desirable and more congested areas, and are unwelcome in white districts. We do need to know what causes the economic factor of property depreciation, and we also need investigation as to how the housing difficulties are solving themselves since the migrants have had time to become adjusted and since Negro areas have had opportunity to expand.

In view of the fact that the manifestations of disease,

crime and immorality among colored groups are affected by their age, sex and marital status, consideration of these factors should be included in discussions of the health situation and the crime rate among Negroes. Moreover, problems of crime, health, and housing, are so closely allied to the economic standing of the race that we need more emphasis upon the relation between them. It would also be valuable to make a closer distinction between northern and southern Negroes in the study of occupations, success in industry, and relation to the unions.[1] Negroes are by no means a homogeneous mass with identical capacity, training and personality, and their differences should be more fully considered in future investigations.

Above all, future studies of the Negro's status in the North would do well to seek a basis for understanding the factors which are involved in the formation of public opinion in regard to race relations. The Chicago Race Commission has made a valuable beginning in such investigations and further surveys of this type are desirable. Are Negroes being thrown into more intimate and friendly contacts with the whites than they were in the South, so that there is opportunity for the development of understanding and tolerance between the races, or are they being separated from white people by a growing spirit of discrimination and antagonism, and by segregation? There are indications that the North is seeking adjustment to the presence of a large colored population by the method of separation and inequality which prevails in the South. It is necessary to have more exact information concerning the nature of the contacts between whites and blacks in northern cities and the factors which have led to the evidences of race prejudice which have already appeared.

[1] Considerable progress in this direction has been made by Spero and Harris, and by the National Urban League.

All too frequently in the past the attitudes and opinions of northern white people have been based on insufficient knowledge, and have contained the dogmatic finality which accompanies emotional bias—antagonistic or sentimentally sympathetic.   Conditions which are conspicuously prevalent among colored groups have been dismissed as due to inherent racial characteristics: the Negro's absence from industrial positions and labor unions is regarded as the result of his unfitness for anything but menial labor and of his inability to organize; a high rate of crime and immorality is explained as an ineradicable Negro trait; retardation in schools is assumed to be the consequence of the Negro's natural intellectual inferiority; congested, unsanitary housing conditions are attributed to the colored man's inherent gregariousness and uncleanliness.   If a study of the surveys which have been made among Negro groups in the North does nothing else, it points out clearly the complex factors which are involved in all these situations. Fundamentally, the Negro's problems are based on his economic condition, and the first real step toward improving his lot in regard to education, crime, health and housing, must lie in giving him economic opportunity comparable to the white man's and a chance to earn a decent wage.

The constantly increasing presence of colored people in our northern cities constitutes one of the most vital present-day sociological problems.   At all times the activities and developmental processes of a group are profoundly influenced by the size of that group and by the characteristics of its members.   The migration of colored people is affecting the extent and composition of the social aggregate in northern centers, and results in the augmented interaction of two population elements that are likely to be swayed by prejudice and attitudes acquired unconsciously and unintelligently.   If the North is to attain a more satisfactory adjustment between the races than has been evolved in the South, there is need for tolerance, understanding and unbiased information.

APPENDIX

PART A.—GENERAL BIBLIOGRAPHY.

1. Abell, John
   a. "Southern Negro in Northern Industry," *Trade Winds,* March 1924, pp. 17-20; same, *Economic World,* vol. 27, pp. 620-2, May 3, 1924.

2. Albany City Club
   a. *Survey of Albany's Negro Population,* Albany, New York, City Club Bulletin, vol. 9, no. 5, March 1929, 15 pp.

3. Allison, Thomas W.
   a. "Population Movements in Chicago," *Journal of Social Forces,* vol. 2, pp. 529-33, May 1924.

4. American Management Association
   a. Survey Report No. 5, *The Negro in Industry,* New York, American Management Association, 1923, 28 pp.

5. Baker, Ray Stannard
   a. "The Negro Goes North," *World's Work,* vol. 34, pp. 314-9, July 1917.

6. Barnett, Claude A.
   a. "We Win a Place in Industry," *Opportunity,* vol. 7, pp. 82-6, March 1929.

7. Barton, J. W.
   a. "Negro Migration," *Methodist Quarterly Review,* vol. 74, pp. 84-101, January 1925.

8. Beales, Le Verne
   a. "Negro Enumeration of 1920," *Scientific Monthly,* vol. 14, pp. 352-60, April 1922.

9. Boie, Maurine
   a. "Analysis of Negro Crime Statistics for Minneapolis," *Opportunity,* vol. 6, pp. 171-3, June 1928.

10. Brawley, Benjamin G.
    a. *Short History of the American Negro,* New York, Macmillan, 1919, 280 pp.
    b. *Social History of the American Negro,* New York, Macmillan, 1921, 420 pp.

239

11. Brown, H. V.
    a. " Pro and Con of Negro Migration in America," *Southern Workman,* vol. 53, pp. 348-52, August 1924.

12. Brown, T. I.
    a. *Economic Cooperation Among the Negroes of Georgia,* Atlanta University Publications No. 19, Atlanta, Georgia, Atlanta University Press, 1917, 56 pp.

13. Bunche, R. J.
    a. " Negro Political Laboratories," *Opportunity,* vol. 6, pp. 370-3, December 1928.
    b. " The Thompson-Negro Alliance," *Opportunity,* vol. 7, pp. 78-80, March 1929.

14. Burgess, Ernest W.
    a. " Residential Segregation in American Cities," *Annals of American Academy of Political and Social Science,* vol. 140, pp. 105-15, November 1928.

15. Calverton, V. F.
    a. " The New Negro," *Current History Magazine of the New York Times,* vol. 23, pp. 694-8, February 1926.

16. Carpenter, Niles
    a. *Nationality, Color and Economic Opportunity in the City of Buffalo,* University of Buffalo Studies, vol. 5, no. 4, June 1927, pp. 95-194.
    Also published separately, New York, *The Inquiry.*
    b. " Feebleminded and Pauper Negroes in Public Institutions," *Annals,* vol. 140, pp. 65-76, November 1928.

17. Chicago Race Commission
    a. *Negro in Chicago,* A study of race relations and a race riot, Chicago, Illinois, University of Chicago Press, 1922, 672 pp.

18. Clark, J. T.
    a. " Negro in Steel," *Opportunity,* vol. 4, pp. 87-8, March 1926.

19. Consumers League of the City of New York
    a. *A New Day for the Colored Woman Worker,* a study of colored women in industry in New York, New York, 1919, 39 pp.

20. Dabney, T. L.
    a. " Organized Labor's Attitude Toward Negro Workers," *Southern Workman,* vol. 57, pp. 323-30, August 1928.

21. Davis, P. O.
    a. " Negro Exodus and Southern Agriculture," *American Review of Reviews,* vol. 68, pp. 401-7, October 1923.

22. Detroit Bureau of Governmental Research
   a. *The Negro in Detroit,* Mimeographed, 12 Sections, 1926.
   b. "Report of the Mayor's Committee on Race Relations," *Public Business,* vol. 14, no. 3, March 10, 1927, 15 pp.

23. Detweiler, Frederick G.
   a. *The Negro Press in the United States,* Chicago, Illinois, The University of Chicago Press, 1922, 274 pp.

24. Donald, Henderson
   a. *The Negro Migration of 1916-1918,* Washington, D. C., The Association for the Study of Negro Life and History, 1921, 116 pp.

25. Dowd, Jerome
   a. *The Negro in American Life,* New York, The Century Company, 1926, 611 pp.

26. Dublin, Louis I.
   a. *Broadening the Life Span of the American Negro,* Metropolitan Life Insurance Company, Statistical Bulletin, vol. 4, no. 9.
   b. "Effect of Health Education on Negro Mortality," *Opportunity,* vol. 2, pp. 232-5, August 1924.
   c. *Health and Wealth,* Chapter 12, New York, Harper and Brothers, 1928, 361 pp.
   d. "Health of the Negro," *Annals,* vol. 140, pp. 77-85, November 1928.
   e. "Life, Death and the Negro," *American Mercury,* vol. 12, pp. 37-45, September 1927.
   f. "Recent Improvement in the Negroes' Mortality," *Opportunity,* vol. 1, pp. 5-8, April 1923.

27. Du Bois, W. E. B.
   a. "Hosts of Black Labor," *Nation,* vol. 116, pp. 539-41, May 9, 1923.
   b. "Passing of Jim Crow," *Independent,* vol. 91, pp. 53-4, July 14, 1917.

28. Duke, Charles S.
   a. *The Housing Situation and the Colored People of Chicago,* Chicago, Illinois, April 1919, 35 pp.

29. Duncan, Hannibal G.
   a. *The Changing Race Relationship in the Border and Northern States,* Philadelphia, Pennsylvania, 1922, 127 pp.

30. Dutcher, Dean
   a. *The Negro in Modern Industrial Society,* soon to be published.

31. Emlen, John T.
    a. "Negro Immigration in Philadelphia," *Southern Workman*, vol. 46, pp. 555-7, October 1917.

32. Epstein, Abraham
    a. *The Negro Migrant in Pittsburgh*, Pittsburgh, Pennsylvania, 1918, 74 pp.

33. Evans, Leona
    a. "In the Promised Land," *Opportunity*, vol. 5, pp. 114-5, April 1927.

34. Evans, Maurice S.
    a. *Black and White in the Southern States,* a study of the race problem in the United States from a South African point of view, New York, Longmans, Green and Company, 1915, 299 pp.

35. Farnham, Dwight T.
    a. "Negroes, a Source of Industrial Labor," *Industrial Management*, vol. 56, pp. 123-9, August 1918.

36. Foster, A. L.
    a. "A Cooperative Adventure in the Field of Race Relations," *Opportunity*, vol. 7, pp. 98-9, March 1929.

37. Frazier, E. Franklin
    a. "Chicago, a Cross Section of Negro Life," *Opportunity*, vol. 7, pp. 70-3, March 1929.

38. Fry, C. Luther
    a. "The Negro in the United States — a Statistical Statement," *Annals*, vol. 140, pp. 26-35, November 1928.

39. Gist, F. W.
    a. "Migratory Habits of the Negro under Past and Present Conditions," *Manufacturers Record*, vol. 85, pp. 77-9, March 13, 1924.

40. Gold, H. R., and Armstrong, B. K.
    a. *A Preliminary Study of Interracial Conditions in Chicago*, New York, Home Missions Council, 1920, no paging.

41. Granger, Lester B.
    a. "Race Relations and the School System," *Opportunity*, vol. 3, pp. 327-30, November 1925.

42. Gwinnell, William B.
    a. "Shifting Populations in Great Northern Cities," *Opportunity*, vol. 6, p. 279, September 1928.

43. Hain, A. J.
   a. "Our Immigrant, the Negro," *Iron Trade Review*, vol. 73, pp. 730-6, September 13, 1923.

44. Harris, Abram
   a. "Negro Migration to the North," *Current History Magazine of the New York Times*, vol. 20, pp. 921-5, September 1924.
   b. *Negro Population in Minneapolis*, a study of race relations, Minneapolis, Minnesota, Minneapolis Urban League and Phyllis Wheatley Settlement, 1926, 77 pp.
   c. "The Negro and Economic Radicalism," *Modern Quarterly*, vol. 2, pp. 198-208, February 1925.
   d. "Negro Labor's Quarrel with White Workingmen," *Current History Magazine of the New York Times*, vol. 24, pp. 903-8, September 1926.

45. Harris, H. L.
   a. "A High Mortality Rate—Why," *Opportunity*, vol. 7, p. 81, March 1929.

46. Haynes, George E.
   a. "Effect of War Conditions on Negro Labor," *Proceedings of Academy of Political Science*, vol. 8, pp. 299-312, February 1919.
   b. "Negro at Work," *American Review of Reviews*, vol. 59, pp. 389-93, April 1919.
   c. "Negro Migration and its Implications North and South," Address before the 77th Annual Meeting of the American Missionary Society, Springfield, Massachusetts, October 1923.
   d. "Negro Migration—its Effect on Family and Community Life in the North," *Proceedings, National Conference of Social Work*, 1924, pp. 62-75.
   e. "Negro Migration, its Effect on Family and Community Life in the North," *Opportunity*, vol. 2, pp. 271-4, 303-6, September and October 1924.
   f. *Negro Newcomers in Detroit*, New York, Home Missions Council, 1918, 42 pp.
   g. "Negroes Move North," *Survey*, vol. 40, pp. 115-22, May 4, 1918.
   h. "Negroes Move North," *Survey*, vol. 41, pp. 455-61, January 4, 1919.
   i. "Race Riots in Relation to Democracy," *Survey*, vol. 42, pp. 697-9, August 9, 1919.
   j. *Trend of the Races*, New York, Council of Women for Home Missions and Missionary Education Movement of the United States and Canada, 1922, 205 pp.

k. "The Church and Negro Progress," *Annals,* vol. 140, pp. 264-71, November 1928.

m. "The Migration of Negroes into Northern Cities," *Proceedings, National Conference of Social Work,* 1917, pp. 494-7.

47. Hill, Joseph A.

a. *Recent Northward Migration of the Negro,* Pamphlet—Reprint from *Monthly Labor Review,* vol. 18, pp. 475-88, March 1924; same, *Opportunity,* vol. 2, pp. 100-5, April 1924.

b. *Women in Gainful Occupations, 1870-1920,* Chapter 13, Washington, D. C., Government Printing Office, Census Monograph IX, 1929.

48. Hill, T. Arnold

a. "Labor," *Opportunity,* vol. 7, pp. 23, 57, 189, 316, 350, January, February, June, October, November 1929.

b. "Negro in Industry," *American Federationist,* vol. 32, pp. 915-20, October 1925.

c. "Negro Labor," *American Federationist,* vol. 35, pp. 1452-6, December 1928.

d. "Present Status of Negro Labor," *Opportunity,* vol. 7, pp. 143-5, May 1929.

e. "Recent Developments in the Problem of Negro Labor," *Proceedings, National Conference of Social Work,* 1921, pp. 321-5.

49. Holmes, Samuel J.

a. "Will the Negro Survive in the North?", *Scientific Monthly,* vol. 27, pp. 557-61, December 1928.

50. Home Missions Council

a. *Annual Report*—1918, pp. 21-32.

b. *The Negro Migration,* Report of Committee on Negro Work, New York, Home Missions Council, 1919.

51. Horwill, H. W.

a. "Negro Exodus," *Contemporary Review,* vol. 114, pp. 299-305, September 1918.

52. Houghteling, Leila

a. *Income and Standard of Living of Unskilled Laborers in Chicago,* Chicago, Illinois, University of Chicago Press, 1927, 274 pp.

53. Housing Editorials

a. "Housing the Migrants," *Opportunity,* vol. 1, p. 290, October 1923.

b. "Housing War," *Opportunity,* vol. 3, pp. 323-4, November 1925.

54. Hughes, Elizabeth A.
   a. *Living Conditions for Small Wage Earners in Chicago,* Chicago Department of Public Welfare, 1925, 62 pp.

55. a. "Increase of Negro Prisoners in Cleveland," *Survey,* vol. 38, pp. 511-2, September 8, 1917.

56. a. "Industrial Employment of the Negro in Pennsylvania," *Monthly Labor Review,* vol. 22, pp. 1224-7, June 1926.

57. Johnson, Charles S.
   a. "Black Workers and the City," *Survey,* vol. 53, pp. 641-3, March 1925.
   b. "Changing Economic Status of the Negro," *Annals,* vol. 140, pp. 128-37, November 1928.
   c. "How Much is the Migration a Flight from Persecution?", *Opportunity,* vol. 1, pp. 272-4, September 1923.
   d. "How the Negro Fits in Northern Industries," *Industrial Psychology,* vol. 1, pp. 399-412, June 1926.
   e. "New Frontage on American Life" in Alain Locke's *The New Negro,* New York, Albert and Charles Boni, 1925, pp. 278-98.
   f. "Negro Migration, an Economic Interpretation," *Modern Quarterly,* vol. 2, pp. 314-26, July 1925.
   g. "Negro Population of Waterbury, Connecticut," *Opportunity,* vol. 1, pp. 298-303, 338-42, October and November 1923.
   h. "Negro Workers and the Unions," *Survey,* vol. 60, pp. 113-5, April 15, 1928.
   i. "Negroes at Work in Baltimore," *Opportunity,* vol. 1, pp. 12-9, June 1923.
   j. "Negro Workers in Los Angeles," *Opportunity,* vol. 6, pp. 234-40, August 1928.
   k. "Present Trends in the Employment of Negro Labor," *Opportunity,* vol. 7, pp. 146-8, May 1929.
   m. "Some Economic Aspects of Negro Migration," *Opportunity,* vol. 5, pp. 297-9, October 1927.
   n. "Substitution of Negro Labor for European Immigrant Labor," *Proceedings, National Conference of Social Work,* 1926, pp. 317-27.
   p. "The American Migrant: The Negro," *Proceedings, National Conference of Social Work,* 1927, pp. 554-8.
   r. "When the Negro Migrates North," *World Tomorrow,* vol. 6, pp. 139-41, May 1923.

58. Johnson, Everett
   a. "A Study of the Negro Families in the Pinewood Avenue District of Toledo, Ohio," *Opportunity,* vol. 7, pp. 243-5, August 1929.

59. Johnson, Guy B.
  a. "Negro Migration and its Consequences," *Journal of Social Forces*, vol. 2, pp. 404-8, March 1924.

60. Johnson, James Weldon
  a. "Changing Status of Negro Labor," *Proceedings, National Conference of Social Work*, 1918, pp. 383-8.

61. Joint Committee on Negro Child Study in New York City
  a. *A Study of Delinquent and Neglected Children Before the New York City Children's Court*, The Committee, 1927, 48 pp.

62. Jones, Eugene K.
  a. "National Urban League," *Opportunity*, vol. 3, pp. 12-4, January, 1925.
  b. "Negro in the North," *Current History Magazine of the New York Times*, vol. 15, pp. 969-74, March 1922.
  c. "Negro Migration in New York State," *Opportunity*, vol. 4, pp. 7-11, January 1926.
  d. "Negroes, North and South: a Contrast," *Missionary Review*, vol. 45, pp. 479-82, June 1922.
  e. "Negro's Struggle for Health," *Proceedings, National Conference of Social Work*, 1923, pp. 68-72.

63. Jones, William H.
  a. *Housing of Negroes in Washington, D. C.*, Washington, D. C., Howard University Press, 1929, 191 pp.
  b. *Recreation and Amusement Among Negroes in Washington, D. C.*, a sociological analysis of the Negro in an urban environment, Washington, D. C., Howard University Press, 1927, 216 pp.

64. Kent, F. R.
  a. *Democratic Party*, New York, The Century Company, 1928, 568 pp

65. King, Willis J.
  a. *The Negro in American Life*, New York, Methodist Book Concern, 1926, 154 pp.

66. Kingsley, H. M.
  a. "The Negro Goes to Church," *Opportunity*, vol. 7, pp. 90-1, March 1929.

67. Klugh, Eolyn C.
  a. "Colored Girls at Work in Boston," *Opportunity*, vol. 6, pp. 295-9, October 1928.

68. Knapp, J. W.
  a. "An Experiment with Negro Labor," *Opportunity*, vol. 1, pp. 19-20, February 1923.

69. Lasker, Bruno
   a. "Some Obstacles of Race Cooperation," *Opportunity*, vol. 3, pp. 101-4, April 1925.

70. Lett, H. A.
   a. "Migration Difficulties in Michigan," *Southern Workman*, vol. 56, pp. 231-6, May 1927.
   b. "Negro Welfare in Michigan," *Southern Workman*, vol. 55, pp. 206-8, May 1926.

71. a. "Letters of Negro Migrants 1916-1918," *Journal of Negro History*, vol. 4, pp. 291-340, 412-65, July, October 1919.

72. Lovejoy, Owen R.
   a. "Justice to the Negro Child," *Opportunity*, vol. 7, pp. 174-6, June 1929.

73. a. "Lure of the North for Negroes," *Survey*, vol. 38, pp. 27-8, April 7, 1917.

74. a. "Lynching Industry—1919," *Crisis*, vol. 19, pp. 183-6, February 1920.

75. McAfee, J. E.
   a. "Churches and Race Relations," *Opportunity*, vol. 7, pp. 39-41, February 1929.

76. McDougald, Elise J.
   a. "The School and its Relation to the Vocational Life of the Negro," *Proceedings, National Conference of Social Work*, 1923, pp. 415-8.

77. McDowell, Mary E.
   a. "Hovels or Homes?", *Opportunity*, vol. 7, pp. 74-8, March 1929.

78. McGhee, Ethel
   a. "The Northern Negro Family," *Opportunity*, vol. 5, pp. 176-8, June 1927.

79. McKenzie, H. B.
   a. "The South, the Cotton and the Negro," *North American Review*, vol. 219, pp. 486-95, April 1924.

80. Manly, A. L.
   a. "Where Negroes Live in Philadelphia," *Opportunity*, vol. 1, pp. 10-5, May 1923.

81. Mark, Mary Louise
   a. *Negroes in Columbus, Ohio*, Columbus, Ohio State University Press, Ohio State University Studies, Contributions in Social Science, no. 2, 1928, 63 pp.

82. Melden, Charles M.
    a. *From Slave to Citizen*, New York, Methodist Book Concern, 1921, 271 pp.

83. Merriam, Charles
    a. *Primary Elections*, Chicago, Illinois, University of Chicago Press, 1928, 448 pp.

84. *Michigan Law Review*
    a. Note on disfranchisement, vol. 23, pp. 279-84, January 1925.

85. a. " Migration of Negroes from Southern to Northern States in the Year Ended August 31, 1923," *Economic World* n. s., vol. 26, p. 626, November 3, 1923.

86. a. " Migration to Philadelphia," *Opportunity*, vol. 1, pp. 19-20, May 1923.

87. a. " Migration: The Macon Telegraph," *Crisis*, vol. 19, pp. 109-10, January 1920.

88. Miller, Kelly
    a. " Enumeration Errors in Negro Population," *Scientific Monthly*, vol. 14, pp. 168-77, February 1922.
    b. " The Negro as a Workingman," *American Mercury*, vol. 6, pp. 310-3, November 1925.

89. Missouri, State of
    a. *Bureau of Labor Statistics, Red Book, Report for 1921-1922.*
    b. *Negro Industrial Commission Biennial Reports.*
    c. " Negro Industrial Commission Report," *Monthly Labor Review*, vol. 20, pp. 988-9, May 1925; vol. 16, pp. 1187-9, June 1923.

90. Moffat, Adelene
    a. " New Problems Caused by the Importation of Colored Labor," *National Federation of Settlements*, 1918, pp. 18-9.

91. Moffett, L. W.
    a. " Careful Selection of Negroes Urged," *Iron Age*, vol. 112, pp. 892-3, October 4, 1923.

92. Moss, R. Maurice
    a. " American Cities—Grand Rapids," *Opportunity*, vol. 7, pp. 12-5, January 1929.

93. Mossell, Sadie T.
    a. " The Standard of Living Among 100 Negro Migrant Families in Philadelphia," *Annals*, vol. 98, pp. 173-218, November 1921. Also published separately, 50 pp.

94. Moton, Robert R.
    a. "Migration of Negroes from the Southern to the Northern States and its Economic Effects," *Economic World*, n. s., vol. 25, pp. 688-91, May 19, 1923.
    b. *What the Negro Thinks*, Garden City, N. Y., Doubleday, 1929, 267 pp.

95. Murchison, Carl A.
    a. *Criminal Intelligence*, Worcester, Massachusetts, Clark University, 1926, 291 pp.

96. National League on Urban Conditions Among Negroes
    a. "Industrial Problems in Cities," *Opportunity*, vol. 4, pp. 68-72, 93-4, February, March 1925.
    b. Bulletins and annual reports.
    c. Unpublished reports of surveys in Trenton, New Jersey; Denver, Colorado; Worcester, Massachusetts; Fort Wayne, Indiana; Buffalo, New York; Springfield, Illinois; Milwaukee, Wisconsin.
    d. *Negro Membership in American Labor Unions*, Ira De A. Reid, Director. In press.

97. Nearing, Scott
    a. *Black America*, New York, Vanguard Press, 1929, 275 pp.

98. a. "Negro and Immigrant Labor," *Opportunity*, vol. 5, p. 320, November 1927.

99. a. "Negro Crime Rate," *Opportunity*, vol. 5, p. 160, June 1927.

100. a. "Negro Housing Situation in Baltimore," *Monthly Labor Review*, vol. 19, p. 898, October 1924.

101. a. "Negro Migrants in Philadelphia in 1923," *Monthly Labor Review*, vol. 19, pp. 998-9, November 1924.

102. *Negro Year Book*, Nashville
    a. 1925-1926.
    b. 1921-1922.
    c. 1918-1919.

103. a. "Negro's Brighter Outlook," *Nation*, vol. 105, pp. 627-8, December 6, 1917.

104. New York
    a. Association for Improving the Condition of the Poor, *Health Work for Mothers and Children in a Colored Community*, Publication 131, 1924, 15 pp.
    b. State Department of Labor, *Unemployment in Buffalo* (November, 1929), Special Bulletin no. 163, 48 pp.

c. New York Urban League, *Housing Among Negroes in Harlem,* 1917.

d. New York Urban League, *2,400 Negro Families in Harlem.*

105. Newman, Bernard J.
   a. *Housing in Philadelphia,* Annual Report of Philadelphia Housing Association 1922 to 1927, See index.
   b. "Housing of Negro Immigrants in Pennsylvania," *Opportunity,* vol. 2, pp. 46-8, February 1924.

106. Odum, Howard
   a. *Rainbow Round My Shoulder,* the Blue Trail of Black Ulysses, Indianapolis, Indiana, Bobbs-Merrill Company, 1928, 322 pp.
   b. *Man's Quest for Social Guidance,* The Study of Social Problems, New York, Henry Holt, 1927, 643 pp.

107. Park, Robert E.
   a. "The Bases of Race Prejudice," *Annals,* vol. 140, pp. 11-20, November 1928.

108. Payne, E. George
   a. "Negroes in the Public Elementary Schools of the North," *Annals,* vol. 140, pp. 224-33, November 1928.

109. Pendleton, Helen B.
   a. "Cotton Pickers in Northern Cities," *Survey,* vol. 37, pp. 569-71, February 17, 1917.

110. Pennsylvania, Commonwealth of, Department of Public Welfare
   a. *Negro Survey of Pennsylvania,* Harrisburg, Pennsylvania, 1927, 97 pp.

111. Phelps-Stokes Papers
   a. *Preliminary Outline on Inter-racial Organization in Northern Cities,* Typewritten

112. Philadelphia, Armstrong Association
   a. *Study of Living Conditions Among Colored People* in Towns in the Outer Part of Philadelphia and in other suburbs both in Pennsylvania and New Jersey, 1915, 57 pp.
   b. *The Negro in Business in Philadelphia,* Pamphlet, 14 pp.

113. Pickens, William
   a. "Negro Migrations: Migrating to Fuller Life," *Forum,* vol. 72, pp. 600-7, November 1924.

114. Pittsburgh Council of the Churches of Christ
   a. *The New Negro Population,* Report on the Recent Influx of Negroes to Pittsburgh, Pittsburgh, Pennsylvania, February 1918 (pamphlet).

115. a. "Problem of the Negro Laborer," *Iron Trade Review*, vol. 60, pp. 836-7, April 12, 1917.

116. Quillen, F. U.

   a. *Color Line in Ohio*, Ann Arbor, Michigan, G. Wahr, 1913, 178 pp.

117. Ragland, J. Marshall

   a. "The Negro in Detroit," *Southern Workman*, vol. 52, pp. 533-40, November 1923.

118. Reid, Ira De A.

   a. "American Cities—Albany, New York," *Opportunity*, vol. 7, pp. 179-82, June 1929.

   b. "Negro Life on the Western Front," (Denver, Colorado) *Opportunity*, vol. 7, pp. 275-81, September 1929.

   c. *The Negro in the Major Industries and Building Trades of Pittsburgh*, 1925. Typewritten.

   d. *Social Conditions of the Negro in the Hill District of Pittsburgh*, 1929. Typewritten.

119. Reuter, Edward B.

   a. *The American Race Problem*, New York, T. Y. Crowell Publishing Company, 1927, 448 pp.

120. Robinson, J. H.

   a. "Cincinnati Negro Survey and Program," *Proceedings, National Conference of Social Work*, 1919, pp. 524-7.

121. Rockwood, H. L. (M.D.)

   a. "Effect of Negro Migration on Community Health in Cleveland," *Proceedings, National Conference of Social Work*, 1926, pp. 238-44.

122. Root, William T., Jr.

   a. *A Psychological and Educational Survey of 1916 Prisoners in the Western Penitentiary of Pennsylvania*, Pittsburgh, Pennsylvania, 1927, 246 pp.

123. Scarborough, William S.

   a. "The Negro Farmer in the South," *Current History Magazine of the New York Times*, vol. 21, pp. 565-9, January 1925.

124. Scott, Emmett J.

   a. *Negro Migration During the War*, New York, Oxford University Press, 1920, 189 pp. (Carnegie Endowment for International Peace, Preliminary Economic Studies of the War, no. 16.)

125. Scroggs, W. O.
   a. "Interstate Migration of Negro Population," *Journal of Political Economy,* vol. 25, pp. 1034-43, December 1917.

126. a. "Segregation," *Opportunity,* vol. 6, p. 384, December 1928.

127. Seligmann, H. J.
   a. *The Negro Faces America,* New York, Harper & Brothers, 1920, 319 pp.

128. Sellin, Thorsten
   a. "The Negro Criminal," *Annals,* vol. 140, pp. 52-64, November, 1928.

129. Sewall, J. L.
   a. "Industrial Revolution and the Negro," *Scribner's Magazine,* vol. 69, pp. 334-42, March 1921.

130. Skaggs, William H.
   a. *The Southern Oligarchy,* New York, Devin-Adair Company, 1924, 472 pp.

131. Smith, William Roy
   a. *Negro Suffrage in the South,* Studies in Southern History and Politics, New York, Columbia University Press, 1914, pp. 231-56.

132. a. "Southern Negro in Cleveland Industries," *Monthly Labor Review,* vol. 19, pp. 41-4, July 1924.

133. Spero, Sterling and Harris, Abram
   a. *The Negro in the Labor Movement,* soon to be published.

134. Stephenson, G. T.
   a. *Race Distinctions in American Law,* New York, D. Appleton & Company, 1910, 388 pp.

135. Stone, Alfred H.
   a. *Studies in the American Race Problem,* New York, Doubleday, Page & Company, 1908, 555 pp.

136. Taylor, Alva W.
   a. "When the Negro Comes North," *Christian Century,* vol. 40, pp. 691-2, May 31, 1923.

137. Taylor, Paul S.
   a. Unpublished material on employment of Negroes in certain industries from 1910 to 1928.

138. Thomasson, Maurice E.
   a. "The Negro Migration," *Southern Workman,* vol. 46, pp. 379-82, July 1917.

139. Thompson, Anna
    a. " Survey of Crime Among Negroes in Philadelphia," *Opportunity*, vol. 4, pp. 217-9, 251-4, 285-6, July-September 1926.

140. Toledo, Ohio
    a. Untitled article on industrial conditions, *Opportunity*, vol. 2, p. 28, January 1924.

141. United States Bureau of the Census
    a. *Increase of Population in the United States 1910-1920*, Census Monograph I, Chapter XI, Washington, 1922.
    b. *Negro Population in the United States*, 1790-1915, Washington, Government Printing Office, 1918, 844 pp.

142. United States Congress, House of Representatives
    a. *East St. Louis Riots,* House Document 1231, Serial no. 7444, July 15, 1918.

143. United States Department of Agriculture
    a. Bulletin 1269, Brannen, C. O., *Relation of Land Tenure to Plantation Organization*, October 18, 1924.
    b. Farmers Bulletin 848; Hunter, W. D., *Boll Weevil Problem*, August 1917, 40 pp.

144. United States Department of Interior, Bureau of Education.
    a. Bulletins 38 and 39, Jones, Thomas Jesse, *Negro Education*, 1916, Washington, Government Printing Office, 1917, 2 vols.

145. United States Department of Labor
    a. Bureau of Labor Statistics, *Handbook of Labor Statistics, 1924-1926*, Miscellaneous Series 439, " Living Conditions of Small Wage Earners in Chicago," pp. 187-91.
    b. *Ibid.*, " Negro in Industry," pp. 395-412.
    c. *Negro at Work During the World War and Reconstruction*, Washington, D. C., Government Printing Office, 1921, 144 pp.
    d. *Negro Migration in 1916-17*, Washington, D. C., Government Printing Office, 1919, 158 pp.
    e. Office of the Secretary, " Inclusion of Negro Workers into Northern Industry," Press Release July 9, 1923.
    f. *Ibid.*, " Negro Migration Nears Half-Million Mark," Press Release October 24, 1923.
    g. Women's Bureau, Bulletin 20, *Negro Women in Industry*, Washington, D. C., 1922, 65 pp.

146. United States Treasury Department, Public Health
    a. Gover, Mary, and Sydenstricker, Edgar, *Mortality Among Negroes in the United States*, 1928, Public Health Bulletin 174, 63 pp.

b. "Study of the Trend of Negro Infant Mortality," *Public Health Reports,* vol. 44, no. 45, November 8, 1929, pp. 2705-31.

147. University Commission on Southern Race Questions
a. *Five Letters,* John F. Slater Fund, Occasional Papers, no. 24, Charlottesville, Virginia, Michie Company, 1927.

148. a. "Urbanization and the Negro," *Opportunity,* vol. 1, p. 323, November 1923.

149. Walrond, Eric
a. "From Cotton, Cane and Rice Fields," *Independent,* vol. 117, pp. 260-2, September 4, 1926.
b. "Negro Exodus from the South," *Current History Magazine of the New York Times,* vol. 18, pp. 942-4, September 1923.

150. Washington, Forrester B.
a. "Health Work for Negro Children," *Opportunity,* vol. 3, pp. 264-9, September 1925.
b. "Health Work for Negro Children," *Proceedings, National Conference of Social Work,* 1925, pp. 226-31.
c. "Recreational Facilities for the Negro," *Annals,* vol. 140, pp. 272-82, November 1928.
d. "The Detroit Newcomers' Greeting," *Survey,* vol. 38, pp. 333-5, July 14, 1917.

151. Wesley, Charles H.
a. *Negro Labor in the United States,* 1850-1925: A Study in American Economic History, New York, Vanguard Press, 1927, 343 pp.

152. White, Walter
a. "Success of Negro Migration," *Crisis,* vol. 19, pp. 112-5, January 1920.
b. "The Sweet Trial," *Crisis,* vol. 31, pp. 125-9, January 1926.

153. a. "Why the Negroes Go North," *Literary Digest,* vol. 77, May 19, 1923, pp. 13-4.

154. Wilmer, S. G.
a. "Negro Exodus as Viewed in North and West," *Manufacturers Record,* vol. 85, pp. 79-83, April 17, 1924.

155. Wilson, E. E.
a. "Responsibility for Crime," *Opportunity,* vol. 7, pp. 95-7, March 1929.

156. Woodson, Carter G.
a. *A Century of Negro Migration,* Washington, D. C., The Association for the Study of Negro Life and History, 1918, 221 pp.

b. *The Negro in Our History*, Washington, D. C., The Association for the Study of Negro Life and History, 1928, 628 pp.

157. Woofter, Thomas Jackson, Jr.

    a. *Basis of Racial Adjustment*, New York, Ginn & Company, 1925, 258 pp.

    b. "Negro and Industrial Peace," *Survey*, vol. 45, pp. 420-1, December 18, 1920.

    c. *Negro Migration*, Changes in Rural Organization and Population of the Cotton Belt, New York, W. D. Gray, 1920, 195 pp.

    d. *Negro Problems in Cities*, New York, Doubleday, Doran & Company, 1928, 284 pp.

158. Work, Monroe N.

    a. *A Bibliography of the Negro in Africa and America*, New York, H. W. West Company, 1928, 698 pp.

    b. "Taking Stock of the Race Problem," *Opportunity*, vol. 2, pp. 41-6, February 1924.

159. *World Almanac 1930*.

PART B.—Bibliography Classified by Subject Matter and Page.

(References refer by number to the General Bibliography, Part A of Appendix) [1]

1. Characteristics of Recent Negro Migrations

    See references:

        2(a), p. 5; 7(a), pp. 89-92; 8(a); 22(a), sec. ii; 25(a), part v; 39(a), pp. 77-9; 42(a), p. 279; 43(a), pp. 730-1; 44(a), pp. 921-5; 46(d), p. 62; 47(a); 57(c), pp. 272-4; 57(n), pp. 317-8; 81(a), pp. 10-14; 85(a); 86(a); 88(a), pp. 168-77; 89(a), pp. 421-4; 92(a); 94(a), pp. 688-9; 102(a), pp. 438, 441; 110(a), chap. 2; 118(a); 124(a), pp. 38 *et seq.*; 125(a), pp. 1034-43; 141(a), chap. 11; 141(b), pp. 40-1, 65-6, 75-6, 93; 145(d), pp. 11, 15-9, 51-8, 73-4, 77, 80-6, 91, 97, 115-8; 145(e); 145(f); 149(b); 151(a), pp. 230-1, 283-6; 156(a), pp. 174 *et seq.*; 157(c), p. 120.

2. Causes of Migration

    (1) Economic Conditions in the North

        See references:

            17(a), pp. 83-4, 357-9; 46(a), p. 304; 46(f), pp. 6-7; 46(g),

---

[1] A few references from Part A have been omitted because they were too general to classify, furnishing merely a background for the study of migration, or were partial repetitions of material already cited.

pp. 115-22; 46 (j), pp. 27-8; 51 (a), pp. 301-2; 57 (c), pp. 272-4; 57(m), pp. 297-9; 57(p), pp. 554-8; 71(a); 98(a); 124(a), pp. 17-18, 50-4, 102-3; 145(d), pp. 22-3, 62, 100, 110, 116-9, 125; 151(a), chap. 10; 157(a), pp. 44 *et seq.*

(2) Agricultural Situation in the South

See references:

5(a); 17(a), pp. 80-1, 358-9; 21(a); 22(a), sec. ii, p. 18; 39(a); 44(a), p. 922; 46(e), p. 272; 46(g), p. 117; 51(a), pp. 300-1; 57(m), p. 297; 59(a); 71(a); 102(a), p. 7; 119(a), pp. 238-40; 124(a), pp. 6, 13-16; 125(a), pp. 1034, 1036, 1041; 143(a); 143(b); 145(d), pp. 11, 37, 58-60, 76-80, 86, 100, 104-5; 151(a), p. 291; 156(a), pp. 169 *et seq.*; 157(a), pp. 76-85; 157(c), pp. 29-32, 50, 64, 69-73.

(3) Social Causes

(a) Political Situation

See references:

11(a); 17(a), p. 86; 27(b); 34(a), pp. 150-2; 64(a), pp. 229-30; 83(a); 84(a); 94(b), chap. 7; 119(a). pp. 150-4; 131(a); 134(a), chap. 11; 135(a), chap. 8; 145(d), p. 32; 151(a), p. 292; 156(a), p. 168; 157(a), pp. 26, 165-6.

(b) Mob Violence

See references:

12(a), pp. 28-9; 15(a), p. 696; 17(a), p. 84; 29(a), pp. 20-21; 34(a), chap. 19; 46(f), p. 7; 46(g), p. 118; 51(a), p. 300; 57(c), pp. 272-4; 57(d), pp. 402-3; 57(f), p. 321; 62(c); 119(a), chap. 15; 124(a), p. 22; 125(a), p. 1041; 145(d), pp. 12, 37, 77, 88, 107; 151(a), p. 292.

(c) Discrimination in Court Procedure

See references:

7(a), p. 94; 12(a), pp. 28-9; 34(a), chap. 17; 46(e), p. 272; 46(f), p. 7; 46(g), p. 118; 94(b), chap. 7; 119(a), pp. 351-63; 124(a), pp. 19-22; 128(a), pp. 54-6; 130(a), chap. 13; 134(a), pp. 247-72; 138(a), p. 379; 141(b), pp. 436-43; 145(d), pp. 11, 21, 58, 88, 105-6; 156(a), p. 168; 157(a), chap. 7; 157(c), pp. 121, 141-4.

(d) Segregation

See references:

94(b), chap. 5; 119(a), pp. 154-6, 396-400; 124(a), pp. 21-2; 134(a), chap. 9; 145(d), p. 105; 156(a), pp. 157-8; 156(b), pp. 477 *et seq.*; 157(a), pp. 238-39; 157(c), pp. 138-41.

(e) Lack of Educational Facilities

See references:

11(a), p. 350; 46(e), p. 272; 46(f), p. 7; 46(g), p. 120; 51(a), p. 300; 71(a); 82(a), p. 161; 94(b), chap. 6; 102(a), pp. 285-300; 119(a), chap. 11; 124(a), p. 18; 125(a), p. 1041; 130(a), chaps. 9 and 10; 134(a), chap. 8; 141(b), p. 404; 144(a); 145(d), pp. 11, 21, 38-9, 58, 68, 88, 94, 106; 156(a), p. 155; 157(a), chap. 9; 157(c), pp. 146-7; 157(d), chaps. 12 and 13.

(4) Socio-psychological Causes

(a) Appeal of Labor Agents

See references:

46(g), p. 118; 124(a), pp. 36, 46; 145(d), pp. 12, 27, 58, 62, 86, 119-21; 151(a), p. 292; 157(a), pp. 48, 117; 157(c), p. 120.

(b) Appeals of the Negro Press

See references:

5(a), pp. 314-5; 17(a), pp. 86-92; 23(a), pp. 73-6; 46(g), p. 119; 57(f), p. 323; 71(a); 124(a), pp. 29-30, 34; 145(d), pp. 12, 29-30, 103; 151(a), pp. 292-3; 156(b), pp. 551-3.

(c) Effect of Returned Migrants

See references:

5(a), p. 314; 46(g), p. 117; 124(a), p. 36.

(d) Letters from Migrants

See references:

17(a), p. 86; 57(d), p. 404; 57(f), p. 324; 71(a); 124(a), pp. 34-5; 145(d), pp. 12, 19-20, 29, 58, 66, 100; 151(a), p. 292; 157(a), p. 44; 157(c), p. 14.

(e) Pressure of Public Opinion

See references:

17(a), p. 86; 57(c), p. 272; 57(f), p. 324; 71(a); 124(a), pp. 26, 39-48; 145(d), pp. 76, 87, 101; 157(c), p. 121.

(5) Miscellaneous Causes

See references:

22(a), sec. ii, p. 18; 46(e); 57(f), p. 323; 124(a), p. 44; 145(d), pp. 12, 28.

3. Occupations of Negroes in the North

See references:

1(a), pp. 621-2; 2(a), p. 11; 6(a); 16(a), pp. 139, 155, 162,

168; 17(a), pp. 140, 166, 358-72, 623; 19(a); 22(a), sections 3 and 4; 30(a); 32(a), pp. 21-2, 30-3; 40(a); 44(b), pp. 16, 18, 24-5; 46(a), p. 306; 46(d), pp. 68-9; 46(f), pp. 15, 19, 34; 46(h), pp. 456-7; 46(j), pp. 30-1; 47(b); 48(a); 48(b), p. 917; 48(c); 48(d); 48(e); 57(a); 57(b), pp. 131-4; 57(f), p. 324; 57(g), pp. 299, 301-2; 57(i); 57(j); 57(n), pp. 322-5; 57(r), pp. 139-41; 58(a); 60(a), p. 384; 62(b), p. 971; 62(d), p. 480; 67(a); 70(a), pp. 234-5; 81(a), pp. 41-2; 92(a); 93(a), pp. 175, 181, 185; 96(a); 97(a); 110(a), pp. 14-7, 27-8; 114(a), p. 4; 117(a), p. 534; 118(a); 118(b); 118(c); 119(a), pp. 230, 241-2; 120(a), p. 525; 124(a), pp. 113-5, 122, 129;136(a), pp. 691-2; 140(a); 145(c), pp. 32-51, 58, 89, 95; 145(d), pp. 125-8; 145(e); 145(g); 149(a), pp. 261-2; 151(a), pp. 298-301; 156(a), p. 190; 157(b), pp. 420-1; 157(c), pp. 157-8.

4. Wages and Hours
See references:

2(a); 16(a), pp. 162-3; 17(a), pp. 168, 365, 398-9, 624; 22(a), sec. iii; 32(a), pp. 22-3; 44(b), pp. 28-30; 46(f), pp. 16-7; 46(h), p. 457; 57(g), p. 338; 57(i), p. 19; 57(j), p. 235; 92(a); 93(a), pp. 185, 214; 96(a); 97(a), p. 101; 110(a), p. 21; 124(a), pp. 97, 103, 124, 129; 136(a), p. 692; 145(c), pp. 33, 41-9; 145(d), pp. 22-3; 151(a), pp. 293-4.

5. Race Contacts Involved in the Industrialization of the Negro
(1) Contacts Between White and Colored Workers
See references:

17(a), pp. 343, 393-8; 22(a), sec. iii, p. 29; 32(a), p. 32; 40(a); 44(b), pp. 37-9; 48(e), p. 322; 57(a), pp. 718-9; 57(j); 65(a), p. 89; 92(a); 103(a), p. 627; 110(a), pp. 22-3; 124(a), pp. 101, 116; 129(a), p. 339; 142(a); 145(c); 145(d), p. 126, 135; 157(c), pp. 159-61.

(2) Negroes and Organized Labor
See references:

16(a), pp. 113-4; 17(a), pp. 405-35, 627-9; 20(a); 25(a), pp. 21-2; 32(a), pp. 36-45; 40(a); 44(b), pp. 36-40; 44(c); 44(d); 46(a), p. 303; 46(b), pp. 390-1; 48(b); 48(c); 48(e), pp. 322-3; 57(a), p. 719; 57(b), p. 135; 57(g), p. 339; 57(h); 57(i), pp. 12-9; 57(j), p. 239; 57(n), p. 326; 57(p), p. 558; 57(r), p. 140; 60(a). p. 384; 65(a), pp. 91-3; 96(a); 96(d); 102(a), p. 11; 103(a), p. 627; 110(a), p. 22; 111(a), p. 2; 119(a), pp. 243-4; 124(a), pp. 147-9; 129(a), p. 339; 133(a); 145(c), p. 26; 145(d), p. 135; 151(a), pp. 266-74, 280; 154(a); 156(a), pp.

190-1; **156(b)**. pp. 539-41; **157(a)**, pp. 51, 113-5; **157(b)**, p. 421; **157(c)**, pp. 159-61.

(3) Colored Workers and Employers

See references:

16(a), p. 116; **17(a)**, p. 396; **22(a)**, sec. iii; **32(a)**, p. 32; **44(b)**, pp. 26-7, 38; **57(j)**, p. 236; **57(p)**, p. 558; **157(b)**, p. 420.

6. The Negro's Industrial Achievement

(1) Success of the Negro Worker

See references:

1(a), p. 620; **4(a)**, pp. 8-9, 14-5, 21-5; **5(a)**, p. 317; **6(a)**, pp. 82-6; **16(a)**, p. 109; **17(a)**, pp. 372-8, 400; **22(a)**, sec. iii; **32(a)**, pp. 32-3; **35(a)**, pp. 126-7; **40(a)**; **43(a)**, p. 733; **44(b)**, p. 27; **46(a)**, pp. 300-3; **46(d)**, pp. 69-70; **46(f)**, pp. 17, 19; **46(j)**, pp. 29-31; **56(a)**; **57(d)**, pp. 407-8; **57(g)**, p. 302; **57(i)**, p. 17; **57(j)**, pp. 237-8; **57(n)**, p. 325; **57(r)**, p. 140; **60(a)**, p. 384; **65(a)**, pp. 56-7; **69(a)**, p. 103; **88(b)**, p. 313; **91(a)**, p. 892; **96(a)**; **102(a)**, pp. 9-10; **111(a)**, p. 2; **115(a)**, p. 836; **117(a)**, p. 534; **119(a)**, pp. 241-2; **120(a)**, p. 526; **124(a)**, pp. 125, 130; **127(a)**, pp. 202-5; **129(a)**, pp. 337-9; **145(c)**, pp. 42-4, 93, 117; **145(d)**, pp. 13, 109; **145(g)**; **149(a)**, p. 262; **151(a)**, pp. 296-7, 303; **152(a)**; **154(a)**; **157(a)**, pp. 51, 105-6; **157(b)**, p. 420; **157(c)**, p. 157.

(2) Labor Turnover

See references:

1(a), p. 621; **4(a)**, p. 25; **5(a)**, p. 317; **17(a)**, p. 377; **22(a)**, sec. iii; **32(a)**, pp. 21, 34; **35(a)**, p. 126; **43(a)**, p. 735; **102(a)**, p. 10; **110(a)**, p. 39; **111(a)**; **124(a)**, p. 117; **132(a)**, p. 42; **145(d)**, pp. 122-4, 150; **151(a)**, p. 303; **157(a)**, p. 106.

(3) Other Aspects of Success

See references:

1(a), p. 621; **10(a)**, p. 173; **17(a)**, pp. 372-3; **22(a)**, sec. iii, p. 19; **32(a)**, p. 34; **35(a)**, p. 126; **43(a)**, pp. 733-4; **46(a)**, p. 302; **46(f)**, pp. 18, 34; **46(h)**, p. 460; **68(a)**; **124(a)**, pp. 115, 125, 130; **132(a)**, p. 42; **145(c)**, pp. 12-3, 19-21; **145(d)**, pp. 127, 151-3; **150(d)**, p. 334.

(4) Success of Negro Women

See references:

17(a), pp. 380-5, 625; **129(a)**, p. 338; **145(g)**; **151(a)**, pp. 303

(5) Retention of Negroes in Industry
See references:

17(a), pp. 402-3, 626-7; 18(a); 22(a), sec. iii, pp. 6-7; 48(a); 48(e), p. 325; 57(j); 57(k); 96(a); 104(b), pp. 11-15; 110(a), p. 17; 137(a); 151(a), pp. 304-5.

7. Composition — Age, Sex, and Marital Condition — of Negro Groups
See references:

17(a), p. 93; 22(a), sec. ii, pp. 6-10; 32(a), pp. 18-9; 38(a), pp. 28-9; 44(b), p. 14; 57(a), p. 718; 57(g), p. 300; 63(a), p. 113; 81(a), pp. 35-7; 118(a); 119(a), pp. 51-5, 209-11; 120(a), p. 525; 157(c), pp. 149, 152, 171; 157(d), p. 34.

8. Housing

(1) Segregation
See references:

3(a), p. 532; 14(a), pp. 105, 108, 112-5; 17(a), pp. 106, 114-36, 194-6, 606-12; 22(a), sec. v; 32(a), pp. 7, 16; 44(b), p. 14; 46(f), pp. 9-10; 46(h), p. 460; 53(b); 57(g), pp. 299-300; 57(r), p. 140; 63(a); 65(a), p. 94; 80(a); 81(a), pp. 11-27; 93(a), p. 177; 110(a), p. 31; 119(a), p. 219; 124(a), pp. 104-6; 127(a), pp. 212-5; 151(a), p. 287; 152(b), pp. 125-9; 154(a); 156(a), pp. 179-80; 157(d), pp. 19, 69-73, 75-7.

(2) Deterioration of Property Values
See references

14(a), pp. 113-4; 17(a), pp. 194-215, 608-10; 22(a), sec. v, pp. 25-32; 40(a); 63(a), pp. 65, 78-80; 65(a), p. 95; 81(a), pp. 27-9; 110(a), pp. 39-40; 119(a), p. 219; 154(a); 157(d), pp. 74-5.

(3) Housing Conditions
See references

2(a), pp. 7-9; 3(a), p. 532; 10(a), p. 172; 10(b), p. 347; 14(a), pp. 108-9, 114; 16(a), p. 179; 17(a), pp. 93, 106, 152-94, 209; 22(a), sec. v; 28(a); 29(a), pp. 22-4, 83; 31(a), p. 557; 32(a), pp. 8, 11-18; 40(a); 43(a), pp. 735-6; 44(b), p. 17; 46(d), p. 71; 46(f), p. 21; 46(h), p. 460; 54(a); 57(d), p. 409; 57(f), p. 325; 57(g), p. 301; 57(r), p. 140; 58(a); 62(b), p. 970; 63(a); 65(a), p. 94; 70(b), p. 206; 77(a); 80(a); 81(a), pp. 46-7, 51-63; 90(a), pp. 18-9; 92(a); 93(a), pp. 175, 194-6, 205, 217; 94(b), chap. 6; 100(a); 104(c); 104(d);

105(a), index; 105(b); 109(a), p. 571; 110(a), pp. 31-6; 112(a); 114(a), p. 3; 115(a), p. 836; 118(a); 118(d); 119(a), pp. 219-20; 120(a), p. 526; 121(a), p. 239; 124(a), pp. 97, 104-6, 120-2, 126, 135, 139-41; 127(a), pp. 187, 210-3; 136(a), pp. 691-2; 145(c), pp. 89, 110; 145(d), pp. 23, 145-9; 150(d), p. 334; 154(a); 156(a), pp. 187-8; 157(d), pp. 17, 78-95.

(4) Rent

See references

16(a), pp. 174, 179; 17(a), pp. 93, 162-4, 199; 22(a), sec. v; 32(a), pp. 13, 17; 43(a), p. 735; 46(f), p. 17; 52(a), index; 57(g), pp. 300-1; 57(r), p. 140; 63(a); 81(a), pp. 47-56; 93(a), pp. 194, 217; 100(a), p. 898; 105(a), index; 105(b), p. 47; 110(a), pp. 36-7, 41; 114(a), p. 3; 118(a); 124(a), pp. 105, 140-2; 145(c), p. 89; 145(d), pp. 23, 148-9; 150(d), p. 334; 154(a); 156(a), p. 187; 157(d), chap. 7.

(5) Lodgers

See references

17(a), pp. 155-65; 22(a), sec. v, pp. 5-10; 25(a), p. 37; 57(d), p. 409; 63(a), p. 112; 78(a), p. 178; 81(a), p. 54; 110(a), p. 39; 157(d), pp. 86-8.

(6) Home Ownership

See references

2(a), p. 7; 17(a), pp. 216-20; 22(a), secs. iv and v; 32(a), p. 24; 46(d), p. 71; 63(a), chap. 6; 110(a), pp. 26-7, 38; 151(a), p. 294; 157(d), pp. 106-8, 136-43.

9. Vital Statistics and Health

See references:

2(a), p. 9; 16(a), p. 179; 22(a), sec. vi; 26(a); 26(b); 26(c); 26(d); 26(e); 26(f); 32(a), pp. 54-61; 38(a), pp. 27-8; 44(b), pp. 42-54; 45(a); 46(d), pp. 70-1; 48(e), p. 322; 49(a); 57(a), p. 642; 57(d), pp. 409-10; 57(g), p. 341; 62(b), p. 974; 62(e); 101(a), p. 999; 104(a); 109(a), p. 571; 110(a), pp. 33-4, 44-52; 118(a); 118(b); 119(a), pp. 172-9, 189-91; 121(a); 145(d), pp. 143-5, 153; 146(a); 146(b); 148(a); 150(a); 156(a), p. 189; 157(a), pp. 41, 52-3, 62; 157(c), p. 171; 157(d), pp. 33-6, 90.

10. Social Maladjustment

See references:

1(a), p. 620; 2(a), p. 13; 9(a); 17(a), chap. 7, pp. 327-56, 621; 22(a), secs. ix and xii; 25(a), p. 49; 32(a), pp. 47-54;

33(a); 46(j), pp. 37-8; 55(a); 57(g), p. 341; 61(a); 70(a), p. 235; 72(a); 76(a), p. 416; 92(a); 95(a); 99(a); 110(a), pp. 69-72; 111(a); 114(a), p. 4; 118(a); 118(b); 119(a), pp. 345-9, 355-7, 361-3; 120(a), p. 527; 122(a); 128(a); 139(a); 145(d), pp. 138-43; 154(a); 155(a); 156(a), pp. 188-9; 157(a), pp. 127-8, 131; 157(c), p. 171; 157(d), pp. 227-8.

11. Migration and the Educational Situation
    See references:

2(a), p. 13; 17(a), pp. 93, 238-70, 614-5; 22(a), sec. viii; 25(a), pp. 66-71; 31(a), p. 556; 32(a), pp. 71-2; 41(a); 43(a), p. 731; 44(b). pp. 19-24; 57(g), p. 340; 78(a), p. 178; 81(a), pp. 42-4; 89(c), p. 988; 92(a); 93(a), p. 177; 94(a), p. 690; 108(a); 110(a), pp. 57-61; 111(a), p. 1; 117(a), p. 538; 118(a); 118(b); 120(a), p. 526; 126(a); 145(d), pp. 11-12; 153(a); 157(d), pp. 18, 173-200.

12. Migration and Politics
    See references:

13(a); 13(b); 17(a), p. 3; 22(a), sec. xi, p. 7; 25(a), chap. 6; 32(a), pp. 30-1; 37(a); 59(a), p. 406; 62(b), p. 973; 94(a), p. 690; 110(a), p. 90; 114(a), p. 4; 136(a), p. 692; 145(d), pp. 124-5; 153(a).

13. Migration and Church
    See references:

17(a), pp. 94, 142-6; 22(a), sec. x; 32(a), p. 24; 46(d), p. 72; 46(f); 46(k), pp. 266-7; 57(a), p. 642; 58(a); 63(b), p. 65; 66(a); 75(a), p. 39; 81(a), pp. 45-6; 92(a); 94(a), p. 690; 110(a), p. 62; 118(a); 119(a), pp. 332-3; 124(a), p. 144; 153(a); 157(c), p. 162.

14. Migration and Recreation
    See references:

2(a), p. 11; 17(a), pp. 341, 271-97, 616-9; 22(a), sec. vii; 37(a); 46(f), p. 25; 57(g), p. 301; 58(a); 63(b); 72(a); 92(a); 93(a), p. 217; 110(a), pp. 53-6; 118(b); 145(d), pp. 152-5; 150(c); 150(d), p. 334; 157(d), part 4.

15. Effect of Migration on Race Relations
    See references:

2(a); 10(a), pp. 171-3; 10(b), pp. 347-8; 17(a), chaps. 1, 2 and 6, pp. 244-325, 614-21; 22(a), sec. ii, pp. 19-20; 25(a), pp. 54-65; 29(a); 36(a); 44(b); 46(d), p. 73; 46(i); 53(b);

57(d), p. 406; 57(f), p. 325; 59(a), pp. 406-7; 62(b), pp. 969-70; 63(b); 65(a), p. 89; 70(a); 70(b), pp. 206-7; 81(a), p. 26; 92(a); 93(a), p. 177; 94(a) p. 690; 94(b), chap. 9, pp. 174-83; 107(a), pp. 15-6; 110(a), pp. 53-6; 111(a); 113(a), p. 603; 119(a), pp. 418-9; 120(a), p. 527; 123(a), p. 565; 124(a), pp. 39-45, 100; 127(a), pp. 187, 212-3; 136(a), pp. 691-2; 142(a); 145(c), pp. 26-7, 30; 145(d), pp. 129-35; 150(c); 152(b); 153(a); 156(a), p. 179; 156(b), pp. 515, 532-3, 538; 157(c), pp. 167, 171; 157(d), pp. 17, 68, 77.

16. Migrant and Northern Negroes
   See references:

   22(a), sec. ii, pp. 18-21; 27(a); 46(f), p. 10; 46(h), p. 455; 81(a), p. 10; 93(a), pp. 177, 216; 110(a), pp. 88-91; 113(a), pp. 602-3; 117(a), p. 539; 124(a), pp. 112, 136, 164; 150(d), p. 334; 156(a), pp. 186-7; 157(c), pp. 155-6.

17. Effect of Migration on Activities of Welfare Organizations
   See references:

   10(a), p. 173; 10(b). pp. 348-9; 17(a), pp. 141-51, 192-4; 31(a), p. 557; 32(a), p. 68; 36(a); 46(d), pp. 72-3; 48(e), p. 322; 62(a); 93(a), p. 176; 110(a), pp. 77, 82; 118(b); 124(a), pp. 103-5, 121, 126-9, 137-8; 145(d), pp. 23, 152-5; 150(d), pp. 334-5; 151(a), p. 288; 157(d), chaps. 14 and 16.

INDEX

Abell, John B., 62, 126
Age composition of Negro groups, 135-7, 142, 155, 187-8, 192, 236-7
Alabama, 25, 28-31, 35, 38
Albany, 60-1, 89
American Federation of Labor, 106
American Management Association, 125
American Statistical Association, Journal of, 27
Arkansas, 25, 27-8, 30-1, 35
Armstrong, B. K., 62
Armstrong Association, 227
Atlanta, 34

Baltimore, per cent increase, 34; nature of survey in, 60-1; wages, 98; housing, 160; recreation, 209
Birmingham, 34
Birth rate, see Vital statistics
Boie, Maurine, 63, 185
Boll weevil, 46-8
Bombing, 147-8, 168, 215, 218-9
Boston, 60-2
Brown, Phil H., 35
Buffalo, nature of survey in, 60-2, 66-7; occupations, 77, 82, 89, 93; unions, 107; housing, 154, 160-1, 165; education, 193-4
Burgess, Ernest W., 146, 154

Carpenter, Niles, 62, 82, 93, 107, 160
Causes of migration, before 1915, 9; economic situation in North, 10, 35, 41-4, 48, 71, 112, 135, 231; ease of communication and travel, 36, 56; agricultural situation in the South, 41, 44-8, 231; discrimination against Negroes in the South, 41, 48-52; discussion, 41, 52, 54,

231; letters, 41-2, 53-4; newspapers, 41, 53; desire to join relatives and friends, 41, 55; suggestion and imitation, 41-2; increasing knowledge, 42, 52, 56; wages, 44, 47; disfranchisement, 48-9, 52; mob violence, 49-50, 52; legal injustices, 50, 52; educational situation, 50-2; segregation, 51-2; labor agents, 53; visits of migrants, 53; rumors, 55; miscellaneous, 55; same as those of white and European migrants, 56-7
Center of Negro population, 27-8
Charleston, 34
Chester, Pa., 194
Chicago, per cent of state population in, 32; per cent increase, 34; nature of survey in, 60-2, 66-7; occupations, 73-6, 78-80, 82, 86-7, 89-90; white and colored workers, 108, 219; unemployment, 132-3; industrial success, 115, 126-7; age, sex and marital status, 135; 139-40; housing, 145, 147-9, 151, 154, 159-60, 162, 165, 167-8, 219; vital statistics and health, 172, 175, 177; crime, 183, 190; education, 194, 196-9; churches, 203; recreation, 207; politics, 219; race relations, 213, 215-21; race riot, 215, 218-20; work of welfare agencies, 226-7
Chicago Defender, 53
Chicago Race Commission, 62, 67, 78-9, 82, 87, 89, 97-8, 103-4, 108, 111, 115, 119, 123, 127-8, 133, 148, 151, 154, 159, 165, 167, 183-4, 194, 196-7, 199, 213, 216-7, 220, 237
Churches, 60-1, 65; growth in, 202-3, 206; activities of, 203-6, 208, 226; segregation in, 203; hold on Negroes, 202, 205

265

success in, 117, 121, 126; sex and marital status, 139-41; housing, 145, 154, 157-8, 160, 162, 165; vital statistics and health, 172, 175; crime, 183, 186; education, 196; politics, 202; work of welfare agencies, 227

Pittsburgh Council of Churches, 64

Political situation, in the South, 48-9; in the North, 60-1, 65, 201-2, 219, 233

Prostitution, 90, 185, 187

Race prejudice, 85, 92-3, 104, 108, 111-2, 114, 131, 143, 147, 151-2, 168, 187, 207, 211-5, 217-8, 221-2, 233-4, 238

Race relations, 60-1, 65, 212-23, 233-4, 237; in industry, 60-1, 65, 95-8, 101-5, 214, 216-9, 232; friction in, 60-1, 65, 104, 218-21; discrimination shown in, 60-1, 65, 95-8, 100, 106, 110, 132-3, 193, 209, 211-7, 221-3, 233-4, 237; in housing, 143, 146-9, 152, 168, 214, 216-8; in schools, 192-5, 214, 216-7; in public places, 214, 217; in transportation, 214, 217; in recreation, 209-10, 214-5, 217

Race riots, 104, 215, 218-21

Recreation, 50-1, 65, 188-9, 204, 206-11, 215-7

Reid, Ira de A., 105

Rents, 60-1, 65, 150, 161-7, 169

Retention in northern industry, 94-5, 112, 130-4

Reuter, E. B., 116-7, 160-1, 187, 205, 221

Richmond, 34

Robinson, James H., 62

Rockwood, H. L., 62

Savannah, 34

St. Louis, 34, 66, 140, 172, 175

Scott, Emmett J., 65-6

Segregation, in the South, 51-2; in the North, 85, 101, 103, 106, 143-9, 168-9, 192-6, 200, 203-4, 208-10, 213, 215-7, 225, 232, 234, 237

Selection of employees, 121-3, 125, 127

Sex composition, 135, 140-2, 155, 171, 188, 236-7

Share tenancy, 44-6

South Carolina, 25, 29, 31, 35, 38, 46

South Dakota, 25

Spero, Sterling, 105, 237

Success of Negro workers, 60-1, 65, 114-30, 233, 237; efficiency, 117, 119, 123; reliability, 117-9; regularity and absenteeism, 117-20, 125; labor turnover, 117, 120-5; migrant and northern Negroes, 125-7; work of welfare agencies in connection with, 127-8; of Negro women, 128-9

Surveys of Negro groups, nature of, 12-3, 58-67

Tennessee, 25, 28-9, 31, 35, 38

Texas, 25, 28, 31, 35, 38

Thompson, Anna J., 64

Toledo, 66, 141, 172

Travelers Aid, 227

Unemployment, 132-4

United States Census Bureau, 27, 29, 38, 174

United States Department of Labor, 34-5, 65-6, 83, 99, 122, 127-8, 156, 184

Urban trend, 10, 32-4

Virginia, 25-6, 29-31

Vital statistics, 170-81, 236

Wages, 44, 47, 60-1, 65, 90, 95-100, 123, 125, 164, 167, 233

Washington, Forrester B., 65-6, 210

Washington, D. C., 12, per cent increase in, 34, nature of surveys in 60-1, 64; housing, 144, 147, 162-3, 165-6; recreation, 209, riot in, 215

Waterbury, nature of survey in, 60-1, 64; occupations, 89; age composition, 137; housing, 146, 154; crime, 183

Welfare organizations, activities of, 60-1, 65, 179, 207-8, 226-8

Wesley, Charles H., 83, 124

STUDIES IN THE ECONOMIC DEVELOPMENT
OF INDIA

3

PRICING AND FISCAL POLICIES

Studies in the Economic Development of India

PRICING AND FISCAL POLICIES

A STUDY IN METHOD

EDITED BY

P. N. ROSENSTEIN-RODAN

*Director of The Indian Project
Center for International Studies
Massachusetts Institute of Technology*

THE M.I.T. PRESS

MASSACHUSETTS INSTITUTE OF TECHNOLOGY
CAMBRIDGE   MASSACHUSETTS

PRINTED IN GREAT BRITAIN
in 10 *point Times Roman type*
BY SIMSON SHAND LTD
LONDON, HERTFORD AND HARLOW

CONTENTS

THE ECONOMIC AND SOCIAL OBJECTIVES
OF
INDIA'S FIVE YEAR PLANS[1]

P. N. ROSENSTEIN-RODAN

Development is not only a technical but a social and economic problem. A technical problem considers a multiplicity of means apt to achieve one given end. An economic problem considers a system (multiplicity) of means apt to achieve a system (multiplicity) of ends. Where there is not one but a multiplicity of ends various ends may not be harmonious but may be in substantial or partial conflict with each other. To achieve more of one end may be possible only at the expense of achieving less of another end. An ethical (moral) valuation has to attach different weights of relative importance to various ends. In this way the national community will determine explicitly or implicitly a hierarchy of ends. By contrasting a system of means (given human and natural resources and ways of using them made possible by a given technology) with a system (hierarchy) of ends the society expresses its choice of economic and social policy.

Over the past decade through the Five Year Plans India has formulated her objectives in two main groups: economic ends to secure a rising standard of living for all citizens; and social ends to achieve social justice, i.e. equality of opportunity, and a reduction in inequalities of income, wealth, and economic power—which constitute a 'socialist pattern of society'.

Let us consider the implications, conflicts, and choices involved within each and between these two groups of ends.

ECONOMIC OBJECTIVES

In order to secure a rising standard of living a high rate of growth (5 per cent) has to be achieved and sustained. In order to sustain the

[1] This essay is essentially identical to the Occasional Paper of similar title written by the author for the consideration of the Indian Planning Commission in February 1961.

rate of growth over the future, substantial investments have to be made which limit the achievable improvement in the standard of living in the immediate future. Without providing for future growth a 6 or 7 per cent increase in consumption could be secured for the next five years; providing for some future growth will confine it to 5 per cent; providing for a higher rate of growth in the future would further lower it below 5 per cent. A series of choices between eating ('somewhat' or 'much') less today for the sake of eating ('somewhat' or 'much') more tomorrow has to be made.

In order to achieve self-sustaining growth in fifteen years costly (i.e. greater) import-saving and export-gaining investments have to be made which will further limit the achievable improvement in the standard of living over the next five or ten years to only 4 per cent per annum, i.e. 2 per cent per head.

A higher rate of growth will in the long run lead to more employment. In the short run, however, there is a conflict between 'maximum output' and 'maximum employment'. More labour-intensive but less efficient methods of production can increase employment today at the expense of producing a lower-value output, and notably less surplus which provides investible funds for more output and employment tomorrow. A choice has to be made: more employment in the 1960s may mean less employment than would otherwise have been possible in the 1970s.

A nation's choice of social time preference is a value judgment on how much the present can sacrifice for the future generation. A development conscious community builds for the future—but the present generation has also a right to live.

SOCIAL OBJECTIVES

The conflict between maximizing output or maximizing employment is primarily a social problem. It reveals two out of the three types of income inequalities in India:

1. Inequality of income between the employed and the unemployed.
2. Inequality of income between the bulk of the agricultural (rural) and the bulk of the industrial (urban) population.
3. Inequality of income (and wealth and power) between the 95-97 per cent of the very poor or poor and the 3-5 per cent of the rich or very rich people.

12

While the third type of inequality hits the eye and understandably causes indignant heartbeats, the first two are not so much in the foreground of public conscience although they are quantitatively and qualitatively more important.

Full employment is undoubtedly the first step for providing a minimum of equality of opportunity and for establishing a socialist pattern of society. This is India's fundamental aim. It is hoped to establish it within a generation. Full employment in an under-developed country is a structural problem quite different from that in developed countries. The conflict between raising the standard of living and greater equality in income distribution makes it impossible to establish it overnight. The road to a greater personal (and regional) equality may lead through a short-run greater (personal and regional) inequality in the sense that some areas ('growing points') and people in them increase their income at a higher rate than others. The diffusion of the increase in income which marks the integration of a national economy can come only at a second later stage. These are the social growing pains of an underdeveloped economy. What matters primarily is not to lose sight of the final goal and to see to it that vested interests should neither delay nor prevent its achievement. Some alleviating welfare measures can make the path less painful even though they may well prolong it. Economic development planning can both accelerate growth, i.e. shorten the interval before a satisfactory standard of living for all is reached, and indicate the selection of some welfare measures which do not widen the interval excessively. The economic development operation is unavoidably painful, but progress in economic knowledge in the twentieth century can make it shorter and can provide partial anaesthetics which did not exist in the nineteenth century.

Raising agricultural output to 100 million tons by 1966, providing the social overhead capital in transport and energy, and making industrial investment in both capital and consumer goods are the main ingredients of the planned 5 per cent rate of growth. They will absorb the major part of investible funds, will raise employment, but will be insufficient to lead to full employment by 1966. A special effort in drive and organization as well as a small part of investible funds (say, 10 per cent) should be diverted into rural public works in secondary road building, digging, fencing, bunding, terracing, etc., which contribute to agricultural capital formation without at first producing more agricultural products. Such activities absorb very little capital goods or foreign exchange, but they can usefully employ millions of unemployed or underemployed people in rural India. If five million people were employed for 200 days a year in such '1 rupee a day' rural public works, 100 crores per annum would have to be found and spent—of which one half would be spent by the additionally employed on food and another 25–30 per cent in home produced textiles and household goods—and another 20–25 crores of capital goods may have to be added. Rural technical education in the form of six to ten month courses is a necessary corollary to such activities. There is no doubt that resources for this form of useful employment-creating activities can be found. The real problem here is organization rather than capital. Other forms of public works, welfare activities, and protection to labour-intensive small enterprise form the bulk of 'anaesthetics' where 10 per cent of national investment may create a multiple proportion of additional employment.

EQUALITY OF OPPORTUNITY

In a somewhat longer run education is the main instrument of additional employment. This is so fundamental that it has to be discussed separately as the main avenue to equality of opportunity.

Equality of opportunity rather than equality of income is the basic tenet of a modern society. Incomes in some occupations may well be higher than in others, provided the entry into those occupations is free and equally accessible to everybody. Full employment, i.e. the possibility of earning a living by work, represents a minimum of equality of opportunity. Even for that insufficient minimum, widespread educational and training facilities have to be provided. Some training may enable workers to find jobs quickly and thereby to increase national income. General education will reveal its economic effects—decisive fundamental and not substitutable effects—only after a longer gestation period of ten to twenty years. Input of education today will increase national output the day after tomorrow. General education is in this sense a true social overhead capital with indirect and delayed economic effects. From an inadmissibly narrow economic point of view which discounts future increases in product it might appear that poor countries cannot afford to invest more than a minimum in this field. Free access to education for everybody irrespective of income is, however, the only way to ensure equality of opportunity. A socialist pattern of society must attach a higher value to it—even if it can only be realized in fifteen to twenty years' time—than to increases in material goods above the minimum of subsistence which can be realized much more quickly. A high proportion of total national expenditure must therefore flow into education.

To raise the rate of growth from 3 to $4\frac{1}{2}$ or 5 per cent per annum is a great achievement, which, if sustained, will change the Indian society in one generation. Such a change represents a revolution achieved by evolutionary methods. To raise the rate of growth from 5 to 7 per cent per annum may not be mere difference in degree; it may be a difference in kind passing a 'supersonic barrier' of development, a discontinuous jump requiring a thorough shake-up of society while preserving its fundamental freedoms. Only a tremendous effort vastly increasing the quantity and quality of education could achieve it. It would make the masses of rural India mobile, vibrant and eager. High productivity in agriculture as well as in industry can best be achieved by such an educational revolution. Though it will thoroughly reshape old established attitudes and institutions, although it will disrupt continuity, it need not endanger national cohesion and unity. We cannot foresee the paths of single social and economic molecules—we cannot describe in detail the mechanism of this change, beyond believing that 'where there's a will there's a way'—but the general pattern of change can be visualized.

It is not beyond our range of possibilities to plan for such a change. Increases in expenditure on education beginning from 100 crores in the first year and rising by 100 crores per annum to additional 500 crores in the fifth year of the Plan seem to be in approximate order of magnitude. At least half of this expenditure will be spent on food, of which at first there might be increased imports of surplus products which may be replaced gradually by rising domestic production during the Fourth Plan. The other half of the expenditure must come either from increased savings or from a cut in some other investments.

REDUCTION IN INEQUALITIES OF WEALTH AND POWER

This is the most difficult part of establishing a socialist pattern of society. The conflict between equity and efficiency—i.e. between social justice and the rate of growth—is deeper and more difficult to

15

resolve in an underdeveloped than in a developed country. Concentration in many industrial sectors is the unavoidable corollary of efficient rapid growth. Even in highly developed countries, where entry of new firms and potential competition is possible, monopolistic tendencies are imperfectly controlled by anti-monopoly legislation and less imperfectly by a low-tariff import policy which adds international to the imperfect national competition. In an underdeveloped country lack of capital, management, and technically competent personnel on the one hand and the small size of the market on the other hand limit the entry of new firms. Moreover, shortage of foreign exchange makes it impossible to use imports as a price controlling device. Even at a later stage technological trends do not stop concentration of management at least, if not of ownership. Enlargement and modernization of existing firms are in many cases cheaper than the creation of new units.

Price control may be thought of as an effective device. The experience in many countries is not encouraging, and the handling of price control under foreign exchange scarcity and import licensing imposes an even greater burden on this inadequate tool. The fundamental difficulty lies elsewhere, however. The price-mechanism is an essential tool for efficient allocation of resources and should not be used for controlling either income distribution or concentration of industry. Nor should income distribution and concentration of industry be always correlated. Income distribution can be somewhat corrected by fiscal devices: progressive income, capital gains tax, and differentiation between earned and unearned income and between income gained and income consumed plus estate duties. Compensating measures must be taken so that income-redistribution will not unduly lower the saving potential. Concentration of industry cannot be avoided where there are economies of scale, but it can be controlled by special tax devices (different amortization periods, for instance) beyond the point of diminishing costs and in those industries in which there are no diminishing costs. Public investment in monopolistic sectors of industry may maintain a higher degree of competition. Institutional changes in the capital market, for instance, government holding a proportion of non-voting shares with private management, are worth exploring. All these measures are palliatives, not perfect solutions. Social stratification, a strong independent civil service, universities, and writers with different often 'monastic' value may create a social countervailing force which will limit the concentration of power without restraining technical progress and concentration of industry.

The social sciences do not indicate unequivocal principles of social engineering. We do not know precisely how to avoid the dangers of excessive concentration of economic power without reducing economic efficiency and the rate of growth. A tentative groping for pragmatic solution will throw more light on this intricate set of problems. It will notably probe what slight sacrifice of efficiency for the sake of a notable increase in equity may be worthwhile. New social and economic institutions and forms may emerge in this process. Awareness of the costs and the results will mark the building of a socialistic pattern of the Indian society.

REGIONAL ALLOCATION OF RESOURCES IN INDIA[1]

L. LEFEBER

1. Efficiency of regional resource allocation is crucial for increasing the capacity for investment and economic growth.

2. It is a paradoxical but inevitable fact that in order to accelerate the future development of retarded regions the growth of industrially more advanced areas must be encouraged. If the latter is stifled by insufficient investment the over-all capacity to save will be diminished and the advancement of retarded areas will be delayed even longer.

3. At the same time, retarded areas need not be neglected. On the one hand, a somewhat greater national effort than the current one would provide resources for regional advancement over and above the requirements for maintaining a 5 per cent rate of national growth. On the other hand, rational pricing and transportation policies and certain other methods would efficiently allocate industrial investments in agricultural producing regions.

4. State and local governments must be persuaded that greater concentration of industrial resources in certain limited areas works out to their long-run advantage. However, this can be done only if rational and explicit long-run planning is introduced.

5. In the meantime improvement of pricing policies and consideration of the viability of individual projects in particular areas would result in rapid improvement in the efficiency of allocation.

I. INTRODUCTION

The purpose of economic development is to increase the standard of living of the masses of people in low-income groups. To attain

[1] This essay is essentially identical to the Occasional Paper of similar title written by the author for the consideration of the Indian Planning Commission in February 1961. The ideas expressed here benefited from discussions with Professor Thomas Balogh of Oxford and Professor P. N. Rosenstein-Rodan of MIT. However, the responsibility for the ideas and errors contained here lies entirely with the author.

this goal national income must grow at a faster rate than the increase in population, and the benefits of income growth must be distributed equitably.

Increase in living standards and redistribution can be attained by alternative patterns. Which one to select depends on many not always clearly specified and frequently contradictory social goals.

To specify all social goals in India and to attach relative weights to each might be exceedingly difficult. However, there seems to be clear and overwhelming national consensus about the desirability of ending unemployment 'as soon as possible'. Also, national consensus would support the notion that all unemployed without regard of racial, religious, or regional affiliation have equal rights to the feasible opportunities for future employment. If these two very general principles are accepted, then it follows that those new employment patterns are desirable which minimize the time needed to achieve meaningful full employment for the nation as a whole. Furthermore, equitable distribution of income in the context of India requires first and foremost the creation of regular employment opportunities at a faster rate than the increase in the potential labour force. In other words, when unemployment exists on a broad scale, income redistribution in favour of the unemployed must take precedence over redistribution among those who enjoy a regular income at or above a level which is just sufficient to maintain a minimum socially acceptable standard of living.

In order to provide a sufficient increase in employment opportunities to keep abreast of unemployment in the future, capital formation would have to take place at a rate faster than it did during the Second Plan or foreseen in the Third Plan. Increased capital formation must be matched, however, with corresponding increases in saving.

There are at least two major weapons to be used for achieving suitable increases in savings: fiscal policy and rigorous observation of the rules of efficient resource use. For effectiveness both have to be supported with moral suasion by the highest political authority.

Fiscal policy is needed to ensure that those who enjoy regular incomes, including earners at the minimum acceptable level, should not appropriate further benefits from development as long as large-scale unemployment exists. Hence, in addition to the upper classes, the increasing numbers of employed urban and rural labour must also be reached by taxation.

19

Efficiency in resource use as a method for increasing savings is not traditionally discussed in economic analysis since it is assumed to be assured by the working of competitive markets.[1] This is at best a questionable assumption in developed market economies and certainly untenable in underdeveloped countries where regular competitive market checks may not exist at all.

Inefficiency in resource use implies that one or several outputs could be produced in greater amounts with the same amount of inputs. For any level of effort efficient resource use will increase investment potential in the short run because more projects can be realized with the same amount of resources; increase savings in the intermediate run because returns on investments will be larger; accelerate the rate of growth and employment in the long run because of the above beneficial effects.

In the context of a planned economy conscious policies to maintain efficient resource allocation are crucial. They must be based on pricing policies that properly reflect changes in the demand and supply conditions prevailing in diverse markets; and investment policies must be responsive to the signalling of the price system.[2]

II. REGIONAL ALLOCATION OF RESOURCES

Regional distribution of resources is an important aspect of over-all efficiency in allocation. It determines the rate of growth of each particular region; hence the growth of the entire nation is also determined. The question is: What are the principles on which regional allocation should be based?

It is quite clear that regional distribution of resources cannot be considered entirely as a non-political decision. Here national and regional social goals are in conflict: On the one hand there is the understandable desire of each state to develop its own resources and increase the standard of living of its own population as fast as possible; on the other hand rapid national growth may require the concentration of larger resources in particular areas.

---

[1] Efficiency in this context implies that the production of no output can be increased without sacrificing some other output. Under such conditions scarce productive inputs are fully employed and in the light of technological feasibilities optimally used; i.e. the economy operates on its production possibility surface.

[2] In this respect current price policy in India is entirely deficient; the term is used to denote a type of anti-inflationary policy which is not only inefficient but also may itself be inflationary in the long run.

This unfortunate conflict arises from the very nature of the growth process. Some areas are better endowed with natural resources than others. The exploitation of certain resources has greater urgency than others for phasing development. Investment is lumpy: many projects must be undertaken in large chunks in order to attain a minimum efficient scale in production. Furthermore, there is a powerful motivation to agglomerate industrial investment at selected areas because of external economies consisting of sharing the same social overhead facilities, service industries, skilled labour pools, and expert management. Then again, markets are also unevenly distributed, requiring uneven development in transportation and market-oriented activities. And in addition to all these influences there is a natural tendency for agglomeration because the proportion of resources used in diverse branches of production can be more economically adjusted if larger pools of the different resources are pulled together.

Regions which have existing advantages can grow at a faster rate than others. In the process of growth, employment opportunities increase and a flow of labour from other regions is attracted, which should have beneficial effects both on the industrializing areas and on the more stagnant regions. Furthermore, the rapidly growing areas can yield surpluses for future investment. Such surpluses arise from the profits of the expanding private and state enterprises and from increasing private incomes which in turn yield larger savings and taxes. Initially a good part of these savings must be used to maintain growth in the vigorous centres. But as savings continue to increase and new investment outlets are needed, more and more resources can be channelled to the development of other areas, which in turn will raise the living standard of the local population and create new surpluses and resources for continued development. The latter will manifest itself in the creation of new 'growing points' in other previously stagnant or slowly moving areas. In good time the number of growing areas should increase to a density which is adequate to provide a satisfactory regional balance. It is a paradoxical conclusion that for developing the retarded areas the growth of the more advanced regions must be encouraged. If the latter is stifled because of insufficient investment on an uneconomical scale, surpluses will be insufficient and stagnant regions which are unable to raise their own savings must be doomed to an even longer period of waiting and poverty.

21

The implication is not that some areas should receive all the attention and others none. It is a matter of social decision to what degree the benefits from realized progress should be used to bring immediate relief to those who are not only underprivileged but also tied by immobility to their retarded regions. The question is how to realize such an object in a way which is compatible with the goal of maintaining a high rate of national economic growth and rapid elimination of unemployment.

Barring some special and obvious cases, most industrial investments, if located in retarded areas, would have very low current yields, if any at all, and only questionable higher returns in the distant future. Similarly, many government sponsored rural programmes would be of the low-yield type. It might be argued that either approach to increase 'regional balance', i.e. low-yield type rural programmes or arbitrary location of industrial investment, is more in the nature of a transfer payment to improve income distribution than a contribution to economic development. In effect, it uses resources which otherwise would be available to increase national economic growth. It follows that expenditures budgeted for retarded areas must be such as to minimize per rupee spent their adverse effects on savings and growth.

Resources needed for the creation of 'economic' investments, i.e. industrial and agricultural capacity that directly or indirectly can yield immediate high returns, should be allocated with the strictest regard for economic efficiency. The surpluses from these projects are essential to maintain future investment and growth. Investments undertaken with the purpose of bringing relief to retarded areas should be based on low-cost rural labour and locally available materials. They should be oriented to prepare the ground for national integration and future development. In addition to local irrigation, land reclamation, reforestation, and other projects some of which can have high immediate returns, public works which increase communication and mobility should be emphasized. Among these, road building and rural school construction programmes are of primary importance.

Since low-yield investment in retarded regions competes for resources with investment needed to maintain the rate of economic growth, the amount of effort which can be devoted to regional balance is determined by, first, the minimum level of politically acceptable national growth rate and, second, the over-all savings effort the nation is willing to undertake over and above the one needed to maintain the desired national growth.

According to the Third Plan five per cent compound growth is the goal. However, given the existing level of effort, resources available to attain and maintain this rate even with most efficient utilization seem to be barely sufficient. The implication is that extensive efforts to increase 'regional balance' would interfere with the desired rate of development.

Nevertheless, approaches could be explored for large-scale rural labour mobilization for labour intensive projects of the type discussed above. Even if five million people would benefit on a rupee-a-day basis, the total annual cost over two hundred days a year, including organizational and capital expenditures, should not exceed say 1·5 billion rupees. Whereas this is still a considerable monetary commitment, the real resource equivalent is very low because a very large part of the total expenditure would have to be matched by food grain provisions which in turn could be covered by P.L. 480 supplies.

While it is true that only large-scale rural labour mobilization of the type mentioned above could bring immediate relief to retarded areas, it is also clear that it is necessarily a short-run measure. Long-run relief can come only from the gradual accumulation of viable, economically efficient industrial and agricultural investments. For this reason it is important to note that many projects, if allocated with strict economic rationality, would benefit industrially retarded areas if efficiency in price policy and allocation were given greater consideration. For instance, railway rates for carrying grain discourage milling in the producing areas where it logically should take place since the commodity loses weight and bulk in processing. Furthermore, there are many small-scale industrial projects in either local consumer oriented industries or in agricultural processing which logically belong to the agricultural producing areas. To promote these types of industries the Plan should give greater attention both to their requirements and to improvements in transportation and pricing policy.

Agricultural development encouraged by suitable regional price stabilization based on crop shortage and crop insurance schemes both in grain and in cash-crop farming are also crucial for growth. Farmers must be protected against the short-run vagaries of free markets and the vagaries of nature if they are to adopt costlier but more efficient production methods. Such protection would have

23

immediate beneficial employment effects. The example of the US farming policies shows that industrial investment is not the only way to increase regional betterment of living standards. Encouragement given to agricultural export and to import-substituting output would also be efficient in the Indian context and conducive to wider regional distribution of resources.

Another neglected project is the broadening of the social and regional base of middle and higher education, another area where national and regional interests coincide. In addition to increasing future skill requirements for national development, a broadened educational base would have a most desirable effect on income distribution, and on improving equality of opportunity. Furthermore, the lack of elementary technical skills in the countryside is an obstacle to a meaningful rural labour mobilization.

Unfortunately state governments frequently compete for certain types of industrial investments not on economic grounds but out of political necessity or misguided eagerness. In effect, regional self-sufficiency in fertilizer production or in petroleum refining is almost a status symbol and the sign of an active state government. Rational economic evaluation of regional production patterns and real cost-benefit calculations would demonstrate that many of these projects are wasteful from the point of view of both the nation and the state. The national interest is to make use of the economies of large-scale production, standardization, and other advantages in order to achieve efficient resource utilization for any desired level of output. The states' interest is to obtain the largest return on whatever funds for investment is available to them. Frequently fewer resources than needed for 'conspicuous investments', if skilfully employed, can accomplish more for the welfare of the local population than badly located larger investments. The latter are usually capital intensive and hence do not provide great employment opportunities; since they cannot be competitive, instead of providing surpluses, they must be subsidized.

A nationally integrated economy implies, of course, anything but regional self-sufficiency in major industrial activities; and the less industrialized states must be persuaded that faster industrial growth in some other areas will in turn enhance their own economic development. However, they can be persuaded only if a comprehensive long-run plan is provided for the entire country which develops goals, phasing, and resource development by their geographical and time patterns.

Without such a master plan, the logic of which is open to inspection and can be continuously reworked and improved over time, democratic planning cannot take place. Without it regional governments cannot be expected to sacrifice or to wait patiently for the advancement of their own areas, which, as far as they know, may never come.

At present a long-term plan does not exist. However, even before such a plan is brought into existence there are a number of measures which could immediately improve the efficiency of resource allocation, regionally and otherwise. These consist of the reworking of the price mechanism for planning purposes and the application of basic criteria to project evaluation.

III. CRITERIA FOR EFFICIENT RESOURCE ALLOCATION

Correct allocation of industrial investment involves the application of competitive principles, particularly when government ownership is prevalent. Efficient allocation can take place only if there is a suitable norm to channel resources into activities that will maximize the real value of national income for given supply-and-demand relationships. Such a norm is provided by an efficiently working pricing mechanism.

Since free-market determination of prices may not be desired by India because of the distortions that might be caused by the prevailing income distribution and certain shortcomings of free markets, the price system must be adjusted suitably to reflect desirable conditions of production and marketing either in a real or in a 'shadow' price mechanism. Actually, with markets of diverse characters and income-distribution problems, a combination of the two might be desirable.

In the context of regional allocation of resources the following pricing rules should be followed:[1]

1. Prices of commodities and rates for services should reflect real costs (including real interest and foreign exchange rates) at the place of production and at the place of consumption.

2. Prices of homogeneous goods should be the same at a given location without regard of origin and should differ from location to location by the marginal cost of transportation *if* the commodity is transported and at most by that cost if not transported between two separate locations.

[1] A detailed analysis is contained in my monograph *Allocation in Space*, The North Holland Publishing Company, Amsterdam, 1958.

3. The present discounted value of the investment at the optimal location should be larger than or equal to the present discounted value of the same project computed for any other location (basing the computation on real costs and interest).[1]

The violation of these principles results in wasting resources and in diminishing future savings and growth potential. A few examples will illustrate this.

Example 1: Railway rates of certain commodities are below cost of hauling, and total revenues barely cover total railway expenditures. The rate for coal is illustrative. Since the railways are unable to make adequate profits from the existing rate, they cannot finance badly needed improvements and new railway investment to keep up with demand. New locational decisions by investors (private or public) are made in terms of the money cost of transportation rather than the real costs; hence they have no motivation to seek out the most economical location, and production costs must increase. Other modes of transportation (particularly coastal shipping) cannot move coal at the same monetary rates even though on long-distance movement their real costs are less than those of the railway; hence there cannot be rational distribution of cargo among alternative modes. Furthermore, discriminatory rates in favour of low-value bulk commodities result in larger flows of goods than needed to sustain a given level of national income at a time of a transportation bottleneck.[2] The remedy is to undertake, say, a five-year programme to 'rationalize' the rate system.

Example 2: Pithead prices of approximately equal quality coal from mines in Madhya Pradesh and Bihar-West Bengal are fixed at levels close to each other. Monetary transportation costs from the pitheads to Bombay differ by, say, six rupees (which is less than the real cost difference). The consequence is that either the Bombay buyers pay differential prices for comparable fuel, the most 'influential' ones taking the benefit, or an intermediary such as a dealer or a mining or transportation official reaps the transport difference for his private gain. With rational pricing policies the pithead price of M.P. coal should be higher than the Bihar-West Bengal price by the real transport cost, and this differential should

---

[1] The present discounted value of the project at the optimal location must be, of course, at least as great as its cost.

[2] Arguments which claim that such rates are needed to encourage economic growth and/or to avoid inflation are of doubtful validity. See L. Lefeber and Datta Chaudhuri, *op. cit.*

be maintained as long as both areas are needed to supply the Western Seaboard. Thus the price of coal in Bombay should be FOB West Bengal plus transport cost without regard of origin.[1] The increased revenues of M.P. mines should be used for intensified exploitation of M.P. mines, or, alternatively, for other investments of possibly higher priority. Thus funds from illegitimate private gains would be channelled to saving and investment, and the burden on the railways would decrease. Also, in the long run coal prices would be favourably affected.[2]

Example 3: Here the need to consider the present discounted value of investments in locational decisions will be shown. The present discounted value of a project is the sum total of the yearly net revenues over its lifetime discounted by the market rate of interest in a free enterprise, or by a shadow rate of interest in a controlled economy. In general, for industrial investments with marketable outputs the present discounted value must exceed or be at least equal to its cost if the project is to be undertaken. If this condition cannot be met, the indication is that the investment is not worth undertaking as its output would have to be subsidized.

The discounting must be done with a rate that adequately reflects the market forces that determine investment; in the case of India 10 per cent can be considered as a minimum.[3] The larger the rate, the greater weight will be given by the discounting process to returns

[1] Actually, one should determine prices by simultaneous consideration of the demands for and supplies of coal in all areas. This can be readily done by programming techniques.

[2] Many other examples of detrimental pricing policies can be provided. The 'equalization funds' in steel and fertilizer industries must lead to the over-utilization of the inefficient and the underutilization of the efficient producers. The decision to sell steel at equal prices at any geographical point without regard to transportation cost is reminiscent of the very detrimental 'basing point' system of the American steel industry, which caused irreversible distortions not only in the development of the latter but also in the locational choices of steel using industries. The harmful effects in all these policies can be demonstrated by simply reasoning.

[3] The relationships which lead to the estimation of the real rate of interest cannot be readily discussed in the context of this paper. It is sufficient to point out that the smaller the initial saving effort, the larger the interest rate must be to accumulate a desired feasible level of capital stock. Conversely, given any level of initial savings, the larger capital stock we want to accumulate, the larger the interest rate must be. Either proposition would imply that in a country like India the interest rate should be on the high side. In effect, there is much empirical evidence to support this contention. In addition, my own statistical measurements indicated that the real rate of interest computed after taxes is about 10 per cent for the economy as a whole.

accruing in the near future, and distant ones will barely be registered. This has, of course, important implications for phasing of projects and choice of industrial location. It suggests that industrial projects which bring their fruits only in the distant future are wasteful and hence not to be undertaken. Also, projects which are desirable may have a net discounted surplus value in some locations and may be unprofitable in other locations.

A good example is the Assam refinery project. First, it is well recognized that refineries are best located in the proximity of markets since the transport of diverse outputs is more expensive than that of crude. At this point there is no market which warrants an efficient-scale refinery in Assam. Second, the capacity of the refinery is below optimal whereas the economies of scale in refining are very large. The implication is that the bulk of the output will have to be transported away at excessive transport cost which will further augment the already prohibitive unit cost of production. The output in the market areas will not be competitive with the output of the Bihar refinery or the product imported by way of Calcutta. Hence production will have to be subsidized. The counter argument says that, while it is true that for the time being there is insufficient market in Assam, this capacity will be needed at a later date when development begins. This argument, of course, completely neglects the question of economies of scale. But even more important is the fact that prospects distant in time cannot justify the tying up of capital when alternative investments or choices of location would provide positive immediate returns. Had the present discounted value of the Assam refinery investment been considered relative to its cost, the decision could not have been in favour of constructing it.[1]

IV. CONCLUSION

The process of economic development in its geographical setting requires growth at different rates in different areas. Attempts to

---

[1] Assam provides particularly good opportunities in rational and bold planning. In addition to its under-populated fertile soil it has vast unutilized natural resources. For instance, a large-scale project of land clearing would provide agricultural opportunities for great numbers of landless families. Large-scale paper pulp production and its transportation to other states for processing could be offset by opposite flows of commodities needed in Assam. Such plans would result in efficient production patterns according to comparative advantage and in optimal utilization of transportation facilities. Assam, as other states, must be encouraged to integrate gradually with the national economy rather than to strive toward regional self-sufficiency.

industrialize retarded regions ahead of time and at the cost of slowing down the growth of more vigorous areas must necessarily put off the date of bringing relief to the former. Inefficient regional allocation of investments results in wasting of scarce resources and in unnecessary burdening of the transport system. Losses in the saving and investment potential go hand in hand with higher costs of production. Inefficient plants operating in unsuitable locations require subsidies which are frequently hidden in complex administered pricing formulas. Such pricing policies lead to further wastes along with increases in the price level.

The short-run solution is to apply more vigorous criteria to regional investment choices in accordance with a rationally adjusted pricing mechanism. In the long run, however, the states cannot be expected to co-operate unless the distant benefits of current patience and sacrifice are spelled out in the form of explicit long-term plans. Without such plans the democratic approach to development will have to be replaced by fiat.

3

TAX POLICY AND THE THIRD PLAN

I. M. D. LITTLE

PREFACE

The following essay was finished in June 1959 just before the author left India after a nine-month stay. During this time, there was a division of opinion in official and other circles about the size of the Third Plan. The advocates of a 'large' Third Plan (that is, a plan of about the size envisaged for the Third Plan when the Second Plan was drawn up) settled on the round figure of Rs. 10,000 crores of investment. This essay was written with the intention of showing that such a plan could be financed without inflation, even given the low figure of foreign assistance of Rs. 1,100 crores.

The essay refers to an earlier unpublished essay ('Public Finance and the Third Plan') which estimated that very roughly extra taxes amounting to Rs. 3,000 crores over the five-year period would be required if Rs. 10,000 crores of investment were to be achieved with only Rs. 1,100 crores of net external aid.

Already by the time the present essay was written, it was becoming evident from the work of others that my initial working assumption of only Rs. 1,100 crores of net aid was impossibly low, and that, however great the internal savings or taxation efforts that India made, the investment plan envisaged could not be achieved without much greater foreign help—simply because the required capital goods and raw materials could not be produced in India in that time. This would, of course, reduce the extra taxation required. There was, however, no need for my figure of foreign aid to be realistic provided only that it was not needlessly high. For, the more aid, the more certain it was that a large Plan would not impose an impossible budgetary problem.

The actual Third Plan, published two years later, is for a total investment of Rs. 10,400 crores. But the definition of investment has been changed and prices have risen. Without much research, it is difficult to compare this actual Third Plan with what I had in mind.

30

Probably it is a little smaller in real terms, but nevertheless the large plan advocates have got most of what they wanted. The expected increase in national income is only very slightly less than what I was envisaging.

The actual Third Plan envisages Rs. 2,650 crores of net foreign aid and Rs. 1,710 crores of additional taxation (including additional profits from public enterprise), as compared with my Rs. 1,100 crores and Rs. 3,000 crores respectively. The higher figure for net foreign aid is undoubtedly a far more realistic assessment of what will be needed. But one cannot add together the official figures for foreign aid and additional taxation (Rs. 4,360 crores) and simply compare the result with my corresponding figure (Rs. 4,100 crores). There are many reasons why the comparison would be misleading, such as:

(i) The actual plan is rather differently shaped, and may be smaller than that which I had in mind. Certainly public sector investment is smaller.

(ii) Net foreign aid raises available savings rupee for rupee, which taxation does not.

(iii) The official estimates are after, and mine before, the additional taxation enacted in 1960–61. This would reduce my estimate by roughly Rs. 140 crores.

(iv) The official figures are based on later budgetary information two years more recent than mine. It appears that the revenue has been rather more buoyant than I anticipated.

These factors all suggest that if I were making a new estimate of the extra taxation needed it would be lower than the official one. But I cannot be at all sure of this, since there are many other factors affecting the estimate which I have not re-examined.

If, as I think, one can safely assume that Rs. 1,710 crores extra taxation (Rs. 1,100 crores for the centre, and Rs. 610 for the states) is not too low a figure, then I suggest that the current essay shows that India has not set herself a herculean task. The tax measures of the 1961–62 central budget, designed to give an increase in central revenue of about Rs. 61 crores for that year, should yield about Rs. 350 crores for the full plan period, leaving only another Rs. 750 crores for the centre to raise. No more than similar budgets in each subsequent year are needed to reach the total—and this ignores any measures taken to improve the profitability of public enterprise.

*   *   *

I. INTRODUCTION

In 'Public Finance and the Third Plan'[1] which forms Part I of the present study of Public Finance in India it was suggested that about Rs. 1,000 crores of extra taxation might need to be raised by 1965–66, given Rs. 10,000 crores of investment in the Third Plan. Over the whole five years the figures for extra taxation (always excluding the increasing yield of present taxes) might be about Rs. 3,000 crores, rising from about Rs. 250 crores in 1961–62 to the Rs. 1,000 crores mentioned above in 1965–66.

This figure could be fairly wide of the mark; moreover it depends on the nature as well as the magnitude of the investment, and probably also to some extent on its split between the public and private sectors. If investment is mainly labour intensive, then wage payments will form a high part of the investment expenditure, and consequently there will tend to be a large increase in consumption; if it is more capital intensive, then wage payments are smaller and overheads are higher, and consequently the taxation required to restrain consumption is also less. Turning to the public/private split, it is not of course true that the Government need tax one crore less for every crore of investment which is in the private, rather than the public sector: for taxation is required to balance over-all supply and demand; and investment expenditure, whether public or private, creates demand without any immediate increase of current supply to satisfy it. But if the private sector has a greater load of investment to undertake, it will almost certainly tend to save more itself. Faced with the problem of itself raising more capital for investment, it will tend to distribute less in dividends.

From the above it follows that it is in principle illogical to estimate required taxation in advance of decisions about the shape as well as the size of the investment programme. Also, of course, one does not have to have a plan for taxation years in advance. What then was the sense of making such an estimate, and how is it to be regarded?

The answer is that one needs to have an idea of the magnitude of the task in order to satisfy oneself that it would be a possible achievement. If it is likely to be impossible, then either there must be a smaller plan, or greater reliance must be placed on foreign aid. These things *do* need to be known far in advance.

The figure of Rs. 1,000 crores should consequently be interpreted

[1] This is an unpublished (and outdated) paper. See the author's Preface.

as follows. If one cannot see how this amount could possibly be raised, then a different Third Plan would be necessary: for at least one can say that there is a risk that as much taxation as this might be needed. Indeed Rs. 1,000 crores was not estimated as a maximum. More might be required. But it seems unlikely that significantly more would be necessary; and also, as a last resort, the plan could again be saved by the greater use of foreign aid than planned. Indeed, it is worth noting that the figure of Rs. 1,100 crores of net aid allowed for in Part I may well be an underestimate of the minimum necessary, however great the internal effort made.

Consequently this paper is designed to investigate whether Rs. 1,000 crores of extra taxation by 1965–66 is possible: and also show that it would not represent an undue burden on the Economy.

II. THE SUPPLY AND DEMAND FOR CONSUMPTION GOODS

In 'Public Finance and the Third Plan' it was shown that private consumption could be allowed to increase at 5 per cent per annum provided the national income increased at 6 per cent per annum. This means that, after allowing for a higher level of investment, and for some improvement in the balance of payments, supplies of consumption goods could be planned to increase at 5 per cent per annum. But if there was no extra taxation, the demand for them would probably increase by about 6 per cent per annum. The function of the extra taxation is to hold the rate of increase of demand down to the level of the rate of increase of supplies.

The extra taxation should also be planned so as to preserve a balance of supply and demand for both food and non-food items independently. This is true because there is little substitutability between agricultural and non-agricultural products. One cannot first raise the taxes, and then look to see what effects this would have on the demand for food and non-food, and then divide the available real sources between food and non-food production in such proportions as will give a balance in both markets. This latter procedure is, however, one that can be carried out (within limits) *within* the agricultural sector, and within the industrial sector—because the supply of one crop can fairly readily be expanded at the expense of another, and similarly with many of the consumption goods produced by the industrial and service sectors.

Let us then proceed by first estimating the supply and demand for food on the assumption that total consumption expenditure is restrained to a 5 per cent rate of increase by a system of extra taxes which is *neutral* as between food and non-food, i.e. the extra taxes affect both the total demand for food and non-food only in so far as they reduce expenditure (a general expenditure tax can be taken as the imaginary hypothesis required).

I think that the best estimate that can be made of the demand for food, in the conditions of the previous paragraph, is that it will rise at the rate of $4\frac{1}{2}$ per cent per annum, given that total private expenditure rises at 5 per cent per annum, and the population at 2 per cent per annum. Within the framework of a Rs. 10,000 crore Plan it has been assumed that the net output of agriculture would rise at 5 per cent per annum. Since the use of certain inputs, principally fertilizers and irrigation, will rise much faster it is implied that the gross output of agriculture will rise at $5\frac{1}{2}$ per cent per annum, i.e. 30 per cent in the plan period. This rate of increase of gross output is reconcilable with an increase of domestic demand for food of $4\frac{1}{2}$ per cent. Of the 1 per cent divergence, $\frac{1}{2}$ per cent is accounted by the cessation of grain imports for current consumption. The other $\frac{1}{2}$ per cent could, and should, be taken up by a relatively higher growth of exports, and of the industrial use of agricultural products, and, some of it, by an increase in stocks.

Since, with a tax system that is neutral between industrial and agricultural products, it appears that the supply of, and demand for, agricultural products should grow in balance, it follows that one should actually plan the increases in taxation to be approximately neutral. But here it needs to be said that the output of agriculture is plainly one of the least predictable and plannable magnitudes. If gross agricultural output lags behind, and does not grow at $5-5\frac{1}{2}$ per cent, the result would probably be a rise in food prices and/or higher imports. Higher food prices can restore the balance of supply and demand, provided that wages and industrial prices can be to some extent insulated from the inflationary contagion. If, on the other hand, agricultural output rises faster, then there will be the opposite phenomenon of falling food prices, possibly resulting in great hardship for those farmers who have not shared in the increase in output.

It is important that the tax system should be used to mitigate the unfortunate consequences of an imbalance in the food market. If food prices are tending to rise (because of an inadequate trend of increased production), then the tax system can help in two ways.

34

First, more tax can be extracted from those who tend to demand the most food, and less from those who eat less. This means greater taxation of farmers. In such circumstances, the farmers would be growing richer at a faster rate than others (since the demand is inelastic, the increase in price would more than compensate them for the relatively slow rate of increase of output postulated), and consequently higher taxation of farmers would not only tend to restore the balance of supply and demand, but would also be equitable. Furthermore farmers would strive to produce more if taxed more heavily, provided that the tax was assessed on the land itself rather than on production. Secondly, the tax system should, in these circumstances of an excess demand for food, be made to work in the direction of reducing the prices of industrial products, thus stimulating the demand for them relative to food. Thus everything would point towards taking tax off industry and putting it on agriculture if there were to emerge a chronic tendency for food prices to rise. *Mutatis mutandis*, similar remarks apply if there were a long run tendency for food prices to fall.

But it emerged earlier that, so far as can be guessed, there should be no tendency for food prices to rise or fall if the increase in taxes are 'neutral'—that is if they do not seriously disturb present price relationships (or, more exactly, those prevailing on average in the years 1952–56 when the NSS surveys, on which our food demand estimates are based, were made) or relative incomes. Consequently I shall proceed to suggest increases in taxes which are approximately neutral in this sense, and which should permit both farmers and others to grow richer at about the same rate.

III. THE DIRECT TAXATION OF AGRICULTURE

The Need

All inquiries show that on the average farmers in India pay less tax than the rest of the community. Since they are also poorer, there is nothing unreasonable in this. But averages may be misleading. It is certain that wealthy individuals whose income is derived largely from the land escape much more lightly than those whose income is derived from other sources. There is thus already a strong case for increasing taxation of the wealthiest farmers and rent-receivers. On the other hand, if the policy of land ceilings becomes general, and effective, the above remarks do not apply because a farmer even with 30–50 acres would not earn an income which would pay much taxation if taxed at general income tax rates.

The suggestions which follow are based mainly on the requirement that, both for reasons of equity and food prices, farmers should not on the average grow richer much faster than others. Within the average the poorer farmer *should* be allowed to grow richer faster, while some of the richest might actually be made worse off.

Let us suppose that agricultural income enters the Third Plan at a level of Rs. 6,000 crores[1] and that Rs. 110 crores are paid in taxation, leaving disposable incomes of Rs. 5,890 crores. At the planned rate of increase the Rs. 6,000 crores would grow to about Rs. 7,700 crores in 1965–66, and pay land and agricultural income taxes of about Rs. 123 crores, leaving Rs. 7,577 crores. Now with an anticipated growth in the non-agricultural labour force of just over 3 per cent per annum,[2] the numbers directly dependent on agriculture are likely to grow by about 1½ per cent per annum. If their expenditures are to increase at the average permissible rate of 3 per cent per head, it follows that total agricultural expenditure should grow at 4½ per cent per annum. If their savings rate remains unchanged (and I can think of no good reason why it should not) agricultural disposable incomes should thus be allowed to grow also at 4½ per cent per annum, i.e. from Rs. 5,890 to Rs. 7,320 crores. This implies that Rs. 257 crores of extra tax should be levied. But as against this there is the fact that farmers are poorer than urban dwellers on the average and so a rather lower target might be more equitable.

The Means

There are two methods of taxing agriculture directly (a) Land Revenue, and (b) Agricultural Income Tax. Much greater reliance has, in the past, been placed on the former. Land revenue has, from an economic point of view, great advantages. First, being assessed on the land (or the value of land), it leaves the whole of any extra product obtained by harder or more efficient work in the hands of the producer. Where greater production is so urgently needed, this alone is probably decisive. But, secondly, agricultural production and incomes are hard to assess, and evasion must be easy. A land tax is

---

[1] It may be noted that any given percentage error in the base results only in the same percentage error in the tax calculation—and is not therefore at all critical.

[2] This is quite consistent with a growth in the urban population of 4 per cent per annum.

not nearly so easy to evade. The land is visibly and unalterably *in situ*, and so no parcel of land can escape taxation. It is true that if the land tax is made progressive, falsification of ownership may result in its paying a lower rate than it should. But this is a minor matter compared with the falsification of incomes where non-declaration results not merely in a lower rate of tax, but also and more important, a smaller basis of assessment.

It may be held that land revenue has two major disadvantages. First, it is regressive. Secondly, as a result of not varying with the product, it is harsh. When the crop fails, or prices are very low, there is no reduction in taxation. But these disadvantages can be overcome. First, it can be made progressive. How to do this will be considered below. Secondly, the harshness can be greatly mitigated on the following lines:

(a) By making the tax progressive, the poorest farmers (those in general with the smallest holdings) will either pay no tax anyway or pay tax only at the present very low rates of about Rs. 3 per acre or less.

(b) By a policy of the partial stabilization of agricultural incomes through the operation of buffer stocks in a few of the more important products.

(c) By permitting tax payments to be deferred (but never waived) when it is established that the vagaries of the monsoon have seriously damaged production in particular areas (interest would be charged on the deferment to give an incentive not to seek for it unnecessarily). It is understood that this is already done.

A start can be made to raising land revenue and making it progressive by a system of surcharges based on the amount of land revenue paid at present. But assessments of the value of the land have not been made for many years, so that the relative assessments of holdings must, in many cases, have become unrealistic. With average land revenue at a level of less than Rs. 3 per acre any resultant inequity is unimportant. But if the revenue is to be considerably increased it will become important. While for most of the Third Plan reliance will have to be placed on surcharges, it is suggested that the longer-term aim should be to make land revenue progressive according to the value or 'standard acreage' of the

37

family holdings. It is assumed that such reassessment could be carried through by 1965–66.

Naturally what constitutes a 'family' would require careful definition. The same applies to the 'holding'. I am assuming that all land over which a family has permanent hereditable occupancy rights constitutes the holding. It is realized that there would result from this both a genuine division of holdings with the split-up of erstwhile joint-families (it is presumed that this is not in itself undesirable— and in any case ceiling legislation must have the same effect), and attempts at evasion by bogus transactions. Possibly the law could be changed in such a way that *mala fide* transactions would result in risking the loss of all ownership rights, which should serve to prevent significant evasion.

The assessment would be made on the economic rent. But for the illustration which follows in Table 1, it is made on 'standard acres', evaluated in such a way that the total number of standard acres is equal to the actual total number of acres (having assessed the value of

TABLE 1

Size (Standard Acres)	Marginal Tax per Acre	Average Tax per Acre	Total Tax Payable at Top of Range
0–5	0	0·00	0
5–6	6	1·00	6
6–7	7	1·86	13
7–8	8	2·62	21
8–9	9	3·33	30
9–10	10	4·00	40
10–11	11	4·64	51
11–12	12	5·25	63
12–13	13	5·85	76
13–14	14	6·41	90
14–15	15	7·00	105
15–16	16	7·56	121
16–17	17	8·12	138
17–18	18	8·67	156
18–19	19	9·22	175
19–20	20	9·75	195
20–21	21	10·30	216
21–22	22	10·70	238
22–23	23	11·30	261
23–24	24	11·90	285
24–25	25	12·40	310
25–26	26	12·90	336
26–27	27	13·40	363
27–28	28	14·00	391
28–29	29	14·50	420
30+	30	15·00	450

all holdings, the total value can be divided by the total number of acres to produce the value of a standard acre). Each holding can then be translated into terms of standard acres.

The scale in the Table suggests itself for the following reasons:

(1) The poorest farmers should be relieved of tax. Tax begins only on the sixth acre. It does not reach present levels unless at least seven acres are owned.

(2) The highest marginal rate should be such as to make it very unattractive to hold so much land but which would not be so high as to make it impossible to show a profit even on the last acre. If it were impossible, the taxation would be confiscatory— and holders could rightly complain that the Government was actually forcing them to sell to avoid outright loss. Since such sales would undoubtedly depress land values, they might complain of 'expropriation' without adequate compensation. If, however, the rate of tax was just so high that capital invested in large holdings could earn only very little, then the holdings would be unattractive, but not impossible to work without loss. Bearing in mind that the scale would attain the suggested height only by 1965–66, when production is assumed to be 30 per cent higher, I have taken Rs. 30 per acre as the suggested maximum rate. But this figure is only a suggestion based on inadequate knowledge.

(3) A progressive land tax scale of the above kind would serve most of the purposes of ceilings on land holdings. All, or almost all, holdings of over thirty acres would be reduced in size. If Rs. 30 an acre was insufficient to have this result, the tax scale would be made even heavier at about the 30 acre size. The aim of establishing a virtual ceiling could thus be achieved without the necessity of the State's paying compensation. But the aim of renting the surplus land resulting from 'ceiling' legislation to landless labourers would not be realized. However, as against this argument, State Governments could buy land, for the purpose of giving it to landless labourers, with the compensation money saved. The difference between the methods is not great. In one case the holder is compelled to sell for 'fair compensation'. In the other case he is so taxed that he wants to sell at the going market price. The high taxation of large holdings would tend to depress the market price of land, though this tendency would be offset by Government pur-

chases; whether it would be partly or entirely offset would, of course, be governed by the amounts of land which State Government decided to purchase. Finally it should be noted that, even if ceiling legislation is passed and made effective, a progressive land tax should first be brought into force, because it would help to reduce the amount of compensation which need be paid to large holders.

A moderately good estimate of the yield of such a tax scale can be worked out. This is done in Appendix A. The estimate comes out at Rs. 222 crores, i.e. about Rs. 120 crores extra. This is well short of the figure given above. There is a dilemma here. More is likely to be needed if the landowner is not to get richer faster than the rest of the community. But *less* is needed if he is not to be more heavily taxed than an equally well-off urban dweller who derives his income from other sources. The situation at present is that the landowner with up to about 25 acres pays more direct tax than other persons with equivalent incomes; this being at least partly offset by the fact that he pays less indirect tax. But a landowner with more than about 30 acres pays *less* tax—direct and indirect. On our proposed scale all landowners with more than five acres would pay more direct tax than others with equivalent incomes. On the other hand, while our proposal increases the prevailing inequity of treatment of moderate sized landowners (those with holdings between about eight and about twenty-five acres) as compared with those with incomes from other sources, it greatly reduces the present inequity whereby larger landowners pay the same rate of tax per acre as smaller ones.

In spite of the fact that it is undoubtedly inequitable that holdings of less than five acres should pay any tax at all, it may be felt that it is inexpedient to reduce any taxation even if it is inequitable. Also it may be argued that small burdens which have long been shouldered are not felt. If holdings of less than five acres were not exempted, but continued to pay land tax at approximately present rates, say Rs. 3 an acre, then the suggested scale could be modified as follows:

TABLE 2

Size (Standard Acres)	Marginal Tax per Acre—Rs.	Average Tax per Acre—Rs.	Total Tax Payable—Rs.
0–8	3	3·00	0–24
8–9	6	3·33	30
9–10	10	4·00	40
10–11	11	4·64	51

and so on as in Table 1.

This modification would increase the extra yield from about Rs. 120 crores to about Rs. 150 crores. It is felt that this is probably about the most that can reasonably be raised from taxation of the land. Although considerably less than the figure of Rs. 257 crores mentioned above, it should be noted that the incidence of at least one of the indirect taxes proposed below—that on kerosene will be mainly on the rural community.

IV. DIRECT TAXES ON INDIVIDUALS
(Income Tax, Wealth Tax, Expenditure, Gifts)

Consider first the minor taxes, wealth, expenditure, gifts. It is impossible to believe that extensions of these taxes can make any significant contribution to the restraint of consumption required for the Third Plan. This is because they fall only on the very wealthy. The consumption of the very wealthy is not of quantitative significance. Not only that, but the very wealthy can maintain their consumption for a long time by saving less or by actually reducing their assets. Finally, tax on the very wealthy is already very high (theoretically anyway). This is not, of course, to say that these taxes should not be levied. Far from it, if the relatively poor are to be taxed, then the rich must be taxed heavily. But it is difficult to believe that much good results from taxing them even more heavily. Positive harm could result, where incentives are of some importance. But this scarcely applies to unearned incomes, and the high maximum rates on unearned incomes might come into force at rather lower levels of income than at present.

The expenditure tax is, in principle, an excellent tax. Its present yield is so low that it ought to be abandoned, or improved and extended. There would seem to be a good case for extending its range, and reducing the offsets—and in general for using it as a substitute for the higher income tax rates. But it has received so much consideration that nothing further need be said here, other than that it had probably better be left out of consideration as a significant means of raising resources for the Third Plan.

Let us therefore turn now to the main tax on individuals, the income tax (including 'super tax'). Income tax starts at an income of Rs. 250 a month for those without children, the first block (Rs. 3,000–5,000 per annum) being assessed at 3 per cent. At Rs. 1,000 per month (earned) the average rate is 6·3 per cent (and the marginal

41

rate 11·5 per cent). At Rs. 2,000 it is 14·1 per cent and at Rs. 4,000 31·5 per cent (the respective marginal rates at these levels being 31·5 per cent and 57·8 per cent). The rate then climbs to a top level of 77 per cent on earned income and 84 per cent on unearned (including surcharges).

The rates on high incomes are very high, exceeded only in the UK, where there is no wealth or expenditure tax. In fact, taking these into account, the rates are probably the highest in the world over a level of about Rs. 4,000 a month. Below about this level, where the expenditure tax is not operative, and wealth tax is likely to be significant in only a few cases, the average rates of tax are below UK levels. They are much below those of some other countries, e.g. Germany and Japan.

Two questions can be raised, first whether the lower limit should be reduced, and, secondly, whether the rates below the level of Rs. 4,000 per month should not be increased. The first question cannot be answered without detailed knowledge of the cost of administration involved in collecting small sums from a relatively large number of people. But it is worth noting that the Japanese tax scale begins below Rs. 100 a month for an unmarried person and at Rs. 210 a month for a married person with two children. I shall, however, assume that it is not worth while reducing the lower limit and that extra resources to be collected from those with incomes below Rs. 250 per month is better collected in other ways.

As far as the second question goes, my own feeling is that there is a strong case for raising the rates within the range Rs. 250–4,000 a month. The following arguments are, of course, very much a matter of ethical judgment but possibly no less worth putting forward for that reason.

For the sake of putting the argument, focus attention on a man who earns Rs. 1,000 a month, is married, and has two young children. He pays only Rs. 56 a month in tax (5·6 per cent of his income). In Japan, this is an income of 907,200 Yen per annum, on which tax of 126,800 Yen would be paid. Thus a similarly situated Japanese would pay 14 per cent of his income in tax, against the Indian's 5·6 per cent. At the level of Rs. 2,000 a month the Indian pays 14·1 per cent, the Japanese 24·2 per cent.[1] In the UK, the rate of tax at the

[1] The Japanese rates are those of 1958. I believe that the average rates have been somewhat reduced for 1959 by an increase in personal and dependent's allowances.

level of Rs. 1,000 a month (= £900 per annum) is closely similar to that in India. But here it should be remembered not only that the UK rates were much higher ten years ago but also that the Indian with Rs. 1,000 a month is very rich compared to the poorest people in India. He is *forty* times as rich as the lowest paid worker; while the Englishman with £900 per annum is only *twice* as rich as the lowest paid worker. To an outside observer it appears that the quantitatively significant inequalities are between the middle classes and the manual workers and small farmers, and also between the better paid manual workers with secure jobs, and those without.

Against the thesis that the middle classes are very lightly taxed in India, there is admittedly the argument that in other countries they obtain more free services from the Government. For instance in the UK, the Government pays one-third of the cost of the Health Service (the rest being paid for by employer and employee contributions not included in the figure given for tax paid), and there is also free education up to fifteen years,[1] and numerous grants for further education. But this does not alter the fact that India urgently needs the resources to develop itself, and the fact that the middle classes are lightly taxed, both relative to some other countries, and in relation to their comparative wealth in India.

Table 3 on p. 44 is illustrative of what might be done to raise direct taxation. The example is for a married man with two children. The scales given are not intended as well worked out suggestions; they could very probably be improved. For instance, the maximum rate of 70 per cent might be made to operate at about Rs. 50,000 on unearned incomes. But the scale will suffice to give one an idea of the magnitude of the extra tax which might be raised. It is also worth noting that the very low Indian rates on the first few taxable blocks have been considerably raised. There is no good reason why the initial shock of entering the taxable range should be so slight as in India. In Japan the first block is charged at 10 per cent. In the UK it is 8¾ per cent but has been as high as 12½ per cent without giving rise to any serious difficulties. The raising of the low block rates also means that more is collected from those with over Rs. 40,000 a year without an increase in the marginal rate they pay and therefore without any distinctive effect.

---

[1] In fact, a considerable proportion of the middle classes do not avail themselves of the free education partly for snobbish reasons and partly because it is still inferior to much private education.

TABLE 3

Range Rs. per annum	Present Block Rate—% (excl. surcharge)	Suggested Block Rate—% (excl. surcharge)	Extra tax payable at top of range. Rs. per annum (excl. surcharge)
0–3,600	0	0	0
3,600–5,000	3	10	98
5,000–7,500	6	13	273
7,500–10,000	9	16	448
10,000–12,500	11	20	673
12,500–15,000	14	25	948
15,000–20,000	18	30	1548
20,000–25,000	30	35	1798
25,000–30,000	40	45	2043
30,000–40,000	45	50	2548
40,000–50,000	55	55	2548
50,000–60,000	60	60	2548
60,000–70,000	65	65	2548
70,000–80,000	70	70	2548

A very rough estimate of the number of assessees in each class, plus a planned rate of growth of incomes of 6 per cent per annum, suggests that the yield of such a raising of rates might have been about Rs. 30 crores in 1956–57, and would be about Rs. 50 crores in 1965–66.

With the above rise in rates, the man with an earned income of Rs. 1,000 a month would (or should) pay Rs. 111 a month including surcharge, 11 per cent against the present 5·6 per cent. The man with Rs. 2,000 a month would pay 21·4 per cent against the present 14·1 per cent. The first of these rates would still be low by Japanese standards.

Some further increase in direct taxes on individuals might result from attacking evasion. A popular estimate of evasion is Rs. 200 crores. The grounds for this figure are very shaky and it may well be an overestimate. Nevertheless a figure of Rs. 50 crores extra by 1965–66 is probably not too much to hope for.

Some modest increases from the minor direct taxes operating on the very wealthy could also probably be engineered. But it would appear that it would be very difficult indeed to exceed the figure of an extra Rs. 150 crores from direct taxation of individuals. We may put a rough provisional target at Rs. 100–150 crores.

V. COMPULSORY SAVINGS

Below the income tax level of Rs. 250 a month, it may be cheaper and more feasible to elicit direct contributions to economic development by means of a scheme of compulsory saving than by a reduction of the level at which income tax becomes operative. It may also be regarded as more equitable. It would certainly be far more popular. Many individuals would, paradoxically, choose to be compelled to save.

Compulsory saving already exists in the form of provident funds, affecting over 3 million employees. Net contributions (receipts less benefits paid out) from all provident funds in 1958 were about Rs. 27 crores. It seems probable that a large part of this represents savings which would not otherwise have been made. To the extent also that they are compulsory, such payments are, from a macro-economic point of view, very closely analogous to taxation. Indeed the part paid by the employer is indistinguishable from a tax on the employment of labour. The probability would seem to be that employees will not in general accept any reduction in wage rates as a result of the employer's contribution, and consequently that this part of the contribution increases the cost of labour to the full amount. It is also not impossible that even the employees' contribution increases the cost of labour in some cases. For if such a compulsory deduction is made, people may be willing to work only for higher wage rates. But in general it will be assumed that they will suffer the compulsory deduction without demanding higher wages.

The question arises as to whether this kind of compulsory savings can be greatly extended. It might be extended to all employees whatever, excepting only agricultural labourers who are often paid in kind. But, for the following reasons, I can see grave difficulties in the way of any much wider extension of the present type of industrial employee's provident fund schemes (which apply to factories employing fifty men or more in thirty-eight specified industries):

(1) The employer's contribution is $6\frac{1}{4}$ per cent and there is talk of raising the rate to $8\frac{1}{3}$ per cent. In addition the employer may have to pay contributions to other State schemes for medical benefits. This means that the tax rate on the employment of labour may be over 10 per cent. My feeling is that this is a most undesirable tax in a country in which labour is insufficiently employed. For this reason alone it would be most undesirable to extend the present schemes. They are a way of adding to the privileges of those who are already securely employed and

45

hence relatively well off compared to the great majority of Indians.[1] Any tax on employers should rather be used to increase capital and employ more labour in a more productive manner: also taxes on employers should *not* be assessed on the amount of labour they employ.

(2) The employee's contribution of $6\frac{1}{4}$ per cent seems high if the scheme is to be extended to include many of the lowest paid workers.

(3) The receipt of the employer's contribution by the beneficiary is dependent on long service. Thus the scheme is used to tie the employee to a particular employer (the employer is tied to the employee in other ways). Whatever the merits of this in large-scale industry—and they are surely debatable—it would not be at all appropriate for such employees as domestic servants, casual labour, or those employed in very small establishments.

(4) The contributions are paid to the Employees' Provident Fund organization. There is apparently often some trouble involved in collection of the amounts due. If the organization had to deal with employers who employed only a very few workers—often even only one—the administrative cost would clearly become prohibitively wasteful.

I believe that, if it had not been for the existing provident funds, it would have been best to have only a progressive employee's contribution. The employer's contribution does nothing but harm. Companies can be taxed as heavily as is economically desirable in other ways and the money can be used far better for development than for benefiting those who already have secure jobs. But, in view of the fact that the provident funds already exist, it would evidently be very difficult indeed to have a further compulsory saving scheme for other employees with no employer's contribution. It would also, I imagine, not be feasible to abolish the present system.

In view of the considerations (1) that the employer's contribution

---

[1] I would here like to refer the reader to 'Wage Patterns in Indian Industry', an article by S. D. Mehta, *The Economic Weekly*, March 28, 1959. After pointing to 'the presence of pockets where wages are excessive in relation to per capita income or the quality of industrial skills required, side by side with areas of the wage economy where a man may earn only to starve' he concludes: 'It is a tragedy that so much of our effort as a nation is dedicated to the justification, maintenance, and further extension of the former, and so little of it to the elimination of the latter.'

should at least be kept very low, and (2) that the employee's contribution cannot be made high on low incomes, and (3) that the total contribution cannot easily be made much less than under the present scheme, it becomes to my mind necessary to have a Government contribution in the case of the lowly paid if any scheme of compulsory saving is to be made to apply to very many more workers.

I would suggest tentatively that contributions might be as in Table 4 below:

TABLE 4

Income per Month	Employer's Contribution	Government Contribution	*Percentages of Earnings* Employee's Contribution	Total Contribution
0–75	5	3	4	12
75–125	4	2	6	12
125–250	3	0	9	12

The considerations which suggest the above arrangements are:

(a) The total contribution should be comparable to present provident funds.
(b) The employer's contribution should be kept low.
(c) The employee's contribution should be kept progressive.
(d) The employer's contribution should probably be higher on the lower incomes to help prevent conspiracy between employer and employee to obtain the Government contribution.

In the range up to Rs. 125 a month the employee would do approximately as well as present members of provident funds (provided that contributions are not, as I should hope, raised). He would do worse over Rs. 125. I would suggest that this must be tolerated. Employers would prevent anyone under-declaring his wage or salary, for that would involve them in a contribution, or a larger contribution. But employees with over Rs. 250 might be allowed to come in as if they were self-employed. On the other hand, see last paragraph on p. 48.

The question is sure to be raised whether the Government's contribution does not make the scheme self-defeating from the point of view of raising resources. This is not so. But the objection can be dealt with only after discussing the terms of withdrawal of money deposited, and the conditions of administration.

Every person in employment (other than certain excepted classes, e.g. agricultural labourers), or taking up employment, would obtain a book from the Post Office or other specially established office. The book would contain a description of the owner (probably a photograph would be necessary), his stated age, and space for stamps. The book would be given to the employer. The employer would be obliged to stick in stamps of value equal to his own contribution plus the employee's contribution every month for all employees whom he employed for more than a specified part of the month. He would deduct the employee's contribution from the latter's wages. Once every, say, six months the employee could take the book to the Post Office. For every month in which the employer's and employee's stamps had been correctly inserted, the Post Office would add a stamp for the Government's contribution if the value of the stamps indicated that the earnings fell within the range of the Government's contribution. The Government's stamp could be coloured pink, the employer's blue, the employee's green.

The value of the stamp would automatically appreciate at, say $3\frac{1}{2}$ per cent compound interest. Each stamp could have printed on it (a) its purchase price, and (b) its value after, say, seven and fourteen years.

The employer's and Government contributions would in any case not be cashable for, say, seven years, unless the owner reached a certain age. The employee's could be cashed before seven years— but clearly some inducement *not* to cash, or alternatively some rules preventing encashment, except in an emergency, must be provided. A financial barrier against encashment would be administratively much the simpler. If the employee had to obtain a doctor's certificate of disability the cost of it might in any case be the only barrier. I would therefore suggest that all interest be forfeited and also a tax of, say, 10 per cent be paid if the employee's stamps were cashed before seven years—and, subject to this, there be no bar on encashment.

The scheme could not be extended to the self-employed except on a voluntary basis. But this should probably be done. Of course, the self-employed man would enter the scheme only to get the Government contribution. So he would always buy stamps (employer's and employee's) of a sufficiently low denomination to entitle him to a Government contribution. What is the economics of this? Any self-employed person whatever could apply for a book and proceed to stick in stamps of value Rs. 6·75 a month (9 per cent of Rs. 75 a month), thus obtaining a Government contribution of Rs. 2·25 a month. After seven years he could cash all these stamps and obtain

9×1.0357 Rs.[1] = roughly Rs. $11\frac{1}{2}$. Consequently his own contribution of Rs. $6\frac{3}{4}$ has, as it were, grown to Rs. $11\frac{1}{2}$ in seven years.[2]
This is an effective compound interest rate of about $7\frac{3}{4}$ per cent.
Consequently, anyone would probably prefer to make the first block
of his small savings (or all of them if they were sufficiently small) in
this way rather than by subscribing to the small savings movement.
But, from the point of view of the Government, there is the great
advantage that the savings obtained would have a strong barrier
against withdrawal for seven years. It would seem to be worth paying
what is in effect a higher interest rate both for this reason, and
because the higher interest rate is in any case likely to attract more
savings. Consequently there need be little worry about the self-
employed (even those with salaries of more than Rs. 250 a month)
coming and paying both the employer's and employee's contribution.
On the other hand, if it were thought to be wasteful to give this high
rate of interest on a small part of the savings of the better-off people,
it can easily be made illegal for anyone to buy stamps, or have them
bought on his behalf, if his income exceeded Rs. 250 a month. There
would be little evasion of this, for the penalty would be that the
stamps illegally bought would be forfeited. The man would also know
that his income could be ascertained from the Central Board of
Revenue. In other words, it would be possible to restrict the scheme
to those below the income tax range.

There is no doubt that the scheme would quite often be evaded.
For instance a man might employ a domestic servant on the understanding that there was to be no sticking in of stamps. But it would
be made illegal to employ anyone for, say, more than fifteen days in a
month without buying the stamps. Any employer who did so would
run the risk of the employee making a complaint. There would need
to be a tribunal to investigate such complaints, and occasionally
institute criminal proceedings against employers *pour encourager
les autres*.

Administratively the scheme should be very cheap. There would be
only the cost of making the books and stamps, and issuing and
cashing them, plus the cost of investigating evasion and instituting

---

[1] Interest would be compounded only annually (partly because it saves interest,
and partly for administrative simplicity).

[2] The maximum value of stamps which the man could buy and still qualify
for a Government contribution would be Rs. 12·5 (10 per cent of Rs. 125) per
month. He would then get a Government contribution of Rs. 2·5. This would
result in an effective rate of interest of rather under 7 per cent.

occasional proceedings. It is important to note that the scheme is not an insurance scheme. There would be no insurance fund to administer. It is simply a method of compulsory selling of non-negotiable Government securities of low value (the stamps).

Of course, if both the number of employees and the wage level ever stabilized, the Government would eventually pay out more than it received. But this is true of all forms of borrowing—interest must be paid. The great advantage of the scheme would be that no (or rather very little) interest would be paid on the net borrowing, for say, seven years—a seven years which is probably of crucial importance in India's economic development.

The scheme could take the place of the present provident funds. I think it would be economically advantageous if it did. But this would no doubt be opposed. Let us rather suppose that existing schemes are frozen, and not extended to more industries, or to factories with less than fifty employees. There seem to be no figures as to the number of non-agricultural employees.[1] But it may be reasonable to suppose that by 1965–66 an extra 10 million employees would be in the new scheme (over and above the 3 million odd covered by present schemes). We shall take no credit for the self-employed who enter, because most of what they save would have been saved anyway.

To estimate the yield of the scheme we also have to know what the average earnings, and the distribution of earnings, of all non-agricultural employees (excluding those covered by present schemes) will be in 1965–66. There are no figures on which to base such an estimate. Table 5 embodies a guesstimate which, it is hoped, may be plausible. It gives an average income per employee of Rs. 78 in 1965–66.[2]

Per annum, the employer's contribution per 100 workers is Rs. 4,032 and the employee's contribution is Rs. 5,148. So for ten million workers we may estimate a yield of Rs. 40 crores from the employers and Rs. 52 crores from the employees, making Rs. 92 crores. From

[1] Incidentally the scheme itself would provide valuable evidence of the number of employees and the degree of their employment (by sample checks of books handed in to receive the Government stamp).

[2] The average wage in Census of Manufactures Industries in 1954 was Rs. 96 a month. The average wage outside organized industry was certainly far lower than this. It is to be hoped that the wages of these lower paid workers will increase a little faster than the average. An average level of Rs. 78 outside organized industry may not be too much to hope for by 1965–66 if the national income rises at 6 per cent per annum.

TABLE 5

YIELD PER 100 EMPLOYEES PER MONTH *Rupees*

Income Range	No. of Employees	Average Income	Total Income	Employer's Contribution	Worker's Contribution	Govt. Contribution	Total Contribution
0–75	55	60	3300	165	132	99	396
75–125	40	90	3600	144	216	72	432
125–250	5	80	900	27	81	0	108
	100	78	7800	336	439	171	936

this there needs to be subtracted the cost of the scheme, and the out-payments during the year, which would be negligible, since the scheme would not by then have been operating for seven years. Also, however, one must make allowances for the fact that part of the employee's contributions would have been saved anyway. But this is likely to be small, and it may be balanced by new savings from the self-employed. The employer's contributions are, in effect, a tax all of which may be counted. I would suggest that one can estimate the net contribution of the scheme towards financing the plan as Rs. 75–100 crores in 1965–66, depending very much on how many people could be got into the scheme.

VI. INDIRECT TAXES VERSUS DIRECT COMPANY TAXATION

These taxes are first discussed together because they are similar in one important respect, and because they are to some extent alternatives so far as raising the balance of required taxation.

The important similarity is that they are both paid by enterprises. This is naturally true of company taxation; but the vast majority of indirect taxes are also paid to the Government by enterprises. This is the basic reason why these taxes must bulk very large, for it is easier to collect from enterprises than from individuals. This is especially true where the enterprise is a company. In the case of small non-corporate enterprise the distinction between enterprise and individual begins to vanish.

The important difference lies in the manner in which they may affect the incentive of the business; this stems from the fact that indirect taxes are assessed either on the volume or the value of the gross product while direct taxes are assessed either on the income or the wealth (or, more strictly, the 'net worth') of the enterprise.

Indirect taxes increase the direct or prime cost of manufacture or

51

distribution. By thus raising costs they affect the amount of the product which can be sold, and which the private businessman will plan to sell. They in no way affect the businessman's incentive to produce that amount. Of course, in the short run, a change in indirect taxation may have a very large effect on a company's profits, because it will alter the relation between output and capacity. But in the long run capacity will adjust itself to output. If one compared two countries in equilibrium, equal in all respects except that one had very high indirect taxation and the other not, one would expect the business world to function in much the same manner, and the rate of profit to be much the same.[1] The taxes would all be passed on to the consumer.

If *all* consumption goods could be taxed indirectly, there could not possibly be any arguments as to whether sufficient taxation could be raised. Any required amount could be raised by this means—provided only that it permitted a level of consumption which was politically feasible, and this we have already allowed for. Any difficulty arises only (1) because one cannot in practice tax all consumption goods, and hence the danger arises of an undesirable shift of demand towards the untaxed items, and (2) because it is difficult to make an indirect tax system sufficiently progressive. Just what consumption goods can be taxed will be discussed again in the next section. But first let us turn to a brief preliminary consideration of the direct taxation of enterprises.

Direct corporate taxes are assessed on profits or 'wealth'. But in any case 'wealth' taxes must be paid out of profits. If profits were a functionless residual then the taxes would not be passed on. But in fact profit is far from functionless; it is the driving force of private enterprise, and the magnet for new private capital and enterprise itself. Thus, to the extent that profit is a real cost it is to be expected that taxes on profit will be passed on to the consumer. But some profits arise from monopolistic positions, and taxes on these profits will not be passed on, for they are functionless and more of a residual character. In fact, historical analysis of the period when company taxes in the USA and UK were greatly raised (during the war) suggests, as one would expect, that although they are passed on to a very large extent—nevertheless the rate of profit on capital was probably reduced a little.

[1] There might be certain differences owing to economies of scale; but this does not damage the more fundamental point which is argued in the text.

Provided they are not too high, there is a point to direct taxation of company profits. So long as the desire of private industry to invest and produce is not driven below the level which is desirable, taxation will help to prevent increases of dividends, it will assist controls to keep investment in check, and it will help to prevent wasteful expenditure. In other words it is in principle desirable to raise company taxation to the point where private companies are just willing, but not overwilling, to perform the tasks allotted to them in the Plan. If they are overwilling, greater taxation will absorb profits which have no function in the system, and they will not be passed on. If taxation is too great then either the taxes will be passed on, and/or there will be a danger of private investment becoming too sluggish. However, this latter danger can be, and is, guarded against by generous depreciation and investment allowances.

But if private industry is over-willing to invest there is to some extent an alternative to increasing taxes on profit. One can allot the private sector a larger part of the Plan. Ideology apart, this may have important advantages—(a) it is not necessary to raise so much in tax, for the private sector will then invest its surplus profits to a greater extent, and may actually increase its savings, and (b) the private sector may have some existent organizations which the public sector has to create, and (c) one is more likely to attract private foreign capital. (Private foreign capital can never play a major role in developing India, but there is no point in sneezing at it even if it adds only a little spice to the massive dishes of public borrowing.)

We may now briefly turn to the forms of company taxation and distinguish 'wealth' and profit taxes. The wealth tax has an important advantage. With given capital equipment, it permits any increase in profits resulting from more intensive use of the capital to be retained by the enterprise. It is analogous in this respect to a tax on land. Thus its desirable qualities should be obvious in a country which suffers from capital scarcity. One particular important respect in which wealth tax on companies would help is in promoting double-shift working. Where it is really profitable there is no difficulty with double-shift working in India. The social costs are small (compared with more advanced countries). Thus no one would dream of anything but double-shift or even treble-shift working in very highly capital-intensive industries. There is a great need to shift the line of profitability of double-shift working down the list of industries as arranged on a capital-intensive scale.

Looked at in another way, putting a wealth tax on companies is rather like raising the rate of interest on capital. If there were a general rise in interest rates, this would undoubtedly help to promote a more efficient use of capital. It is really an anomaly that India is a low interest rate country. But Governments are reluctant to raise interest rates (a) because it means increasing expenditure on debt payments, (b) because it tends to enrich rentiers, (c) because the fall in capital values is sometimes financially embarrassing. The wealth tax is an attractive alternative.[1] It performs many of the functions of high interest rates, without any of the above disadvantages (except, possibly, to a small extent (c)). In the long run, i.e. in so far as decisions about increasing the amount of capital used are concerned, there is little distinction to be drawn between taxes on profits and taxes on wealth.

The last Budget took a highly important and advantageous step in the field of company taxation. It cast off the remaining shreds of the British system, and adopted the American so-called double taxation system. But the repeal of the wealth tax on companies seems to have been an unfortunate retreat in the direction of British orthodoxy.[2]

The wealth tax was assessed not on assets (as, in theory, it should be) but on net worth, i.e. paid up capital plus reserves. This gives an important advantage to companies with old equipment (bought at lower prices and largely depreciated). If a heavy wealth tax on companies were to be imposed, some means might have to be found to make the treatment of old and new assets more equitable. This should not be impossible. Another difficulty which lies in the way of a heavy wealth tax is that it is an inescapable 'prior charge'. Thus a wealth tax is *not*, in this respect, equivalent to a raising of interest rates, for interest on equity or preference capital need not be paid if a company is in difficulties. A 2 per cent wealth tax on a company

[1] Another interesting alternative to higher interest rates, which has been suggested, is a tax on bank lending. This is worth exploring as much for its economic effects in promoting economy in the use of capital, as for its value as a source of revenue.

[2] The same might be said of the withdrawal of the discrimination against distributed profits. The excess dividends tax was based on a nominal rate of distribution on capital which might bear no relation to real capital employed. It was thus an inequitable tax which deserved repeal. But the same argument does not apply to a simple discrimination against distribution, whereby corporation tax is assessed at a higher rate on all profits distributed regardless of any relation to capital.

would be as though a 6 per cent debenture equal to one-third of its present capital was imposed on the company. The resulting capital structure would be more top heavy than reasonably prudent financing would suggest. Probably this consideration would limit the height of a wealth tax on companies to one per cent. But this level should be tolerable especially with an exemption period for new companies—this is necessary because new companies cannot employ their capital productivity without some lag.

There are various other aspects of direct company taxation which may need review, especially the accelerated depreciation allowances and the investment or development allowance. It is not obviously correct to give such allowances if there is no sign of private investment being too sluggish. It would thus be anomalous to give these allowances indiscriminately if at the same time private investment was being held back by shortages or by administrative action.

The main aim of the above very brief discussion of direct company taxation has been to explore the extent to which further taxes should be direct company taxes, or indirect taxes. The fact that the basic rate of direct company taxation, 45 per cent, is already high by international standards is bound to influence one, though against this the offsets by way of relief for investment, for new firms, and for small firms, are also exceptional. Furthermore, the extent to which companies should be taxed depends to some extent on the magnitude of the investment they are expected to undertake. I think, therefore, that it is almost impossible to say so far in advance whether there is much room for further corporation taxation; this is going to depend on the willingness to increase its commitments which the private sector in fact exhibits. Merely for the sake of giving an order of magnitude to the amount of taxes which must be raised by the remaining method—indirect taxation—I put a range of Rs. 0–50 crores in 1965–66 (Rs. 50 crores in 1965–66 might correspond to about Rs. 30 crores now). This figure is, of course, additional to the 'natural' increases which will flow from the present tax rates as total profits increase.

VII. INDIRECT TAXES
(INCLUDING PROFITS ON PUBLIC ENTERPRISE)

Let us first recapitulate the previous estimates as in Table 6 on p. 56.

TABLE 6

	Extra Taxes to Yield Stated Number of Rs. crores in 1965–66
Land Revenue	150
Direct Taxes on Individuals	100–150
Compulsory Savings	75–100
Direct Taxation of Companies	0–50
Total	325–450

If the above total is subtracted from the 'target' of Rs. 1,000 crores, we get a residual of Rs. 550–675 crores to be raised by indirect taxes. Let us take about the middle of this range, and so investigate the economic possibility of raising as much as Rs. 600 crores by increased indirect taxation.

The Problem of a Shift to Agricultural Goods

As we have said, this would be no problem if all consumption goods could be taxed. But since they cannot be, the question that needs to be investigated is whether one can try to raise Rs. 600 crores on the 'taxables' without there being a self-defeating induced switch to the consumption of untaxable goods.

A crucial assumption which we shall make is that foodgrains are untaxable. This is not strictly the case, for those foodgrains sold off-farm are taxable. But it is presumed that the political objections to taxing them would be overwhelming even if the tax were partly hidden in the form of profits of state trading. Now if the imposition of Rs. 600 crores of indirect taxation raised the non-agricultural price level significantly, it would tend to cause a switch to untaxed food and so destroy the aim of a more or less neutral tax system, as between food and non-food, from which we started. This is the problem we shall first investigate.

In the above paragraph we spoke only of consumption goods. It is important to realize that, from the point of view of raising resources for investment and current Government expenditure, there is no point whatever in taxing goods which are predominantly investment goods or which are predominantly bought by the Government. There is no harm in transferring money from one pocket to another but no good results either. This does not mean that only final consumption goods should be taxed. It is also perfectly proper to tax raw materials or intermediate goods where these go primarily into making consumption goods. For instance, it is reasonable from this point of view to tax electricity (or have larger profits in public electricity undertakings). Although the amount of electricity used directly by households is a small part of the total output, the total proportion of electricity used directly and indirectly (through buying consumption goods which take electricity to make) must be quite large. Similar remarks apply to coal. A counter example is steel. In India only a very small proportion of steel enters directly or indirectly into final consumption.

We require to make, then, an estimate of the average rate of indirect taxation on the non-agricultural consumption-good sector of the economy, and to see what this average rate would have to be in 1965–66 if an extra Rs. 600 crores of taxation is to be collected. The 'non-agricultural' sector is here taken to include all processed food. Thus sugar cane is the output of the agricultural sector, but sugar that of the non-agricultural sector; tobacco leaf that of the agricultural sector, but cigarettes of the non-agricultural sector and so on. With relatively trifling exceptions all indirect taxes are paid by the non-agricultural sector (though this does not mean that the incidence is necessarily upon the non-agricultural sector).

A study of the pattern of consumption for 1952 suggests that about 52 per cent of consumption at market price is devoted to non-processed agricultural outputs (cereals, pulses, milk, vegetables, fruit, meat, eggs, and fish).[1] At factor cost this is equivalent to about 54 per cent. In 1957–58 total consumption was probably of the order of Rs. 10,000 crores. So consumption of non-agricultural products and services (in the sense of the previous paragraph) may have been around Rs. 4,600 crores (factor cost).[2] Indirect taxation in that year was Rs. 676 crores (excluding taxes on exports). Of this total we roughly estimate that Rs. 550 crores fell on the non-agricultural, non-investment, non-Government sector. Thus the average indirect tax rate on this sector was about 12 per cent. In 1965–66 total consumption should have grown to Rs. 13,250 crores (see 'Public Finance and the Third Plan'). Consumption of non-agricultural products may then be of the order of Rs. 6,250 crores. An independent calculation of the size of present indirect taxation at that date (taken

[1] NSS No. 13 Consumer Expenditure, Vol. 1, Table 2.3, p. 7.

[2] This is probably a minimum estimate, since it is known that NSS estimates of food consumption are higher than are consistent with National Income figures; also it is possible that the proportion of food in total consumption may have fallen a little.

from 'Public Finance and the Third Plan') and its distribution, suggests that the rate of indirect taxation on this sector will remain at approximately 12 per cent, i.e. indirect taxation falling on this sector will have grown to about Rs. 725 crores. If Rs. 600 crores extra is to be raised, the average rate of taxation of the non-agricultural sector will have to rise from about 12 per cent to about 21 per cent.

Can the above increase in indirect taxation be accommodated without raising the price level? I believe the answer is 'Yes'. But first let us see what price rise would be implied if there were no other changes in costs, and if the tax were wholly passed on. Taking factor costs throughout as 100, we see that the final price would rise from 112 to 121 between now and 1965–66—i.e. the price level of the non-agricultural sector would rise by $1\frac{1}{2}$ per cent per annum. Even if this happened, it can reasonably be concluded that the extra taxation would not cause a significant shift of demand to agricultural products.

But there is no need for the above result. There are three other factors affecting the price level, (a) higher wages, (b) increased efficiency, and (c) a possible squeeze in profit margins. The wage factor will, of course, tend to make for higher prices. We must here remember that there is room for people to get better off at 3 per cent per annum per capita. Does this not mean that wage rates must rise? Yes, but it is important to note that only a part of the increased per capita consumption of the non-agricultural workers ought to come from increased wage rates. Much of it ought to come from fuller employment, and upgrading—that is from the movement of workers to better paid jobs as the number of these increases, and from the normal operation of piece rates or other bonus systems which to some extent tie earnings to output. At best, there will be very little room for increased wage rates.

Turning to increased efficiency, there are a number of factors to be considered. First, we may note that the implied growth in the over-all labour productivity of the non-agricultural sector during the Third Plan period has been, in effect, assumed to be almost 4 per cent per annum. That is, non-agricultural output is assumed to grow at almost 7 per cent per annum, and the non-agricultural labour force at 3 per cent per annum. This does not mean that the total of wages and indirect taxes per unit of output can grow so fast, i.e. at 4 per cent, because the increased productivity will occur partly as a result of more capital per head—and capital also demands its 'reward'.

What unambiguously permits higher taxes and wage payments to be absorbed without affecting final prices is greater efficiency in the sense of more output for given quantities of *both* labour and capital, or, in general, anything which reduces cost per unit of output.

The main factors which will lead to greater efficiency in the above sense are:

(a) the reinvestment of depreciation provisions in more modern equipment.
(b) the extension of capacity with equipment which is better than the already existing average.
(c) the production of import substitutes at lower cost than the imports.
(d) the fuller utilization of existing capacity in the consumption goods industries.

The main factor on the other side is the production of import substitutes at *higher* cost than the imports.

Before leaving the problem of the impact of higher indirect taxes on non-agricultural prices, one may ask what would be implied if the price level *were* forced up. Since the over-all figures show that consumption per head *can* increase at 3 per cent per annum (and disposable incomes at about the same, or a slightly higher rate), it would show that either profit receivers or wage earners or both were struggling to obtain more. In the process industrial prices would rise. But with reasonable restraint it would appear that there need be no rise in the price level, always provided output rises as rapidly as has been postulated.

The Problem of a Shift to Non-Taxables within the Non-Agricultural Sector

Having said something about the problem of the non-agricultural sector versus the agricultural, we should now consider the fact that by no means everything is taxable in the non-agricultural sector. Excluding most services as non-taxable it would appear that about 65 per cent of the non-agricultural sector output consists of goods which are in principle taxable (that is, about one-third of total consumption consists of taxables). So the average rate of indirect tax on 'taxables' must rise from about 18 per cent at present to about 31 per cent.

Although there are many incomparabilities it may at this point be worth looking at the corresponding rates of tax in the UK. For this purpose I have excluded food as roughly corresponding to the agricultural sector, and also services other than travel and entertainment, this latter adjustment broadly excluding the non-taxables in the non-agricultural sector. The result is presented in Table 7 below:

TABLE 7

£ Million-Current Prices

Year	Consumers' Factor Cost Expenditure excluding Food and Services other than Travel and Entertainment	Indirect Taxes on the same items excluding rates on property	Column (3) as a percentage of Column (2)
(1)	(2)	(3)	(4)
1938	2083	425	20·2
1948	3681	1591	43·2
1949	3909	1549	39·6
1950	4080	1606	39·4
1951	4370	1707	39·0
1952	4572	1691	37·0
1953	4856	1730	35·6
1954	5222	1797	34·4
1955	5575	1932	33·6
1956	5805	2051	35·2
1957	6197	2099	34·0

The corresponding percentage for India is, as we have seen above, about 18 per cent. Rs. 600 crores extra by 1965–66 implies a rise in the percentage to about 31 per cent, roughly comparable with the UK now. But on total consumption the average rate would then be 10 per cent, against 21 per cent in the UK—the difference, of course, resulting from the fact that the proportion of non-taxable food expenditure to total expenditure is far higher in India.

In spite of the non-comparabilities, these UK figures, which have been achieved without any serious, indeed noticeable, diversion to non-taxables, serve to show that the problem of raising enough by way of indirect taxes in India is an administrative and not an economic problem. To put the point in another way, provided that the taxation is widely spread over all, or almost all, goods which are administratively taxable, it seems very unlikely that the elasticity of substitution between taxables and non-taxables would be so high as to make it impossible to have rates of tax averaging about 30 per cent over the whole taxable non-agricultural field. In this connection it should be noted that all final consumption goods, except most indigenous food, and coal, electricity, and books, are taxed in the UK.

The rates, however, vary widely as Table 8 giving 1957–58 tax rates shows:

TABLE 8

1957 UK INDIRECT TAX COLLECTION AS PERCENTAGE
OF FACTOR COST CONSUMPTION

Tobacco	364%
Alcohol	85%
Pharmaceuticals, Cosmetics, Toilet Articles	36%
Entertainment	24%
Durables	23%
Travel (including motoring)	23%
Household Goods	15%
Clothing	5%

It is impossible to give any similar table for India because of the absence of reliable, independent, and recent consumption estimates,[1] but there is little doubt that the effective rate of tax collection is far lower on most categories, cloth being the main exception.

It seems clear that the primary difficulty, perhaps indeed the only difficulty, in the way of achieving a sufficient level of indirect taxation in India, is the fact that in the case of many goods there is a very large number of very small producers and distributors. In order to be able to include sufficient of the products of small-scale industry within the net it might be necessary to prohibit the sale of some products except via recognized and taxable channels—e.g. licensed wholesalers and retailers who must pay a purchase tax. State trading is a particular example of this. At the same time, the danger of high levels of taxation diverting production from organized and taxable industry to small-scale enterprise which, whether legally or illegally, may pay no tax, can probably be exaggerated, for in many cases the superior and increasing efficiency of organized industry will enable them to swallow the tax and still produce more cheaply.

For various reasons I shall make no attempt to produce a precise programme of indirect taxation to yield Rs. 600 crores in 1965–66. The main reasons are:

(a) the problem is largely administrative, demanding greater knowledge of the conditions of production and distribution channels than I possess.

(b) it is, in any case, difficult to know in advance the problems which will arise. Seven more years will elapse before taxation

[1] The latest NSS figures are for 1952. Also the consumption categories do not generally overlap the tax categories; where they do, e.g. alcohol and tobacco, consumption is likely to be more or less understated.

of this order of magnitude is needed. During this time more knowledge will be acquired. In particular it must be emphasized that taxation should never, if possible, be used in such a way as to create excess capacity. Thus it is doubtful whether any more tax on cotton or cotton textiles will be desirable for several years, but it is almost impossible to know at present how much extra taxation will be compatible with full capacity working of the industry by 1965–66; though if any, it should be noted that extra taxation on other things will tend to help the demand for cotton goods.

But in many important cases there is no problem of the under-utilization of present capacity or of capacity which is in the course of being created. In some cases also there is not likely to be any serious administrative problem. A few of these cases are examined below.

The products to which I have directed most attention are those of the oil industry. This was because these products are, for good reasons, a favourite target of Finance Ministers. But heavy taxation of them is apt to create serious and costly distortions of supply and demand for the particular products. This whole problem is examined in Appendix B where suggestions for increased taxation are made. Depending on the attitude taken towards the taxation of kerosene the estimated extra yield works out at Rs. 100–150 crores in 1965–66.

There also appears to be a strong case for greater profits from electricity supply or, alternatively, for further taxation of electricity. The gross surplus of the government-owned public electricity supply undertakings is estimated in 'Public Finance and the Third Plan', Appendix G, at Rs. 2·5 crores per billion kWh, i.e. at 2·5 n.p. per unit. Approximately the same rate of gross surplus applied to the whole of the public electricity supply. New capital invested (book value) per kW of installed capacity was Rs. 1,192. One kW of installed capacity at the prevailing load factors would have produced about 3,350 kWh per annum, giving a gross surplus of 83·75 rupees. This is a gross yield of only 7 per cent per annum, to cover interest and depreciation. Having regard for the fact that the capital cost per kW is now much higher (at least Rs. 1,500 per kW) and for the fact that some surplus over and above normal provision for interest and depreciation should be realized, I would suggest that a gross surplus of 4–4½ n.p. per kWh generated should be aimed at, i.e. an extra 1½–2 n.p. per unit. If capacity costs Rs. 1,500 (for generation and distribution), and the load factor improves to 45 per cent, this would give a gross yield of $10\frac{1}{2}$–12 per cent on what is probably a low estimate of replacement cost. This would be a more reasonable figure. In 1965–66 generation of electricity may be expected to reach 45 billion kWh, so that $1\frac{1}{2}$–2 n.p. extra per unit generated would yield extra resources of Rs. $67\frac{1}{2}$–90 crores. But from this should be subtracted about Rs. 20 crores on account of the yield of present sales taxes in 1965–66, which have not been included in the above discussion. The upshot is that it would be reasonable to expect about Rs. 50–70 crores extra from electricity generation in 1965–66.

From the figures given in 'Public Finance and the Third Plan', Appendix F, it also appears that gross profits of the nationalized coal industry are extremely low. I do not know whether private coal supply also makes so low a return. But in any case any more favourably placed mines should be expected to earn a rent; and the capital sunk in marginal mines should earn at least a normal return. It appears that the gross return is only about Rs. 1 a ton, and that the required investment per ton is of the order of Rs. 50. An extra Rs. 5 a ton would, if these figures are approximately correct, do no more than establish reasonable profitability. It is accordingly suggested that at least Rs. 5 a ton extra should be realized (whether by larger profits, or via an excise tax). The yield of this in 1965–66 would be about Rs. 50 crores. But this could well be regarded as a minimum. Rs. 10 a ton would be by no means excessive, for the price of Indian coal is less than half of that in the other main producing countries. I would therefore put the extra surplus to be realized from coal at Rs. 50–100 crores by 1965–66.

To sum up, the fuel and energy field could reasonably be expected to yield an extra Rs. 200–320 crores by 1965–66—between one-third and one-half of the extra indirect taxation which may be required.

It should be emphasized that the rates of tax (or profit) proposed are by no means exceptional. The oil taxation rates proposed would still be lower than corresponding rates of tax in several European countries. The extra surplus suggested for electricity would probably not bring the total realized surplus on capital to normal private commercial levels. Finally, the surplus proposed for coal would probably not bring its price to more than the level of long-run marginal cost in India: and it should be axiomatic that at least this should be realized; finally, the price of coal would still be far below the cost of obtaining equivalent energy from abroad.

There is often strong opposition to taxing or in any way raising the price of basic industrial inputs. It is represented that because energy enters into the cost of so many things it has a peculiarly virulent effect on final prices. This is a myth. Even if any resultant increase in cost is fully passed on, the effect on the price of the final output is no more than the tax raised. In practice normal increases in productivity should permit such increased costs to be absorbed and they may even induce economies in the use of energy which partly offset the increases in input prices.

Finally, we may briefly consider some other possibilities without, however, drawing up any quantitative programme.

(1) Transport is a promising field as demand is likely to continue to press heavily on resources available. The extra taxation of diesel oil proposed will of course raise the cost of road transport. But consideration should also be given to a tax on diesel engines which, taken together with the extra tax on diesel oil, would suffice to bring the petrol engine back into favour at least for some transport purposes. Further taxation of tyres and private automobiles also can be considered. Finally these extra taxes on road transport should permit increased profits in, or taxation of, railway transport, especially passenger transport which is still extremely cheap. Furthermore, very similar remarks apply to the railways as to electricity and coal so far as the rate of return on capital goes. At present the gross rate of return on capital at charge is only about 7 per cent. The estimated future gross surpluses of the railways, as given in 'Public Finance and the Third Plan', imply a fall in the rate of return, possibly to about $5\frac{1}{2}$ per cent in 1965–66—assuming that capital at charge will by then have risen to Rs. 3,000 crores. This in turn implies a very low gross yield indeed on the new capital invested, probably about $3\frac{1}{2}$ per cent. It is clear that much larger surpluses than those predicted at present freight rates, should be aimed at. If a gross return of 10 per cent were aimed at, and this is still a very modest rate, about Rs. 135 crores extra surplus would result. The extra proposed taxation of diesel oil, tyres, etc., would probably increase the costs of road transport by enough to make railway prices still competitive; but if there were any danger of undue transfer of passengers and freight to the roads, so as to threaten full

capacity operation of the railways, still further taxation of road transport could be effected (this, of course, all needs more detailed consideration than I have had time for).

(2) Tariff rates on consumption goods, and on intermediate goods which require little further processing before consumption, could be raised. The aim should be to eliminate any windfall profits consequent on obtaining licences for such goods. At the same time excise taxes can be levied on (or raised where they already exist) home produced substitutes.

(3) Tobacco duties could be raised considerably (smoking in India seems very cheap to an Englishman).

(4) Much alcohol is untaxed which would pay tax if prohibition were abandoned.

(5) Many consumption goods appear to be untaxed or only taxed at very low rates—motor-cycles, bicycles, razor blades, fans, air conditioners, footwear, etc.

(6) But, of course, apart from food, textiles form by far the largest item of consumption. Here extra taxation depends on increased demand taking up the present excess capacity in the industry. But, if, as appears to be the case, more capacity will be required by 1965–66, then there should also by then be room for further taxation of textile products especially in view of the fact that there will be considerably greater taxation of other goods.

(7) Some processed food items, such as sugar, spices, oils, tea, and coffee, could be more highly taxed. It is probable that part of the incidence of such taxes will fall on the larger farmers who can spare land for cash crops, and thus to some extent these taxes can be regarded as a supplement to progressive land taxation.

There are, of course, still other possibilities besides those considered. The aim has been merely to show that one can fairly easily suggest indirect taxes and public surpluses, which would not be administratively difficult or costly and which would go a long way towards the suggested target of Rs. 600 crores by 1965–66, without proposing rates of tax which are very high by the standards of some other countries, and without proposing more than quite normal rates of return on capital.

Conclusion

(1) The aim of the paper has been to investigate whether it seems

feasible to collect enough taxes to prevent consumption rising faster than 5 per cent per annum, given a 6 per cent per annum increase in income and a 2 per cent per annum increase in population.

(2) In a more industrialized and developed country there would be little or no difficulty about such a programme. But there is greater difficulty in India partly because such a high proportion of production is from small holdings and small enterprises and partly because so small a proportion of the population can easily be brought within the direct tax net.

(3) Nevertheless it would appear that something at least very near to what might be necessary to achieve Rs. 10,000 crores of investment (with only Rs. 1,000 crores of net aid from abroad) is feasible without resorting to exceptional methods. But it would probably mean that nearly every opportunity of taxation and public profit which is economically and administratively sound would need to be exploited to the full. Resourceful and brave Finance Minister will be a *sine qua non*.

(4) The rough suggested split up of the extra taxation for 1965–66 is as follows:

	Rs. Crores
Land Revenue	150
Direct Personal Taxation	100–150
Compulsory Savings	75–100
Company Taxation	0–50
Indirect Taxes (and profits of public enterprise)	550–675
	875–1125

(5) So far as can be judged now, these taxes should not be inconsistent with stable final prices on average in both the agricultural and non-agricultural sectors, though naturally some of the products and services on which there is a large increase in taxation must rise in price.

APPENDIX A

THE YIELD OF A PROGRESSIVE LAND-OWNERSHIP TAX

(1) The distribution of holdings between five and thirty acres is assumed to be that given in the NSS 'First Report on Land Holdings, Rural Sector'. (Table 1.0, page 47.) The distribution of standard

acres is also assumed to be the same as that of actual acres; it is not known whether this introduces any systematic bias.

(2) The distribution mentioned is given only in blocks of 5–7½, 7½–10, 10–15 acres, etc. It was necessary to interpolate the number of holdings of each size by acres, i.e. to estimate the number of holdings in the range 5–6, 6–7, acres etc., in such a way that the total number of acres owned in each five acre block was the same (or very nearly the same) as that given in the Table referred to. The resultant distribution is given below in Table 9 together with the tax yield:[1]

TABLE 9

Size	No. of Holdings (1,000)	Tax per Holding (Rs.)	Total Tax (Rs. Crores)	Acreage ('000)
0–5	48,873	0	0·00	51,956
5–6	2,600	6	1·56	14,300
6–7	2,000	13	2·60	13,000
7–8	1,600	21	3·36	12,000
8–9	1,253	30	3·76	10,700
9–10	1,000	40	4·00	9,500
10–11	920	51	4·70	9,660
11–12	780	63	4·91	8,970
12–13	639	76	4·86	8,000
13–14	560	90	5·04	7,560
14–15	460	105	4·83	6,670
15–16	420	121	5·08	6,510
16–17	366	138	4·64	6,100
17–18	340	156	5·30	5,950
18–19	315	175	5·51	5,830
19–20	300	195	5·85	5,850
20–21	237	216	5·12	4,860
21–22	210	238	4·96	4,520
22–23	185	261	4·83	4,160
23–24	165	285	4·70	3,890
24–25	145	310	4·49	3,560
25–26	143	336	4·81	3,650
26–27	140	363	5·08	3,710
27–28	140	391	5·46	3,860
28–29	140	420	5·87	3,990
29–30	140	450	6·30	4,130
	64,074		117·62	222,886

(3) It will be seen that the distribution accounts for 64,074,000 holdings and about 223 million acres out of the NSS total of

[1] For simplicity of calculation it is assumed that fractions of an acre count as an acre. If this were regarded as unfair a very small increase in the rates would recover the revenue thereby lost.

65,659,000 holdings and about 310 million acres. The remaining 1,585,000 holdings totalling about 87 million acres are greater than thirty acres. We assume that all these latter holdings will be split up and that none will exist over thirty acres. But in addition we assume that the land tax will apply to 420 million acres in all as compared with the NSS total of 310 million acres. Consequently we have 197 million acres unaccounted for. We assume that these 197 million acres either are in, or will settle down into, the same pattern as that of Table A. Consequently we simply multiply the Rs. 117·62 crores of tax shown in Table A by 420/223 = 1·885. This gives a final estimate of Rs. 222 crores.

APPENDIX B

A NOTE ON OIL TAXATION IN INDIA

A. *Oil Taxation and the Relative Supply of and Demand for Petrol, Diesel Oil and Kerosene*

Where products are in joint supply, a free market mechanism will adjust relative demands to relative supplies. In extreme cases one of the joint products may become free. For instance, coke was given away in parts of England in the nineteenth century.

Heavy specific taxation of one of the products prevents this adjustment, and may result in part of the product running to waste. This is particularly likely to happen when the products can be easily substituted for each other.

In many countries of the world heavy taxation of motor-spirit illustrates the above principle and has resulted in a switch to diesel oil. Indeed, the present author has already had occasion to write something rather similar to what follows in the UK, in Italy, and generally for the OEEC countries.

The main oil products which are substitutes for each other are petrol, high-speed diesel oil, and kerosene. Take the first pair first. On the average in India petrol is taxed at about Rs. 1·75 a gallon and diesel at about Rs. 1·00 (after the increase in excise duty in the last budget). At these levels of taxation the advantage lies over-whelmingly with diesel for heavy and long distance transport. The increase in the diesel tax in the last budget will do nothing, even in the long run, to change the relative demand for petrol and diesel oil. In the UK there is equal specific taxation of both products, but heavy motor transport is nevertheless almost exclusively diesel. Heavy taxation, even if equal on both products, causes a switch to diesel, because it puts a premium (an unwarranted premium) on thermal efficiency—and the diesel engine has higher thermal efficiency although it weighs more and costs more. It is only in the USA where the taxation of oil products is very low that the swing to diesel fuel has not been embarrassing.

Consider now the pair, diesel oil and kerosene. Kerosene can be used in diesel-type internal combustion engines. Until the recent increase in the duty on diesel oil there was no significant difference in the price; moreover there was the convenience of diesel oil being available at the pump. So kerosene was not used in this way. But now there is a likelihood of a serious switch to kerosene. This would be economically harmful for two reasons. First, the deficiency of supply of kerosene from India's own refineries is, and will continue to be for many years, greater than the deficiency of supply of diesel, even without any switch. Secondly, there will be a loss of revenue since kerosene is very lightly taxed. Thus a rise in the price of diesel oil, if there is no other change, will have a greater tendency to increase the demand for kerosene than the demand for petrol. To this extent, the higher tax on diesel oil is harmful.

Finally, petrol and kerosene are also substitutes. At present this is true mainly in aviation where the usage is not sensitive to prices at all. But it is now known that the fuel J.P.4, or 'wide-out' petrol, can be successfully used in 'diesel' engines. This is already being done in Europe. The use of J.P.4 could hardly be economical for the operators if petrol is taxed more heavily than either of the other fuels, for J.P.4 *is* petrol for fiscal purposes.

Thus, if nothing is done, India is faced with the situation that the demand for diesel oil will increase very rapidly, that for kerosene nearly as rapidly, and that for petrol very little or even not at all. India already has a small surplus of petrol. With the refineries planned, this surplus will rapidly increase, while the home production of the other products will be insufficient to meet the demand. India will be lucky indeed to find a market for the petrol because the switch to diesel oil is taking place everywhere. At the same time there will be a deficient supply of kerosene and diesel which will have to be imported. If more oil were found and refineries built, India might be self-sufficient in diesel and kerosene but only at the cost of having even more surplus petrol. It is very doubtful if it is worth building

69

more refineries with the prospect of wasting 20-40 per cent of the product.

Rather more precise figures can be given to support the previous paragraph. Let us consider the demand for the main products, motor-spirit, kerosene, high-speed diesel, light diesel, and furnace oil, in order, given present policies:

(a) *Motor Spirit*

The demand for motor spirit in 1958 was about 5 per cent lower than in 1951. This reflects the heavy switch to diesel of the last few years. The oil companies do not expect any increase over the present level of about 750,000 tons; indeed, they expect a further fall. But I do not want to exaggerate the problem of refinery imbalance and, in view of the fact that the switch to diesel must be almost complete, it is not implausible to suppose that a slow growth in demand will reassert itself. I accordingly allow a growth to 800,000 tons in 1965.

(b) *Kerosene*

The demand over the past ten years has grown at the arithmetic rate of 100,000 tons a year. The continuance of this trend would yield a demand of 2,300,000 tons in 1965. But, if anything, the trend of increase is likely to be greater. Population will be growing faster than in the past (since kerosene is used chiefly for light, the number of families must have an influence on the demand), and it is planned that incomes should grow faster. As against this the increase in rural electrification has not been observed to have any visible impact and in any case it will not be very large in relation to the number of villages. Making a modest allowance for the forces making for an increased trend, I put the demand in 1965 at 2,500,000 tons. *This makes no allowance for any switch to kerosene from diesel for inter-combustion engines.* It also excludes its use as a turbine fuel. Thus 2,500,000 tons is surely an underestimate of the total demand.

(c) *High-Speed Diesel* (*HSD*)

The rate of increase per annum in the past four years has been over 25 per cent. In 1957 it was over 33 per cent. Obviously this reflects in large part the switch from petrol and the growth cannot continue for long at this rate. The future rate of increase will depend very much on policy towards road transport and on the production possibilities of lorries and buses, but it may plausibly be assumed that the Government will not want to stand too much in the way of what is likely to be a rapid increase in road transport from its present low level. Another use of high-speed diesel which is likely to increase very rapidly is that of the railways. We allow for a growth of diesel use from 900,000 tons in 1958 to 2,500,000 in 1965. This represents a growth rate of 16 per cent per annum.

(d) *Light Diesel Oil (LDO)*

In the last ten years, usage (mainly in stationary engines) has risen by 25,000 tons a year on average. A reduction in its use for small-scale electricity generation is expected. This may be more than offset by increased use for irrigation. A projection of the past trend seems to be the best guess, yielding an estimate of about 700,000 tons in 1965.

(e) *Furnace Oil*

The rapid increase from about 900,000 tons in 1955 to about 1,400,000 in 1958 is believed to be due to its use in two electricity generating stations. If there is no further growth in oil-fired electricity generation (and this can easily be prevented, if necessary) the growth is likely to become more modest, reaching about 2,100,000 tons in 1965.

Summing up the above results we have a total demand for these products of 8·6 million tons, split as follows:

Demand	
Motor Spirit	800,000
Kerosene	2,500,000
HSD	2,500,000
LDO	700,000
Furnace Oil	2,100,000
	8,600,000

Let us now consider what the respective balances of supply and demand are likely to be if India herself refines a total of 8·6 million tons of these products. The present refineries and those planned at Gauhati and Barauni will not be able to produce so much. There

71

would need to be roughly 2–2½ million tons of new capacity to give a total capacity of close to 10 million tons of crude oil refined, in order to give an output of 8·6 million tons of the products under consideration.[1] Thus to guess what the situation would be requires a guess as to the characteristics of the crude oil (assumed to be Indian) upon which the extra refining capacity is to be based. Let us assume that this production will have the same characteristics as that from Barauni and Gauhati. The respective shares of each product in the total output of the five products from these refineries are thought likely to be approximately as follows:

Motor Spirit	35%
Kerosene	20%
HSD	25%
LDO	5%
Furnace Oil	15%

The result of this assumption is that the supply of 8·6 million tons would be split up as in column (1) of the following table:

	Supply	Demand	Excess (+) Deficiency (−) Million tons
Motor Spirit	2·36	0·80	+1·56
Kerosene	1·48	2·50	−1·02
HSD	1·97	2·50	−0·53
LDO	0·66	0·70	−0·04
Furnace Oil	2·13	2·10	+0·03
	8·60	8·60	0·00

The result is an excess supply of 1½ million tons of motor spirit with a deficiency of 1 million tons of kerosene and ½ million tons of high speed diesel. As already remarked the deficiency of kerosene is very probably an underestimate. The other two products, LDO and Furnace Oil, are likely to be in balance.

It is abundantly clear that no extra refining capacity, after Barauni and Gauhati, should be built without action being taken to see that the motor spirit can be usefully disposed of at home or sold at a reasonable price abroad. The latter is, to say the least, highly problematical. Since there will already be a surplus of nearly a million tons of motor spirit without any such extra capacity, it follows that more than a third of the output of such capacity would

[1] It is believed that this capacity is not far different from the present provisional targets of the Planning Commission.

probably be wasted unless something were done to solve the problem. Moreover 1·6 million tons would still have to be imported at a c.i.f. cost of about Rs. 35 crores.

What can be done? We have seen that even an equalization of the prices of petrol and HSD would probably not cause any switch back to ordinary petrol engines. Such a switch back would in any case take four or five years even if it were made financially attractive to transport operators. In the long run this switch back could, of course, be engineered by a sufficiently radical change in taxation. But high taxation of petroleum products is essential in the interests of development (see p. 74). If there is to be such high taxation a switch back to petrol engines can be brought about either by having a much higher tax on diesel oil than on petrol, or by having a very heavy vehicle tax based on the weight of the vehicle (or in its value—since value and weight are closely correlated), or by actually taxing diesel engines directly.

If there were no technical possibilities of using (wide-cut) petrol in diesel type engines, such a radical revision of orthodox ideas on petroleum product and allied taxation would be indicated. But even this could do no better than switch ½ million tons from diesel to petrol, still leaving a heavy surplus of petrol and deficit of kerosene. It seems clear that every effort should also be made to discourage the growth in the consumption of kerosene and, above all, to prevent its being used in internal combustion engines.

It seems clear that the best solution to the problem lies in the production of wide-cut petrol, both at Barauni and Gauhati, and in later refineries. *For the wide-cut petrol to find acceptance it must not be more expensive than either HSD or kerosene.*

On these grounds there is therefore urgent need to equalize the tax rates on petrol, HSD and kerosene (though it might be possible to have a slightly higher rate of tax on high-octane motor spirit). Since the pre-tax prices of these products are likely to be almost equal, there can, for greater administrative convenience, be an equal specific duty. This should suffice to permit the oil companies to achieve a balance of supply and demand for each product by suitable variations of the pre-tax prices.

The necessity for having a well co-ordinated and economically sound system of indirect taxation of oil strongly suggests that oil taxation should be reserved to the Centre. The nuisance and waste involved in different rates of tax in different States should be avoided.

Furthermore, the cost of collection of excise duties on oil must be far less than that of sales taxes and no evasion is possible with the former.

B. *Oil Taxation and Development*

There is no doubt that large increases in taxation will be required if there is to be a large Third Plan. There is also no doubt that a large part, at least a half, of the increased taxation must be indirect taxation. In the main text of this paper I have suggested that about Rs. 600 crores of extra indirect taxation may be needed by 1965. There is doubt as to whether so much can be raised if any good administrative opportunities for economically sound increased taxation are neglected. There is no doubt that oil taxes are ideal indirect taxes; oil as a whole is in highly inelastic demand, and there are very few producers or importers so that the cost of collection is negligible.

All that is necessary for very high rates of tax to be possible is that care must be taken to see that the demand for different kinds of oils is kept in balance, which is precisely what has not been done. It may also be argued that high oil taxation 'distorts' the development of transport and unduly favours the railways. There is little or nothing to this argument. In principle where it appears that road transport is most economical from the country's point of view, it is easy to ensure that road transport is used, either by refraining from building a railway or, where the railway exists, by charging sufficiently high freight or passenger rates for the class of freight or passenger which it is desired to divert to the road. Finally, the argument that the taxation of transport in general inhibits development is little or no more than special pleading; the bottleneck of Indian development is capital, not the effective size of the market for particular goods. Moreover the rate of tax suggested, Rs. 1·75 a gallon, is not extremely high. It is, for instance, only just above the UK rate (2/6d a gallon), and there road transport thrives in competition with the railways.

Thus I would suggest that the optimum solution from an economic point of view is that the rates of excise tax and tariff rates on petrol, high-speed diesel, and kerosene, should all be equalized immediately, the rate being brought to a level of Rs. 1·75 a gallon for each product, and that State sales taxes on these products be abolished. Let us estimate the yield of such taxation and compare it with the yield given present policies.

74

We have estimated the total demand for these products as 5·8 million tons in 1965–66. Given present policies, it would be split as to 255 million gallons of motor spirit and 720 million gallons of both kerosene and high-speed diesel oil. The tax yield (excise and customs) would be Rs. 44·5 crores for petrol (Rs. 1·75 a gallon), 72 crores for diesel (Rs. 1 a gallon) and Rs. 13·5 crores for kerosene (Rs. 1·875 a gallon) totalling Rs. 130 crores. The increase in the rate on high-speed diesel to Rs. 1·75 would be unlikely to make a significant difference to the total demand for petrol, J.P.4, and diesel, taken together. But some reduction in the demand for kerosene should result. Let us guess that, instead of rising from 1·6 to 2·5 million tons between 1958 and 1965, it rises only to 2·0 million tons.[1] Then the total demand for all these products would be 5·3 million tons, or about 1,530 million gallons. At Rs. 1·75 a gallon, the yield would be Rs. 268 crores—i.e. Rs. 138 crores extra.

Let us look also at the new balance of supply and demand for the products. For this purpose we may now lump petrol (including J.P.4) and high-speed diesel together since, on our assumptions, they could not be in independent excess supply or demand. The result is given in the table below.

	Supply	Demand	Excess (+) or Deficit (—)
Motor Spirit ⎱			
J.P.4 ⎬	4·10	3·30	+0·80
HSD ⎰			
Kerosene	1·40	2·00	—0·60
LDO	·60	0·70	—0·10
Furnace Oil	2·00	2·10	—0·10
	8·10	8·10	0·00

It can be seen that the balance has been considerably rectified. The algebraic sum of the surpluses and deficits is only 1·60 million tons against 3·18 million tons before. A surplus of petrol (or HSD) remains but it has been halved. If the surplus can be arranged to be HSD it can almost certainly be marketed abroad. The foreign exchange cost of importing products has been reduced to Rs. 12 crores from Rs. 35 crores. If the surplus product is marketed abroad, there should actually be small net earnings of foreign exchange.

---

[1] Instead of costing about Rs. 1·50 a gallon, kerosene would cost about Rs. 3·00 a gallon. Thus we assume that doubling the price would reduce the demand by 20 per cent.

To sum up the above results, the revision of oil taxation suggested would probably save building over half a million tons of refining capacity and at the same time save Rs. 20–35 crores of foreign exchange. It would also raise about Rs. 140 crores of urgently needed resources for economic development. The economic arguments seem to be overwhelming.

The main objection to the above programme is, of course, that an extra tax of rather over Rs. 1½ a gallon on kerosene would fall heavily on poor rural families. The average annual consumption of a rural household must be about 5–6 gallons a year at present; so the burden would be. say, Rs. 8–10 a year. For small landholders, some compensation might be made by abolishing land-tax on small holdings (it would cost only Rs. 12–15 crores of taxation to abolish tax on all holdings under five acres). But, of course, this would not compensate either the landless families or those with very small holdings. But it is submitted that the enormous economic advantages of a fairly heavy tax on kerosene make it very important to discover means of making such a tax politically and socially possible. It should, in this context, be remembered that the presumption of a Rs. 10,000 crore plan is that gross agricultural output rises at about 5½ per cent per annum. If this can be achieved the great majority of the poorest families should see enough of the fruits of development to be able to pay up to Rs. 10 a year.

At the same time it must be recognized that it is most unlikely that politicians would be willing to raise the kerosene tax to Rs. 1·75 per gallon. Suppose that only Rs. 0·75 per gallon was thought to be politically possible. This would reduce the total tax yield by about Rs. 50 crores to Rs. 188. If only this lower rate of tax on kerosene is felt to be possible, then it will most probably be necessary to take administrative action to stop its use in internal combustion engines, and perhaps to ration it.

Some increase in the tax on light diesel oil and fuel oil (in this latter connection it may be remarked that the price of the main substitute, coal, should also be allowed to rise) could be arranged. Also lubricants could be taxed. Taxation of these products could yield Rs. 12–20 crores.

In total then extra oil taxation could yield Rs. 100–150 crores, depending mainly upon the weight of tax on kerosene.

THE REAL COST OF LABOUR, AND THE CHOICE BETWEEN CONSUMPTION AND INVESTMENT[1]

I. M. D. LITTLE

Although the primary intention of this article is to make a theoretical point, it is believed that this point is of relevance to a country such as India. Certainly the author's arguments were developed with the Indian economy in mind. But they should also apply to many developing economies.

The point is to establish an efficiency condition for maximum output when consumption enters into the cost of production. Under special circumstances, when the aim is to maximize investment, and hence presumably growth, it is shown that the efficiency condition can be satisfied only if there is a shadow wage rate equal to the actual ('subsistence') wage rate multiplied by the marginal propensity to consume—where the increment to consumption is the total increment and not simply that of the newly employed man.[2]

To make the point potentially useful and valid, three assumptions are required. First, the marginal productivity of labour in the consumption goods industries must be zero. Second, it must be positive in the capital goods industries. Third, the government must be unable or unwilling to take steps to see that more labour can be employed without an increase in total consumption. Until the last section of this article, the economy is treated as closed: but this assumption is for simplification of argument, and is not essential.

If conditions conform to the above assumptions, it is easy to

[1] This is connected with my experience as a member of the Center for International Studies project in India in 1958–59. It arose more directly out of a paper given to a Massachusetts Institute of Technology seminar in January 1960. I am indebted to several members of the seminar for comments. I am also much indebted to Mr. Caff, student of Nuffield College, for mathematical assistance. (Originally published in *Quarterly Journal of Economics*, February, 1961.)

[2] Professor P. N. Rosenstein-Rodan has previously applied this result in his mimeographed M.I.T. Italy Project paper 'Disguised Unemployment and Underemployment'. But the conditions for its validity were not set out, nor the result proved.

see that there is some opportunity cost of labour in the capital goods industries—for more labour there implies the diversion of capital to the consumption goods industries to provide the extra consumption resulting from the extra employment. In passing, it may be noted that the case is dissimilar to that of a developed economy in a slump: for, in the latter case, machines are unemployed in the consumption goods industries; it is because of this situation that the opportunity cost of employing men to make capital, or dig holes and refill them, is zero.

I. A SIMPLE MODEL

A theoretical article is not the place for deploying full support for the assumptions made. But the author believes that they are reasonably justifiable for India—and so a brief discussion follows.

It is assumed that more men can be employed in the capital goods industries without any fall in production elsewhere. To support this, there is ample evidence of severe underemployment, with a small quantity as yet of open unemployment.[1] So far as the towns are concerned there is little doubt that the marginal productivity of the underemployed—most of whom are semi-employed in providing services—is zero. In the country the figures do not throw sufficient light because of the seasonality of employment. In many areas at least, the labour force is probably fully employed at planting and harvest time. But it seems to be widely agreed that substantial quantities of labour could be released, even at peak periods, with no effect on production if other measures were taken; if holdings were reorganized, thereby reducing the labour required; if many small holdings were eliminated (many are too small to offer full employment even at peak periods); if people worked harder (which they would do if necessary); and if they helped each other more (co-operation!). Some of the above 'ifs' would require organization—but little or no capital. Furthermore, there is no reason why industry should not release labour back to the land at peak periods, in particular if factories are situated in small towns.

Our assumption was, however, not merely that the marginal product of the underemployed was zero, but more particularly that the marginal product of those employed or semi-employed in the consumption goods industries was zero; and the argument has so

[1] Cf., e.g., National Sample Survey, Report No. 14, and P. C. Mahalanobis, 'Science and National Planning', *Sankhya*, Vol. 20 (Sept. 1958).

far left out of account non-agricultural consumption goods, produced in factories or workshops. Here there is a positive marginal product, presumably equal to the wage paid. But it is not a serious distortion to neglect these goods. First, they form a rather small part of total consumption—probably about 25 per cent. Consequently, it remains true that total consumption could not be significantly expanded without the use of more capital. Secondly, in any case, only a little more employment and output could be achieved before the marginal product of labour would fall to zero in this sector also.

Turn now to the assumption that the marginal product of labour is positive in the capital goods industries. By analogy with factory-made consumption goods, it might appear that, although the marginal product was equal to the wage, nevertheless very little more output and employment could be achieved before the marginal product would become zero. If this were true, it would seriously affect the interest of our argument. But most reports on Indian agriculture testify to the fact that a vast amount of work could be undertaken, virtually without equipment, for the formation of agricultural capital —such as contour bunding and terracing, levelling, drainage, minor irrigation works, local roads, village godowns, fencing.[1] It is recognized that there are obstacles, in particular the small size of holdings, to carrying out such work. Even so, it seems fair to assume that much more could be done if the government or state governments, could see their way to spending more without inflationary consequences.

This brings one to the third assumption—that the government is unwilling or unable to take steps to see that more labour can be employed without any resultant effect on total consumption. Possible means of doing this are voluntary unpaid labour, compulsory procurement of supplies from agriculture (without payment or with inadequate payment), or sufficiently increased taxation. There is a severe limitation to the amount that is likely to be achieved by the first; the second is probably politically impossible. So far as the last is concerned, the author's belief is that more could be done. But, nevertheless, it very probably remains true that it is practically impossible for the Indian fiscal system to redistribute consumption in favour of the newly-employed sufficiently to permit as much employment as would otherwise be possible. This is in spite of the

---

[1] Cf., e.g. 'Report on India's Food Crisis and Steps to Meet It', produced by the Agricultural Production Team, sponsored by the Ford Foundation (New Delhi, 1959).

fact that it is a rising level of consumption which would need to be sufficiently redistributed.

Let us now introduce the simplest model which will suffice to prove the point made. A more complicated and more realistic one will follow. Consider the following:

$$
\begin{align}
I &= k(K_k, L) \tag{1} \\
S_x &= x(K_x) \tag{2} \\
D_x &= f(L) \tag{3} \\
S_x &= D_x \tag{4} \\
K &= K_k + K_x \tag{5} \\
Y &= W_k I + W_x x \tag{6}
\end{align}
$$

Equation (1) expresses the output of capital goods as a function of the capital and labour employed. Capital goods are everlasting, and comprise both machines, which need machines and labour for their construction, and land works requiring only labour. Nevertheless, and unrealistically, capital goods are like meccano sets in that they can be instantaneously switched between the consumption and investment good sectors (this unreality is removed in the second model).

Equation (2) expresses the output of consumption goods as a function only of the capital employed. This gives formal recognition to the assumption, already discussed, of a zero marginal productivity of labour in this sector.

Equation (3) expresses the assumption, already discussed, that consumption is an increasing function of employment in the investment goods sector. Obviously, this is not intended to imply that consumption does not also increase for other reasons. For instance, as agricultural production increases, there will be increases in peasants' consumption, which are not directly connected with increased employment in the investment goods sector as a result of the movement to that sector of members of peasants' families. Peasants apart, there will also be claims for increased consumption from those already employed in industry and government, and so on. The more successful is the government in moderating the consumption increases of those already employed, and of the peasants, as it increases employment, the smaller will be the extra consumption— that is, the lower will be dx/dL in the model. Formally speaking, dx/dL is a total differential which takes into account all compensatory action which the government can and is willing to take to prevent excessive consumption from limiting the numbers which can be usefully employed without inflation.

The remaining equations speak for themselves, but there are other points to be noticed. First, stocks are ignored. Second, intermediate goods are regarded as assignable to one sector or the other. This limits the applicability of such a model,[1] especially in a country which has experienced only the backwash of Professor Leontief. But then it should be obvious that the model is intended only to give formal emphasis to, and yield a proof of, the point being made.

Let us now derive the condition for maximum output, the only freedom of choice being the division of K between K_k and K_x. From equations (1), (4) and (6) we have:

$$\Delta Y = W_k \Delta I + W_x \Delta x = W_k \left\{ \frac{\partial k}{\partial K_k} \Delta K_k + \frac{\partial k}{\partial L} \Delta L \right\} \tag{7}$$
$$+ W_x \left\{ x'(K_x) \Delta K_k \right\} = 0,$$

where W_k and W_x are the weights attached to investment and consumption respectively.

From (2), (3) and (4) we have:

$$\Delta L = \frac{x'(K_x)}{f'(L)} \Delta K_x.$$

From (5) we have:

$$\Delta K_k = -\Delta K_x.$$

Substituting the latter two results into the first we get:

$$\Delta K_x \left\{ -W_k \frac{\partial k}{\partial K_k} + W_k \frac{\partial k}{\partial L} \frac{x'(K_x)}{f'(L)} + W_x x'(K_x) \right\} = 0.$$

Whence we have:

$$\frac{\partial k}{\partial K_k} \ \bigg/ \ \frac{\partial x}{\partial K_x} = \frac{\partial k}{\partial L} \ \bigg/ \ f'(L) + \frac{W_x}{W_k} \tag{8}$$

The significance of this optimum condition can be brought out by introducing prices, and seeing what happens under perfectly competitive conditions. Let p_x, p_k and W be the prices of consumption

---

[1] See E. Domar, *Essays in the Theory of Employment*, Chap. IX, 'A Soviet Model of Growth', pp. 227–28.

goods, and capital, and the wage, respectively.[1] Then the condition of equalization of returns to capital gives

$$\frac{\partial k}{\partial K_k} \bigg/ \frac{\partial x}{\partial K_x} = \frac{p_x}{p_k} \tag{9}$$

The labour demand condition gives

$$\frac{\partial k}{\partial L} = \frac{W}{p_k}. \tag{10}$$

In general it can be assumed that the extra consumption resulting from the employment of one more man is less than his wage; for even if he does not save, his family, with one less mouth to feed, will consume less. Hence

$$f'(L) = \frac{\alpha W}{p_x} \qquad (\alpha < 1). \tag{11}$$

Now if (8) is to be fulfilled we must have

$$\frac{W_x}{W_k} = \frac{\partial k}{\partial K_k} \bigg/ \frac{\partial x}{\partial K_x} - \frac{\partial k}{\partial L} \bigg/ f'(L). \tag{8*}$$

But, using (9), (10) and (11), the R.H.S. of 8* becomes equal to

$$\frac{p_x}{p_k} \left\{ 1 - \frac{1}{\alpha} \right\}.$$

This expression is negative, whence it follows that (8) cannot be produced by perfect competition, except in the special case when $W_x = 0$, and $\alpha = 1$.

Now introduce a divergence between the wage cost of a man to entrepreneurs (S — the shadow wage), and the actual wage (W — as before). The labour demand condition becomes

$$\frac{\partial k}{\partial L} = \frac{S}{p_k}, \tag{10*}$$

Whence, using (8), (9), (10*) and (11), we have

$$\frac{W_x}{W_k} = \frac{p_x}{p_k} \left\{ 1 - \frac{S}{\alpha W} \right\}$$

or

$$S = \alpha W \left\{ 1 - \frac{W_x}{W_k} \frac{p_k}{p_x} \right\}. \tag{12}$$

[1] These prices are determined by the market in the normal competitive manner. But the labour supply is assumed to be perfectly elastic at a given real wage. There is therefore only one value of W/p_x consistent with equilibrium, and if there is an excess of demand for consumption goods a new equilibrium cannot be attained by a fall in real wages; but only by a fall in employment.

Thus the government can impose the 'optimum' condition by subsidizing wages, for, whatever the weights, S must be less than W. The shadow wage cannot be determined independently of the prices established in the market, but must conform with them. In principle the right solution could be achieved by trial and error.

It is important to note the optimum condition which emerges when no value is put on consumption for its own sake. Then we have

$$S = \alpha W. \tag{13}$$

The shadow wage rate is now independent of the prices. The only value attaching to consumption goods derives from the fact that they 'produce' labour, and hence capital. Thus

$$W_x \text{ (derived)} = W_k \frac{\partial k}{\partial L} \bigg/ f'(L)$$

or, $$\frac{W_x \text{ (derived)}}{W_k} = \frac{\partial k}{\partial L} \bigg/ f'(L) = \frac{p_x}{p_k}. \tag{14}$$

Thus the relative derived weights and the relative market prices become equal when the situation has been optimized by setting the shadow wage rate equal to αW. Since the consumption goods weight is now derived, and not indicative of intrinsic value, the 'optimum' condition can be interpreted as an 'efficiency' condition which ensures that one cannot have more investment as well as (incidentally) more consumption.

It is perhaps worth noting that the situation analysed above can be described in terms of external economies. Thus private and social cost diverge (a) because the market gives no indication to the capital goods sector that additional employment is at the expense of equipment (since equipment must be diverted to making consumption goods), and (b) since wages do not reflect the marginal product of labour in alternative uses. These divergences work in opposite directions. But only if consumption has no direct social value, and if $\alpha = 1$, do they offset each other exactly so that the wage paid becomes equal to the social cost of labour. Otherwise, if maximum growth is desired so that consumption has no social value, and if $\alpha < 1$, the social cost of an extra man employed is equal to the extra consumption engendered. Provided there is perfect competition so that the marginal value product of capital is equal in the capital and consumption goods sectors, this seems intuitively clear.

It is sometimes assumed that the correct shadow wage is zero since the marginal product of labour is zero (in agriculture). This is true if it is assumed that the relative prices (which would be established for capital and consumption goods, if such a shadow rate were used) correctly reflect social utilities (see equation 12). But if, as seems most probable, it is held that investment is more valuable than would be implied by the commodity prices established under such extraordinary conditions, then the correct shadow wage is greater than zero.

It has been remarked earlier that it is important to note that the optimum or efficiency condition holds even if the aim is to maximize investment. It is important because the powerful desire of many leaders of opinion in most underdeveloped countries to develop as fast as possible may be interpreted to mean that capital equipment should grow, for some years at least, as fast as possible albeit subject to a tolerable minimum pattern of consumption growth. What is regarded as tolerable might be zero, or even negative, but would generally be positive. Certainly in India where the population is growing at about 2 per cent per annum and desperate poverty is widespread, probably 4 to 5 per cent might be taken as the tolerable minimum.

It may still be asked why if a still greater rate of growth of consumption were possible within the planning period under consideration, it should be sacrificed for a more rapid rate of growth of capital equipment. It is not enough to say that, of course, consumption in later periods *could* be still higher if its growth were to be moderated in the initial period. This is a merely hypothetical statement and gives no categorical reason for preferring to moderate consumption growth initially. But there are a number of powerful reasons for the preference which are enumerated in the following paragraph.

First, India is heavily dependent for investment goods on foreign sources, she has a heavy balance-of-payments deficit, and her export prospects are rather dim. Consequently, a withdrawal or reduction of foreign aid might well leave her in a position where her development was limited by the capacity of her capital goods industries rather than by savings. Secondly, there is a risk that the rate of population increase is accelerating, so that the tolerable minimum rate of growth of consumption may rise. Thirdly, there is the risk of having to appropriate more for defence. Fourthly, there is a forgivable desire to be capable of defence production on her own account.

In the above circumstances, our analysis which suggests that it is possible to set the rate of growth of consumption too low, even if the aim is to maximize investment, may be of some interest. It could be argued that, surely, a rate of growth of consumption of 4 per cent per annum should permit the whole slack of underemployment to be taken up, if that were possible on other grounds. This is true, provided that the growth of 'extraneous' consumption—by which is meant in this context that which does *not* arise from extra employment—is sufficiently limited. The view of the author is that it is quite probable that it will not be sufficiently limited—and consequently that consumption may partly need to be held back by restricting employment, and output, and investment, below what is economically possible. In other words, it seems probable that India is, and will be, operating at a point at which there could be more investment if there were more 'functional' consumption.

If 'extraneous' consumption could be sufficiently limited, so that $\frac{dx}{\partial L}$ became zero, then the shadow price of labour would be zero until such time as there was no underemployment, and the marginal productivity of labour rose. Certainly insufficient attention has been paid to the manner in which the growth of 'extraneous' consumption —which comes not only from the peasants (this is well recognized), but from the wages of already employed factory workers and from other members of the middle classes—limits the growth of employment, output; and investment in a country like India.

II. A MORE COMPLICATED MODEL

A more complicated non-instantaneous model is now introduced, which is without several of the most glaring unrealities of the first model.[1] But, since exactly the same results emerge, most readers may skip it without loss. Consider the following equations:

$$K_{t+1} - K_t = k(K_{kt}, L_{kt}) \qquad (1)$$
$$C_{t+1} - C_t = l(K_{ct}, L_{ct}) \qquad (2)$$
$$K_t = K_{kt} + K_{ct} \qquad (3)$$
$$L_t = L_{kt} + L_{ct} \qquad (4)$$
$$S_{xt} = x(C_t) \qquad (5)$$
$$D_{xt} = f(L_t) \qquad (6)$$
$$S_{xt} = D_{xt} \qquad (7)$$

[1] The model can also be regarded as an exercise in intertemporal welfare economics in the manner of Chap. XII of Dorfman, Samuelson, and Solow, *Linear Programming and Economic Analysis* (New York: McGraw-Hill, 1958).

In this model there are two kinds of capital, both produced by capital and labour. But capital of type K cannot be used in the consumption goods industry. Similarly capital of type C cannot be used to make machines. Thus, in any period, the operative decision is how to divide capital and labour between producing capital which will make more capital, and capital which will make consumption goods. The model is no longer 'instantaneous', since a decision to switch, say, labour from K to C does not result in more consumption goods industry equipment, and hence more consumption, and hence the employment of more labour, until the following period. There are also two degrees of freedom since both capital and labour can move between K and C. This does not mean that K must still consist of meccano sets. Once the model is solved, it is known beforehand how K should be divided between K_k and K_c, and, provided only that the specific nature of K_o is far in the past, the appropriate kinds of plants or machines can be made. In other respects, the model is the same as before.

We shall take it that the problem is to maximize the value of terminal equipment after T years, subject to some weight being given to consumption. This implies that some weights or values are given to the amounts of the two different types of capital, K_t and C_t, existing at the end of the planning period of T years. It will be seen that the attachment of a certain value to consumption goods capital at the end of T years will determine the amount of consumption goods capital in each previous year—and hence will determine the amount of consumption in each previous year. The resultant pattern of consumption growth will be higher or lower according as a higher or a lower weight is attached to the terminal consumption goods capital: but, unless an independent weight is attached to such capital at each period of time—i.e. a weight which is not derived from the aim of maximizing terminal capital at the end of T years—there is no room for a variation of the pattern of consumption growth within the planning period. To avoid complication, it is thus assumed that the precise pattern of consumption growth within the planning period is a matter of indifference.

It must also be noted that the optimum consumption path from the end of the planning period until eternity must in principle be decided before the relative values of consumption goods and investment goods capital can be fixed for year T. Since machines can make machines to make, and so on *ad infinitum*, there is no definite limit to the period for which a present decision projects its echoes into the future. Obviously then the values fixed for the different items of terminal capital equipment must be a trifle arbitrary. But since, tautologically, the future is both unknown in its pattern and duration, there is no more to be said.

We may now turn to the problem which is to maximize $W_{kt}K_t + W_{ct}C_t$.

To simplify the algebra, transform the first two equations into:

$$K_{t+1} - K_t = k(K_{kt}, C)_{kt} \qquad \text{1(a)}$$
$$C_{t+1} - C_t = l(K_{ct}, C_{ct}) \qquad \text{1(b)}$$

where $C_{kt} + C_{ct} = C_t$.

This can be done since L_t is, via equations (5), (6) and (7), a function of C_t. Thus the choice, open to us, of switching L_t between L_{kt} and L_{ct} can be represented as a choice of switching C_t between C_{kt} and C_{ct}. It is as if we chose to devote agricultural capital either to producing food to feed workers in sector K or to feed workers in sector C. Since we assume labour is homogeneous it follows that:

$$\frac{dL_t}{dC_t} = \frac{dL_{kt}}{dC_{kt}} = \frac{dL_{ct}}{dC_{ct}}. \qquad (8)$$

To maximize $W_{kt}K_t + W_{ct}C_t$ we have:

$$\Delta(W_{kt}K_t + W_{ct}C_t) = 0.$$

Hence from 1(a) and 1(b):

$$W_{kt}\left\{ \Delta K_{t-1} + \frac{\partial k}{\partial K_{c(t-1)}} \Delta K_{k(t-1)} + \frac{\partial k}{\partial C_{k(t-1)}} \Delta C_{k(t-1)} \right\}$$
$$+ W_{ct}\left\{ \Delta C_{t-1} + \frac{\partial l}{\partial K_{c(t-1)}} \Delta K_{c(t-1)} + \frac{\partial l}{\partial C_{c(t-1)}} \Delta C_{c(t-1)} \right\} = 0.$$

Since $\Delta K_{t-1} = \Delta K_{k(t-1)} + \Delta K_{c(t-1)}$
and $\Delta C_{t-1} = \Delta C_{k(t-1)} \Delta C_{c(t-1)}$
it follows that:

$$\left\{ W_{kt} + W_{ct} \frac{\partial l}{\partial K_{c(t-1)}} \right\} \Delta K_{t-1} + \left\{ W_{ct} + W_{kt} \frac{\partial k}{\partial C_{k(t-1)}} \right\} \Delta C_{t-1}$$
$$+ \left\{ W_{kt} \frac{\partial k}{\partial K_{k(t-1)}} - W_{ct} \frac{\partial l}{\partial K_{c(t-1)}} \right\} \Delta K_{k(t-1)}$$
$$+ \left\{ W_{ct} \frac{\partial l}{\partial C_{c(t-1)}} - W_{kt} \frac{\partial k}{\partial C_{k(t-1)}} \right\} \Delta C_{c(t-1)} = 0. \qquad (9)$$

But $\Delta K_{k(t-1)}$ and $\Delta C_{c(t-1)}$ can be chosen independently of each other and of ΔK_{t-1} and ΔC_{t-1}.

87

Letting

$$W_{k(t-1)} = W_{kt} + W_{ct} \frac{\partial l}{\partial K_{c(t-1)}} \text{ (def)} \tag{10}$$

and

$$W_{c(t-1)} = W_{ct} + W_{kt} \frac{\partial k}{\partial C_{k(t-1)}} \text{ (def)} \tag{11}$$

we have the optimum conditions

$$\frac{\partial k}{\partial K_{k(t-1)}} \bigg/ \frac{\partial l}{\partial K_{c(t-1)}} = \frac{\partial k}{\partial C_{k(t-1)}} \bigg/ \frac{\partial l}{\partial C_{c(t-1)}} = \frac{W_{ct}}{W_{kt}} \tag{12}$$

and

$$W_{k(t-1)} \Delta K_{t-1} + W_{c(t-1)} \Delta C_{t-1} = 0. \tag{13}$$

Equation (12) is the 'normal' optimum condition which says that the relative marginal productivities of the two 'factors' in the two activities should equal both each other and also the relative value of the two activities. If we transform back to the terms of the original equations (1) and (2) we get the same result, as follows:

$$\frac{\partial k}{\partial C_{k(t-1)}} = \frac{\partial k}{\partial L_{k(t-1)}} \frac{dL_{k(t-1)}}{dC_{k(t-1)}}$$

and

$$\frac{\partial l}{\partial C_{c(t-1)}} = \frac{\partial l}{\partial L_{c(t-1)}} \frac{dL_{c(t-1)}}{dC_{c(t-1)}}.$$

Whence, using (8), we have:

$$\frac{\partial k}{\partial K_{k(t-1)}} \bigg/ \frac{\partial l}{\partial K_{c(t-1)}} = \frac{\partial k}{\partial C_{k(t-1)}} \bigg/ \frac{\partial l}{\partial C_{c(t-1)}}$$
$$= \frac{\partial k}{\partial L_{k(t-1)}} \bigg/ \frac{\partial l}{\partial L_{c(t-1)}}. \tag{14}$$

Thus equation (12) is rather uninteresting. But it should be noted that it yields the traditional result—that is, the relative marginal productivities should equal the relative weights—only because the ultimate period is being considered. Thus consumption goods have no influence on capital formation in the next period, only because there is no next period. The normality thus arises only because one has to stop the model this side of eternity.

The penultimate period is more interesting. Consider equation (13). Since this is the condition of maximizing $W_{k(t-1)}K_{(t-1)} +$

$W_{c(t-1)}C_{(t-1)}$, we can immediately write down conditions analogous to (12) and (13), writing $(t-_2)$ for $(t-_1)$, and substituting (10), (11) and (14) into (12) and (13). Thus:

$$\frac{\partial k}{\partial K_{k(t-2)}} \Big/ \frac{\partial l}{\partial K_{c(t-2)}} = \frac{\partial k}{\partial L_{k(t-2)}} \Big/ \frac{\partial l}{\partial L_{c(t-2)}}$$

$$= \frac{W_{ct} + W_{kt}\dfrac{\partial k}{\partial C_{k(t-1)}}}{W_{kt} + W_{ct}\dfrac{\partial l}{\partial K_{c(t-1)}}}. \tag{15}$$

The relative weights on the R.H.S. have become, as it were, adjusted for the influence which more capital of both kinds in the penultimate period will have on capital formation in the ultimate period.

Now, as was done with the first model discussed, let us see what would happen under conditions of perfect competition. First consider the R.H.S. of equation (15) and suppose that prices at the terminal date are correctly set so as to reflect the 'true' values W_{ct} and W_{kt}.[1] Then we have the expression:

R.H.S. (15) $= \dfrac{p_{ct} + p_{kt}\dfrac{\partial k}{\partial C_{k(t-1)}}}{p_{kt} + p_{ct}\dfrac{\partial l}{\partial K_{c(t-1)}}}$

But $\dfrac{\partial k}{\partial C_{k(t-1)}} = \dfrac{\partial k}{\partial L_{k(t-1)}}\dfrac{dL_{t-1}}{dC_{t-1}} = \dfrac{\partial k}{\partial L_{k(t-1)}}\dfrac{x'(C_{t-1})}{f'(L_{t-1})}$

using equations (8), (5) and (6).
Therefore:

R.H.S. (15) $= \dfrac{p_{ct} + p_{kt}\dfrac{\partial k}{\partial L_{k(t-1)}}\dfrac{x'(C_{t-1})}{f'(L_{t-1})}}{p_{kt} + p_{ct}\dfrac{\partial l}{\partial K_{c(t-1)}}}.$

Now, letting W, r_c, and r_k, be respectively the wage rate and the rents of K and C, we have under perfect competition:

[1] In principle, the government can stand ready to buy the terminal equipment at the appropriate prices. The market then establishes the prices of the preceding periods.

$$\frac{\partial k}{\partial L_{k(t-1)}} = \frac{W_{t-1}}{p_{kt}}$$

$$x'(C_{t-1}) = \frac{r_{c(t-1)}}{p_{x(t-1)}}$$

$$f'(L_{t-1}) = \frac{\alpha W_{t-1}}{p_{x(t-1)}}$$

$$\frac{\partial l}{\partial K_{c(t-1)}} = \frac{r_{k(t-1)}}{p_{ct.}}$$

Inserting these equations into the R.H.S. we have:

$$\text{R.H.S. (15)} = \frac{p_{ct} + \dfrac{r_{ct(-1)}}{\alpha}}{p_{kt} + r_{k(t-1)}} \qquad (16)$$

Similarly, under perfect competition we have:

$$\text{L.H.S. (15)} = \frac{p_{c(t-1)}}{p_{k(t-1)}} \qquad (17)$$

But the returns to capital of both kinds would also be equalized. Allowing for capital gains, this implies:

$$\frac{p_{ct} + r_{c(t-1)}}{p_{c(t-1)}} = \frac{p_{kt} + r_{k(t-1)}}{p_{k(t-1)}}$$

or,

$$\frac{p_{ct} + r_{ct(-1)}}{p_{kt} + r_{k(t-1)}} = \frac{p_{c(t-1)}}{p_{k(t-1)}} \qquad (18)$$

Thus perfect competition reproduces equation (15) only if $\alpha = 1$. This is the same result as was deduced from the first model. It similarly follows that the shadow wage rate, which will produce the efficiency condition, given perfect competition in other respects, is αW. Finally, it can easily be verified that the same result holds if we push the analysis back to the prepenultimate period, and so on back to the beginning of the plan.

III. SIGNIFICANCE OF THE ASSUMPTIONS OF A CLOSED ECONOMY AND PERFECT COMPETITION

A few points remain to be cleared up. First, only a closed economy has been dealt with. But it seems intuitively clear that opening the economy would make no difference to the result: this is because the essential conditions for the result to be valid—that more labour, used to produce investment goods, results in more consumption which cannot be provided merely by employing more labour—is in no way affected by the introduction of international trade. Of course, consumption goods can be imported—but then they must be paid for by exports. If one could export the things which labour can make by hand—local roads, irrigation ditches, etc.— there would be no problem. But since one cannot do this, more labour employed on agricultural works (which do not produce an immediate return) implies importing more food and fewer machines, and also implies some extra investment in consumption goods other than food. Even the existence of economic aid does not alter the picture—provided it is limited. In fact, only the assumption of sufficient *free* food imports, which would solve by far the most important part of the problem of providing the extra consumption, would alter the emphasis of our results. If this could be assumed, then the marginal propensity to consume Indian output, and the 'shadow' wage rate—would become zero—in which case our results are no different from those arrived at by looking directly at the marginal productivity of labour in alternative 'employment'.

Finally, the references to perfect competition, together with an implicit assumption of equilibrium prices, should emphatically not be taken to mean that such are reasonable assumptions. They were made only to bring out the significance of the 'efficiency' condition arrived at. In practice, there are prima facie reasons for believing that all important prices in India may diverge seriously from the prices which would ensure over-all 'economic efficiency'.

There are no conclusions at this point: such as there are, were drawn in the first section.

NUFFIELD COLLEGE,
OXFORD.

TRANSPORTATION POLICY IN INDIA[1]

LOUIS LEFEBER
Massachusetts Institute of Technology
and
M. DATTA CHAUDHURI
Indian Statistical Institute

Transportation plays a crucial role in the development of India. The point needs no special elaboration. If transport capacity turns out to be insufficient to carry the traffic required for the attainment of the goals of the Third Plan, then the goals themselves will have to be abandoned.

There are, moreover, some roundabout but equally important ways in which the transportation industry exerts crucial influence. For instance, transport rate and investment policies can directly, or through the responses of affected industries indirectly, affect the amount of resources needed for the realization of rapid economic growth. The following discussion intends to bring into focus some of the direct and indirect relationships between the transportation sector and the rest of the economy, all of which have an important bearing on Indian economic planning.

[1] The original version of this paper was presented to the Indian Planning Commission in the spring of 1961. It was mimeographed and distributed by the Perspective Planning Division and adapted for publication in a forthcoming volume by the Indian Statistical Institute. After the writing of this paper the official estimates of the demand for transportation during the Third Plan Period were revised upward. Also, there was some increase—though in the author's estimate insufficient—in the rates charged by the Indian Railways.

The co-operation of and helpful information made available by Mr Pitambar Pant, Chief of the Perspective Planning Division, is gratefully acknowledged. The authors are indebted to Mr V. V. Sarwate of the same Division for his contribution to the material contained in Appendix B. Grateful reference should also be made to useful information obtained from Mr L. A. Natesan of the National Council of Applied Economic Research and to the helpful suggestions of Mr V. K. Ramaswami, Economic Adviser, Ministry of Commerce and Industry.

THE DEMAND FOR AND SUPPLY OF TRANSPORTATION
SERVICES DURING THE THIRD PLAN

There are indications that transportation was in short supply during much of the Second Plan period. The capacity shortages developed in spite of the fact that the railways completed their scheduled investment programme and that the demand for coal and other bulk commodities did not reach its targeted level in several sectors. The implication is that transportation requirements were underestimated —or investments in the transportation plant misallocated—in the Second Plan. There is reason to believe that a similar development may take place also during the Third Plan.

The Third Plan targets provide for an increase in railway capacity to facilitate the movement of 85 billion ton-miles by the end of 1965–66. In addition there are provisions for increasing the production of trucks to a capacity to accommodate 24·5 billion ton-miles. The two estimates add up to about 109 billion ton-miles of commodity movements by rail and road.

The above railway target consists entirely of long-distance traffic.[1] The target for road transportation includes the amount projected for local and feeder traffic along with road transportation's contribution to long-distance movement. Assuming that about 30 per cent of the truck capacity will be devoted to long-distance motor transport (70 per cent being utilized for local and feeder traffic), the implication is that the total capacity available in 1965–66 for long-distance transport will be about 92 billion ton-miles. If this figure is translated into capacity required in terms of traffic tons originating, we find that provisions are made for the movement of at most 268 million tons of long-distance traffic.[2] Finally, if we account for about 3·5 million tons of commodities carried by coastal shipping, we reach the conclusion that the transportation provisions of the Third Plan

[1] By the term long-distance traffic we denote movement which is other than local or feeder traffic.

[2] The explanation of our assumption concerning the share of long-distance transport in the total road transport capacity is given in Appendix A. The Third Plan estimates were converted by us from ton miles into tons originating on the basis of the currently prevailing 348 miles for the railways and 300 miles for long-distance road transport as the average lead of movement. The average lead of the railways, however, increased at a yearly rate of about eight miles over the past six years. If the trend continues, it may reach about 390 miles by the end of the Third Plan. Hence the text emphasizes that the targeted capacity consists of at most the quoted tons originating for long-distance transportation. Larger average leads would yield of course a lesser capacity in terms of tonnage.

for long-distance movement on land and sea amount to a grand total of at most 272 million tons of commodities.[1]

Contrary to the above estimates we have found that requirements for total long-distance traffic (i.e. services rendered by all three modes of transportation) will be in the neighbourhood of 305 million tons of commodities if the over-all production targets of the Third Plan are to be met. This estimate was obtained by considering the volume of outputs in diverse sectors as they relate to long-distance transportation; i.e. the projection was based on historical transport coefficients by sectors as well as the consideration of the targets of the Third Plan.[2] But the conclusions reached by this method were also supported by the admittedly less reliable correlation of aggregate output and railway transportation observations of the last decade. The implication is that the transportation capacity for long-distance movement targeted by the Third Plan will be at least 33 million tons short of actual requirements.

Given the estimated total number of trucks available (projected from the current park and production targets of the Plan) we have eliminated that part of the road-transport capacity which is required for local and feeder traffic to sustain a long-distance movement

---

[1] The transportation targets of the Third Plan seem to be supported by the Neogy Committee's report on *Transportation Policy and Co-ordination* (New Delhi, 1961). The projections for required railway services correspond very closely to the provisions of the Plan. The projections for road transport contain one estimate somewhat in excess of the target of the Plan; two alternative estimates show magnitudes which are about 30 per cent below the target level. On closer inspection, however, the statistical procedures in the context of the data prove to be inadmissible (see footnote 3 on page 95). Furthermore the estimate for railway traffic based on the 'coefficient method' contains a fatal computational error. The sixteen commodities shown in Annexure I of Appendix XIII (2) account for 60 per cent of the total railway freight traffic. This is correctly concluded on historical evidence and acknowledged by the explanatory note (Appendix XIII (2), page 3). The sixteen commodities in Annexure I total 169 million tons for 1965–66; hence, the total railway tonnage must be 281 millions in that year as opposed to the Plan target of 243 million tons. Table 4 of the same Appendix is computed on the basis of an assumed average lead of 345 miles; hence, railway ton-miles for 1965–66 must be about 97·5 billions as opposed to the figure shown.

[2] See Tables of Appendix A and explanatory notes. In the estimating procedure we have noted that the volume of outputs related to freights carried by the railways from 1950–51 to 1955–56 are indicative of total transport requirements as in those years long-distance transport by other modes of transportation was insignificant. After 1955–56 the estimated total long-distance volume carried by road and water—but particularly by road—was steadily increasing. It is to be kept in mind that this development, if uncorrected for, provides a downward bias in projections of total transport requirements based on railway statistics.

of 305 million tons of commodities. The remaining road-transport capacity yields 24 million tons for long-distance movement.[1] Historical projections of coastal shipping indicate a capacity of 3·5 million tons by 1965–66.[2] The total railway capacity in the last year of the Plan would have to reach at least 277·5 million tons as opposed to the targeted 243 million tons, if our projections are correct. A linear regression line covering the years 1953–54 through 1959–60 fitted to a scatter of gross turnover (i.e. total value of production plus imports) and tons originating on the railways indicates a demand of 276 million tons for railway transport alone by 1965–66; this supports our estimate. A parabolic fit over the years 1950–51 through 1959–60 gives 289 million tons. Both of these are based on railway statistics and exclude the gradually increasing demand for long-distance road transport over the period of fitting.[3]

One further point may be worth mentioning. The estimates of the Third Plan are provided in ton-miles while we confined ourselves to estimating tons originating. Ton-miles—apart from their questionable value in measuring units of transport services—contain implicit information about the distances travelled by individual commodities. As indicated above, the average lead of traffic in railways increased at the rate of about 8 miles over the last 6 years. Preliminary figures indicate that the lead for 1960-61 may have further increased to 355 miles. The projection of the trend would give about 390 miles

[1] See Appendix A, Table 2. The 24 million ton estimate was derived on the basis of current capacity utilization. However, the latter could be improved by removing administrative hindrances to motor transport. With improved utilization the road transport industry could carry about 30 million tons of long-distance traffic with an average load comparable to that of the railways.

[2] See Appendix A, Table 2.

[3] The correlations contained in Appendix XIII (2) of the Neogy report are misleading. First, straight lines fitted to scatters which indicate marked curvilinearity or abrupt changes in slope are of questionable predictive value. The data show a marked increase in the rate of change in transportation requirements relative to output from 1953–54 onward. The explanation lies in the change in the rate of industrialization in response to the First Plan. Hence, straight lines fitted over the span 1950–51 to 1958–59 are bound to give underestimates.

Secondly, the steady increase in average lead is ignored by the Report. To demonstrate the consequences: after accounting for the trend in the Report's estimated 82 billion railway ton-miles (Table 6, Appendix XIII (2)) the latter translates itself into only 210 million tons traffic by rail in 1965–66, which is nonsensical. Note that our estimates based on ton-mile data projected for 1965–66 indicate a requirement for railway traffic in excess of 110 billion ton-miles (See Appendix A). After accounting for the trend in average lead these estimates result in about 290 million tons of railway tonnage for the same year.

as average lead by 1965–66. Whereas it is by no means certain that the lead will continue to increase at this rate, this may very well happen. Forces which work to restrain further growth in lead (increasing weight of coal and ore movement for steel in the total transport bill, the dispersion of certain industries such as cement, etc.) are offset and possibly outweighed by powerful counterforces, such as the gradually increasing national economic integration and the replacement of steel, paper, and other imports by domestic production. Furthermore, the discriminatory rate structure of the railways in favour of low-value commodities and the government price policy for steel and other goods encourage excessive distances in movement. It is a fact that an estimate of traffic requirements can be obscured unless the demand for distance moved is differentiated from tonnage to be handled by the different modes of transportation. In transportation planning both must be separately considered since capacity adjustment for increasing lead (given tons) is not equivalent to adjustment for increasing tonnage (given lead).

In summary our projections for the last year of the Third Plan consistently indicate a requirement of about 305 million tons demand for long-distance transportation with a possibly continuing increase in the average lead of movement. Against this demand the capacity based on the provisions of the Plan will be at most 272 million tons given that the lead remains constant. If our reasoning is correct, a demand for at least another 33 million tons of long-distance traffic is unaccounted for.

The implication is that insufficiency of transportation services may prove to be the most significant bottleneck in the economic development of India. More efficient utilization of existing facilities and improved investment allocations in the railway system or in road transport, or in both in some suitable combination, are required to attain the additional capacity for handling 33 million or more tons originating. Improved utilization of road transport, i.e. elimination of the arbitrary legal and other barriers to long hauling, could diminish the gap by as much as 6 million tons, in which case a demand for at least 27 million tons of additional capacity would still remain.[1]

----

[1] Whereas some part of this required added capacity could be allocated to coastal shipping it is quite clear that the bulk of it would have to be accommodated by either rail or road.

THE RELATIONSHIP BETWEEN YIELD, CAPACITY, AND INVESTMENT IN THE INDIAN RAILWAYS

It is a well-known fact that at this point the railway capacity to speedily move bulk commodities and other cargo is insufficient. This is attested by increasing complaints about coal deliveries to crucial sectors (e.g. steel) as well as by the large amounts of outstanding registration. This capacity shortage developed in spite of the fact that several targets of the Second Plan relying on heavy uses of coal and other bulk commodities were not fully attained.[1]

Excessive demands on the transportation plant are partly caused by a rate of industrial activity faster than the plant is equipped to cope with and are partly self-inflicted through reliance on a discriminatory rate policy. Discrimination in the rate structure of the Indian railways takes place in favour of low-value bulk commodities which are rated at or below the level of corresponding operating costs. The resulting losses in overhead and other costs are charged to the rates quoted for commodities of relatively high market value.

This type of discrimination is an anachronistic inheritance from the early Western railway monopolies. Originally its purpose was to encourage the movement of bulk commodities when excess capacity in the plant existed and, incidentally, also to defeat those competitive modes of bulk transportation (coastal shipping) which had no opportunity to discriminate.

What can be rational in the face of excess capacity is not always warranted under conditions of overutilization. As long as discrimination prevails unnecessary added demand for railway services is generated. The monetary cost of transportation does not reflect its real costs; hence, when decisions of industrial location are made, the true costs of investment and production are not taken into account either. Furthermore, as the real cost of delivered goods is obscured, comparisons between the monetary costs of substitutable raw materials also become illusory. As an illustration, one can point to the excessive reliance on coal in western India. If the rates for coal were higher, many new plants which heavily rely on the use of coal would locate nearer to the coal regions. The already established industries would at least partially substitute residual fuel oil for coal. Both responses would facilitate the easing of the transport problem.

[1] It should be remembered that the railways completed their investment programme scheduled for the Second Plan.

Given a mounting pressure on capacity, an efficiently working pricing mechanism would respond by increasing the rates for transportation services. This in turn would discourage further demands on the system, and the increased profitability would indicate the need for expanding the capacity. Incidentally, it would also provide resources (in the form of increased profits) toward financing the new capacity requirement. With increasing capacity the rates would gradually settle at a level which leaves room only for 'normal' returns to capital investment.

The lesson we can learn from the working of a competitive price mechanism is that rates should be such as to equate the demand for transportation to the available supply or capacity. Furthermore, the desirability of new capacity is determined by measuring its yield against alternative possible investments; when profits increase relative to other investments, capacity increase is in order; and when yields on the margin are equalized, we know that there is a balanced distribution of capital resources. Thus the function of yields and prices is to guide resources into those lines of activities which are the most efficient from the point of view of the economy. And though short run fluctuations in prices and rates may be undesirable, the use of the price system for balancing capacity and demand and for providing long-run measuring rods for the efficiency of investment is crucial particularly in the context of a modern planned economy.[1]

The need to rely more on the pricing mechanism is illustrated particularly well by the example of the Indian railways. The rate structure obscures rather than reflects the real cost of transportation, encourages excessive movement, and results in no profits, with no indication of the type and size of capacity increases required to alleviate the evident scarcity. Large investments are scheduled in the railway plant to be effected during the Third Plan—about Rs. 1,300 crores; yet according to our earlier computations the scheduled capacity targets will be some 33 million tons short of the actual demand by the end of the Plan. Furthermore, if the current rate structure were maintained and operation were to continue at losses or at best with zero profit, a substantial part—20 per cent—of the total scheduled public investment resources would be tied up in activities which do not contribute to the surpluses needed for future investment.

The yield (or opportunity cost) of the project should be carefully

[1] Note the increasing reliance of socialist economies on the pricing mechanism.

98

considered in order to evaluate the desirability of new investment in the railway plant. This requirement is far from being an anachronistic leftover of the nineteenth century spirit of free enterprise. The yield reflects income-creating opportunities from investment projects which could be undertaken as alternatives and which are lost to the society. In other words, the efficiency of new investment can be measured only in terms of its yield; in order to be undertaken it should be at least as profitable as other new investments. If this condition cannot be met, the project should be abandoned. Furthermore, if alternative methods exist for the provision of substitutable goods or services, for selection the return on each should be compared with that on the others. If these rules are not observed by private investors, the penalty is bankruptcy. Unfortunately, no such penalty exists for the government investor.

The evidence seems to be that private investors in India operate on the basis of at least 20 per cent yield on new investment before taxes but after depreciation.[1] This is of course a social yield since about 50 per cent of the returns goes into income taxes. From the point of view of private resource allocation investments are made in the expectation of at least 10 per cent yield after deducting income taxes.

The road transport industry—which provides a service substitutable for those of the railways—operates at private average yields which range from about 14 to 30 per cent on capital invested (net of depreciation and before profit taxes), and the indication is that the incremental yield (profit on new investment) is in excess of the above

[1] A computation of the marginal rate of return over cost for India gives a rate which fluctuates between 19 and 21 per cent between 1950–51 and 1957–58. This is of course before taxes but after depreciation. (The computation was based on the framework of Capital Formation and Economic Growth: A Theoretical and Empirical Analysis by R. S. Eckaus and L. Lefeber, *Review of Economics and Statistics*, May 1962, included in Vol. II of this series. The statistical work for the Indian economy was done by Mr G. V. L. Narasinham of the Perspective Planning Division.) This rate signifies the expectations for the last investment item in all lines of activities undertaken by entrepreneurs; hence it is to be interpreted as the minimum expectation of the new investors. It follows that many new projects may have larger returns on the investment. In effect, our private investigations and discussions with Indian industrial consultant engineers have convinced us that the expected return in no branch of manufacturing industries is less than 13 per cent after depreciation and taxes. Profitability is of course obscured by complex accounting procedures; hence it is not readily evident to the uninitiated. The profit rates given by the Reserve Bank of India are irrelevant as they refer to average rather than marginal returns. Furthermore, they are based on arbitrary and unreliable balance sheet information.

quoted 20 per cent. Its social yield also includes the taxes and duties paid on fuel, transport, licensing, etc.[1]

The implication is that additions to railway plant should not be undertaken if the expected yield on the incremental investment cannot approximate 20 per cent net of depreciation. While this rate on additional investment in a 'national enterprise' may offend the post-office socialist, it should by no means be considered prohibitive. It has to be remembered that present railway rates for bulk commodities are too low in terms of the costs of operation and the excessive demands put on the current plant. If these rates are adjusted to a realistic level and if incremental investments are undertaken primarily to ease congested routes and to improve the efficiency of railway operations, excess demand would be eliminated and the yield on the new investment might readily attain the quoted rate.

The demand for transportation services on the railways is assumed to be inelastic in the short run and quite elastic in the long run. The short-run inelasticity is explained by three facts: in the absence of free capacity on other modes of transportation, traffic cannot be shifted; established plants operating in protected markets have an inelastic demand for inputs; there is an excess demand for consumer goods and final producer goods in the country. As a consequence the immediate response to a rate increase would be little or no change in the demand for rail transportation but a significant improvement in the yields.

The long-run elasticity is assumed to be larger, however, because plants seeking new locations would consider the real rather than the

[1] It is of course true that the total profitability of road transport must be related also to the cost of building and maintaining the highways. Our preliminary finding is that the taxes and duties obtained from the industry cover these costs. Furthermore, it must be remembered that road building is based heavily on unemployed rural labour and its real resource equivalent is small. The contention that road transportation is being subsidized by the state cannot be readily accepted. Nor can the contention be accepted that profitability in road hauling is due to the exploitation of cheap labour by fly-by-night operators. At least one large company operating several hundred buses and trucks, known to the authors, obtains adequate average yields even though it assumes responsibility for several 'social overhead' activities such as education of labour force and public road maintenance. At the same time it is among the best employers within the region of its operations.

An excess demand also faces the road transport industry. The acceptance of significantly higher transport rates in road hauling is rationalized by the significantly higher speed, house-to-house service (railway rates do not include collection and delivery), lesser packaging and handling costs, smaller accident and pilferage rates, and prompt payment of claims.

monetary cost of transport, partial shifting of traffic to coastal shipping would take place, and the substitution of raw materials (for instance coal vs. residual fuel oil) would become profitable. As a consequence the combination of a suitable rate and investment policy would work towards eliminating inefficient excess demands on the plant and maintain a suitable social yield on investment.

What type of policies are needed to make the railways both more efficient and profitable? Clearly increased efficiency of plant utilization is required; the plant will also have to be enlarged to accommodate the new traffic generated during the Third Plan. The new investment would have to be concentrated, however, in those lines where demand for transportation warrants it. Furthermore, the rate structure would have to be revised—its level raised and discrimination diminished—in order to put the railways in the black and to eliminate the social diseconomy caused by the disparity between the monetary and the real cost of transportation.

The investment allocation to the railways amounts to Rs. 1,298 crores in gross and Rs. 978 crores in net terms for the Third Plan. Out of these investments, however, at most Rs. 708 crores relate to increasing traffic capacity to the targeted 243 million tons; the other investments relate to diverse items including the construction of new (marginal) lines and staff quarters and other expenditures (Table 7, Appendix B). The latter unproductive items are in response to regional political demands for the extension of the network on the one hand and to misguided application of socialist principles on the other. If economic efficiency is to be the criterion for the reorganization of transportation, items which do not yield appropriate returns should be eliminated from railway investment.[1]

The above quoted investment figure of the Plan would have to be increased if the railways will also have to accommodate the added 27 million tons of traffic which according to our estimate will be generated by the end of the plan period over and above the official

[1] From the nation's point of view economic efficiency as a way to increasing savings and income growth is crucial. Regional demands must be satisfied by methods which do not damage the efficiency of resource allocation. Furthermore, the provision of housing and other facilities for staff, paradoxically, increases rather than decreases income inequality. For in a society with vast unemployment the foremost method of increasing equality is to increase savings and productive investment in the interest of industrialization. Hence those who are employed should not appropriate further gains from industrialization while unemployment continues and even increases. See the paper on *Regional Allocation of Resources in India* by Louis Lefeber in this volume.

101

projections.[1] Our rough and preliminary estimates indicate that Rs. 850 crores (net) is appropriate to meet the requirements of a 270 million ton traffic target in the railways which then would close the projected traffic gap.[2]

Let us now investigate the profitability of new investment under alternative conditions in the Indian railways.[3] First, we assume that the rate structure remains unchanged—i.e. will be maintained exactly as it was in 1960–61—during the entire plan period. Furthermore we assume that the net investments undertaken correspond to the Rs. 978 crores as foreseen by the Plan to attain a capacity for 243 million tons by 1965–66. The estimated gross profit (gross earnings minus working expenditures) for 1960–61 came to Rs. 134 crores. The gross profit in 1965–66 based on the Plan target is estimated to reach Rs. 171 crores. Hence the incremental gross profit is Rs. 37 crores in response to an investment of almost a thousand crores, i.e. the yield gross of depreciation is not more than 3·6 per cent of the value of the investment. If the marginal line and housing constructions are excluded along with some other trimmings (Table 7, Appendix B) and net investment is reduced to Rs. 708 crores, then the gross yield becomes a bit higher than 5 per cent. If we assume that depreciation charges are 4 per cent, the incremental net yield becomes negative in the first and about 1 per cent in the second computation.[4]

The investment becomes somewhat more promising if the 27 million tons of added demand for transportation will be allocated to the railways. In that case, of course, the investment will have to be enlarged, but revenues—and costs—will also increase. According to

[1] Our estimate of total shortage is 33 million tons. However, we pointed out that better utilization of road transport facilities for long distance movement could accommodate 6 million tons of the added demand.

[2] This investment also allows for the projected increase in passenger traffic. The figure is reached by an increase of investment requirements proportionate to goods traffic.

[3] The figures of the subsequent argument are summarized in the Tables of Appendix B.

[4] As far as depreciation charges are concerned, a flat 4 per cent, i.e. 25-year depreciation of assets, seems to be more realistic than the current practice of the Indian railways. Whereas a large part of the railway plant consists of assets older than twenty-five years, it is also true that had the railways undertaken a more vigorous depreciation and renewal policy in the past, their plant would be more adequate to cope with current demands. Furthermore, with increasing technological progress in railway transportation, obsolescence will have to be given greater weight in the depreciation policy.

our estimates in 1965–66 revenues (based on current rates) will reach Rs. 708 crores and costs 466 crores, resulting in a gross profit of 242 crores.[1] The incremental gross profit under these conditions becomes Rs. 108 crores (242 minus 134 crores). Assuming that the investment required to handle the increased traffic (net of trimmings) is Rs. 850 crores, the gross incremental yield becomes about 12·5 per cent and net of depreciation 8·5 per cent.

This is an interesting outcome which highlights the most difficult financial problem of the railways. The yield of the investment increased by more than 7 per cent due to increasing the capacity to 270 million tons. The explanation lies in the fact that the last 27 million tons of traffic can entirely consist of higher-rated commodities whereas the traffic accounted under the originally projected 243 million tons capacity contains an overwhelming proportion of low-rated commodity flows. Since the primary business of the railways is to transport bulk commodities, the high-rated commodities are necessarily the first ones to be forced out to other modes if capacity limitations and/or inefficiency of delivery prevails on the railways. The implications are obvious. As time goes by and road transportation gradually acquires capacity, an increasing proportion of the high-rated traffic will shift to road transport. This development is bound to happen if not during the Third Plan then in subsequent years. In the meantime the evidence seems to be that the demand for bulk commodity movement as per cent of total railway transportation is growing at a faster rate than the demand for the transport of high-value commodities. On both accounts—because of competition from road transport and the trend in the demand for bulk movement —the long-run salvation of the Indian railways from bankruptcy will have to come from attaining profitability on the basis of the transportation of low-value bulk commodities. This can be done only by raising the rates of bulk commodity transportation, which currently are insufficient to cover costs including a realistic rate of depreciation.

There are other reasons too, however, to increase transportation rates on the railways. As mentioned above, other investment— including road transportation—operates at or above 20 per cent yield before profit taxes and after depreciation. If the Indian railways cannot obtain comparable yields on new investment, the shifting of

---

[1] For the estimation of costs and revenues see Appendix B.

new capacity to other modes of transportation—particularly road transport—should be considered.

What increase in total revenues would be necessary to provide a comparable—and desirable—marginal return on railway investment? Assume that we could retroactively increase the estimated Rs. 464 crores railway revenues for 1960–61 by say 28 per cent or Rs. 132 crores, in which case total revenues would amount to Rs. 596 crores for the same year. Assume also that about 70 per cent of the increase is obtained from an upward adjustment of the rates charged for low-value bulk commodities with the remainder met by increased charge for unprofitable services rendered to the government (military, etc.) and by raising passenger fares for all classes and particularly for higher-class coaching and sleeper services.[1] Then the corresponding over-all average earning per ton of commodity over the distance of the average lead (348 miles) would come to Rs. 25·5. Assume that the rate structure underlying the above hypothetical revenues is carried forward to 1965–66 and applied to 270 million tons goods traffic, and that other earnings are correspondingly adjusted.[2]

Given the hypothetical rate adjustment, gross profits in 1960–61 would amount to Rs. 266 crores and in 1965–66 to 453 crores. The difference indicates an incremental gross profit of Rs. 187 crores over the Plan Period (see Table 6, Appendix B). This incremental profit is in response to the Rs. 850 net investment (net of trimmings); i.e. the gross incremental yield would be 22 per cent, or the yield net of depreciation would be 18 per cent. This yield is now in a range comparable to that of other investments.[3]

To summarize the argument, if investment in the railways is to be made worthwhile, two fundamental conditions have to be met: investments have to be concentrated in lines where the demand for traffic ensures capacity utilization (which excludes marginal lines and other investments); and the rate structure has to be raised in such

[1] It is a peculiar phenomenon inconsistent with the ideals of the Indian state that while revenues from third-class passenger transport seem to cover more than the cost of services, higher-class passenger services are provided at a loss. To put it bluntly, the third-class passengers subsidize the travel of the well-to-do.

[2] In this computation we have assumed that the average lead remains constant. An increase in average lead should not damage our argument since costs increase less than proportionately in response to increases in the lead.

[3] Adding in the cost of marginal lines, staff housing, etc., the total investment would come to Rs. 1,120 crores and the gross and net yields would drop to about 16·5 and 12·5 per cent respectively.

a way as to increase the profitability of transporting bulk commodities. The elimination of discrimination by corresponding
increases in the rates for bulk commodities would discourage
unnecessary growth in the demand for railway transportation. But in
the long run it would also save the railways from bankruptcy. The
trend is for an increasing proportion of bulk commodities relative
to the total tonnage transported. Unless rates are suitably adjusted,
increasing proportions of traffic will have to be carried at or below
operating costs.

What does the above suggested increase in revenues imply from
the short-run point of view? If we stay with our hypothetical revision
of the rate structure, the current average yield (profits in terms of
capital) of the railways would drastically improve. Assuming that the
current capital value of the railway plant is Rs. 1,900 crores, the
suggested revision would give a 10 per cent average yield (net of
depreciation).[1]

A 10 per cent average yield or capital charge is not excessive. It is
commensurate with the average profitability (before taxes) of other
Indian enterprises in general and road transport in particular. More
importantly, when capacity is lagging demand, rates should be high
enough to encourage only the most efficient utilization of the plant.
To put it differently, when marginal costs are above average costs,
profits are indicated. And the size of outstanding registrations
indicates that considerable profits could be earned. Furthermore,
returns on investments in the transport plant undertaken during the
previous plan periods should have reflected their opportunity cost.
A 20 per cent return (which corresponds to the real rate of interest
in India) on the incremental investment undertaken over the last
ten years would imply at least a 10 per cent yield on the utilization
of the entire plant.

It is not advisable to force a drastic change of such magnitude
on the users of the railway services suddenly and in a single discontinuous jump. Instead the adjustment could be accomplished by
gradual increases, say over a five-year period. However, the major

[1] Current railway accounting does not reflect the value of the plant based on
which depreciation and capital charges could be assessed. Valuation is, of course,
an impossible task if scholarly standards are applied to it. However, a pragmatic
estimate can be obtained which could then provide a basis for future assessments.
Our estimate of Rs. 1,900 crores is built upon the Indian Government outlays in
acquiring the plant, subsequent investments and yearly depreciation on a 4 per
cent basis. The figure is a crude estimate.

burden of the rate increase would have to fall on bulk commodities. And this is exactly where the political problem arises.

ARGUMENTS AGAINST THE RATIONALIZATION OF THE RATE STRUCTURE

Opposition to the rationalization of the rate structure is to be expected from many quarters. It could be motivated by concern for the effects of rate increases on production costs (particularly of export goods). Less intelligent arguments against rationalization would focus on the question of equitable (in an undefined sense) regional distribution of resources and on the propriety of obtaining profits on a government enterprise.

It is true that an increase in the transport cost of bulk commodities would have cost effects. However, these should not be exaggerated. For instance, since the value created per ton of coal in manufacturing is very large, in most industries a significant increase in its transport cost would still have only negligible cost effects. And precisely those industries which are noticeably affected are the ones which should be encouraged to either substitute other fuel (such as residual fuel oil in western India) or seek location at more economic points.[1] One of the industries which might be heavily affected by the suggested rate increase is cement manufacturing. In response to the entire five-year rate adjustment the increase in the cost of cement would be about 5 per cent for a plant located at a distance of the average lead from the pithead. This is still not an alarming cost increase. The significant point is that the short-run cost effects of the rate adjustment would be

---

[1] The fear that industrial activity would suffer and that coal flows to existing industries would diminish is unfounded. Plants which are located already have an inelastic demand for coal and would continue production. They would, however, undertake a gradual shift to more economical fuels or sources of power if such is economical.

A rise in the price of delivered coal by Rs. 10 per ton might result in cost rises of final outputs ranging from about 0·1 per cent in general and electrical engineering and 0·5 per cent in cotton textiles to about 2·5 per cent in paper, glass, and steel industries. In the case of electricity coal can play an important role. However, excepting some electrolytic processes, the value of final output created by a unit of electric power is very large; hence the increase in the price of delivered coal would have again small effects on the costs of final outputs.

Tables 8 and 9 of Appendix B provide consumption norms of coal in various industries for the entire economy and separately for Bombay, where about 50 per cent of the coal consumption originates from West Bengal.

sufficiently small so that longer-run economies coming from improved resource utilization could offset them.

The competitive position of Indian export industries is a legitimate concern. Those industries, however, which face an inelastic demand (e.g., jute and tea) would not be unfavourably affected. In the case of the industries which have difficulties at the going exchange rate direct export subsidies would be preferable to subsidization through railway rates since those can be dispensed without causing widespread distortion in the economy. Devaluation of the rupee might be an alternative policy which could result in the elimination of all subsidies (but also in the creation of export taxes for goods facing inelastic demands).

The question of regional equality in the distribution of resources is too large a topic to be taken up here.[1] However, it is to be emphasized that the fastest road to developing retarded regions is to increase the country's saving potential and with it the rate of new investment. The inefficiencies caused by the discriminating rate structure are not conducive to this result. Furthermore, several industrial activities could be taken up in rural areas if raw materials were made to pay their full transportation cost. Agricultural processing (for instance, grain milling) is a case in point.

Finally, there is the question of profits in government-owned enterprises. It is again true that under certain conditions and for particular well-specified purposes the government should produce goods or services which are sold below cost or given away free of charge. This is the case with education and welfare services. In the industrial field the government may want to induce increased consumption of certain goods or services by selling below the average costs of production because of external economies or because average costs are falling in response to an increase in output (i.e. social marginal costs are below average costs). These conditions are, however, patently absent in the case of the Indian railways; i.e. capacity can barely keep up with increases in demand, and plant utilization is at a level where marginal costs are sharply rising.

Government ownership of productive facilities in India is motivated also by income distribution considerations. However, the desire to restrict private profits to a socially acceptable level does not imply that government enterprises must operate without profits. On the contrary, in a country like India, where the supply of private

[1] See 'Regional Allocation of Resources in India', in this volume.

savings and the taxation of incomes are very limited, profits of government-owned enterprises should be one of the important sources of savings.

RAIL VERSUS ROAD

No discussion of transportation problems can be complete without some reference to the competition among alternative modes of transportation, particularly the rail *versus* road controversy. The railways are justifiably concerned with the gradually increasing (though as yet insignificant) share of road transportation in the long-distance movement of goods. Trucks are ideally suited for the transport of high-value commodities, and the fear is that they will gradually appropriate that share of the traffic which currently offsets the railways' losses on bulk commodity transport. These fears are substantiated by the Western experience where the combined effect of discriminatory railway rate structures and rapid growth in road transportation put most railways on the brink of bankruptcy if not deeply in the red.

The Indian railways' response to the threat is to attempt to curb the development of long-distance road transport. This was also (and still is) the response of Western railways. Efforts to curb road transportation, however, are doomed to fail in the long run—as they did in the West; furthermore they are not in the nation's interest. Road transportation is a valuable form of technological progress, and its comparative advantage in hauling high-value commodities (over long distance) should not be suppressed. Enlightened railway policy must realize that the primary advantage and importance of railways lies in the rapid and efficient movement of bulk commodities. Hence the rate structure must be adjusted to make the railways financially viable even if they must rely exclusively on bulk commodity movements. New investments in the railway plant should increasingly be oriented to attain greater efficiency in the movement of bulk commodities. With an enlightened policy that ensures the financial viability and continued vital role of the railways, the curbs and restraints on road transportation (which are particularly detrimental at periods of acute transportation shortage) can and must be lifted.

The above general principles do not give any indication of the proper balance between new investments in railways and highway transportation. The answer is beyond the scope of this paper. At this stage only obvious conclusions can be reached which are none the less worth mentioning. The railways should concentrate greater amounts of new investment than currently scheduled to alleviate conditions on congested routes and should intensify efforts to promote speed and efficiency on existing trunk lines. At the same time they should gradually retire from commitments on unprofitable lines and should resist regional pressures for new lines where no assured steady flow of bulk commodities warrants their installation. In these areas motor transportation is evidently more suited to the conditions. The road system can be built with the help of an under-employed rural labour force and with a real resource counterpart that is insignificant (i.e. P L 480 grain could cover most requirements). The rolling stock, the number of trucks servicing these rural routes, is optimally adjustable to the small and slowly changing needs.

Simple-minded cost and benefit comparisons are meaningless. Cost accounting for alternative modes must include all costs attributable to the provision of services; for instance, the cost of local and feeder traffic and the effects of delays and risk of damage on inventories are part of the total cost of long-distance transportation. Foreign exchange requirements must be accounted for at a 'shadow' exchange rate rather than at the official one. Most importantly, policy decisions should be based on the rational evaluation of feasible alternatives rather than on an implicit assumption of constancy of conditions currently prevailing in the Indian economy. For instance, fuel problems should be viewed in the context of the growth of the Indian petro-chemical industry; particular taxes which directly affect transportation should be considered as adjustable.

CONCLUSION

There is a danger that transport may become a bottleneck in the Third Five Year Plan. The shortage of physical capacity is aggravated by discriminatory railway rate policies which encourage unnecessary demands on the plant.

These rate policies, moreover, have other equally important consequences. On the one hand they threaten the financial viability of the Indian railways and significantly subtract from the limited resources available for the Plan. On the other hand they cause distortions in the choices of industrial location and the regional distribution of economic activity. The real costs of production are increased, scarce resources are wasted, and the balance of regional development is, if anything, adversely affected.

The remedy is in raising the rates for bulk commodities to a level which properly reflects all costs of transportation including those of depreciation and capital charges.

Attempts to curb road transportation will neither save the railways from bankruptcy nor contribute to the easing of the transport shortage. On the other hand, an enlightened rate policy will re-establish the railways' financial position even if they have to rely on revenues from bulk transportation alone. In the competition with road transport, that is where their comparative advantage lies.

The price effects of a rate increase should not be exaggerated. Furthermore, they would soon be offset by the resulting economies in resource utilization. To understand this, one must keep two facts in mind. First, the value created per unit of raw materials is very large; hence the increases in transportation charges translate into small fractions of the value of the finished products. Secondly, discrimination in favour of bulk commodities is a blanket subsidy to all users of raw materials whether such is economically justifiable or not. Subsidy to established industries is a waste of resources and should not be necessary. In the case of infant industries direct subsidies are preferable since the total resource equivalent can be maintained at the level of the intended subsidy without paying the hidden resource costs of distortions in the entire economy.

APPENDIX A

ESTIMATES OF LONG-DISTANCE GOODS TRAFFIC

1. Methods employed in forecasting the volume of goods traffic in 1965–66 are:

   (a) extrapolation of transportation coefficients; and
   (b) regression analysis.

2. Table 1 gives a breakdown by commodity groups of tons originating in railways from 1950–51 to 1959–60. The relationships between volumes of output and freight tons are expressed as percentages of total production. Assuming that similar or somewhat increasing percentages of the volume of production of various commodities will require long-distance movement by all modes of

transportation in subsequent years, an estimate of total freight traffic (in tons-originating) is worked out based on the production plans of the various sectors of the economy. Most of the coefficients merely reflect the historical trend; in the case of coefficients where the trend was rejected the alternative assumptions are explained as follows:

(a) Food grain movement is taken to increase at the rate of 4 per cent per annum, corresponding to the expected rate of urban population growth.

(b) Pig iron for sale and finished steel are taken to require two stages of transportation after production—once to secondary industry and then to consuming centres. In the past, rail movement of iron and steel was as high as 180 per cent of production plus imports. But then the bulk of imported steel was usually in finished form and was consumed largely in port towns. By the end of the Third Plan the bulk of domestic demand will be met by home production—at steel plants situated away from the big cities. Hence the increased coefficient.

(c) A similar argument applies for paper and paper board. With the Central Indian Newsprint and other domestic industries replacing imports, particularly in the consumption of the port cities, the coefficient of movement is likely to go up.

(d) 'Others' (other than the seventeen listed commodities) are taken to provide 38 per cent of the total long-distance traffic in 1965–66. During the last decade this group accounted for 37 per cent to 40 per cent of total rail movement. Moreover, motor transport was taking an increasing share of long-distance traffic. The latter was to a large extent confined to this group of commodities. If this is taken into consideration, then one should establish a rising trend of the ratio of this group to the total long-distance traffic. We have retained 38 per cent as our coefficient. Thus our estimate is bound to be on the conservative side.

On the basis of the coefficients and targeted production it is found that about 305 million tons of goods will require long-distance movement in 1965–66.

3. Motor transport is expected to take an increasing share of total long-distance traffic in the future. From the production programme of

111

the automobile industry and on the assumption of fifteen years' life for a truck we find that the maximum number of trucks available in 1965–66 will be about 303,000, roughly two-thirds of which will be diesel-run. Taking CTPC's estimate of vehicle utilization (100,000 ton-miles and 40,000 ton-miles per annum for diesel and petrol trucks respectively), the total capacity of motor transport in ton-miles was estimated. Table 2 shows our estimate of the requirements of local and feeder traffic assuming that the relative share of animal-drawn carts will diminish according to the historical trend. The capacity on road available for long-distance traffic was obtained by residual. In 1950–51, under 'Code of Principle and Practice', motor transport could not for all practical purposes participate in long-distance traffic. We have assumed that the entire capacity on road in that year was devoted to local and feeder traffic. The ratio of total capacity on road to the volume of long-distance traffic in 1950–51 was 70 ton-miles per ton-originating in long-distance. Based on this ratio, we obtained the requirements of local and feeder traffic. The residual capacity goes to long-distance traffic. Taking an average lead of 300 miles, we get the tons-originating of long-distance traffic on road. If 305 million tons of goods need to be moved over long distance in 1965–66 by all modes of transportation, about 25 million tons of these goods can be carried by road, given the planned expansion programme in the automobile industry. Historical evidence suggests that about 3·5 million tons will be carried by coastal shipping in that year. The residual is 276·8 million tons, of which the railways have planned for 243·5 million tons.

4. Total freight traffic on railways during the last decade has been functionally related to various indicators of economic activity. Projections on the basis of these equations give estimates of goods traffic on railways under the assumption that the growth of the other modes of transportation is independent of railway traffic.

4.1 Let us denote the variables as follows:

T = freight traffic on railways (in billion ton-miles).

Y = net domestic products at fixed prices (in Rs. billion).

X_1 = income originating in goods producing sector, excluding non-marketed agricultural products at fixed prices (in Rs. billion).

X_2 = value of gross outputs of the goods producing sector plus imports at fixed prices (in Rs. billion).

112

The time series of the variables are given in Table 3. We fit the following equations by the method of least squares:

$$\text{(i)} \quad \log T = -3\cdot2191 + 2\cdot3714 \log Y \qquad (r_1 = 0\cdot94)$$
$$\text{(ii)} \quad \log T = -1\cdot3273 + 1\cdot770 \ \log X_1 \qquad (r_2 = 0\cdot94)$$
$$\text{(iii)} \quad \log T = -2\cdot8229 + 2\cdot0909 \log X_2 \qquad (r_3 = 0\cdot95)$$

If the first three years (i.e. 1950–51, 1951–52, and 1952–53) are excluded, a straight line fit is meaningful. That is given by

$$\text{(iv)} \quad T = -69\cdot94 + 0\cdot841 \ X_2 \qquad (r_4 = 0\cdot98)$$

Correlation coefficients (r's) are given along with the equations as measures of the closeness of fit.

4.2 Projections to 1965–66 on the basis of the above equations are

(i) 113·1 billion ton-miles goods traffic on railways
(ii) 112·3 billion ton-miles goods traffic on railways
(iii) 113·6 billion ton-miles goods traffic on railways
(iv) 111·1 billion ton-miles goods traffic on railways

Implicit in the series of ton-miles is a rising trend of average lead. If we divide these ton-miles estimates by the approximate trend value of average lead in 1965–66 (i.e. 390 miles), the estimates of railway goods traffic in tons originating are obtained as

(i) 290 million tons
(ii) 288 million tons
(iii) 291 million tons
(iv) 285 million tons

5. Next, tons-originating (in millions) of goods traffic in railways (denoted by T_1) have been related to X_2. The fitted equations are

$$\text{(i)} \quad T_1 = -116\cdot069 + 1\cdot821 \ X_2 \qquad (r_5 = 0\cdot98)$$
$$\text{(from 1953–54 to 1959–60)}$$
$$\text{(ii)} \quad T_1 = 21\cdot142 + 0\cdot59 \ X_2 + 0\cdot0055 \ X_2^2 \qquad (r_6 = 0\cdot98)$$

Projections to 1965–66 on the basis of these equations give:

(i) 276 million tons originating on railways
(ii) 289 million tons originating on railways

TABLE 1

LONG-DISTANCE GOODS TRAFFIC
(IN THOUSAND TONS-ORIGINATING)

Sl. No.	Commodities		1950-51 Railways (actual)	1951-52 Railways (actual)	1952-53 Railways (actual)	1953-54 Railways (actual)	1954-55 Railways (actual)	1955-56 Railways (actual)	1956-57 Railways (actual)	1957-58 Railways (actual)	1958-59 Railways (actual)	1959-60 Railways (actual)	1960-61 (all-modes)	1965-66 (all-modes)
			(2)	(3)	(4)	(5)	(6)	(7)	(8)	(9)	(10)	(11)	(12)	(13)
1.	Coal	production	32307	34432	36303	35980	36880	38226	39434	43500	45336	47028	52000	97000
		transport	30423	32782	35411	32544	35119	38158	38158	40517	43001	44616	49847	92000
		per cent	94·2	95·2	92·0	90·5	95·2	96·8	96·8	93·1	94·9	94·8	95·8	95·0
2.	Cement	production	2613	3195	3537	3780	3927	4487	4969	5602	6072	6828	7750	13000
		transport	2432	2794	3023	3382	3345	3956	4291	5077	5012	6058	7208	12090
		per cent	93·1	87·5	85·5	89·5	85·2	88·2	87·1	90·6	82·6	88·7	93·0	93·0
3.	Iron and Steel	production and import	1422	1476	1487	1507	1864	1858	1897	1747	3093	3704	—	8000
		transport	2707	2636	2497	2555	2763	3655	4237	4861	5592	6602	7308	16000
		per cent	157·0	161·1	148·0	147·9	128·9	137·5	117·0	142·0	180·7	178·2	—	200·0
4.	Iron and other Ores	production	3655	4376	4601	4459	5054	5405	5744	5973	6644	8677	12500	34000
		transport	3007	3816	3338	4040	4330	4314	4630	5351	5807	8558	10489	30600
		per cent	82·3	87·4	72·5	90·6	86·7	80·0	80·7	89·6	87·4	98·6	83·9	90·0
5.	Foodgrains	production	50235	51175	58266	70178	67770	66494	70168	66091	78680	75557	76000	100000
		urban consumption	10000	—	—	—	—	12000	—	—	—	—	15000	18000
		transport	7682	8755	8345	8311	8122	9044	9685	11076	11933	12287	11580	13860
		per cent of urban consumption	76·8	—	—	—	—	75·4	—	—	—	—	77·0	77·0
6.	Oil seeds	production	5076	4949	4659	5285	6208	5643	6176	6051	6907	6352	7080	9800
		transport	1570	1389	1509	1359	1521	1766	1642	1641	1497	1467	2478	3430
		per cent	30·9	28·1	32·4	25·7	24·2	31·3	26·6	27·1	21·7	23·1	35·0	35·0

	C1	C2	C3	C4	C5	C6	C7	C8	C9	C10	C11	C12
9. Raw Cotton production and import	714	761	697	806	867	818	966	914	887	782	946	1230
transport	517	560	560	650	716	739	703	680	541	531	946	1230
per cent	72·4	73·6	94·7	80·7	82·5	90·3	72·8	74·5	61·0	67·9	100·0	100·0
10. Cotton manufacture production	498	543	616	647	635	715	736	770	727	738	940	923
transport	465	469	495	466	499	548	482	484	430	394	688	858
per cent	93·4	86·4	80·0	72·0	78·6	76·0	65·5	62·9	59·1	53·4	93·0	93·0
11. Raw Jute production	586	835	820	552	523	712	766	724	925	812	767	1140
transport	465	562	497	466	485	512	720	688	728	799	805	1140
per cent	93·4	67·3	60·6	84·4	92·7	71·9	94·0	95·0	78·7	98·4	105·0	100·0
12. Jute manufacture production	839	875	852	869	928	1027	1093	1030	1062	1051	1100	1100
transport	267	247	256	232	241	290	269	259	261	253	352	352
per cent	31·9	23·2	30·1	26·7	26·0	28·2	24·6	25·2	24·6	24·1	(32·0)	(32·0)
13. Salt production	2620	2732	2824	3171	2715	2979	3265	3626	4135	3128	4400	5000
transport	1551	1558	1521	1682	1716	1858	1715	1880	1781	1952	2640	3000
per cent	59·2	58·1	53·9	53·1	63·2	62·4	52·5	51·9	43·1	62·4	(60·0)	60·0
14. Tea production	271	286	301	263	288	284	298	303	320	316	324	379
transport	261	272	239	293	256	274	274	285	285	260	309	360
per cent	96·3	95·1	79·4	111·4	88·9	92·0	92·0	89·1	89·1	82·3	(95·0)	95·0
15. Paper and paper board production and import	215	219	240	266	286	324	330	311	344	366	(369)	820
transport	184	190	185	206	235	256	267	306	364	411	369	820
per cent	88·1	86·8	76·5	77·6	82·4	79·0	82·5	92·0	105·8	112·2	100·0	100·0
16. Sugarcane production	56150	—	—	—	—	59587	66998	68019	70456	75038	79610	105000
transport	2774	—	—	—	—	3408	3712	3324	2627	3141	4777	6300
per cent	4·9	—	—	—	—	5·7	5·5	4·9	3·7	4·1	(6·0)	6·0
17. Manganese ore production	883	1292	1462	1902	1414	1584	1687	1650	1256	1168	1800	3000
transport	867	997	1468	1987	1291	1378	1647	1620	974	1173	1680	2850
per cent	98·2	77·2	100·4	104·5	85·6	87·0	97·6	98·2	77·5	100·4	93·3	95·0
18. Others transport	35055	—	—	—	—	44954	49888	52562	52760	54000	63600	115730
per cent of total	38·4	—	—	—	—	37·4	40·2	39·7	39·0	37·4	(38·0)	(38·0)
TOTAL	91400	—	—	—	—	114000	124100	132400	135200	144200	167400	304550

TABLE 2

AVAILABILITY OF LONG-DISTANCE TRANSPORT FACILITIES BY RAIL, ROAD, AND COASTAL SHIPPING

	unit	1950–51	1955–56	1960–61	1965–66
1. Railway	million tons	91·4	114·0	155·0	243·5
2. Coastal shipping	million tons	2·0‡	2·5	(3·0)	(3·5)
3. Sub-total (1) + (2)	million tons	93·4	116·5	158·0	247·0
4. Motor transport capacity	billion ton-miles	3·3	5·5	10·0	24·5
5. Animal drawn carts capacity	billion ton-miles	3·2	3·5§	(3·8)	(4·1)
6. Sub-total (4) + (5)	billion ton-miles	6·5	9·0	13·8	28·6
7. Feeder and local traffic*	billion ton-miles	6·5	8·3	11·6	21·3
8. Long-distance motor traffic	billion ton-miles	—	0·7	2·2	7·3
9. Long-distance motor traffic†	million tons	—	2·3	7·3	24·3
10. Unaccounted traffic	million tons	—	—	—	33·3
11. Total long-distance traffic (3)+(9)+(10)	million tons	93·4	118·8	165·3	(304·6)

Figures in brackets are estimated.

* Requirement of local and feeder traffic per ton originating of long-distance traffic is 70 ton-miles per ton-originating, assuming that entire motor transport (and of course, bullock-carts) in 1950–51 was engaged in local and feeder traffic. This ratio is taken to remain constant over the whole period.

† Assuming an average lead of 300 miles.

‡ 'Report of Chief Engineer on Road Development Plan for India 1961–81,' New Delhi, 1958.

§ 'Goods Traffic Survey,' Delhi, 1957 Table 2.40.

TABLE 3

BASIC DATA

(1) Year	(2) Net domestic product at 1948–49 prices (Rs. billion)	(3) Income originating goods producing sector (excluding non-marketed agricultural product) in 1948–49 prices (Rs. billion)	(4) Value of gross output of goods producing sector plus imports at 1960–61 prices (Rs. billion)	(5) Railway Freight Traffic (in freight traffic million tons)	(6) Tons originating billion (in ton-mile)	(7) Average lead of Railway goods traffic (in miles)	(8) Number of trucks on road
1950–51	88·7	36·5	104·7	27·0	91	295	81,888
1951–52	91·6	38·4	110·3	29·0	97	299	84,013
1952–53	94·7	40·3	112·5	28·9	97	298	91,425
1953–54	99·5	42·6	118·6	29·5	98	301	92,513
1954–55	102·8	45·2	123·7	32·1	106	302	—
1955–56	104·8	45·2	125·9	36·4	114	320	119,097
1956–57	109·9	47·8	134·2	40·2	124	324	124,628
1957–58	109·0	47·2	130·2	44·6	132	338	—
1958–59	117·0	51·1	140·5	46·7	135	346	145,048
1959–60	—	—	141·5	50·1	144	348	—
1960–61	—	—	—	—	—	—	160,000
1965–66 (anticipated)	167·3	84·7	215·3	—	—	—	303,000

APPENDIX B

OPERATIONAL COSTS AND EARNINGS OF RAILWAYS

1. Estimates of operational costs have been worked out on the following assumptions:

  (a) Cost per train-mile in 1965–66 will remain the same as in 1959–60.

  (b) The ratios of freight tonnage and passengers to goods train-miles and passenger train-miles respectively will remain the same in 1965–66 as in 1959–60.

2. Total train-miles on Indian railways was 235·2 million in 1959–60 (Indian Railways, 1959–60 Table VIII). Total cost of operation (excluding provision for depreciation and interest payments) was Rs. 302·8 crores (see Table 4). Cost per train-mile is taken as the ratio of the two, i.e. Rs. 12·90.

3. In 1960–61, the estimated volume of passenger traffic (estimated on the basis of first eight months' data given in 'Review of Performance etc.', Feb., 1961, page 14) was 1,632 million. Taking the railways' estimate of 15 per cent increase, it will be 1,877 million in 1965–66. Required train-miles on a pro rata basis come to 155·1 million.

4. On an analogous computation the required goods train-mileage for 243·5 million tons of cargo comes to 185·8 million, and that for 270 million tons, 206·0 million.

5. Total requirements of train mileage on the basis of railways' estimate of traffic in 1965–66 is 340·9 million and on the basis of our estimate (the same passenger traffic and 270 million tons of goods) is 361·1 million. Operational costs (excluding depreciation and interest) for the two estimates are Rs. 440 crores and Rs. 466 crores respectively.

6. Table 5 gives the breakdown by commodities of the revenue-earning part of the 270 million tons of goods traffic in 1965–66. Non-revenue traffic is kept at 41 million tons in spite of the fact that with increasing traffic non-revenue movement of coal and materials for the railways should also increase. However, the increase on margin cannot be substantial, and a corresponding adjustment would not alter the conclusions. The gross earnings on the basis of 1959–60 rate structure come to Rs. 503·5 crores on the remaining 229 million tons.

If the 5 per cent surcharge on freight imposed since 1959–60 is added to this, gross earnings come to Rs. 528·7 crores. By adding passenger, other coaching, and sundry earnings to this we get a total of Rs. 708 crores as gross earnings. In Table 6 the estimates of total gross earnings corresponding to the railways' targets are given (adopted from the Report of the Railway Convention Committee, page 19) along with those based on our estimates. It is to be noted that in these calculations the average lead for each commodity is taken to remain at 1959–60 level.

7. The value of capital assets of the railways at historical costs in 1960–61 is estimated to be about Rs. 1,900 crores. If the proposed Third Plan investment programme is fulfilled, it will come to about Rs. 2,900 crores in 1965–66. The whole of net investments envisaged in the Third Plan for railways cannot be considered strictly necessitated by only the demand for additional traffic. If such items of investment as staff quarters, certain new lines, etc., are separated, about Rs. 708 crores of investments remain as those due to additional traffic. Table 7 gives a rough and tentative breakdown of this estimate. This is based on crude calculations, hence it gives only a rough idea of the order of magnitude. On a proportionate basis it is estimated that about Rs. 850 crores of investments may be strictly necessary during the Third Plan for achieving the target of 270 million tons of goods traffic and 1,877 million passenger traffic.

8. In Tables 8 and 9 consumption norms of coal in various industries are given for the entire economy and separately for Bombay.

TABLE 4

COST OF OPERATION ON RAILWAYS, 1959–60

	(in Rupees crores)	
	Gross Expenditure (excluding suspense and credit)	*Net Expenditure (allowing for suspense and credit)*
1. Administration	37·8	36·3
2. Repairs and maintenance	110·2	94·1
3. Operating staff	65·9	57·9
4. Fuel	66·6	58·0
5. Other operating expenses	32·0	28·5
6. Labour welfare	30·0	28·0
Total 1 to 6	342·5	302·8
7. Suspense	6·5	—
8. Credits and recoveries	302·8	302·8

119

TABLE 5

ESTIMATES OF GROSS EARNINGS OF RAILWAYS
IN 1965–66
(AT CURRENT RATES)

| (1) | 1959–1960 (*Actuals*) | | | 1965–66 (*Estimated*) | |
	Tonnage (*m.tons*)	Earnings (*m.Rs.*)	Earnings per ton (*Rs.*)	(*Traffic 270 m. tons*) Tonnage (*m.tons*)	Earnings (*m.Rs.*)
(1)	(2)	(3)	(4)	(5)	(6)
A. *Revenue-earning traffic:*					
1. Coal for public	27·34	401·4	14·67	71·0	1041·6
2. Food grains	12·28	277·8	22·62	13·5	305·4
3. Iron and other ores	8·56	101·1	11·81	30·6	361·4
4. Manganese ore	1·17	28·2	24·07	2·9	69·8
5. Cement	6·06	102·3	16·88	11·0	185·7
6. Salt	1·95	51·4	26·36	2·8	73·8
7. Sugarcane	3·14	10·5	3·35	4·3	14·4
8. Oilseeds	1·46	45·7	31·30	2·6	81·4
9. Iron and Steel	6·61	263·3	33·83	14·4	487·2
10. Sugar	1·35	57·0	42·22	1·4	59·1
11. Cotton—raw	0·53	37·7	71·13	0·6	42·7
12. Cotton manufactures	0·39	44·7	114·62	0·5	57·3
13. Jute—raw	0·80	26·6	19·50	1·0	19·5
14. Jute manufactures	0·25	15·6	61·52	0·3	18·5
15. Tea	0·26	17·8	68·46	0·4	27·4
16. Paper	0·41	22·1	53·90	0·7	37·7
17. Vegetable oils	0·23	12·1	52·48	0·4	20·6
18. Other commodities	36·11	1090·1	30·19	70·6	2131·4
Total	108.90	2605·0	23·92	229·0	5034·9
					+ 251·7*
					5286·6
B. *Non-revenue earning traffic:*					
Railway coal	17·28			21·0	
Other railway materials	18·01			20·0	
Total	35·29			41·0	
GRAND TOTAL	114·19			270·0	

* Allowance for 5 per cent surcharge on freight imposed subsequent to 1959–60.

TABLE 6

COSTS AND EARNINGS OF RAILWAYS ON THE BASES OF CURRENT COSTS AND CURRENT AND RECOMMENDED RATES

(IN RS. CRORES)

(1)	1960-61 (estimated)		1965-66 On Railways estimates of traffic and investments		1965-66 On our estimates of traffic and investment†	
	At current rates	At recommended rates*	At current rates	At recommended rates	At current rates	At recommended rates
	(2)	(3)	(4)	(5)	(6)	(7)
I. Capital Assets	(1900)	(1900)	2900	2900	2750	2750
II. Costs:						
Working expenses	330	330	440	440	466	466
Total costs	596	596	846	846	851	851
III. Gross Earnings:						
1. Good earnings	304	396	429	621	526	689
2. Other earnings	160	200	182	230	182	230
Total earnings	464	596	611	851	708	919

* If 70 per cent of the Rs. 132 crores deficit in 1960–61, i.e. Rs. 92 crores, are covered by increased rates on goods then the required earnings on 155 million tons are Rs. 396 crores. This means an average earning of Rs. 25·5 per ton of goods over the average lead (i.e. 348 miles) on an average rate of 7·3 nP. per ton mile.

† On the assumptions that (a) the required transportation capacity is allocated to railways, and (b) only Rs. 850 crores of direct investments are necessitated by the additional traffic demand alone.

TABLE 7

BREAKDOWN OF RAILWAY INVESTMENTS IN THIRD PLAN

(in Rs. crores)

sl. no. (0)	plan head (1)	gross investment (2)	net investment (3)	direct net investment for traffic (4)
1.	Rolling stock	505	384	384
2.	Track renewal	170	—	—
3.	Traffic facilities	183	183	183
4.	Signalling and safety	25	21	21
5.	Electrification	70	70	70
6.	Workshop machinery and plants	62	53	—
7.	Bridge work	25	11 ⎤	
8.	Other electric works, e.g. traction renewal	8	—	
9.	Staff quarters ⎱			
10.	Staff welfare ⎰	50	50	
11.	User's amenities	15	15 ⎬	50
12.	New lines	125	125	
13.	Other structural works	15	15	
14.	Road services	10	10	
15.	Stores suspense	35	35 ⎦	
	TOTAL	1298	978	708

TABLE 8

TOTAL VALUE OF OUTPUT PER TON OF COAL CONSUMPTION*
(ALL INDIA)

	1950	1951	1952	1953	1954	1955	1956
1. Wheat flour	6,238·2	5,736·7	5,049·6	6,684·9	6,001·9	5,560·1	7,457·7
2. Rice milling	5,654·8	6,190·1	7,120·2	7,257·4	8,032·9	8,418·0	9,709·0
3. Biscuit making	4,225·4	5,361·7	7,037·0	9,592·8	9,452·2	7,755·6	9,999·8
4. Fruits and vegetable processing	7,496·6	11,487·7	5,742·5	7,480·8	5,727·5	7,988·2	10,655·6
5. Sugar	11,600·5	11,252·1	9,857·2	8,475·1	7,962·0	9,465·9	11,477·7
6. Distilleries and breweries	453·0	491·1	491·5	447·3	472·8	512·6	553·9
7. Starch	3,201·7	3,314·0	2,128·8	1,949·9	1,564·4	1,345·7	1,306·6
8. Vegetable oils	5,965·4	7,044·9	5,338·0	5,452·0	5,711·8	5,259·9	5,973·7
9. (a) Edible hydrogenated oils	—	5,910·4	4,945·2	4,828·7	3,945·3	3,516·7	5,579·9
(b) Paints and varnishes	13,410·2	17,840·3	16,050·4	13,748·3	12,487·8	12,881·8	14,205·9
10. Soap	12,856·3	14,852·9	13,195·5	11,090·4	10,435·0	10,767·7	11,744·6
11. Tanning	14,017·3	19,883·3	16,899·5	16,064·0	16,039·0	18,507·2	19,644·1
12. Cement	214·9	204·7	221·7	198·8	204·8	209·5	196·9
13. Glass and glassware	331·7	396·2	337·5	330·1	357·4	400·7	433·1
14. Ceramics	171·5	194·5	176·9	223·0	278·4	253·1	379·8
15. Plywood and tea chests	2,778·8	2,994·1	3,311·8	2,036·5	2,548·6	3,060·5	3,344·2
16. Paper and paper board	359·3	368·5	384·6	382·6	452·5	438·3	395·2
17. Matches	6,299·0	7,126·3	7,056·9	5,354·8	5,862·1	5,186·8	5,008·9
18. Cotton textiles	1,963·1	2,503·5	2,171·9	2,012·2	2,058·3	2,057·8	2,071·9
19. Woollen textiles	3,227·4	5,666·9	3,451·4	3,707·3	3,648·2	2,921·8	3,441·5
20. Jute textiles	2,383·9	3,481·3	2,738·2	1,583·0	2,042·1	2,136·4	2,215·7
21. Chemicals	1,248·8	1,531·7	988·7	901·1	889·9	1,190·1	1,359·0
22. Aluminium, copper and brass	1,829·0	1,909·8	1,776·1	1,935·7	1,507·7	1,687·1	2,112·7
23. Iron and steel	159·8	169·8	195·5	223·3	306·9	341·1	449·2
24. Bicycles	12,442·6	13,711·3	18,133·7	18,021·7	17,288·6	19,328·9	15,218·5
25. Sewing machines	1,126·4	7,509·3	6,430·2	7,515·7	5,721·0	6,726·9	5,440·3
26. Producer gas	4,244·3	4,695·7	5,088·9	10,834·7	6,013·7	9,200·8	10,554·2
27. Electric lamps	15,646·7	17,947·4	17,799·3	16,079·0	13,801·7	14,067·1	15,569·4
28. Electric fans							
29. General engineering and electrical engineering	5,128·7	5,995·6	6,306·4	6,081·0	6,945·0	7,867·9	8,453·1
TOTAL	1,232·4	1,458·7	1,271·3	1,183·6	1,328·2	1,450·1	1,586·6

* Includes coal equivalent of electricity bought from public utilities

TABLE 9

CONSUMPTION NORMS OF COAL, COKE, FUEL OIL AND OTHER FUELS AND ELECTRICITY IN BOMBAY STATE, 1957

Industry	Consumption norms of Coal, Coke, Fuel oil and other Fuels and Electricity. In value in Rs. per million Rs. of output									In quantity per Rs. million of output						
	Coal	Coke	Char-coal	Fire-wood	Fuel oil	Coal gas	Others	Electricity	Total	Coal (tons)	Coke (tons)	Char-coal (tons)	Fire-wood (tons)	Fuel oil (000 gals.)	Coal gas (000 cu.ft.)	Electricity (000 kw.h.)
(1)	(2)	(3)	(4)	(5)	(6)	(7)	(8)	(9)	(10)	(11)	(12)	(13)	(14)	(15)	(16)	(17)
Wheat flour	170	—	—	—	90	—	—	6400	6600	3·5	—	—	—	0·2	—	122
Rice milling	—	2300	110	1600	29600	—	—	720	30300	—	30·3	0·8	29·6	22·8	—	(10)
Biscuit making	—	210	90	40	4600	2300	—	7800	18700	—	2·5	0·5	0·6	6·9	532	93
Fruits and vetetable preservation	—	40	—	5000	5000	440	210	5300	11100	—	0·7	—	115·3	7·4	110	55
Sugar	2400	20	—	32000	11300	—	37000	100	19000	53·5	0·6	—	804	13·7	—	0·8
Distilleries and breweries	63000	40	—	—	5700	—	—	73000	211000	1780	0·6	—	—	8·4	—	402
Starch	23000	—	—	320	8100	—	370	23000	54000	545	—	—	10·2	8·0	—	358
Vegetable oil	2200	90	20	—	3500	—	90	5400	9300	56·2	1·3	0·2	—	4·6	—	40·6
Edible hydrogenated oil	3100	860	10	220	6400	680	10	3700	15900	94·1	12·0	0·1	3·7	9·5	165	103
Paints and varnishes	50	880	30	—	1700	10	—	2600	7300	1·1	12·9	0·2	—	3·2	1·6	35
Soap	—	—	—	70	10600	—	—	2900	13200	—	—	—	0·9	18·0	—	67
Tanning	2100	—	10	30	1400	—	4100	6400	6400	58·0	—	0·1	0·3	1·1	—	32
Cement	217000	310	390	3000	2400	190	1800	54000	278000	4812	4·4	2·6	76·3	3·4	48	640
Glass and glassware	20000	10	—	350	125000	—	1200	20000	171000	518	0·2	—	11·7	187	—	212
Ceramics	108000	150	10	670	79000	—	—	33000	221000	2517	2·4	0·1	25·5	108	—	251
Paper and paper board	34000	40	—	1300	2200	—	110	45000	82000	1006	0·5	—	75·4	1·4	—	750
Matches	—	—	—	20	10200	40	20	34000	46000	—	—	—	0·5	16·3	9·0	900
Cotton textiles	14000	100	90	10	8200	—	40	20000	42000	324	1·3	—	0·1	13·3	—	378
Woollen textiles	3300	20	90	230	3900	110	300	9800	17400	66	—	0·5	5·3	20·9	26	160
Chemicals	14000	3100	30	1200	11000	—	340	7100	36000	300	42·1	0·2	27·3	17·5	—	108
Aluminium, copper and brass	—	1600	360	—	11400	—	120	7000	21700	0·4	19·5	3·8	1·6	25·8	—	102
Iron and steel	1400	770	—	80	17000	—	—	21000	40000	33·2	11·2	—	0·3	11·0	—	425
Bicycles	40	240	110	20	8600	—	—	7200	16200	1·0	3·0	0·8	—	—	—	120
Electric fans	—	1800	140	—	—	—	—	11000	13000	—	21·0	0·8	—	—	—	126
General engineering and electrical engineering	240	3200	90	290	3300	480	100	5000	12700	5·3	45·9	0·6	5·8	3·6	116	62
TOTAL	11800	700	30	350	8200	90	180	13800	35000	274	9·7	0·2	8·7	12·7	22	249

Source: Census of Manufacturing Industries, 1957.

WORKING CAPITAL IN THE INDIAN ECONOMY: A CONCEPTUAL FRAMEWORK AND SOME ESTIMATES[1]

AMARTYA KUMAR SEN

I. INTRODUCTION

Can the degree of capital-intensity be measured by the *per capita* availability of 'horsepower',[2] or of 'tons of steel'?[3] The answer is, not very well, for while they are both tolerable measures of the physical stock of fixed capital, they do not touch working capital at all. The working capital requirement can be divided into three parts: the work-in-progress, the stock of finished goods, and the stock of raw materials including spare parts and stores. The size of work-in-progress per unit of output flow depends on the cost of recurring inputs (e.g. wages, raw materials) per unit of output flow and the time lags between the application of recurring inputs and the arrival of outputs.

The stocks of finished goods might arise from two main sources: the delay in getting products transferred from producers to buyers (transaction hoards), and an expectation that the price of the goods involved is likely to rise faster, with due consideration of risk-premiums and carrying costs, than alternative forms of hoarding wealth (speculative hoards). There might also be some precautionary hoards, though final products by and large are not very good means

[1] I am indebted to the Center for International Studies for its assistance, which made this work possible, and also to its members, particularly Professor Rosenstein-Rodan, for their valuable comments. I have also received extremely useful advice from Professor Simon Kuznets, and at various stages of this work I have benefited greatly from the comments of Mrinal Datta Chaudhuri, Richard Eckaus, Louis Lefeber, P. N. Mathur, Harendra Mazumdar, Ashok Mitra, Pitamber Pant, I. G. Patel, Vinod Prakash, and Trevor Swan. A. G. Armstrong kindly did the computation.

[2] L. Rostas, *Comparative Productivity in British and American Industry* (Cambridge, 1948), p. 51.

[3] N. Kaldor, 'A Model of Economic Growth', *Economic Journal*, December 1957, p. 592.

of holding precautionary purchasing power. Some products, e.g. gold and silver, are of course eminent exceptions. In some cases a vague fear of inflation might lead to a type of hoarding that falls in between precautionary and speculative stocks.

The transaction delays are normal and are quite comparable in many ways with the delays in the production process. Thus it may be more useful to put transaction hoards of final goods in the same group as work-in-progress. The main category of inventory that is left out of the work-in-progress thus redefined is the speculative type of hoarding, which depends on price expectations, carrying costs over time, risks and uncertainties involved, and peoples' attitudes towards risks and uncertainties.

The same types of considerations apply to the speculative stocks of raw materials. There may be some precautionary hoards, e.g. of raw jute, in case the production of the raw material fails. There may be various mixtures of precautionary and speculative hoards. There will be in addition a stock of raw materials maintained for the normal convenience of production. The distinction between 'productive' inventory (i.e. working capital) and 'unproductive' inventory is discussed in section III below.

Before we proceed further, a general question may be raised about optimization of the size of inventories held. There seems to be a widely held view that optimization requires that 'inventories should increase only in proportion to the square root of sales'.[1] The basic argument can be put in the following way. Let:

a = annual carrying cost per unit of inventory,
b = re-order cost per order,
s = sales of the good per year,
p = purchase price per unit of the good,
C = aggregate cost of meeting sales of s per year,

and q = quantity purchased in each order, to be optimized.

We have $C = a \left(\dfrac{q}{2}\right) + p.s + b \left(\dfrac{s}{q}\right)$ (1)

The first order condition for minimization of C is:

$$\frac{dC}{dq} = 0,$$

[1] W. J. Baumol, *Economic Theory and Operations Analysis* (London, 1961), p. 10; J. F. Magee, *Production Planning and Inventory Control* (New York, 1958), p. 306; T. M. Whitin, *Theory of Inventory Management* (Princeton, 1957).

i.e. $\dfrac{a}{2} - \dfrac{b.s}{q^2} = 0,$

i.e. $q = \sqrt{\dfrac{2bs}{a}} = k.\sqrt{s},$ where k is a constant. (2)

Now this picture is far too simple,[1] but even without bringing in any radically different considerations it may be pointed out that the result is strongly based on very special assumptions. We may suggest a somewhat more general system in the following way. First, carrying cost is likely to rise more than proportionately to inventory, beyond a point, and this rising average cost of carrying can change the result considerably. A second point to note is that just as having too many orders might involve costs for the buyer, it also involves cost for the seller, so that he may well consider it necessary to charge a higher price for smaller orders and a lower price for larger orders. To take a particular example, we may redefine a and p, which instead of being constants, can be taken as:

$$a = (\alpha + \beta.q) \tag{3}$$
$$p = A - \gamma.q \tag{4}$$

Equation three makes the total carrying cost equal to $\frac{1}{2}(\alpha.q + \beta.q^2)$ with increasing average cost property, for $\beta > 0$, and p represent a downward sloping curve, for $\gamma > 0$. We assume these relationships to hold in the relevant limited range rather than for all q, so that we do not necessarily exclude possibilities of decreasing costs of carrying at smaller inventories, nor need we consider $p < 0$ for very large values of q. In this range the total cost will be:

$$C = \alpha \left(\dfrac{q}{2}\right) + \beta \left(\dfrac{q^2}{2}\right) + (A - \gamma.q)\,s + b.\left(\dfrac{s}{q}\right) \tag{5}$$

Now the cost minimization condition of the first order for non-zero q is given by:

$$B.q^3 + \left(\dfrac{\alpha}{2} - \gamma.s\right) q^2 - b.s = 0 \tag{6}$$

The 'square root principle' is the result of assuming $\beta = 0$, and $\gamma = 0$, so that equation (6) reduces to:

$$\dfrac{\alpha}{2}q^2 = b.s$$

[1] See Arrow, Karlin and Scarf, *Studies in the Mathematical Theory of Inventory and Production* (Stanford, 1958).

i.e. $\quad q = \sqrt{\dfrac{2.b.s}{\alpha}}$ (7)

(7) corresponds to (2) above.

If instead we take the 're-order cost' to be negligible, *i.e.* $b = 0$, we have:

$$\beta q^3 = \left(\gamma .s - \frac{\alpha}{2}\right)q^2$$

i.e. for non-zero q,

$$q = -\frac{\alpha}{2\beta} + \frac{\gamma}{\beta} .s = k_1 + k_2.s,$$ (8)

where k_1 is a negative constant and k_2 a positive one.

Here the stocks held $\left(\dfrac{q}{2}\right)$ will rise at a constant rate with respect to sales. If $\alpha = 0$ so that carrying cost is simply $\left(\dfrac{\beta}{2} .q^2\right)$, q and s will be simply proportional to each other.

In the absence of statistical verification there is nothing in principle to indicate that the 'square root' rule for optimization is more valid than the 'proportionality' rule. Indian data do not provide much opportunity for comparing these hypotheses, but in the few cases where some opportunities exist we do not find any better explanation for the size of the inventory by using the 'square root' rule than we get from the simple 'proportionality' rule. Nor do we interpret this to mean necessarily any lack of optimization behaviour.[1] The square root rule is an extremely special case, and no less plausible models can be constructed (as above) that make the 'rule of thumb' of proportionality approximately optimal.

II. SURPLUS LABOUR AND THE SYSTEM OF WAGE PAYMENT

The working capital requirement depends not only on technical factors but also on the nature of the economic organization. A special problem is posed by the value of labour in the pipeline, i.e. the value of labour included in the value of semifinished goods. From the point

[1] Cf. Baumol, p. 10.

of view of the capitalist the value is simply the wages locked up in the process, but from the point of view of the nation we have to look at the alternative use of labour and the additional consumption generated by additional employment.[1] If an economy has a lot of unemployment, the former is unimportant. This is the case with a very large part of India. On the other hand, the additional consumption requirement is still considerable, and the working capital can be measured in terms of the amount of the fund of consumer goods necessary due to the lag between payment to labour and the arrival of the output. To what extent the consumption requirement will correspond to the value of wages in the pipeline will depend on the propensity to consume, but in a country as poor as India the propensity to consume of wage earners is likely to be near unity.

However, in a very big part of many underdeveloped economies the household provides the basis for economic operations, and wage labour is relatively rare. This means that the remuneration to labour in this sector need not increase with additional labour until the fruits of that labour are reaped, so that the working capital requirement in terms of consumer goods fund is to that extent reduced. Take the case of fertilizers being supplied to a group of peasants cultivating land on a family basis. The additional labour they will now put in along with fertilizers will receive no particular additional remuneration until the additional products resulting from this are reaped. If, on the other hand, a wage-based farm employed additional labour to apply fertilizers, the wage-bill would have gone up immediately, and the existence of unemployed labour would not have prevented the requirement of a surplus stock of consumer goods for the employment of additional labour.[2] This means that the

---

[1] For a discussion of the problem of social cost of labour, see the writer's *Choice of Techniques* (Oxford, 1960), Chapter V.

[2] In so far as some additional saving was now done by those who were supporting the unemployed people before they found new employment and/or by the newly employed people themselves, the requirement of the surplus stock will be smaller. The prospect of this providing much voluntary savings is not, however, very great in a poor economy, so that some taxes will be required if a substantial part of the additional working capital requirement is to be met by additional savings from these sources. There might, however, be some voluntary shift in the commodity pattern of consumption which might to some extent ease the process of capital accumulation through a change in the relative prices. For a discussion of this problem see 'Unemployment, Relative Prices and the Savings Potential', by the present writer, *Indian Economic Review*, August 1957; also, 'Unemployment, Relative Prices and the Saving Potential', by Jagdish Bhagwati, *Indian Economic Review*, August 1958.

I   129

household economy achieves a certain saving of marginal working capital that is not possible for the wage-based economy, and since the process of development is also partly a process of conversion of the household-based economies into wage-based ones, the requirement of working capital is likely to grow to that extent more than proportionately to income. This makes the necessity of discussing this aspect of capital all the more important.

We must, in this context, examine the view of Professor C. P. Kindleberger about the relative decline of the requirement of capital represented in 'inventories' with the growth of an economy resulting from a fall in the ratio of agricultural output to total output. He says (in his chapter on 'Capital') 'since agricultural output is produced at one time of the year and consumed evenly over the year as a whole, half of output on the average is in inventories at a given time. This is a higher ratio than industry or services. In consequence, since the proportion of agricultural output in total output declines as income grows, the ratio of inventories to output declines.'[1] Now this argument is certainly valid in so far as 'inventory' is defined as any stock of goods, but it does not tell us much about 'inventory' viewed as capital necessary for production. The crucial difference between a wage and a non-wage economy is relevant here. In a non-wage economy this stock is in the nature of purely a consumption stock without representing a necessity for production at the margin. The size of this stock does not have to be increased prior to expanding production; on the contrary, the expansion of this stock is only a result of a larger size of output.

One should emphasize in this connection the distinction between stocks arising due to the temporal discontinuity (or the seasonal nature) of output in agriculture and the working capital that may be needed due to the time lag between input and output in this sector. The former does not demand any productive investment. Think of an economy where agriculture is permitted only on January 1st, i.e. the output is extremely seasonal, but the seeds sown in the morning are harvested in the afternoon of January 1st, out of which the workers are paid; i.e. the time lag is negligible. There is no need here for any working capital for labour in the pipe-line, and more labour

---

[1] *Economic Development* (New York, 1958), p. 38. See also W. A. Lewis, *Theory of Economic Growth* (London, 1955). 'The capital requirements of agriculture are usually underestimated. . . . The working capital required is large, because the crop is seasonal . . . ' (p. 270).

can be employed without the necessity of the prior presence of an additional stock of wage goods. The stock of output will be gradually spent between one January 1st and another, but this need not be expanded to employ more people on any January 1st. So this does not serve as working capital necessary for expansion.

The effects of a time lag between the application of labour and the arrival of the fruits of that labour are, however, quite different. In agriculture this lag is long, and in one of the Ricardian models of agricultural production working capital arising from this constitutes the whole of agricultural investment.[1] As we have already mentioned, however, in underdeveloped economies with family-based, non-wage cultivation this type of working capital is not necessary from the point of view of application of incremental labour. The under-employed peasants can work a little harder to apply, say, fertilizers, or water from irrigational projects, and they receive their return only when the additional output is harvested.[2] With the growth of an economy there are, therefore, two different trends. As a result of a fall in the share of agricultural output the ratio of 'inventories' to output may well fall in the Kindlebergerian manner. But this will not imply a relative fall in the productive investment requirement for expansion. In fact the decline of family-based production will tend to lead, other things being equal, to a larger requirement of working capital.[3] This possibility of working capital rising more than pro-portionately to output poses interesting problems for planning which development authorities must take into account.

III. 'PRODUCTIVE' AND 'UNPRODUCTIVE' INVENTORY

The discussion in the last section raised the rather general question of the distinction between 'productive' and 'unproductive' inven-tories. The distinction in principle is clear enough. We could define

[1] This provides the basis for the Ricardian position, in contradiction to Robert Malthus, that the profit rate in agriculture determines the profit rate for the whole economy, since it is independent of the relative prices; the output, input, and capital for agriculture being all made of corn. (*Essay on the Influence of a Low Price of Corn on the Profits of Stock*, 1815.)

[2] However, in so far as harder work requires more consumption of food, there will be a certain requirement of incremental working capital in the shape of a stock of food. This will also happen in so far as the cultivator can and wants to borrow more on the security of an expected increase in the forthcoming harvest resulting from an increase in the application of his labour.

[3] In so far as the decline of a family-based production leads to other types of non-wage cultivation, e.g. co-operative joint farming, this will not be so.

it rigidly in the following way. Let (p_i) be the vector of prices and (x_i) the vector of outputs being produced in an economy. Then an inventory could be defined as 'productive' only if an arbitrary increase in its size will allow us to reach an output vector (y_i) such that $(p_i)(y_i) - (p_i)(x_i) > 0$, treating the first item in each multiplication as a row matrix and the second as a column matrix. A sufficient but not necessary condition for this is that for at least one commodity (r), $(y_r - x_r) > 0$, and for all others $(y_i - x_i) \geqq 0$, provided all items of the price vector are positive.

But this definition is really too broad, for some commodities may have minute effects on output flows. If a worker feels cheerful looking at his wife's new bright dress and works a little better to produce a little more, it will still not be fair to put the stock of bright dresses as 'productive' working capital. We can take care of this by redefining the condition in the following way. Let V be the value of the increase in the size of the relevant inventory, then we require that

$$(p_i)(y_i - x_i) \geqq \alpha . \text{V},$$

where α is the appropriate rate of return that we might propose as a qualification test.

While this is the principle, in practice we have to stop way short of all this sophisticated calculation. It is conventional to treat the stocks of commodities held by consumers as unproductive and the stocks held by entrepreneurs as productive. This is a very rough division but it corresponds broadly, though admittedly imperfectly, to the condition described above. More doubts could be entertained about the wisdom of ignoring stocks held by consumers in an underdeveloped country than in a developed one, for the 'efficiency effects' of such stocks will be by and large greater in underdeveloped countries. But it must be remembered that the efficiency will depend more on the flow of consumption than on its stock held, and that the exact extent of the effect will be very difficult to disentangle and will call for a sociological rather than an economic study. We shall therefore confine our estimates to inventories held only by producers.

This last consideration still leaves some questions unanswered, for example, the inventories of consumer goods held by producers-cum-consumers in the shape of peasant-cultivators. There, as we have seen, the stock of food contributes to production, but an increase in its size would not necessarily increase the agricultural output. It is thus correct to argue that stocks of consumer goods held by such consumers-cum-producers should be treated as equivalent to stocks of consumer goods held by consumers and not to those held by producers.

What about stocks carried by traders? If a peasant driven by debts requiring payment, sells all his food stock to a trader after the harvest and buys it back (by fresh borrowing) from him as he needs it, this stock with the trader must be treated as fundamentally similar to the stocks held by peasants. Thus an observation that traders are holding more stocks is no guarantee that it is a 'productive' investment.

The line between stocks of this type and stocks required for genuinely productive transfers will be difficult to draw in practice. But most stocks held by traders will be of a type that will pass our test when different prices are attributed to a commodity with its producer and with its consumer. In India, where there are hardly any reliable statistics on the stocks held by traders, applying any fine distinction will be impossible, but difficulties involved in the problem must be borne in mind.

Finally, what about stocks of finished goods held by manufacturers? Several of those who commented on an earlier draft of this paper expressed unhappiness about including this item in the estimate of 'productive' inventory. Undoubtedly stocks of raw materials and of goods-in-process are necessary for production in a way that stocks of finished goods are not. But stocks of finished goods with the manufacturer should be viewed not as necessary for the manufacture but as an integral part of the next stage, the trade and the use of the commodity in question. In so far as the trader buys not every moment but at intervals to save (say) the 're-order cost', this will tend to give rise to temporary accumulations with the manufacturer. These stocks are therefore necessary parts of trading. An example will make this clear. Imagine a stationary state with perfect certainty, and one manufacturer and one trader, with the latter buying goods from the manufacturer at fixed intervals. Then, with constant (and equal) flows of production and consumption per unit of time, the average stock of finished goods held by the manufacturer will be exactly equal to the average stock held by the trader. And the two together will represent a constant amount of stock carried by the society to deal with the intervals of purchase required for the convenience of trading. Diagram I represents this, when $0, T_1, T_2, \ldots$ represent equidistant points of sale.

133

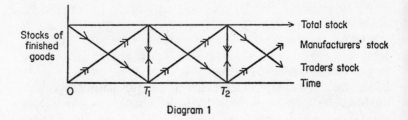

Diagram 1

Imagine now that this economy expands to another stationary state by an exact duplication of the above so that the stocks held by the manufacturers and by the traders will rise in the same proportion. There is no doubt that in so far as the increased traders' stock is treated as necessary for expansion the increased manufacturers' stock should be given the same treatment.

The relationship gets more complex when there are more than one trader and more than one producer, and it is even conceivable, though not likely, that in a case of many traders and few producers each producer's output for any moment will be bought that very moment by one trader or another, so that the traders' stocks will be substantial but producers' stocks negligible. But the part that manufacturers' stocks of finished goods play in trading must be recognized. This is not to deny that a manufacturer might end up with unwanted stocks through overestimation of demand, just as he might end up with a shortage through underestimation of demand, but in the determination of the over-all long-run trend these mistakes will be relatively unimportant. In any case such miscalculations may happen in any field, not merely in this. To conclude, for the reasons quoted above I propose to give stocks of finished goods with manufacturers the same standing of being 'productive' as stocks of raw materials and goods-in-process held by them.

IV. THE INDIAN DATA

We divide the Indian economy into sectors and try to work out incremental coefficients of working capital related to net income. We intend to use these later to approach the total coefficient by looking at the incremental national income divisions.

134

Manufacturers

This is the only sector where there is a reasonably reliable set of data about working capital. The main source consists of the thirteen censuses of manufacturing industries (1946–58) conducted by the Central Statistical Organization, for which reports have already been published.[1] In Table 1 these data are reproduced in a summary form. They refer to all manufacturing industries taken together. 'Value added' is calculated net of depreciation, and the stocks of raw materials, finished goods, and work-in-progress are measured in value terms. We differ from the census practice of including 'cash in hand and in the banks' as working capital, and have excluded it from our picture.

Unfortunately for the first four years no data are available about work-in-progress. It will be noted, however, that for the next five years the value of work-in-progress is almost exactly 10 per cent of the value added, and for the remaining four years quite close to it. In view of the fact that this is a rather small element in total working capital for all years, it was thought reasonable to assume that nothing

TABLE 1

STOCKS AND VALUE ADDED OF MANUFACTURING
INDUSTRIES
(RS. CRORES)

	Net Value Added	Raw Materials Stocks	Finished Goods Stocks	Work-in-progress Stocks	Total Stocks
1946	211	135	69	n.a.	(225)
1947	242	143	84	n.a.	(251)
1948	317	169	117	n.a.	(318)
1949	273	172	110	n.a.	(309)
1950	284	179	109	28	316
1951	347	212	141	35	388
1952	315	202	147	33	382
1953	334	187	128	35	350
1954	373	200	144	38	382
1955	419	213	156	39	408
1956	469	250	188	43	481
1957	468	279	221	48	548
1958	490	280	198	50	528

[1] For data about 1946 to 1955 see the *Tenth Census of Indian Manufactures*, 1955 (Calcutta, 1959), and thereafter see the yearly Census reports. The reports are published from Calcutta by the Government of India.

135

much would be lost by assuming that the figures for work-in-progress in the first four years was also 10 per cent of the value added. The resulting approximate totals are given within brackets. Since work-in-progress is less than 10 per cent of total working capital for each year, this implies that even if we make, say, a 10 per cent error in the figure of the work-in-progress, that will affect the total working capital figure by less than 1 per cent. Furthermore, since we correlate not merely the total working capital series to 'value added' but also individually the stocks of finished goods (thirteen years), raw materials (thirteen years), and work-in-progress (nine years) to 'value added', we also have as much separate information as the actual data give us. The correlation between the total working capital figures and 'value added' as well as between the individual items in working capital and the latter seems quite remarkable. The resulting linear equations obtained as well as the values of r^2 (indicating the closeness of fit) are presented below. We use the following set of notations:

S = total stocks (working capital); F = stocks of finished goods; R = stocks of raw materials; W = stocks of work-in-progress; and V = Value added.

TABLE 2

RELATION BETWEEN STOCKS AND VALUE ADDED IN MANUFACTURING

(RS. CRORES)

Item	Equation	r^2
S	$S = 5 \cdot 62 + 1 \cdot 06\ V$	·94
F	$F = -25 \cdot 01 + 0 \cdot 47\ V$	·92
R	$R = 31 \cdot 15 + 0 \cdot 49\ V$	·91
W	$W = 3 \cdot 20 + 0 \cdot 09\ V$	·93

Two things should be immediately noted. First, the fit is quite close not merely for the total but also for the components. Second, each of the straight lines, particularly the total, go very close to the origin, so that the assumption of proportionality is quite reasonable.

From these it will appear that the marginal coefficients of the requirement of stocks per unit of net income are about 0·47 for finished goods, 0·49 for raw materials, 0·09 for work-in-progress, and 1·06 for the total. There is a very slight difference between the sum of the first three (1·05) and the size of the fourth (1·06), but they are as close as can be expected in statistical approximations of this type. We shall be using the figure 1·05.

It will be interesting to inquire the extent to which the results will be changed by introducing two changes: (a) taking the beginning-of-the-year stock rather than end-of-the-year stock as we have done, and (b) by taking the square roots of 'value added' figures rather than the 'value added' figures themselves. The results are that introducing (b) does not improve the regression, and introducing (a) makes it very much worse. Putting $V_n = $ value added in year n,

$$V_n + 1 = \text{value added in year } (n + 1),$$

and $S_n = $ total working capital on December 31st, year n, we present in Table 3, the results of relating total working capital to V_n, $V_n + 1$, $\sqrt{V_n}$, and $\sqrt{V_n} + 1$.

TABLE 3
ALTERNATIVE EXPLANATIONS OF WORKING CAPITAL OF DECEMBER 31, YEAR n

Determining Variable	Equation	r^2
V_n	$S_n = 5\cdot62 + 1\cdot06\,V_n$	·94
$V_n + 1$	$S_n = 27\cdot42 + 0\cdot93\,V_n + 1$	·73
$\sqrt{V_n}$	$S_n = -354\cdot59 + 39\cdot38\,\sqrt{V_n}$	·93
$\sqrt{V_n} + 1$	$S_n = -306\cdot06 + 35\cdot44\,\sqrt{V_n} + 1$	·73

As far as the value of r^2 is concerned, there is nothing to choose between relating working capital to V_n and relating it to $\sqrt{V_n}$. But it is to be noted that while the former explanation gives us almost a proportionality rule, the latter involves the problem of explaining a very big negative constant in the equation of the stock. Thus formally we gain nothing by adopting the square root explanation, and intuitively we face an additional problem of explaining negative stocks for low values of the value added.

The fact that working capital this December 31st is more closely related to last year's 'value added' than to the coming year's is very significant. There are various possible explanations of this, some of which we cannot explore because of the lack of data. Superficially at least, the problem might look much easier for stocks of finished goods because they would naturally be related to last year's production flow, but for raw materials the same explanation could not be used. However, also for the stock of raw materials, the value of r^2 is around 0·9 for the absolute value or the square root of last year's value added, whereas it is only around 0·6 for the coming year's. This seems to indicate that this year's output and income influence the producers' expectation of the next year's output and income even though this expectation does not always come true. Thus this year's output flow may influence this year's accumulation of raw materials stocks through this indirect way.

Before closing this discussion on the manufacturing sector, it is necessary to refer to another important source for data, the 'finances of Indian joint stock companies',[1] conducted by the Reserve Bank of India. We have two series, one from 1950–55 and the other from 1955–59, but they have different coverage and cannot be put together. For such short series, no sophisticated statistical techniques can be used. Just as a check, however, we might look at the ratios of working capital to value added in each year, as well as the total for the period. Even this is not very easy because the 'value added' figures are not directly given by the Reserve Bank, and the cost-breakdown is such that it is not possible to calculate it accurately. We do get, however, an approximate idea by subtracting from the value of total production (= 'sales' plus 'other incomes' plus change of 'stocks') three items: 'raw materials consumed and other manufacturing expenses', 'excise duty', and 'depreciation provision', in Statement I. This is only an approximation to the net value added. From Statement III we get the value of 'stocks and stores', including 'raw materials', 'finished goods', 'work-in-progress', and 'others' (stores and spare parts). We present the results in Table 4 below and Table 5 on p. 139.

TABLE 4
PROCESSING AND MANUFACTURES: 1950–55
(R.B.I.)

	1950	1951	1952	1953	1954	1955	Total
Net Value Added (Rs. Crores)	233·35	281·27	266·62	282·85	304·02	356·62	1,724·73
Working Capital (Rs. Crores)	241·75	299·36	278·49	265·66	274·03	296·22	1,655·51
Ratio of W.C. to N.V.A.	1·04	1·06	1·04	0·94	0·90	0·83	0·96

[1] *Reserve Bank of India Bulletin*, September 1957, and September 1961.

138

TABLE 5

PROCESSING AND MANUFACTURES: 1955-59
(R.B.I.)

	1955	1956	1957	1958	1959	Total
N.V.A. (Rs. Crores)	404·23	449·79	454·18	492·91	573·81	2,374·92
W.C. (Rs. Crores)	363·61	445·60	493·53	493·13	501·50	2,297·37
Ratio of W.C. to N.V.A.	0·90	0·99	1·09	1·00	0·87	0·97

The average ratio for both the series, although no more than approximations, lend support to the notion that our ratio of 1·05 calculated from the Census data is not unreasonable. However, between the Reserve Bank's ratio of 0·96 or 0·97 and the Census' marginal (and approximately average) coefficient of 1·05 we choose the latter because its coverage is wider, it involves a longer series, it has a definite and good measure of the degree of fit, and its 'value added' figures are more reliable.

Mining

Our only source is the Reserve Bank surveys of the finances of joint stock companies referred to earlier.[1] But the 1950–55 series does not separate out the 'mining expenses' from 'salaries and wages' for 1950–53, so it is of no use in calculating value added. The 1955–59 series is the only one to fall back on.

TABLE 6

MINING: 1955-59 (R.B.I.)

	1955	1956	1957	1958	1959	Total
Net Value Added (Rs. Crores)	24·11	26·79	32·82	34·66	34·10	152·48
Working Capital (Rs. Crores)	5·73	6·14	7·09	8·15	8·80	35·91
Ratio of W.C. to N.V.A.	0·24	0·23	0·22	0·24	0·26	0·24

[1] *R.B.I. Bulletin*, September 1957, and September 1961.

We can do no better than take 0·24. Incidentally, it is to be noted that the year-to-year fluctuations in the ratio are not excessive, and there is hardly any trend in the ratio over the period.

Small Industries

This sector gives us a great deal of trouble. There are very little data about it, and what data there are conflict about working capital requirements. Mr P. N. Dhar's study of *Small Scale Industries in Delhi*[1] gives us some data for the particular year of the survey. The net value added amounted to Rs. 31·95 lakhs, the real working capital (deducting cash, securities, advances, and credit) to Rs. 12·75 lakhs, so that the ratio worked out as 0·40. But this refers only to Delhi, which has the benefit of being near its market and many of its sources of raw materials.

The 'Model Schemes' of small factories published by the Development Commissioner of Small Scale Industries,[2] which go into the financial requirements, seem to suggest a much higher ratio. An estimate made on the basis of this seems to produce an average of Rs. 2,200 of working capital per person, and Rs. 3,700 of 'gross value added' per person,[3] so that the ratio works out as about 0·60. This ratio will be higher if we take the net 'value added' (figures for which we do not have), but this will probably be compensated by the fact that the conventionally defined 'working capital' figures include estimates of financial working capital, which (though small) must be eliminated from real working capital.

Neither the figure 0·40 nor 0·60, nor any other figure that we can get from our very scattered sources of information, can claim to be at all representative of all small-scale industries in India. Unfortunately the sample survey of small-scale industries conducted by the N.S.S. does not give data on working capital. So we have to do with a vague idea of the coefficient being perhaps around 0·40 to 0·60.

Trading

Once again data are very scarce, but two sources could be traced. Some of the joint stock companies covered by the Reserve Bank Survey are trading companies, and their ratios of working capital

[1] Delhi, 1958.

[2] Ministry of Commerce and Industry, Government of India.

[3] 'The Capital and Labour Requirements of Small Factories,' unpublished, a technical study, Planning Commission, section 6–2.

140

to net value added, on the same principles as described before, yield the two following tables.

TABLE 7

TRADING: 1950–55 (R.B.I.)

	1950	1951	1952	1953	1954	1955	*Total*
N.V.A. (Rs. Crores)	9·35	10·49	8·51	7·85	7·66	8·04	51·90
W.C. (Rs. Crores)	12·33	13·93	13·15	11·10	10·14	10·13	70·78
W.C./N.V.A.	1·32	1·33	1·55	1·41	1·32	1·26	1·36

TABLE 8

TRADING: 1955–59 (R.B.I.)

	1955	1956	1957	1958	1959	*Total*
N.V.A. (Rs. Crores)	11·35	12·60	13·07	14·48	19·47	70·97
W.C. (Rs. Crores)	13·65	16·98	14·98	12·85	19·88	78·34
W.C./N.V.A.	1·20	1·35	1·15	0·89	1·02	1·10

The only other estimate of trading inventories we have is that of Mr M. Mukherji and Dr S. R. Sastry.[1] They have two figures, one of which is based on the R.B.I. survey itself, so it adds nothing new to our estimates. The other, based on some estimates of time lag in training, comes to Rs. 1,520 crores for 1949–50. This as a ratio of the income from 'other commerce', i.e. excluding banking and insurance, as calculated by the National Income Committee for 1949–50, comes to 1·22. This is around the same order of magnitude as our R.B.I. averages. We take 1·10 as the required ratio rather than 1·36 or 1·22 because it relates to more recent years, it has wider coverage, and there is some argument for keeping a downward bias in view of the possibility of 'unproductive' stocks discussed in Section III.

Construction

The working capital ratio of this sector is high, but by convention this

[1] 'An Estimate of Tangible Wealth of India,' in *The Measurement of National Wealth*, ed. R. Goldsmith and C. Saunders, *Income and Wealth Series VIII* (London, 1959).

is placed in most countries under fixed capital. The United Nations expresses its approval of this system.[1] In principle this is a queer rule, but practical difficulties of distinguishing finished and semi-finished construction works are great. Since Indian fixed capital figures take into account unfinished buildings and other constructions, we bow to this widespread (if objectionable) convention and put 0 as our coefficient.

Railways

There is no international convention about this, but in India the total of investment in railways is put by convention into fixed capital. This practice is even more indefensible than that of construction but, to avoid possible double counting, we decided to put 0 here also, so that our figures could be treated as entirely complementary to the fixed investment figures used in Indian statistics. It is hoped that at some future date these conventions will be reconsidered.

Agriculture

We noted in Section II that in Indian agriculture we may confine our attention to work-in-progress only as far as the incremental requirement of working capital is concerned. And we expect this requirement to be low because of the non-wage system. We have used here two sources of data, the *All-India Rural Credit Survey*,[2] and the *Studies in Economics of Farm Management*,[3] which are available for Bombay, Punjab, Madras, Uttar Pradesh, and West Bengal for 1954–55 and 1955–56 and for Madhya Pradesh for 1955–56. Neither is very suitable because the latter set covers only some regions, and, while the former Survey selected areas from all over India, it apparently did not choose the sample in a way to make it representative.[4] Still, not having anything else to go on, we might use these two sets of data to see what picture does emerge from them.

According to the *All-India Rural Credit Survey*[5] the total annual 'farm expenditure' per family in cash and in kind is Rs. 495 for 'all-India'. Of this, 'disposals' or 'value of payments made in kind at harvest' (Rs. 93), cash rent paid to landlord (Rs. 18), land revenue

---

[1] *Studies in Methods No. 2. A System of National Accounts and Supporting Tables* (New York, 1953), p. 30.

[2] Reserve Bank of India (Bombay, 1956), Vols. I–III.

[3] Published by the Ministry of Agriculture, Government of India.

[4] *All-India Rural Credit Survey*, Vol. 1, Part 1, p. 11.

[5] Volume 1, Part 1, pp. 842–9.

and other agricultural charges (Rs. 15), and interest paid on loans (Rs. 9) are not involved in work-in-progress as they are paid after marketing the output. We can also ignore the value of non-wage family labour for reasons discussed in Section II. This item is not included in 'farm expenditure', but the item 'owned manure' (Rs. 44) involves imputing market value to non-wage labour. We exclude this item too. This gives us a total of material and wage cost per family of Rs. 316. Assuming an average lag of three months between these various items of expenditure and harvesting, we can take a quarter of this, i.e. Rs. 79, as the average work-in-progress per family.

Of the Rs. 495 of farm expenditure, Rs. 167 represent wages of various types, and Rs. 91 represent rent, revenue, interest, etc., and Rs. 44 represent the value of manure made by family labour, so that Rs. 193 could be taken to represent material expenditures.[1] Since the value of produce per family is Rs. 752 in this sample, the 'value added' can be approximately taken to be Rs. 559. The ratio of work-in-progress (Rs. 79) to this 'value added' thus works out as 0·14. This is a very low ratio, but that is what we expected.

Turning now to the *Studies in the Economics of Farm Management*, we can illustrate the procedure for one estimate, say Punjab, 1954–55, the Cost Accounting Sample.[2] The value of output per acre is Rs. 145. To get the 'value added' we deduct from it the value of seeds (Rs. 8), fertilizers (not 'farm yard manure') (Rs. 2), depreciation (Rs. 5), irrigation charges (Rs. 6), payment to artisans (Rs. 3), and the material cost involved in the maintenance of bullocks. This last is found to be around Rs. 20 since Rs. 32 is mentioned as the cost of 'bullock labour', and the breakdown given elsewhere shows 63 per cent of this to be material costs. The net 'value added' is thus estimated to be about Rs. 101. The costs of 'prepaid' inputs include seeds, fertilizers, artisans, material costs in bullock labour, and hired (as opposed to family-based) human labour. This last works out on an average as Rs. 9 per acre, so that the total 'prepaid' inputs cost Rs. 42 per acre. With an average lag of three months we get approximately Rs. 10·5 as the average work-in-progress. Taking this as a ratio of 'value added', we end up with a figure of 0·10.

We do similar exercises for all the available sets of data. Unfortunately the exercise could not be done for West Bengal and Madras

---

[1] Volume 1, Part 1, pp. 830, 843, 849, 853, and 854.
[2] *Studies in the Economics of Farm Management, Punjab,* 1954–55, pp. 56, 58, and 71.

because of incomplete data (no breakdown of bullock costs), but we have estimates for two samples for two years each in Punjab, Uttar Pradesh, Ahmednagar (Bombay), and Nasik (Bombay), and one estimate for Madhya Pradesh. We present the results in Table 9, where C.A.S. stands for Cost Accounting Sample, S.S. for Survey Sample, D. for Dry Areas, R. for Irrigated Areas, Bombay I for Ahmednagar, and Bombay II for Nasik.

TABLE 9

WORK-IN-PROGRESS AS A RATIO OF VALUE ADDED IN AGRICULTURE

		1954–55	1955–56
1.	Punjab (C.A.S.)	0·10	0·09
2.	Punjab (S.S.)	0·14	0·13
3.	U.P. (C.A.S.)	0·16	0·17
4.	U.P. (S.S.)	0·17	0·16
5.	Bombay I (S.S.) D.	0·27	0·13
6.	Bombay I (S.S.) R.	0·16	
7.	Bombay I (C.A.S.)		0·13
8.	Bombay II (S.S.) D.	0·15	0·11
9.	Bombay II (S.S.) R.	0·26	
10.	Bombay II (C.A.S.)		0·12
11.	M.P.		0·11

There is a great deal of variety in these figures, and the only possible strict answer to the question about the size of work-in-progress in Indian agriculture is that we do not know what it is. If, however, we were obliged to mention a best guess in a situation of this kind, we should probably pick 0·14. Not only is it the ratio given for 'all-India' by the Rural Credit Survey, but also it falls in between the figures obtainable from the Farm Management Studies, with eight figures above it, eight below, and one equal. One hopes that some day Indian agriculture will be better covered and we shall be less forced to rely on guesswork.

Other Sectors

We have not been able to get any calculation for non-railway transport, fishery, forestry, animal husbandry, communications, government services, house property, banking and insurance, and professional and domestic services. Most of these, one would guess, involve very little productive inventories, but we have no data to

144

make any estimate at all. It is shown however in the next section that even assuming that these sectors will require no investment in working capital whatever, the total working capital requirement of the Indian economy is considerably more than double of what Indian planners assume.

V. IMPLICATIONS

We use below the sectorial working capital requirements to get an idea of the over-all investment in working capital. We get figures for increases in income during the Third Five Year Plan from 'Estimates of Production and Income in India: 1960–61 and 1965–66'.[1]

TABLE 10

WORKING CAPITAL REQUIREMENT DURING THIRD FIVE YEAR PLAN

Sector	Increase in Net Income (Rs. Crores)	W.C. Coefficient	W.C. Investment (Rs. Crores)
1. Manufactures	895	1·05	940
2. Mining	148	0·24	36
3. Small Enterprises	357	0·50	179
4. Trading	438	1·10	482
5. Agriculture	1,353	0·14	189
6. Construction and Railways	335	0 (f.c.)	0
7. Rest	1,007	?	?
8. Total	4,534		Over 1,826

This suggests that the ratio of investment in working capital to increase in net income is above 0·40. Since planned investment during Third Plan is Rs. 9,600,[2] this gives us a ratio of required investment in W.C. to net fixed investment of 19 per cent, and a ratio of the former to total net investment of 16 per cent.[3]

The Indian plan documents estimate an absurdly low requirement of working capital and put it only at Rs. 800 crores during the Third

[1] Perspective Planning Division, Planning Commission, New Delhi, 24.12.1960.
[2] *Third Five Year Plan* (New Delhi, 1961), p. 59.
[3] It is interesting that on the basis of studying the inventory ratios of the UK, the USA, Ireland, Netherlands, New Zealand, and Norway, Uma Datta concluded that 'on an average the net increase in physical stocks forms 15 to 20 per cent of net fixed investment'. *Papers on National Income and Allied Topics*, ed. V. K. R. V. Rao and others (New York, 1960), p. 140.

K

145

Five Year Plan.[1] Our estimate even for only the five sectors covered suggests a requirement well over Rs. 1,800, i.e. considerably more than double the provision. Manufacturing alone will require working capital investment considerably in excess of the total provision for the Third Plan.

The Planning Commission of India is gradually changing in the direction of assuming a greater importance of working capital. In the First Plan there was no provision for it; in the Second it was assumed to be 6·5 per cent of total net investment; in the Third the assumed ratio works out as 7·8 per cent. Our estimate puts the requirement (for only the five sectors covered) at 16 per cent. Since there has not been so far any systematic attempt at collecting and putting together working capital statistics, we have not seen any *ex post* study of whether the prognostications of the Planning Commission come out true.

We have found that the conceptual problems involved in the identification and measurement of working capital are considerable, which is perhaps the reason for the paucity of official estimates of this important item of investment. But if our estimates are accepted it will appear that the total investment requirement of increasing Indian output is considerably higher than assumed and that the rates of saving and investment of the Indian economy have been much more than shown in official statistics. Besides, once the magnitude of working capital is correctly estimated, the need for investigating possibilities of economizing it becomes obvious. It is hoped that this paper is a step in the direction of clarifying the conceptual framework of working capital in the Indian economy, and that it will serve to stimulate further and more detailed work on this important branch of capital formation.

[1] *Third Plan*, p. 59.

A NOTE ON THE ECONOMIC PRINCIPLES OF ELECTRICITY PRICING

A. HARBERGER and N. ANDREATTA

I

In this note we attempt to explore the economic principles of electricity pricing. While we shall make some references to theoretically ideal pricing principles, we shall for the most part be concerned with practical rules which can be expected to come reasonably close to the theoretically ideal solutions.

We proceed on the assumption that the rate of return to be earned by capital invested in electricity undertakings is given. This rate of return will presumably be the appropriate 'shadow rate of interest' for the economy in which the electricity undertakings are located. Under some circumstances this shadow rate of interest may not be a unique number but may vary among investments in accordance with their risk; in such a case the rate to be applied to electricity undertakings is that corresponding to the estimated degree of risk of these investments.

One principle which is of primordial importance in the theory of electricity pricing is that the rate structure should foster the full utilization of available capacity. This principle should not be interpreted to mean that full utilization should be sought at all costs, however. The way in which it works can best be illustrated by an example of a single thermal station working in isolation. If under an initially prevailing rate structure the plant is used to full capacity only 50 per cent of the time, it is worth while to reduce the charges for electricity during those periods in which the capacity is not fully used. In some cases a small reduction in the charge will induce additional demand for electricity in the off-peak hours to the point where full capacity utilization is achieved. But most commonly there will be some periods during which even very substantial reduction of tariffs will be insufficient to induce full-capacity utilization. For such periods the minimum admissible tariff is one which covers the marginal costs of generating and distributing the electricity. These include principally the costs of the coal or other fuel necessary to generate electricity during these off-peak hours plus a charge to cover the losses of electricity in transmission and distribution. The practical rule of electricity pricing which we would advocate to cover this case would be that the marginal cost of producing and delivering electricity should be the price during off-peak hours, while during peak hours the tariff should include, in addition to the marginal cost, a charge for the fixed costs of the plant. The appropriate charge could be obtained by dividing the annual fixed costs associated with the plant by the number of kW hours of peak-time electricity generated during the year. If running costs were 4 nP. per kWh, this would be the charge during off-peak hours. If the annual fixed costs associated with the plant were Rs. 8,000/-, and the number of kWh generated during peak times was 100,000 in a year, the extra charge for peak-time use of electricity would be 8 nP. per kWh, and the total charge for peak-time use would be 12 nP. per kWh.

The reader may already suspect the ways in which this rule might lead to trouble. There may have been 100,000 hours of peak-time use of electricity during a prior period in which all kWh were priced at an average cost of, say, 8 nP. But when the charge for these particular hours is raised to 12 nP. per kWh it may be that the system is no longer used to capacity during all of the previous peak-time hours. The theoretical solution which is indicated here is a tariff which varies according to the time of day, and perhaps also according to the season of the year, in such a way as to induce the maximal utilization of existing capacity, subject to the constraint that the charge should never be lower than 4 nP. per kWh. Such a tariff structure could theoretically be obtained for any existing system, and it would be independent of the shadow rate of interest. A tariff which varied in such a way as to ration the available capacity among existing users when their demand exceeded capacity and which offered electricity at marginal cost when demand failed to reach capacity would be ideal from the allocative point of view. If the amounts collected in excess of marginal cost during the times when electricity was being rationed by way of the tariff fell short of an acceptable rate of return on investment, there would be no reason to expand capacity. When, however, these receipts rose above the shadow rate of return on capital, this would be a signal that further investment in capacity was economically desirable.

From the above example it is easy to see that the theoretical solution could not be put into practice in its full detail. However, the essence of this solution—a distinction between peak-time use of electricity (which is charged with the fixed costs of the system) and off-peak use of electricity (which is charged only with the marginal costs of generation and distribution) is preserved in the practical rule which we suggest. This rule, perhaps with minor variations, would be applicable for any system, however large, which was exclusively thermal.

We now consider the case of a system in which thermal and hydro capacity are combined. We assume first a situation in which the hydro capacity is of the run-of-the-stream type. It is the nature of run-of-the-stream projects that both the capacity output of the hydro undertaking and the timing of that capacity output are determined. In some cases the mechanical generating capacity will be sufficiently great to utilize to the full the seasonal maximum flow of water in the stream. In this case the flow of water is the thing which fundamentally determines the capacity output of the hydro part of the system. In other cases the generating capacity may not be sufficient to utilize the maximum flow of water. Here there are likely to be times during the year when capacity output of the hydro operation is determined by the flow of water in the stream and other times when this capacity is determined by the amount of generating equipment installed. For our present purpose, however, this distinction is not important. The important thing is that in any given run-of-the-stream hydro undertaking both the total annual maximum output and its timing are determined. Under such circumstances, and given the fact that the running costs of such a project are virtually negligible, it is pointless to allow any potential output to go to waste. Therefore it is evident that the full capacity of a run-of-the-stream hydro project should be brought into play before any connected thermal capacity is called upon to produce electricity. The run-of-the-stream hydro undertaking should serve as the base load of the system.

The principle of rate making in this case is essentially the same as that discussed above for the purely thermal system. The peak load of the system will be borne by thermal capacity, and the charge per kWh during the peak period should cover both the fixed and running costs of thermal electricity. If thermal electricity is required to supplement hydro electricity during any of the off-peak hours of the

149

system, the appropriate charge for these hours will be the marginal costs of producing thermal electricity. In the remaining off-peak hours, if any, when no thermal capacity is used, and the output of the run-of-the-stream hydro undertaking is below its full potential, the appropriate charge would be the running cost of producing and delivering the hydro power—a charge which would generally be very low indeed.

When thermal capacity is combined with hydro capacity of the storage type the roles of hydro and thermal production are the reverse of those indicated for the preceding case. A hydro storage undertaking differs markedly from the run-of-the-stream operation in that the timing of the production of hydro power now becomes subject to control of electricity authorities. Broadly speaking, the total electricity output which a hydro storage project can produce during the dry season is determined by the amount of water which it can store. But the flow of water through the generators can be cut off at any time the authorities desire, permitting the use of this hydro capacity to accommodate the more extreme variations in the level of total demand of the system. If, as in India, the rainy season is short and the dry season long, one can without great error distribute the total annual cost of the hydro storage operation equally over all the kWh produced during the year. The cost per kWh thus obtained may be considered as the marginal cost per kWh produced by a hydro storage project. But as we shall see, this cost is not likely to be relevant for the purpose of rate making.

The best way to understand the principle of rate making when a hydro storage project is combined with thermal facilities is to visualize a graph in which the total demand for the system's electricity is plotted for the different hours in the year. There may be a few hours in the year when the system is called upon to deliver 200,000 kW, more hours when the system is called upon to deliver at least 160,000 kW, still more hours when at least 140,000 kW are demanded, etc. The rule in this case is to use the hydro storage capacity to accommodate the peak demand of the system. One way in which it might work out would be that hydro capacity would be called into play only when the demand for electricity in the entire system exceeded 140,000 kW, and only to fill the amount by which system demand exceeded 140,000 kW. The way in which the critical level of demand is determined, at which hydro capacity should come into play, is as follows. If using hydro capacity to meet demand in excess of 140,000

150

kW would lead to the exhaustion of the water supply significantly before the end of the dry season, then 140,000 kW is too low a critical level. If, on the other hand, the use of a critical level of 140,000 kW would leave significant quantities of water in storage at the end of the dry season, then this critical level is too high. The critical level should be set in such a way that under normal circumstances the rule of using hydro capacity only to meet demand in excess of the critical level can be expected to lead to a situation in which the amount of water stored in the dam is just exhausted at the end of the dry season.

We now turn to the actual process of rate making this case. Obviously, with hydro capacity serving to meet peak-time demand, the rate charged for truly off-peak use of electricity should be the marginal cost of producing and distributing thermal power. This rate will come into play at those times when the system has some unused thermal capacity. But what is specially interesting about this case is the fact that thermal costs also determine the peak-time charge for electricity even though the brunt of the peak load is borne by hydro power. The way in which this apparently anomalous result emerges is as follows. Any significant increment in peak-time demand will require the raising of the critical level on which hydro capacity is brought into play. For example, a substantial increase in peak-time demand might require the raising of the critical level from 140,000 kW to 160,000 kW. Now the full capacity of the dam would be utilized in providing for electricity about the 160,000 kW point, and if previously the available thermal capacity was only 140,000 kW, the increase in peak-time demand will require the expansion of capacity by 20,000 kW. Both the fixed and the variable costs of this expansion in capacity should be borne by those who demand electricity at peak time. Thus the appropriate charge for peak-time use of electricity will be determined by the cost of expanding thermal capacity.

The existence of storage hydro capacity capable of being used for peaking purposes is likely to lower the peak-time charge for electricity and to broaden the peak period to a greater number of hours. When a system is purely thermal it may have to meet peak demand in, say, four hours of the day, and these peak demands may be very substantially higher than the average volume of electricity demanded during the rest of the day. If hydro capacity is available, it may be able to accommodate not only this very concentrated demand, but also something in addition. The critical level may be below the point associated with a four-hour daily peak. Hydro capacity may, for

151

example, be able to meet the excess demand over a level which is typically achieved in ten or twelve hours of the day. If this is the case, then an increase in peak demand will call for an increase in thermal capacity which can be expected to be utilized for ten or twelve hours in the day. The rate for peak-time use of electricity would accordingly be the rate determined by spreading the fixed annual costs of thermal capacity over ten or twelve hours of the day rather than, say, four hours a day; and the peak-time rate will accordingly be lower than it would have been in a purely thermal system with comparable demand conditions.

One may inquire whether the above rule of rate making would still apply if the rate determined for peak time on the basis indicated was lower than the cost per kWh obtained by dividing the total annual costs of the hydro project by the number of kWh which it generated. That is to say, does the rule still apply if it calls for a rate which would yield an accounting loss to the hydro operation? The answer, we believe, is that the rule should apply even in this case. Incremental peak-time demand can in fact be made at the costs which are indicated by the rule. Moreover, in a situation of growing demand the observation of the rule is likely to lead to progressively greater accounting profits for the hydro operation. When at a given state of development the storage capacity of the dam is very large relative to total demand and to associated thermal capacity, it may work out that the peak of the thermal part of the system is eighteen or twenty hours a day. But as demand grows it is not likely that the storage capacity of the dam will grow along with it. The result is that thermal capacity will have to expand to meet the increased demand. As this occurs, the capacity of the hydro project will become a progressively smaller fraction of the total capacity of the system. The critical level will rise, the peak of the system will become progressively smaller, and the peak-time charge for electricity will become progressively higher. Since for accounting purposes the electricity produced by the hydro capacity should be valued at the peak-time charge, it is clear that the total value of the hydro projects output will rise progressively, and its profitability should also rise.

We turn now to a discussion of the principles of rate making in projects which are purely hydro. In a storage project there is the presumption, already indicated, that the total annual output of electricity is given, and that its timing is subject to a considerable degree of control. As long as this is the case there is no point in attempting to distinguish between peak and off-peak use of electricity. The rule for rate making in this case is to charge an equal amount for each kWh. This amount should in principle be governed by the demand conditions. That is, the available amount of electricity should be rationed among demanders by adjusting the price of electricity. If the available amount of electricity is very large, it may for a time fetch a price which is too low to cover the annual fixed costs of the project including the shadow return on invested capital. But as demand grows, the price which this electricity will fetch is likely to rise. The movement of this price will give the appropriate signal as to when new capacity should be added to the system.

In the case of a run-of-the-stream hydro project, operating in isolation, the principle of rate making is to ration the available amount of electricity, varying the rate per kWh both by time of day and by season. As this principle is difficult to apply in practice, we suggest that a rule which would approximate its effects would be to charge a higher, possibly much higher, rate during peak periods. This peak-time rate should in every case be sufficiently high to maintain demand within the limits of capacity. In some cases this rule might lead to some difficulties, such as a very narrow peak arising when the charge is sufficiently high to contain demand at the time when electricity is most wanted. It may be that at this maximum peak-time price there is a peak of only one or two hours in the day, but if for the remaining hours only running costs are charged, then the demand in some of these other hours will exceed the system's capacity. Under these circumstances the appropriate action is to institute two levels of peak-time tariff—one for the very high peak of one or two hours, and the second a lower tariff for the intermediate hours for which demand is below capacity when electricity is charged at the high peak rate and above capacity when electricity is charged at running cost.

II

The discussion of the preceding section was based on the assumption that any additional marginal capacity to be acquired by a system would be thermal. This assumption is justified by the special characteristics of hydro production. The number of potential hydro-electric sites in an area is always limited, and as demand grows, their capacity is likely to be exceeded. If, for a time, new hydro-power can be obtained more cheaply than additional thermal power, then naturally additional capacity should be hydro, and the principles of pricing should be those outlined for the purely hydro case. But we believe that this situation is not very likely to be important in most areas of India. The continued rapid growth of demand for electricity will surely press on the limits of available hydro sites. Moreover, the continued formation and widening of grid networks will tend to produce systems containing both hydro and thermal plants, and these systems will surely require expanding amounts of thermal capacity to meet expanding demand. Thus the cases discussed in the preceding section are likely to be the most relevant ones for future decision-making in India.

However, in order not to ignore alternative possibilities completely, we here list the ways in which marginal expansion by way of hydro rather than thermal capacity could take place, and we comment briefly on the rate policy and/or investment policy appropriate in each contingency.

1. *Provision of additional storage capacity in a purely hydro project.* New capacity should surely be added, if it is possible to add it, when the output of the new facilities can be expected to yield a sufficient return to justify the added investment. The effort should be made to charge the same basic rate for the full output of the enterprise; in general this will entail a lower rate than the one which would have rationed output prior to the expansion of capacity. On occasion it may be true that the flat rate per kWh which would ration the new output yields a return on the prospective new capacity too low to justify the investment, and yet the investment may in fact be justified. This result can occur because it may be possible to establish a set of tariffs which discriminate among classes of users, among times of day, and/or among seasons of the year, and which would yield sufficient revenue to justify the additional investment. The highest rate charged under this discriminating pattern should, however, be no higher than the basic rate which would have rationed the output of the old capacity among consumers. When computing the return attributable to the new investment in such a case, the total income accruing to new and old capacity should be divided between them in proportion to their contributions to output.

2. *Provision of additional storage capacity in a thermal or hydro-*

154

thermal project. Adding to storage capacity will lower the critical level at which hydro generation comes into play. It will accordingly broaden the peak of the thermal part of the system and lower the peak-time charge. If at the lower charge for peak-time electricity an acceptable return for the new investment is obtained, the investment is justified.

3. *Provision of additional run-of-the-stream base load capacity.* Normally this should have no influence on rates as the tariffs should be determined by the costs of providing peak-time electricity. As long as thermal capacity is necessary for peak use both before and after the addition of the new base-load capacity, there should be no change in peak-time rates. And off-peak rates should change only in the case where the additional base-load capacity causes the displacement of thermal capacity from off-peak hours. To determine whether investment on additional hydro base-load capacity is worth while, the prospective output of the new capacity can for all practical purposes be valued at the rates prevailing before the addition to capacity. Where the additional capacity is built to take advantage of seasonal high flows of water, of course only output over and above the pre-existing capacity should be attributed to it.

4. *Provision of additional generating facilities on a hydro storage project* typically has two effects. First, it increases the output obtainable from the project in the rainy season. This is analogous to run-of-the-stream output and should be treated as base-load output of the system. Second, the additional generating facilities, while not adding to the storage capacity of the dam, do increase the flexibility of use of that capacity by augmenting the maximum instantaneous output which it is possible to generate. While a theoretical case could be made for the charging of a special peak-within-a-peak rate for electricity generated at times when the hydro generating capacity was fully utilized, we do not consider this to be a practical policy. We prefer to look upon the benefits of additional hydro generating capacity in a given storage project as consisting of

(a) the value of the extra base-load electricity generated during the wet season because of this added capacity, and
(b) the extra revenue which can be obtained from stored water during the dry season because of the extra generating capacity.

Paradoxically, the increased generating capacity has the function of *raising* the appropriate peak-time charge for electricity. It does this by increasing the flexibility of use of hydro capacity and meeting peak demands of short duration which might otherwise have to be left unsatisfied. As a result of this flexibility the 'critical level' of thermal output is slightly raised, and the thermal peak slightly narrowed, with the consequence of a slight rise in the appropriate peak-time rate applicable to all the electricity produced by the storage project.

III

The distinction made in the previous sections between peak-time and off-peak rates for electricity requires for its proper implementation that the electricity undertakings be able to measure not only the total amount of electricity used by a consumer but also the amounts used at peak and off-peak times. Meters are available to do this job, but they are too expensive for use in the case of small consumers. They can, however, easily be used for large industrial consumers, and we shall assume that this group's consumption of power is so metered.

In this section we inquire into the possibilities of adopting 'second best' methods which would approximate the effects of a time-tariff for the several classes of small consumers (domestic, small industrial, commercial). What makes such approximate methods possible is the fact that the electricity consumption of each type of user tends to be concentrated on a relatively well-defined period of the day. Thus, while some domestic consumption of electricity takes place in daytime and late-night hours, the overwhelming bulk of it occurs between nightfall and, say, 10 p.m. On the other hand, small industrial consumption is concentrated in the daytime hours, having its peak between around 9 a.m. and around 5 p.m. Commercial consumption tends to have its peak between nightfall and, say, 8 p.m., the precise timing depending on the store hours which are customarily observed.

In the case of purely hydro storage system or of a thermal-cum-hydro storage system one need not worry seriously about the distinction between peak and off-peak hours. In the pure hydro storage system all kWh generated should in any case be charged at the same basic rate. In the thermal-cum-hydro storage system the thermal peak is likely to be quite broad—in the order of 10–14 hours a day, aggregating perhaps to 4,000 or 5,000 hours a year. With such a broad peak, some 80 or 90 per cent of the total thermal output of the system is likely to be at peak-time. The ideal solution would be to charge a basic rate of roughly 4 nP. per kWh in off-peak times (this is a rough estimate of the average running cost of thermal electricity in India) and a basic rate of around 11 nP. per kWh in peak hours. (This is obtained by spreading the estimated annual fixed costs (Rs. 280/-) of thermal capacity over 4,000 peak-time hours and adding the resulting charge to the 4 nP. running cost per kWh.) But since for small consumers there is no way of distinguishing peak from off-peak consumption, the best practical solution is simply to charge the basic rate of 11 nP. for all kWh they consume. The resulting 'overcharge' for electricity taken in off-peak hours will apply only to a small fraction of the total electricity taken by these groups.[1]

In the case of a purely thermal system, or of a system where run-of-the-stream hydro capacity serves as base load with thermal capacity meeting peak-time demand, the situation is a bit more complicated. Here the appropriate rate policy depends on the pattern of demand for the total output of the system. The relevant alternative patterns are three, which differ according to the timing of the system peak. There may be a 'lighting' peak between the hours of, say, 6 p.m. and 10 p.m.; a 'day-time' peak between the hours of, say, 9 a.m. and 5 p.m.; or what we shall call a 'plateau' peak extending all the way from, say, 9 a.m. to 9 or 10 p.m.

The 'plateau' peak has identical consequences for rate making as the extended thermal peak which emerges when thermal and hydro storage capacities are joined in a single grid. For large industrial users peak-time charges in the order of 11 nP. per kWh are indicated, and off-peak charges in the neighbourhood of 4 nP. per kWh. For other users a basic charge of around 11 nP. per kWh is indicated for all the electricity they consume.

The 'lighting' peak occurs when the demands of domestic and commercial consumers together with public lighting requirements more than offset the normal night-time dip of industrial consumption. The peak is narrow, perhaps some four hours a day, or around 1,500 hours a year, and thermal capacity must be built and maintained to meet this peak demand. It is only natural that the peak-time charge

---

[1] An overcharge for off-peak use is inevitable in this case, and there is no point in reducing the peak-time charge below the appropriate level in an effort to sweeten the pill.

required to make this investment pay off should be high. Spreading Rs. 280/– of annual fixed charge per kW of capacity over 1,500 hours of peak-time use gives a fixed charge per kWh of roughly 19 nP., to which must be added running cost of around 4 nP. per kWh. The total basic charge for peak-time electricity is thus around 23 nP. per kWh, and that for off-peak use is around 4 nP. per kWh. Large industrial users should in these circumstances pay the higher rate for peak-time use and the lower rate for use at other times. Domestic and commercial users should pay the 23 nP. basic rate for all the electricity they consume since the great bulk of their consumption takes place during the lighting peak. Public lighting authorities, whose use of electricity extends well beyond the lighting peak, could easily, like large industrial consumers, be charged on a time-tariff basis. Even without special metering it is possible to estimate with great precision the time pattern of electricity use by the public authorities.

Special difficulties arise in the case of lighting peak mainly with respect to small industrial consumers. Since the bulk of their consumption is presumably outside the hours of the lighting peak, one may argue for charging them a basic rate as low as 4 nP. per kWh. On the other hand, charging this rate for all their consumption might cause them to increase their electricity use not only in off-peak hours, when the system has idle capacity to serve them, but also in peak hours. The electricity authorities can safeguard themselves against this possibility by charging this group the basic rates corresponding to a 'plateau' peak (estimated at around 11 nP. per kWh). Since the consumption per hour of this group is certainly less in the 'lighting-peak' hours than in daytime, charging them on a basis which would be appropriate if their consumption were the same in these two periods will yield more than sufficient revenue to cover the fixed charges associated with whatever capacity their peak-time demand requires. Thus, depending on the judgment of the electricity authorities as to how much electricity small industrial consumers are likely to demand during the lighting peak, the appropriate basic charge for these users should be somewhere between 4 nP. and 11 nP. per kWh.

The 'day-time' peak occurs when the concentration of industrial demand in day-shift work outweighs the impact of lighting demand in the early evening. Day-time peaks are typically of the order of eight hours duration, so that (making allowances for Sundays, holidays etc.) peak-time demand would amount to some 2,500 hours per day.

The annual fixed charge of Rs. 280/- spread over 2,500 hours yields a fixed charge per kWh of around 11 nP., which, together with running costs of 4 nP., implies a basic peak-time rate of around 15 nP. per kWh. This is the appropriate basic rate for small industrial consumers in the case of a day-time peak. For commercial and residential consumers the situation would be analagous to that of small industrial consumers when the system has a lighting peak. The appropriate basic rate here would lie between 4 and 11 nP. per kWh, the choice within this range depending on the extent of commercial and residential demand which the electricity authorities estimate will occur during the day-time peak.

IV

In this section we attempt to draw the main implications for rate policy which emerge from this analysis. The first and probably most important of these implications is the dominant role which thermal costs are likely to have for rate setting. In grids containing both hydro and thermal capacity the relevant marginal costs of additions to capacity will almost certainly be thermal costs. Thus only in grids containing essentially no thermal capacity, which are unlikely to be important as demand and grid-formation expand, will one have to look to other than thermal costs in order to find the appropriate levels of tariffs.

The dominance of thermal costs is a particularly convenient fact if one wants to estimate rough 'norms' for electricity rates for a country in which, as in India, a great number of systems or grids exists. This is because the costs of thermal capacity do not exhibit nearly such wide geographical variations as the costs of hydro capacity. Variations in capital costs per kW of thermal capacity stem mainly from differences in the sizes of generating plants. Given that India has by now entered a stage in which most additional thermal plants are in the order of 100 kW or more of capacity, the capital costs per kW of such additions are not likely to be very different as one moves from site to site. For expansions of thermal capacity in the next decade Rs. 700/- per kW can be regarded as a low capital cost, and Rs. 1,000/- per kW can be regarded as a high capital cost, at least so long as the present foreign exchange rate prevails. To this must be added a capital cost of transmission and distribution facilities of some Rs. 500/- per kW of installed capacity and a capitalized

159

charge for interest accumulated during the gestation period (here estimated at 15 per cent of the total invested capital). The plausible range for total capital-at-charge at the beginning of operation of newly added facilities is thus from Rs. 1,380/- to Rs. 1,725/- per kW of new capacity. At a charge of 12 per cent for interest-cum-depreciation the annual fixed charge directly associated with the added capacity would be between, say, Rs. 140/- and Rs. 175/- per kW. To this must be added an annual charge of Rs. 100/- to Rs. 150/- per kW for the maintenance of the capacity in operating conditions and for associated administrative expenses. Total annual fixed charges per kW of capacity are therefore likely to range between Rs. 240/- and 325/-. Running costs per kWh of electricity produced are unlikely to be lower than 3 nP., and unlikely (even in regions remote from the sources of coal) to be higher than 5 nP.

The accompanying Tables 1 and 2 give the range within which electricity rates might be expected to lie if they are to be set on the economic principles outlined in this paper. Table 1 gives minimum levels for rates, obtained by using an annual fixed charge of Rs. 240/- and a running cost of 3 nP. per kWh. Table 2 gives maximum levels, obtained by using an annual fixed charge of Rs. 325/- and a running cost of 5 nP. per kWh. In Table 3 the midpoints of the ranges demarcated by the entries in Tables 1 and 2 are presented to indicate plausible average rates for the different types of systems and categories of consumers. For convenience of reference the ranges emerging from Tables 1 and 2 are denoted in parentheses following each figure in Table 3.

In order for the reader to interpret the electricity rates given in Tables 1–3 we must clarify what we mean by 'basic' rates. These rates might best be considered as f.o.b. wholesale prices of electricity. They apply to high-voltage electricity measured at the generating station. Two adjustments must be made to these rates in order to estimate the retail prices they imply. In the first place, and most important, there is the adjustment for losses in transmission and in transformation to low voltage. These losses are virtually non-existent for high-voltage (large industrial) consumers, but they are quite important for low-voltage (residential, commercial, and small industrial) consumers. Something like a quarter of the power generated is lost in the processes of transformation to and transmission at low voltage. Thus if the basic (wholesale) rate were 15 nP. per kWh, the retail rate for low-voltage consumers would have to be

TABLE 1

PLAUSIBLE MINIMUM BASIC ELECTRICITY RATES
(IN nP./kWh)

CLASSIFIED BY TYPE OF SYSTEM AND CONSUMER CATEGORY

Type of system	Category of Consumer		
	Large industrial	Small industrial	Commercial and residential
Thermal-cum-Hydro Storage			
(a) 12 hour thermal peak	8*	8	8
(4,000 hrs/yr.)	3†		
(b) 9 hour thermal peak	11*	11	11
(3,000 hrs/yr.)	3†		
Purely Thermal, or			
Thermal-cum-base-load-hydro			
(a) plateau peak	8*	8	8
(4,000 hrs/yr.)	3†		
(b) lighting peak	19*	3–8	19
(1,500 hrs/yr.)	3†		
(c) day-time peak	13*	13	3–8
(2,500 hrs/yr.)	3†		

* During system peak. † During off-peak periods.

TABLE 2

PLAUSIBLE MAXIMUM BASIC ELECTRICITY RATES
(IN nP./kWh),

CLASSIFIED BY TYPE OF SYSTEM AND CONSUMER CATEGORY

Type of system	Category of Consumer		
	Large industrial	Small industrial	Commercial and residential
Thermal-cum-Hydro Storage			
(a) 12 hour thermal peak	13*	13	13
(4,000 hrs/yr.)	5†		
(b) 9 hour thermal peak	16*	16	16
(3,000 hrs/yr.)	5†		
Purely Thermal, or			
Thermal-cum-base-load-hydro			
(a) plateau peak	13*	13	13
(4,000 hrs/yr.)	5†		
(b) lighting peak	27*	5–13	27
(1,500 hrs/yr.)	5†		
(c) day-time peak	18*	18	5–13
(2,500 hrs/yr.)	5†		

* During system peak. † During off-peak periods.

TABLE 3

PLAUSIBLE AVERAGE BASIC ELECTRICITY RATES
(IN NP./KWH)

CLASSIFIED BY TYPE OF SYSTEM AND CONSUMER CATEGORY

| | Category of Consumer | | |
Type of system	Large industrial	Small industrial	Commercial and residential
Thermal-cum-Hydro storage			
(a) 12 hour thermal peak	10·5 (±2·5)*	10·5 (±2·5)	10·5 (±2·5)
(4,000 hrs/yr.)	4·0 (±1·0)†		
(b) 9 hour thermal peak	13·5 (±2·5)*	13·5 (±2·5)	13·5 (±2·5)
(3,000 hrs/yr.)	4·0 (±1·0)†		
Purely Thermal, or			
Thermal-cum-base-load-hydro			
(a) plateau peak	10·5 (±2·5)*	10·5 (±2·5)	10·5 (±2·5)
(4,000 hrs/yr.)	4·0 (±1·0)†		
(b) lighting peak	23·0 (±4·0)*	4·0 (±1·0)–	23·0 (±4·0)
(1,500 hrs/yr.)	4·0 (±1·0)†	10·5 (±2·5)	
(c) day-time peak	15·5 (±2·5)*	15·5 (±2·5)	4·0 (±1·0)–
(2,500 hrs/yr.)	4·0 (±1·0)†		10·5 (±2·5)

* During system peak.   † During off-peak periods.

around 20 nP. per kWh simply to take account of transformation and transmission losses. In general, to adjust for this factor, the rates given in the Tables would have to be increased by about a third for the low-voltage consumer categories.

The second and less important adjustment would add a charge for connecting, metering, billing, and otherwise servicing the individual consumer. This charge would appropriately be independent of the volume of consumption and would best be set as a fixed monthly charge for consumers in each category. But if for practical reasons it were deemed advisable to incorporate an allowance for 'Consumer Costs' in the rates per kWh paid by the different classes of consumers, a modest adjustment in addition to that for transmission and transformation would have to be made in the basic rates.

One of the striking features of the rate patterns presented in the Tables is that they contain no rate below 3 nP. per kWh. Yet it is well known that many industrial undertakings in India do obtain electricity at lower rates than this. We shall not here inquire into the individual cases in which lower rates are charged, but shall simply indicate the sorts of situation in which lower rates might be justified.

The first is the purely hydro project which for some reason cannot be effectively integrated into a larger grid so as to complement thermal capacity. The second is the thermal-cum-hydro-base-load system in which the hydro-base-load capacity is large relative to thermal capacity. Under such circumstances it may be unnecessary to use thermal capacity at all during the off-peak hours, thus justifying a lower charge for off-peak use of electricity than that indicated by the marginal costs of producing thermal power. These two types of situations must now prevail in some parts of India; accordingly blanket objections to rates below around 3 nP. per kWh are not justified. But such situations are likely to become less and less prevalent in the future as demand grows and as grid formation proceeds. Thus in long-term planning, in decision-making about industrial locations, etc. the general principle should be to consider the expected marginal costs of thermal power as the minimum admissible price of power. Moreover this minimum should be taken as applying only during the off-peak hours of the system.

The final implication which we wish to draw from our analysis concerns the common practice of charging two-part tariffs for industrial use of electricity. A two-part tariff consists of a fixed monthly charge based on the consumer's level of maximum demand plus a flat rate per kWh consumed. The theory behind the two-part tariff is that the consumer should be made to pay for the fixed charges associated with the capacity which his maximum demand requires, and that once these charges are paid, he should be free to consume all the electricity he wants at its marginal cost of production and delivery. The difficulties with this approach are both theoretical and practical. On the theoretical side, charging all consumers fixed charges to cover the capacity costs associated with their maximum demands will generally lead to more being collected on this account than is necessary to cover the fixed charges of the system. The reason for this is that since the maximum demands of individual consumers are not simultaneous, the same capacity can help to meet more than one consumer's maximum demand. When one contemplates reducing the fixed charges to take account of this objection, the practical difficulties emerge. A consumer whose maximum demand comes at the time when the system is at its peak should really be required to pay for the full cost of the capacity necessary to meet his maximum demand, while a consumer whose maximum demand occurs at an off-peak time should not. No simple two-part tariff will make this

163

vital distinction. If the fixed charge is made somewhat lower than the charge associated with the consumer's maximum demand, the same problem crops up in setting the appropriate rate per kWh consumed. A rate higher than the marginal cost of producing and delivering electricity is too high for the periods when the system has unused capacity; a rate equal to marginal cost is too low for the periods when the system is at its peak.

The way out of these dilemmas is to abandon the two-part tariff in favour of a time-tariff—at least for those (large industrial) consumers for whom a time-tariff can be economically and effectively administered. The time-tariff recognizes that it is possible to supply additional off-peak power at marginal cost, while provision of additional peak-time power requires the expansion of capacity. The principle that the fixed costs of capacity should be borne by peak-time demand is fundamental; any rate-making rule which attempts to by-pass this principle is bound to have less than optimal results. Our analysis thus strongly favours as rapid a transition as possible to a rate structure which distinguishes sharply between peak and off-peak use of power by large industrial consumers.

CONTRIBUTION OF ATOMIC ENERGY TO A POWER PROGRAMME IN INDIA

P. N. ROSENSTEIN-RODAN

I. ATOMIC ENERGY IN DEVELOPED COUNTRIES

Nuclear power prospects for the next decade were considered in 1956 to be of major importance in only two areas of the world, namely, Europe and Japan. Those were the areas in which nuclear power could reach a competitive threshold with conventional power for three reasons:

1. The hydro-electric potential was limited and nearing exhaustion.
2. Coal had to be imported at very high prices, around $20 per ton. At such prices, incidentally, residual fuel oil for thermal stations appeared cheaper than coal.
3. Europe and Japan were highly industrialized areas with electric grids in which installation of large units (150 mW or more) for base load electricity at very high plant factors (75 per cent to 80 per cent) was possible.

Accordingly, ambitious programmes for installation of new power stations were established both in England and in Europe foreseeing installation of 6 million kW in each within ten years. On the basis of the estimates then available, it appeared that the cost per kWh of nuclear power would be around 10 per cent higher than that of conventional thermal power. It was thought, however, that such a margin of 10 per cent might be well worth the end of becoming less dependent on one source of power (notably oil) and also that in a short time cost-reducing technical progress would be greater in the new field of nuclear power stations than in that of conventional thermal stations.

Experiences of the last three years—admittedly a short period—do not seem to confirm these expectations.

1. Coal prices fell in Europe by at least 25 per cent so that a ton

of coal today costs under $14 instead of the previous $20. It is now fully competitive with oil.

2. Residual fuel oil supply has also become more abundant at slightly lower prices.

3. Interest rates in Europe (with the exception of Italy where they were calculated at 7 per cent) rose from 4 per cent to 5–6 per cent, raising thereby the relative cost of nuclear power.

4. Cost-reducing technical progress did not materialize in nuclear power, but it has been achieved in thermal power.

The first two changes may be short-run phenomena, although it has to be remembered that the price of coal imported from the United States has fallen by 25 per cent, mainly because of the collapse of freight rates, and experts doubt that the freight rates will recover to the 1955–56 level. Accordingly, many authorities doubt that one should project $20 per ton of coal for the near future. While opinions may differ about the long-run price prospects of coal and oil, the fact remains that, on the whole, pessimistically high price expectations have given place meanwhile to optimistically lower ones.

More important, however, are the results of technical development during the last three years. Contrary to expectations, cost-reducing technical progress did not materialize in the nuclear field, but it did materialize in the field of thermal electricity. The introduction of large turbo-generators of 200,000 kW and more has reduced fixed investment costs for large thermal electric power stations by about 20 per cent from, say $150 to $160 per kW installed to $120 and $130 per kW. This also benefits large nuclear power stations, but the cost reduction there amounts to under 10 per cent: half that (or less) of large thermal stations. At the same time, the cost of nuclear energy for stations of 150 mW could not be reduced; this can be clearly seen from offers submitted at the international tender under the auspices of the International Bank in 1958 for the Italian E.N.S.I. project. Accordingly, several voices in Europe recently have been advocating a slowing down of the EURATOM and UK atomic power programme, since it appears that the cost of nuclear energy will be higher than that of a conventional one not by a mere 10 per cent but by at least 20 per cent,[1] or, as some people say, by even 40 per cent to 50 per cent.[2]

[1] See *The Economist* (London), May 9, 1959.
[2] See Ferdinand Dierkens, 'L'atome en Belgique', *L'Opinione Economique et Financière*, March 19, 1959.

II. ATOMIC ENERGY IN UNDERDEVELOPED COUNTRIES

While prospects of atomic energy appear, for the time being, to be well below the optimistic expectations even for developed countries like Europe and Japan, all the arguments which made the introduction of nuclear power in underdeveloped countries much less promising remain fully valid. There are, as is well known, at least four reasons against the introduction of nuclear power in underdeveloped countries. They are:

1. Only large power stations (100 mW or more) are suitable for atomic power. In most underdeveloped areas these units may be too large since such large units can normally be well used only if their output can be fed into an electric grid.[1] Most underdeveloped countries, however, are not covered by electrical grids or have them only in very exceptional cases in the neighbourhood of a few large cities.

2. Atomic power stations can only be used for base load electricity on a very high load factor of 75 per cent to 80 per cent. This is due to the fact that capital charges are very high in nuclear power (two-thirds or more of total power costs) while in thermal stations capital charges are lower (about one-third of the cost of power). The condition of a high load factor is much more difficult to meet in an underdeveloped country, and it seems unlikely that the load factor of 80 per cent or even 75 per cent could be obtained in India. Even in Europe, incidentally, the early calculation based on an 80 per cent load factor had to be revised to a 75 per cent load factor since it seemed unlikely that the higher target could be met.

3. Since capital costs form a so much higher proportion of total costs of nuclear power, the rate of interest has a major influence on cost determination. In the EURATOM and UK calculations the rate of interest was raised from the original 4 per cent to about 6 per cent. In Italy, where the scarcity of capital is certainly less than in India, it is calculated at 7 per cent. In underdeveloped countries, where there is a much greater scarcity of capital, the underlying rate of interest should undoubtedly be higher. There is no doubt that in India, for instance, an assumed 'shadow' rate of interest should be

---

[1] This is an even greater obstacle to obtaining high load factors (see next point II.2).

put at around 10 per cent and certainly nowhere near $4\frac{1}{2}$ per cent. Together with the depreciation, the charges on interest and depreciation should be at least 15 per cent.

4. A relatively high over-all efficiency, say 28 per cent, is to be assumed for a nuclear power station. That might also be somewhat lower (say 25 per cent) for an underdeveloped country since the choice between various power stations of different age structure and efficiency to provide for peak loads is much more restricted.[1]

III. THE NEED FOR ATOMIC ENERGY IN INDIA

1. Dr H. J. Bhabha proposes a nuclear power programme of 1 million kW in India for the next decade.[2] He recognizes, albeit platonically, the first two (a minimum large size plant and a very high load factor) of the four reasons against the introduction of nuclear power in underdeveloped countries. He argues, however, that in some places like Bombay and Ahmedabad a very high load factor is obtained already (63 per cent to 69 per cent) and seems to infer from it that an 80 per cent load factor in the future might not be too unrealistic an assumption.

Assuming 9 per cent interest, the costs per kWh of a coal fired power station amount to 8·7 mills, those of atomic power (allowing for the credit for plutonium and assuming the cost of uranium of rupees 400·000 per ton = \$83,330) to 9·6 mills.

We might readily agree that in some Indian towns a relatively big thermal station (150 mW or more) may usefully be installed, but it seems quite unrealistic to assume an 80 per cent load factor. Any realistic comparison should contrast a thermal and a nuclear power station of 150 mW or more but on the assumption of a 65 per cent load factor. If we add to it that the rate of interest in India should be calculated at 10 per cent rather than at $4\frac{1}{2}$ per cent, then the comparative costs per kWh can be assumed to be 9·58 mills for a thermal

---

[1] This point is left out of account in the following text. A 28 per cent efficiency is in fact assumed.

[2] See H. J. Bhabha, *The Need for Atomic Energy in the Underdeveloped Countries*, lecture delivered at the Second International Conference on the Peaceful Uses of Atomic Energy held in Geneva in September 1958, and H. J. Bhabha and N. B. Prasad, *A Study of the Contribution of Atomic Energy to a Power Program in India* (Department of Atomic Energy, dittoed document, 1958).

COMPARISON OF CAPITAL AND POWER COSTS‡

Load factor—80 per cent; Efficiency of nuclear power station—28 per cent
Efficiency of thermal power station—25 per cent;
Fuel burn-up—3,000 MWD/tonne

	Coal-fired power station	Oil-fired power station	Atomic power station First generation	
Unit capital cost	Rs. 1,050/kW*	Rs. 800/kW*	Rs. 1,700/kW	
Unit fuel inventory cost				
at Rs. 300,000 per tonne			Rs.500/kW	
at Rs. 400,000 per tonne				Rs.667/kW
COST OF GENERATION in Rs./kWh				
1. Capital charges				
(a) Depreciation at 5 per cent	·0075	·00571	·01214	
(b) Interest at 4·5 per cent	·00675	·00514	·01092	
(c) †Interest at 9 per cent	(·01350)	(·01028)	(·02184)	
2. Interest on inventory at 4·5 per cent				
Fuel at 300,000/tonne			·00321	
Fuel at 400,000/tonne				·00429
3. Operating Costs	·00125	·00125	·00125	
4. Fuel costs:				
Coal at Rs. 45/ton	·025			
Oil at Rs. 96/ton		·027		
Fabricated uranium at				
Rs. 300,000/tonne			·01488	
Rs. 400,000/tonne				·01984
	·04050	·03910	·04240	·04844
5. Less credit for plutonium at Rs. 56,000/kg.			·00333	·00333
Net cost of nuclear power			·03907	·04511

* This excludes filling and improvements to site.
† Not included in Dr. Bhabha's table.
‡ Table IX, H. J. Bhabha and N. B. Prasad, *op. cit.*

coal fire station against 14·16 up to 15·6 mills for a nuclear power station. These are the only relevant cost comparisons.

I. M. D. Little, in 'Atomic Bombay? A Comment on "The Need

for Atomic Energy in the Underdeveloped Countries",[1] calculated
the following costs on the above mentioned assumptions:

	Coal		Nuclear	
	Rupees	*$ mills*	*Rupees*	*$ mills*
Capital Cost	·01975	4·114	·0518 to ·0542	10·808 to 11·310
Operating Cost	·00125	·260	·0012	·260
Fuel Cost	·02500	5·208	·0148 to ·0198	3·100 to 4·133
Total	·04600	9·583	·068 to ·075	14·166 to 15·625

In this calculation a cost of $156 per thermal kW installed has been
assumed. A larger power station of over 200 mW may nowadays be
installed at a lower cost of $130 per kW. It is thus quite clear that
nuclear power costs 50 to 60 per cent more per kWh than thermal
power. It would be sheer waste to spend twice as much capital on
atomic energy to produce electric power at 50 per cent to 60 per cent
higher costs than that which can be obtained from equivalent
thermal power. This is a decisive argument against the introduction
of nuclear power in India, even disregarding the fact that the foreign
exchange component of nuclear power investment is more than twice
as high as the foreign exchange costs of thermal power. If a shadow
rate of foreign exchange higher than the existing rate were to be
applied in the programming of the Third Five Year Plan—which
would be quite appropriate in view of the foreign exchange gap—
then the argument against nuclear power would be still stronger.

Dr Bhabha, however, produces two additional arguments which
might change, if not redress, the balance in favour of a nuclear
power programme in India. The first is the fact that the present coal
prices in high coal price areas (for instance, Bombay) of 45 rupees
per ton may not reflect the present and certainly will not cover the
future real costs of coal. The second is that, while the comparative
costs of nuclear power may not be attractive for the first and second
generations of nuclear power stations, they will become very much
more attractive for the third generation power stations.

[1] *The Economic Weekly*, November 29, 1958.

170

As to his first argument, it may be readily admitted that the presently very high coal price of 45 rupees per ton in Bombay (among the highest in India) may not fully cover all the indirect costs, notably, of transport and transport equipment. This may be especially the case if we consider that the cost of capital necessary for the maintenance of rail trucks and railway equipment may be based on an interest rate which is too low, say $4\frac{1}{2}$ per cent instead of the more probably correct shadow rate of interest of 10 per cent. Dr Bhabha gives estimates of additional investment costs for the railways and mines, but this is insufficient to determine what the proper coal price is. Dr I. M. D. Little correctly argues, however, that the coal price would have to reach 87 to 103 rupees per ton in Bombay in order to equalize costs of nuclear power stations. 'It is hard to believe that the long-run real cost of mining and getting coal to Bombay is as much as this, or will ever be as much as this over the course of twenty years. Anyway, long short of these figures, oil is cheaper.'

As to the second argument, in the long run the balance of cost charges, at present decidedly against nuclear power costs, may gradually swing more in favour of atomic energy for two reasons: first, because, contrary to the results of the short run of the last three years, cost reducing technical progress may be greater in nuclear than in thermal power; and secondly, because in the long run the real cost of mining coal may rise increasingly. 'But that it might be good to have atomic energy in 20 years, or even in 10 years, is little reason to buy uneconomical plants from the UK or USA now. . . . To put any of her own capital resources into buying the early products of this western research would seem to be a great waste of the very limited savings of the Indian people. As Dr Bhabha says, electricity is in short supply in India. It is likely to go on being in short supply if one uses twice as much capital as is needed to get more.'[1]

Dr Bhabha's main argument in favour of a nuclear power programme in India is his calculation of the third-generation atomic power costs. These costs are assumed to be a mere 50–60 per cent of those of the first- and second-generation atomic power stations. The first- and second-generation atomic power stations should be considered, according to him, as mere stepping-stones or instruments of producing locally uranium U^{233} for the 'third-generation power stations'. Using local monazite, 'with the vast reserves of thorium

[1] I. M. D. Little, *op. cit.*

171

available in India, an additional investment in nuclear power in the first ten years would repay itself within the following ten years and, what is more important, hold out the possibility thereafter of an expansion of the power programme at the maximum rate considered reasonable, namely, doubling every five years for an indefinite period. . . . If India is to benefit from the advantages of nuclear power ten to fifteen years hence, and be in a position to utilize further the technical developments which may be expected by then, an investment in a million kilowatts of nuclear power has to be made within the next seven years.'[1]

Unfortunately the argument and its operational conclusions are wrong for three reasons:

1. *Uncertain cost estimates*

The technology and the cost of the various processes involved in the second- and third-generation stations is not yet firmly established even in the laboratory stage, not to mention on a commercially or practically feasible stage. Dr Bhabha recognizes this difficulty—albeit insufficiently—when saying: 'Since the technology of this reactor (LMFR) is still in its early stages, and no prototype power reactor of this design has yet been built, our discussion at this stage must necessarily be subject to considerable uncertainties'[2] and: 'Our estimates for latter parts of the programme are necessarily invested with much greater uncertainties, and we regard them as indicating only the correct order of magnitude on the basis of present technology.'[3] The uncertainties are so great, however, that even a correct order of magnitudes cannot be estimated at the present stage. Even if the purely technological problems were clearly solved, it would be excessively risky to initiate a nuclear power programme in India before industrially and commercially checked costs estimates can be obtained. In addition, however, a number of purely technological items in Dr Bhabha's argument appear highly doubtful.

2. *Technological doubts*[4]

(i) It appears doubtful whether the doubling time of five years for

---

[1] H. J. Bhabha and N. B. Prasad, *op. cit.*, pp. 34–35, paragraph 47.

[2] *Ibid.*, p. 18, paragraph 27.

[3] *Ibid.*, p. 21, paragraph 31.

[4] The author had the benefit of advice from Professor M. Benedict (M.I.T.) on these matters, who is not responsible, however, either for the interpretation (or misinterpretation) or conclusions here.

U^{233} fuelled plants is not too optimistic. The benefits of the third-generation plants may take 15 or 20 years instead of the 10–15 years assumed.

(ii) The feasibility of any type of U^{233} breeder is not yet practically proved. The internally cooled liquid metal fuel reactor (LMFR) on which the calculations are based[1] disappointed expectations: it will not breed.

(iii) Recycling thorium[2] is unattractive economically because costs of handling irradiated thorium, which will have been made radioactive with Th^{228}, would be much higher than costs of fresh thorium.

(iv) Recent calculations seem to show that costs of power produced in a U^{233} breeder will be substantially higher than in a reactor fuelled with natural or slightly enriched uranium.

(v) It is quite uncertain whether plutonium will fulfil the expectations as to its productive use in the future. Far from basing costly investment decisions on this hope, it appears even highly doubtful whether deducting credit for plutonium produced by the nuclear power station is justified for more than the next few years. It is quite uncertain whether the US and the UK Atomic Energy Commissions will go on paying the present prices for plutonium. Without this credit the costs per nuclear kWh would increase by a further 0·7 mills.

3. *Unwarranted conclusions*

Points 1 and 2 show that the economic and the technological arguments used are at best doubtful. The impression is given that, if they were to reveal themselves as correct after a few years further experience, a failure to initiate a nuclear programme in India now would lose valuable time, since it takes ten years or more before third-generation atomic power stations can be built. This is, however, a completely unjustified conclusion. It appears unnecessarily wasteful to build three generations of reactors. India could then start off with third-generation plants and import U^{235} to start them from the United States, whose U^{235} costs are very low, being based *inter alia* on low hydro-electric costs of 3–4 mills per kWh. As long as U^{235} was available only for a short run, the dependence on one source of supply—even if very much cheaper than own-produced costs—may have been felt to be politically unpalatable. Since purely

[1] H. J. Bhabha and N. B. Prasad, *op. cit.*, p. 18.
[2] *Ibid.*, p. 20.

173

commercial long-run contracts for delivery of U^{235} are available, however, this argument does not apply.

The 'third'-generation atomic power station argument of Dr Bhabha does not justify the initiation at present of a nuclear power programme in India. When a man is hungry he may pay a high price for a meal, but he should not proceed to buy a restaurant.

9

INDIA'S BALANCE OF PAYMENTS PROBLEM

SIR DONALD MACDOUGALL

I. THE PROBLEM AND THE EXPORT FACTOR

It is arguable whether the balance of payments is the most important factor limiting the rate of India's economic development, but it will probably at least be agreed that it is a major limiting factor. Shortage of foreign exchange is certainly holding up production quite seriously at present, and there is a danger that it will continue to restrict output and the rate of growth during the Third Plan and, looking further ahead, in the Fourth and the Fifth.

The Present Situation
Many factories in India are today lying partially idle through lack of imported supplies. A glance at Table 1 shows that there is unused capacity over a wide field, even on a single shift basis, and that few industries are working multiple shifts. The data refer to the year 1959–60, but it seems unlikely that there has since been any general improvement; industrial output has increased substantially, but so has capacity. It is true that the figures may sometimes overstate capacity for statistical reasons; on the other hand, since the table relates production to capacity at the beginning of the year, the percentages of capacity utilized would often be still lower if account were taken of the new capacity installed during the year in many industries.

There are, of course, many reasons other than shortage of foreign exchange for this state of affairs. For example, new factories inevitably have teething troubles; short runs and breakdowns interrupt production even in established factories; capacity may have been installed in excess of current needs where demand is expected to increase; demand may sometimes have been overestimated; and so

175

on. But a substantial part of the unused capacity undoubtedly reflects shortage of imported materials, components, spare parts, and replacements. This is true, for example, of a good many industries using steel, non-ferrous metals, wood pulp, rubber, and intermediates for certain chemicals and drugs. Factories in many fields are held up for lack of some vital bottleneck item; some firms that have agreed to a 'phased programme' of reducing the import content of their production (imposed quite properly to induce progressive import-saving) have fallen behind schedule and are unable to get the imports required for full production.

It seems likely that, say, a further Rs. 100 crores per annum could usefully be imported to meet industry's requirements, given the present level of demand for industrial goods, and that this might increase industrial production by perhaps 15–20 per cent, or by several times the value of the increase in imports. Shortages of home produced goods and services, such as coal, power, and transport, might limit production in certain fields, but these too could sometimes be overcome by imports, at least after a time, were foreign exchange available. Imported oil, for example, might be substituted for coal in coastal regions, and at the same time save transport, while generating plants to be run on oil or water power might be imported to relieve the power shortage.

Industrial production might be further increased if still more foreign exchange were available for imports of materials, etc.; for effective demand might then be allowed to increase with less fear of inflation since some extra supplies would be forthcoming to meet the extra demand.

Increased imports of fertilizers could likewise increase the value of agricultural output by a multiple of the foreign exchange cost. A still further substantial increase in national production and employment might be possible if large-scale public works were undertaken, using under-employed labour and indigenous materials, and if the extra demand of the workers employed could be met by increased imports. (Mr Andrew Shonfield has recently suggested that such imports, at least of food grains and perhaps of cotton, might be obtained from the United States as a gift.)

In these various ways shortage of foreign exchange is a serious bottleneck that is holding up production and preventing the full use of the nation's industrial capacity, land, and labour. Increased aid or exports could make possible an increase in production several times as great in value and, by raising income, raise savings and investment and thus the rate of economic development.[1]

The Third Plan

Shortage of foreign exchange will continue during the Third Plan, and there is a serious danger that it will make impossible the rate of development that is hoped for and that is absolutely essential. Even if foreign aid is forthcoming on the large scale envisaged in the *Draft Outline* (more than twice that received in the Second Plan), this may not be enough; for the import needs may well have been under-estimated, as they were in the Second Plan.

The allowance for development imports[2] implies a very rapid increase in the output of capital goods in India, and any estimate of requirements probably tends to understate the ancillary and unfore-seen types of equipment that have to be imported. The growing tendency for aid to be tied to exports from the aid-giving country, especially the United States, will increase the cost. There is no guarantee that the prices of capital goods generally will not rise in the aid-giving countries, as they have done in the past.

The allowance for maintenance imports (including capital goods for replacement) looks very low. The average for the Third Plan is put at little more than Rs. 700 crores per annum.[3] This is probably no more, and perhaps less, than the present rate of importation, which is severely restricted and, as we have seen, substantially less

---

[1] The following very simple example shows how extra exports may increase savings and investment. It ignores many complications. The figures are purely illustrative.

Curtail home consumption of, say, bicycles by Rs. 100.

Increase exports of bicycles by Rs. 100.

Import Rs. 100 extra raw material.

Put Rs. 75 into production of consumption goods and make an extra Rs. 300 of consumption goods.

Put Rs. 25 into production of capital goods and make extra Rs. 100 of capital goods.

Extra income (wage and profits) is Rs. 225 in consumption goods production, Rs. 75 in capital goods production; total Rs. 300.

Say one-third of this is taxed or saved, i.e., Rs. 100. This finances the extra output of capital goods. Consumption demand out of the extra income goes up by Rs. 200, and this is met by the extra production of consumption goods of Rs. 300, less the fall in purchases of bicycles of Rs. 100.

[2] Capital goods for new investment together with components, etc., for increasing production of capital goods in India.

[3] Rs. 3,750 crores over the five years. *Third Five Year Plan—A Draft Outline*, p. 53.

than is required to give a reasonable use of capacity. Import needs, moreover, seem likely to grow despite the large increases planned in import-saving production if, as is contemplated, industrial output is to grow by about two-thirds over the next five years and national income by something approaching one-third.[1]

There is also the special problem arising from the difficulty of getting aid for maintenance imports. Aid-giving countries usually prefer to finance capital goods and 'projects' that will create monuments to their generosity, although there are welcome signs that this attitude is changing. India is probably in rather an unusual position among underdeveloped countries in that the foreign aid required to supplement her domestic savings tends to exceed her needs for imports of capital goods for new investment; for she is an important producer of capital goods. Part of the aid is thus required for maintenance imports.

There is not necessarily anything improvident about taking aid for such imports. It can help to increase investment just as much as aid to finance new capital goods. A large part of the Marshall Aid given by the United States to Europe was in fact used to finance imports other than of capital goods. It is to be hoped that these facts will be increasingly recognized, but in the meantime there will remain a special problem for India's balance of payments.

(Even if more of India's aid were made free to spend on either maintenance or development imports, there would still, however, in present circumstances, be a problem of how much to switch to the former in order to 'feed' existing unused capacity when some of this might produce less essential goods.)

India enters the Third Plan, faced with all these difficulties and uncertainties, with no cushion against unforeseen contingencies as there was at the beginning of the Second Plan. The reserves cannot be drawn upon to any significant extent. They are little more than Rs. 150 crores compared with nearly 750 crores five years ago, and there are few remaining inessential imports to be cut; on the contrary, as we have seen, imports are insufficient for the proper maintenance of the economy.

For all these reasons it seems unlikely that the Plan can be achieved unless aid, or India's exports, are very substantially increased above the levels contemplated in the *Draft Outline*. If more

[1] *Draft Outline*, pp. 31 and 228.

aid is not received—and I think it should certainly be asked for—exports would probably have to be increased by nearly one-half during the next five years. Even this would leave a very difficult position during the earlier years because exports cannot be increased overnight and some of the more important import-saving investments will bear fruit only in the later years of the Plan.

The Fourth and Fifth Plans

Even if more aid, including aid for maintenance imports, can be obtained in the Third Plan, this should not in any way weaken the export drive. It would still seem necessary to aim at an increase approaching one-half in exports during the next five years to provide a base from which a further massive increase can take place during the Fourth Plan. Such an increase seems necessary if India is to achieve independence of foreign aid in the Fifth Plan. This would probably involve a rate of exportation at the beginning of the Fifth Plan of as much as Rs. 1,500 crores per annum, or more than twice the present rate of under Rs. 650 crores.

Such a very large increase in export needs may come as a shock to some readers, and it clearly requires some justification. No detailed proof can be given, but an increase of this order can, I believe, be shown to be plausible and indeed a minimum one; it would certainly be very hard to argue that a lower level of exports would suffice. In brief, an increase of about two-thirds in exports would be needed merely to pay for the present level of imports; some further rise in import needs seems inevitable to maintain the greatly increased levels of activity which it is hoped to achieve; in addition, there will be heavy repayments of capital and interest on the loans that have already been received from abroad together with those that will be received during the next ten years.

A rather fuller justification will now be attempted. (Table 2 will help readers to understand some of the figures mentioned.)

Maintenance imports[1] at present seem to be around Rs. 700–750 crores per annum and should be nearer Rs. 850 crores to allow industrial capacity to be more fully used. If it is hoped to raise national income by over three-quarters, and to treble industrial production, by the beginning of the Fifth Plan—which would be merely a continuation of the rates of growth implied in the Third

[1] Excluding food imported under P.L. 480.

Plan[1] although an acceleration is really needed—it is hard to see how maintenance imports could be kept below, say, Rs. 1,000 crores at the very least despite a rapid development of import-saving activities. This would mean that the increase in maintenance imports (Rs. 250–300 crores) was only about $2\frac{1}{2}$ per cent of the increase in national income.

I would have put down a larger increase had it not been for the view implied in the *Draft Outline* that maintenance requirements will not rise during the Third Plan. I feel that at least some modest increase must be allowed for, considering the following facts: there have been very few examples of countries achieving a rapid economic development without an increase in imports (although Indian development over the next decade might conceivably provide a unique example of rapid import-saving); the present level of imports is severely restricted; a large expansion of exports will be very difficult unless special types of materials and equipment required to make goods acceptable in foreign markets are imported; a substantial part of the expansion of exports is likely to be directed to the Soviet bloc on a bilateral basis and to some neighbouring countries on what may in effect be a bilateral basis, so that some imports may have to be accepted that would not be regarded as essential if foreign exchange earnings were freely convertible. (In this context it is important to ensure that goods exported to Soviet bloc countries are not re-exported by them to other countries where they replace Indian goods that would otherwise have earned convertible currencies. Trade figures suggest that there may have been some diversion of this sort in certain commodities.)

Development imports in the Second Plan seem to have averaged Rs. 300–400 crores per annum and are expected to exceed Rs. 400 crores per annum during the Third Plan;[2] they may well have to be nearer Rs. 450 crores for reasons mentioned earlier. It is hard to believe that they could be less than, say, Rs. 400 crores per annum at the beginning of the Fifth Plan if, as is hoped, investment is to be raised to over $2\frac{1}{2}$ times the present level (11 to 16 per cent[3] of a national income more than three-quarters higher, and it may be that

[1] *Draft Outline* pp. 31 and 228. The rates of growth are over 5 per cent per annum in national income and about $10\frac{1}{2}$ per cent in industrial production; these have been compounded over the eleven years 1960–61 to 1971–72.

[2] *Draft Outline*, p. 54. Development imports are at present running temporarily at a lower figure.

[3] *Draft Outline*, pp. 6 and 43.

a still higher investment ratio is required). Merely to prevent any increase in the need for development imports will be difficult. Apart from the need for a very large rise in the output of capital goods as a whole, there is the problem of special types of equipment. At the stage of development that India will have reached there seem bound to be as many types that she will still not be able to produce, especially as many new products will be developed in the world during the next decade. At Rs. 400 crores, development imports would be only 10 per cent of India's net investment (though a larger fraction of the capital goods required for net investment).

With maintenance imports at Rs. 1,000 crores and development imports at Rs. 400 crores, total imports would be Rs. 1,400 crores. This would be little more than $5\frac{1}{2}$ per cent of the national income. The lowness of this figure may be appreciated when it is realized that in the United States—a large country with very diversified resources, in the van of technological progress, and with a long history of economic development behind it—high tariffs-imports (c.i.f.) are over 4 per cent of the national income[1] (and were usually $5\frac{1}{2}$ per cent or more until the 1930s). The corresponding figure for the Soviet Union may also be of the order of 4 per cent. Apart from China, there is virtually no other country with an import ratio anything like so low. If India's national income were valued at US prices, the ratio of imports to national income assumed for the beginning of the Fifth Plan would be well under 4 per cent.

Although I have allowed for an increase in total imports above the 1960–61 level, and thus assumed no import-saving in an absolute sense, there would have to be massive import-saving in a relative sense. Imports would have to fall from nearly 8 per cent to little more than $5\frac{1}{2}$ per cent of the national income. The increase in imports would be under 3 per cent of the rise in national income. The rate of increase assumed in the quantity of imports (under $2\frac{1}{2}$ per cent per annum) is little more than half that required by the United States throughout the half century ending in 1929 (over 4 per cent per annum), although the planned rate of increase in the Indian real national income is much higher than that achieved by the United States during this period.

In addition to imports, the service of public external debt (including interest and repayments) may be, say, Rs. 200–250 crores per

[1] 4·1 per cent in 1959. The more usually quoted figure for imports f.o.b. as a percentage of the gross national product is lower (3·2 per cent).

annum even if the bulk of the loans received during the next ten years are on easy terms, and especially if repayments due in the Third Plan are postponed or covered by new borrowing, as was contemplated in the *Draft Outline* (page 55). On the other hand, net invisible earnings (excluding interest on the public external debt) together with net inflow of private capital may provide, say, Rs. 100–150 crores.[1] Exports would then have to be about Rs. 1,500 crores.

It may be argued that there is no need to aim at such a high figure since foreign aid is likely to continue in the Fifth Plan. But it would seem to be rather a dangerous gamble to count on this. Political conditions can change greatly in ten years. Mr Kennedy, for example, will no longer be President of the United States, and there will be many other claimants for whatever aid is available, including many countries whose ability to use aid profitably will be much greater than it is today.

Even if it is assumed that aid will be available to India on a substantial scale in the Fifth Plan, this will not necessarily change the export target that should be aimed at. For if internal savings have been stepped up by the Fifth Plan to a level that can give a satisfactory rate of growth without foreign assistance, India will presumably not wish to accept it; and it would be unfortunate if balance of payments difficulties made the aid necessary. If, on the other hand, internal savings are still inadequate, it will not be difficult to create a balance of payments deficit, if necessary, by stepping up the rate of investment, so that a balance of payments case for aid can still be made and the aid can be absorbed.

It is possible that there will be important discoveries of oil or other natural resources that can be used to replace imports. But it would be imprudent until they have actually been made to count on discoveries that would have a revolutionary effect on the balance of payments. In any case, such resources would take time to develop. I have, moreover, already allowed for very large-scale import-saving. And a completely autarkic policy of import-saving at any cost—of producing anything that it is physically possible to produce in India —would undoubtedly slow down the rate of growth.

[1] These items at present yield under Rs. 100 crores net, excluding also official donations. Earnings from transportation and especially tourism should rise, as should private investment from abroad. On the other hand, there may be significant extra payments of income on such investments.

This is not to say that investment in import-saving activities should not have some preference—and perhaps quite a substantial one—over investment in production that can be exported. I think it should because, for example, of the greater dependence of exports on circumstances outside India's control and of the tendency for a pushing of exports to worsen the terms of trade. But the preference for import-saving should not be absolute. For example, an investment in production for export that required only, say, a 10 per cent export subsidy should normally, I suppose, be preferred to an investment in import-saving that required protection equivalent to, say, a 50 per cent import duty, after allowing a reasonable time for infant industries to grow up in either case.

The Magnitude of the Task

For all these reasons I feel that a target of around Rs. 1,500 crores per annum for exports at the beginning of the Fifth Plan is by no means too high. It would mean, very roughly, an increase of around one-half during the next five years, followed by a further increase of about one-half during the following five years. There is no point, of course, in arguing about the precise figure, for in any case it will probably be agreed that the increase required is very large indeed; but I shall use the figure of Rs. 1,500 crores for purposes of illustration. How practicable is the task?

From the point of view of allocating a sufficient proportion of the nation's investment to export activities, and of reserving a sufficient part of the increase in the nation's output for export, the task does not look unmanageable. Exports would have to rise by about 8 per cent per annum compared with an increase of 5 to 6 per cent in the national income. Less than 8 per cent of the increase in output would have to be devoted to exports. The proportion of the national output exported would merely have to be restored to the level achieved during the First Plan.

These figures refer to output as a whole, and for a time there will be difficult problems in particular fields where home demand will have to be restrained to make room for exports. But the pattern of output can be changed considerably over a period so that, looking ten years ahead, the problem should not be too difficult provided that an appropriate pattern of investment is adopted.

When, however, one considers the problem of selling the goods abroad, the task appears much more difficult, for India's exports would have to increase faster than world trade seems likely to expand. The latter has risen in terms of quantity by about one-third in each of the last two five-year periods (and may, perhaps, grow more slowly in future). The exports of underdeveloped countries taken as a whole have grown considerably less quickly.

While world trade has been expanding quite rapidly, India's exports have been stagnant during the last ten years. This is partly because her share in the world market for certain products has been falling (sometimes mainly for external reasons, sometimes in the main because Indian domestic consumption has been catching up with production). In jute manufactures, for example, Pakistan has entered the world export market and Thailand has entered that for lac. In tea, East Africa and Ceylon have been increasing their share of the UK market at India's expense. India's share in the world market for manganese ore has fallen. In groundnut oil, where once she had a substantial share, her exports have now virtually dried up.

Probably the more important reason, however, why India's exports have fared so much worse than world exports as a whole is that they unfortunately consist to a considerable extent of items where world trade is expanding only slowly if at all. Nearly one-half of India's exports still consists of the three traditional staples—tea, cotton textiles, and jute manufactures. World trade in these items taken together seems unlikely to expand very rapidly in future, barring a striking increase in imports by the Soviet bloc; and the scope for increasing India's share is limited because it is already high in tea and jute manufactures, while an attempt to secure a largely increased share of the world market for cotton textiles—where her share is already substantial—would be likely to provoke restrictive measures abroad. In spite of these difficulties, exports of the three staples must be vigorously promoted; they are at present so important that they must not be neglected. But, while quite a sizeable increase is by no means impossible, it is clear that, if the total exports required are to be achieved, there will have to be a really striking increase in exports of the other items; they may well have to be trebled or more.

Among these other items there are some very promising exports even outside the field of the newer manufactures. There could be rapid increases in the earnings from, for example, iron ore, coffee, fish, vegetable oils, and, in the field of invisible exports, tourism. These are items in which world trade is likely to expand rapidly, or where India's share is small and could be increased substantially, or both. There are also a good many other quite promising items. Exports of all these and other commodities must be pushed hard, but, even on the most optimistic assumptions, they can hardly be relied on to provide anything like the increase in total exports that is required.

A very substantial contribution must thus come from the newer manufactures, exports of which must be increased many times over to several hundred crores per annum. They at present account for only about 5 per cent of India's exports, a share which must be increased to a much more important fraction. Whatever the figure, it seems clear that an almost revolutionary change will be required in the structure of India's export trade.

I must confess that India's export task looks extremely formidable, but I do not think it need be matter for despair, for cutting down or drastically altering the fundamental nature of the Plan, or for giving up hope of achieving a rapid rate of growth with independence of foreign aid within a decade. In products where there has been a decline in India's share of the market it is by no means inevitable that this must continue or that part at least of her previous share cannot be regained, provided really vigorous measures are taken to increase production, to free supplies for export, to make them competitive, and to market them. We have also seen that there are a good many promising commodities of which exports could be rapidly increased. In the case of the newer manufactures it is sometimes argued that the world market will not expand very rapidly in future because of the simultaneous industrialization of a large number of underdeveloped countries. But even if this is true, which is doubtful, it might still be possible for India to carve out the rather small share she needs, perhaps about 2 per cent of the world export market for the relevant products taken as a whole—a smaller share than that of such small countries as Sweden, Switzerland, the Netherlands, or Belgium.

Moreover, India, though poorer than the great majority of other underdeveloped countries per head of the population, is more advanced industrially than most and should thus be able, by keeping one step ahead, to sell them manufactured products that they cannot yet produce. The trading skill of Indians and the large number of Indian traders in many other countries should be of assistance, as should be the selling organizations and experience built up by textile exporting firms over a long period.

It is also possible that more and more international firms selling all over the world will, if they are permitted to do so, choose India as one of their bases for production and export (as some are already doing). Among the low-wage countries, India's claims are high. She has one of the largest home markets; the general political outlook is more secure than in many other countries (although the extent of government control may prove a deterrent); she has a good supply of educated personnel and of industrial facilities generally.

There is then no need for despair, but there is no doubt that the task is a very difficult one indeed. What has to be done if there is to be a chance of success?

II. THE REQUIREMENTS FOR INCREASING EXPORTS

Recognition of the Need to Export

The first and fundamental requirement is a recognition by all concerned of the magnitude of the task and of the vital need to achieve a really massive increase in exports if India's economic development is not to be seriously jeopardized. Exports must no longer be regarded as a means of getting rid of unwanted surpluses that have unfortunately arisen. The government must accept a large increase in exports as a major objective of economic policy and give it high priority. Ministers must take difficult decisions on general policy, involving much more drastic measures than have been taken hitherto; and there must be effective machinery for carrying them out without delay and for taking rapid decisions on the many detailed problems that will constantly arise.

I am no expert on public administration, and I do not know how this can best be carried through in the Indian context, but I can think of some occasions in the past when Britain was faced with similarly urgent problems. There was, for example, the wartime crisis when U-boats were sinking ships at such a rapid rate that Britain was threatened with starvation or at least with a complete dislocation of the war effort at home and overseas. Mr Churchill formed a small but top-level Battle of the Atlantic Committee over which he presided and which met very frequently to take decisions, to check that decisions taken previously had been implemented, and to review their effectiveness. Then there was the Battle of Britain crisis of 1940 when Lord Beaverbrook was given the task of getting as many fighter aircraft ready for service as he could in the shortest possible time. He was very successful although his efforts dislocated war production for some time thereafter.

Since India's export problem is a longer-term one, and the drive for exports must not be allowed to dislocate the economy generally, perhaps another example will be more directly relevant. When the Conservative government returned to power in 1951 they were faced with the need to redeem an election pledge to build 300,000 houses a year as soon as possible, the rate of construction was then only 200,000. Whether this was a wise use of Britain's limited investment resources is beside the point. Mr Churchill appointed Mr Harold Macmillan to achieve this task, Mr Macmillan in turn recruited a business man of considerable experience and determination to assist him and the target was achieved far more quickly than most people had thought possible. An important condition was the ability of Mr Macmillan and his officers, with the full backing of the Prime Minister and the Cabinet, to prevail over other Ministries when their interests conflicted with that of his.

The vital need to export must be brought home again and again to all sections of the community: to officials, who have to take countless decisions that directly or indirectly affect exports; to businessmen, who will have to do most of the actual exporting and make some sacrifices to that end; to the general public, who will also have to make some apparent sacrifices for the sake of exports.

In particular, the general public will have to put up with restraint on the consumption of some goods that can be exported where the supplies are not adequate fully to meet both home and export demand. Even where total supplies could be increased sufficiently through higher investment, it may still be desirable to restrain demand where the products are not essential and the resources for investment can be more usefully employed elsewhere. Restraints on home demand will often involve higher prices which may result either from a higher excise duty or from the charging of higher prices by producers who have to sell abroad at a loss. Restraint may be necessary, at least temporarily, on the consumption of such products as vegetable oils, tea, the better qualities of coffee, leather, and a fairly wide range of manufactures. This will seldom involve an absolute reduction in consumption or even in *per capita* consumption; a moderate slowing down in the rate of growth of consumption will normally suffice.

There is a natural reluctance to restrain consumption, and especially when the goods are produced in India. But the belief that such goods must always be cheap and plentiful reveals a strange asymmetry of thought towards imports and exports respectively. If, say, 90 to 95 per cent of the country's needs of an article are produced in India and the remaining 5 to 10 per cent imported, there will normally be little hesitation in cutting the imports drastically to save foreign exchange and making do with rather smaller supplies, even if this means considerably higher prices and profit margins. In the circumstances it seems a little strange that there should be opposition to a moderate slowing down in the rate of growth of consumption of goods produced in India that could be exported and earn foreign exchange, especially if this is done by excise taxes which accrue to the government.

It must be remembered that restraints on consumption will be recouped several times over in terms of the production of other goods since the extra exports will make possible the import of vital bottleneck items. In general, the public will have to be convinced that, without such restraints, it will be impossible to achieve an adequate rate of development; and that the failure to achieve an adequate rate of development would be a much more serious matter.

It is necessary to convince not only Indians but also the advanced nations of India's need for greatly increased exports. The advanced nations can do much to help or to obstruct India's export drive. They must be convinced that, without a massive increase in exports, India can never achieve self-sustaining growth and independence of foreign aid and at the same time repay the large loans she is receiving. The slogan at the moment must be 'aid *and* trade' if it is ever to be 'trade *not* aid'. In particular, the advanced nations must be convinced of the need for much more competition from the new Indian manufactures, not only in third markets but even in their own home markets. If restrictions are imposed on goods produced with 'cheap' or 'sweated' labour, as with cotton textiles, India's chances of achieving the exports she needs will be considerably reduced.

Merely to refrain from imposing such restrictions will not, however, be enough. More positive action to encourage imports from India (and other underdeveloped countries) is required. The analogy of the Marshall Plan is relevant. The United States, while giving massive aid to Europe, embarked in effect on an import drive to help sales of European goods in the United States (while tolerating severe discriminatory restrictions against her own exports to Europe).

For example, US officials abroad actively sought out European products that might be saleable in the United States; American tourists were allowed to bring back as much as $500 worth of goods purchased abroad without paying duty; local purchases by the American military forces in Europe were encouraged in various ways. (These measures have now, quite rightly, been reversed, as Europe's balance of payments has become much stronger.) The advanced nations could also help by persuading firms with interests in factories in India to waive agreements limiting exports from those factories.

Emphasis on Economic Efficiency

A second general requirement for increased exports is that every effort should be made to reduce costs and increase economic efficiency and that this should be given preference wherever possible over other considerations. This is necessary if India is to compete in world markets without prohibitive subsidies (as well as for other obvious economic reasons).

Where economies of scale are important it is essential to concentrate on large plants even if this means some sacrifice of the benefits of regional dispersion of industries and involves some risk of concentration of economic power. Competition is usually good for efficiency, but the deliberate creation of several undertakings where one could produce far more cheaply is unlikely to achieve the desired result. It may be tempting to give preference to small-scale industries because they employ more labour; but they may be unable to compete in world markets. Larger enterprises, even if they employ fewer people directly, may, if they can export, actually provide more employment in industry as a whole by gaining foreign exchange for the country which can be used to import scarce raw materials, the shortage of which is limiting production and employment.

The need for exports may also conflict with the desire for fair play. For example, foreign exchange must be granted liberally to would-be exporters for travel and sales promotion abroad even though this may lead to some abuse. And in so far as reliance is placed on the State Trading Corporation or other government agencies to sell goods abroad, emoluments will have to be paid that can attract from the private sector the best experts in the various branches of trading even if these are out of line with government salaries.

189

Ensuring Supplies for Export

A third general requirement is that adequate supplies should be available for export. This, as we have seen, can be done in part by restraining domestic consumption. It is also necessary to provide for adequate production of exportable commodities. This means ensuring that sufficient investment is carried out in the industries concerned, that they have adequate supplies of raw materials, fertilizers, etc., and that any other necessary measures are taken (for example, a modification of the legislation on cow-slaughter could increase supplies of hides and leather for export).

In the past the expansion of production of exportable commodities has too often lagged behind that of home demand. This must not be allowed to happen in future. Expansion of production is especially necessary when the commodities meet really essential needs of the mass of the people so that consumption cannot easily be restrained.

Since resources will remain scarce, and especially imported equipment and materials, it is vital to remember the corollary that investment for production that is not absolutely essential, and that will not yield substantial net earnings or savings of foreign exchange, must be severely limited so as to leave room for the more vital projects. This will mean that many schemes, though desirable in themselves and especially if they would benefit only the higher-income groups, will have to be postponed till conditions are more favourable.

Care must also be taken in the allocation of investment resources among activities that can earn or save foreign exchange. The calculations involved are difficult. Profitability in a narrow financial sense is not a sufficient criterion since, among other things, the value to the nation of extra exports or import-substitutes is considerably greater than it appears to be at existing rates of exchange. It is certainly necessary to work out the initial foreign exchange cost of the investment, the continuing annual foreign exchange costs, and the continuing annual earning or saving of foreign exchange. The net annual earning or saving of foreign exchange as a proportion of the initial cost will not yet, however, provide a satisfactory criterion for choosing between investments because the use of scarce domestic goods and services must also be allowed for.

Indirect effects must also be taken into account. For instance, in deciding how many aircraft to buy abroad for use on internal services credit must be taken for the additional foreign tourists who will come to the country (assuming that inadequacy of air transport is

190

limiting their number), and account must be taken not only of the fares they will pay to Indian Airlines Corporation but also of their other expenditure in India. Though such calculations are difficult, they should be more seriously attempted and made more carefully than hitherto. They might suggest ways in which a reallocation of investment would assist the balance of payments.

Making Exports Competitive

Even if sufficient supplies are made available for export, they cannot be sold unless prices are competitive. Measures to reduce costs will take time to bear fruit. In the meantime, if India is to achieve the large expansion in exports that is necessary, it seems essential that a good many exports should be sold below the domestic-price and sometimes even below the cost of production. This will be necessary over a fairly wide range of manufactures as well as for a rather small number of primary commodities, sugar being an outstanding example.

In order to make the best use of the nation's resources, preference should normally be given to products that require a smaller rather than a larger rate of subsidy. (On this criterion sugar looks like a bad bet, at least as a continuing export in the long run unless costs can be very substantially reduced either through a geographical redistribution of Indian production or in other ways. But in the shorter run India clearly cannot afford not to sell the substantial surpluses that have arisen.)

Direct or indirect export subsidies will arouse some antagonism abroad. The rules of GATT are somewhat strict on this matter (and surprisingly more strict than on import restrictions) but India has reserved her position. Trouble may, however, arise with producers both in rival exporting countries and in the importing nations.

India can, however, make a good case for at least temporary subsidies. The urgent need for increased export earnings is apparent. It can also be reasonably claimed that the 'infant industry' argument for protection of import-competing industries applies, *mutatis mutandis*, to infant export industries, of which they are many in India. Moreover, many governments subsidize exports in various ways; and the sale by industrial firms of exports at prices lower than those charged at home is a very common phenomenon.

191

III. EXPORTS OF NEWER MANUFACTURES

It is impossible to discuss the measures required to promote exports of each individual item of India's trade, but it may be useful to explore in a little more detail the special case of the newer manufactures, which will have to play such a vital role in the expansion of India's exports. During the Third Plan their contribution, though important, may not be a major one, but it must be during the Fourth.

How Competitive are They?

There are various reasons why a significant range of these industries seems likely to be capable of exporting at competitive prices and why the range is likely to widen steadily:

1. Possessing very high grade iron ore, India should be able to produce cheap steel, although at present the prices charged by Indian steelworks seem to be higher than those charged by many foreign producers, at least for steel to be made into exports.

2. Indian wages per worker are a very small fraction of wages in the main exporting countries of Western Europe and North America (and probably less than half of wages in Japan). Even if output per worker in manufacturing as a whole were a still smaller fraction, so that wage costs per unit of output were in general higher in India, one would expect to find a fair number of industries in which Indian wage costs were lower. International comparisons show that the relationship between output per worker in one country and another usually varies widely from industry to industry, and one would thus expect to find industries in which India's lower output per worker was more than offset by her lower wages.

In fact, I have found quite a number of firms in which this is so and even some where output per worker appears to be higher than it is abroad, although allowance must sometimes be made for higher costs resulting from lower efficiency of labour that are not reflected in figures of output per man, for example, where tools are used up more quickly. The quality of some Indian products may also be lower than that of foreign goods, but again I have found quite a number of cases where users of Indian products have no complaints on this score.

3. The reports of the Tariff Commission suggest that, while the ratio between costs at home and abroad varies greatly, a fair pro-

portion of India's industries may in fact be competitive. The 'fair ex-works price' of Indian products was found to be lower than the c.i.f. price of imports, excluding duty, in more than one-third of sixty-three cases studied (see Tables 3 and 4). Conclusions about individual products cannot be drawn without further study—since comparisons of this sort are fraught with many difficulties,[1] but the general picture shown may be correct unless the list is seriously unrepresentative of industry generally. The 'fair ex-works price' does not refer to the most efficient undertakings in each industry but rather to a representative firm, and allowance is made for a reasonable profit.

To get a fair picture of India's competitive position in third markets, allowance should, however, be made for the cost of transporting manufactures from Indian factories to overseas countries —perhaps 5 to 10 per cent of the ex-works price on average, including handling, insurance, and miscellaneous charges. To assess India's ability to sell to the countries now exporting to her, it would be necessary to make a further allowance for the cost of transporting their exports to her. If these allowances could be made, it might show that India was competitive in only perhaps one-quarter or less of the products.

4. A wide range of manufactured products (in addition to cotton and jute manufactures) is in fact already being exported, though usually in very small quantities. It is not difficult to draw up a list of around fifty such products or groups of products. Some of them may admittedly, however, be sold at prices that do not cover costs, for example, to secure import licences for machinery under export incentive schemes, to fulfil undertakings to export entered into when the plant was licensed, or to relieve temporary shortages abroad when a foreign collaborator cannot meet the demand in full.

5. India's manufacturing costs should progressively decline, and the quality of her products should improve, as the scale of production is increased, as managements acquire greater experience, as labour is trained, and as better equipment is installed. The process should be faster than it is in the advanced industrial countries since the rise in the scale of production should be more rapid in India, since the advanced nations have largely exploited the economies of mass

---

[1] While most products where the Indian price is lower are exported, there are also some exports of a fair number of products where the Indian price is shown to be higher and sometimes substantially higher.

production in many industries, and since India can benefit greatly merely by taking over techniques which they are already using, while they must rely much more for further cost reductions on new technological discoveries.

The growth in India's relative advantage, or the decline in her relative disadvantage, will, however, be retarded by the need to rely more and more on materials and components produced in the country which, initially at least, may often be more expensive than the imported product. Much will also depend on the rate of increase of wages, but despondency on this score can be overdone. What figures are available suggest that in the engineering industries, for example, wages have risen substantially less quickly than labour productivity over the past decade. If true, this compares favourably with the experience of many other countries.

For these various reasons it seems likely that Indian industry is capable of competing in export markets over a significant range of products and that the range will widen. Even when industries are not yet competitive, the margin of disadvantage is often not very large. India is thus more favourably placed than a good many other under-developed countries where the great bulk of manufacturing industries is sometimes still hopelessly uncompetitive.

Measures to Promote the New Manufactured Exports

The range of industries that is competitive in India does not, however, seem to be wide enough at present to make possible the rapid and substantial expansion of exports that is required and to induce sufficient firms to enter foreign markets, even in a small way, early in the Third Plan so that they can gain experience of marketing which will enable them to achieve the really massive expansion of exports that must come during the Fourth Plan. Concentration on a narrow range of products will not be enough, especially as this would mean securing more substantial shares of the markets for individual products and so increase the danger of protective reactions abroad.

In the United States, which still relies substantially on exports of primary products, probably nearly half the manufacturing industries can produce more cheaply than their competitors abroad. In countries like the United Kingdom and Germany, which rely mainly on manufactured exports, the fraction is probably substantially higher. It would seem that, if India is to achieve the rapid expansion of exports that she needs, something approaching one-half of her industries must now be made competitive, especially when it is remembered that she will often have to sell below ruling prices to get an entry into new markets. Some measure of subsidy is thus necessary until costs have been sufficiently reduced.

In addition, even where Indian producers are competitive the pull of the sellers' market at home, with its strong demand and good prices, seriously weakens any incentive to export. In countries like the United Kingdom, Germany, Belgium, Sweden, or Japan, where a substantial fraction of output is traditionally exported by many manufacturing industries, producers will continue to make efforts and sacrifices in the export market even when home demand is strong. But in India there is no such tradition of exporting manufactures on a large scale outside the cotton and jute industries. Powerful measures to make the home market relatively less attractive are thus necessary.

It may be that a change in the relative profitability of home and export sales equivalent to that which would be brought about by a devaluation of the order of, say, 25 per cent is required, and that the measures taken should include direct and indirect export subsidies of more than half this amount. These guesses are based partly on the evidence given above and in Tables 3 and 4, partly on general experience of the degree of devaluation that has been required in the past by countries needing to achieve a large expansion of exports. A twisting of the relative cost and price structure of this order through general measures seems necessary to provide the background against which specific measures to bribe, bully, or cajole producers to export more can be effectively operated.

Such specific measures will also be very necessary, but it would be unwise to rely on these alone, if only because of the time required to put them into operation on a sufficient scale since so many industries and firms are concerned. The administrative problems also are formidable and the dangers of abuse probably greater than with general measures. Moreover, while businessmen may be persuaded to export provided any financial sacrifice is not too great, they are much less easily persuaded, and much more likely to find ways of getting round a directive, if the sacrifice is substantial.

The choice of general measures will depend on administrative and political considerations and on how far a particular method of, in effect, subsidizing exports is likely to provoke unfavourable reactions abroad. Whatever methods are chosen, it is essential that, taken together, they give an incentive to export of the required magnitude. Five possible types of general measures may be mentioned (and others are conceivable) together with some illustrative orders of magnitude.

1. Drawbacks of customs and excise duties on materials used are already given to exporters (as are certain rebates on railway freights), but the procedure is often complicated and prolonged; and while an exporter is waiting for refunds, he may be short of working capital. Drawbacks might be simplified, consolidated, applied to more products, and made more generous and to cover more taxes; but I do not suppose that the assistance to exports would much exceed, say, 5 per cent on average.

2. A difference of, say, 20 per cent between the prices of steel for the manufacture of home and export goods (obtained partly by raising the former prices, partly by lowering the latter) would reduce the relative costs of engineering products for export by around 5 per cent, assuming that steel accounts for about one-quarter of the cost on average. In some engineering industries, the effect would, however, be smaller. It seems, for example, that iron and steel account for only about one-eighth of the cost of electric fans and bicycles and about one-sixteenth of the cost of sewing machines. Thus the effect of altered steel prices would be negligible in most non-engineering industries, but similar schemes might be introduced for other materials.

3. Additional excise or purchase taxes on an appropriate range of manufactures would help to restrain the growth of consumption, release supplies for export, and force manufacturers to seek out export markets. They would also tend to reduce the price to the manufacturer of sales in the home market and thus the gap which often exists between home and export prices; but a tax of, say, 10 per cent would not usually reduce the home price to the producer by as much as 10 per cent since part at least of the tax would be passed on to the consumer. Taxes on manufactures seem to be moderate and not very widespread at least in comparison with a country like the United Kingdom.

4. Exporters of manufactures could be given a remission of tax on profits. Ideally one would like to reward only those making additional exports, but the danger of collusion might rule this out. (For example, two exporters might agree that one would increase the exports made under his name while the other reduced his by an

equal amount, and that the gain from tax remission would be shared between them.) Since, however, non-traditional exports of manufactures are at present small but should grow rapidly, tax remission on all exports of the newer manufactures would come to more or less the same thing and would involve only a small loss to the revenue for some time to come. If, say, 20 per cent of export proceeds were allowed to be deducted from taxable income, this would be equivalent to an export subsidy of nearly 10 per cent. The loss of revenue could be financed many times over by the indirect taxes described in 3 above or, alternatively, by a somewhat higher rate of tax on profits generally, so that the profit-earning class as a whole would not benefit while the general public was making sacrifices as a result of higher excise taxes and in other ways. Any danger of over-invoicing could presumably be largely avoided if the taxpayer were given credit only for foreign exchange turned in to the authorities.

Schemes of this type are in operation in some other countries, including Germany, Japan, and Ireland. Ireland has been able to administer a scheme applying to additional exports of manufactures and, incidentally, nearly doubled her industrial exports between 1958 and 1960, from the equivalent of Rs. 23 crores to Rs. 45 crores, although the tax relief cannot, of course, be given full credit.

5. Exporters could be allowed, in effect, to retain a fraction of their foreign exchange earnings and to use this to buy imports which could be sold at a substantial profit, as has been done with success in, for example, Pakistan. If any article, including luxuries, could be imported, this would, besides raising certain social problems, add to the import bill, which tax remission would not. Exporters might of course only be given import licences that were then taken away from other importers; but this would not be easy to administer, and the extent of the effective subsidy would vary greatly from article to article and from time to time. Measures of this sort cannot be ruled out, but it might prove better to reserve them for specific incentive schemes, including those where, as at present, the exporter is allowed to import supplies for use in his own factory.

Against a background of general measures such as these, specific measures for individual industries and groups of industries, export houses, etc., would have more chance of success. Individual industries or firms might more easily be induced, for example, to export an agreed, and rising, fraction of their output as a condition for permission to buy vital components or machinery. (It would hardly seem practicable to use a financial sanction since this would in effect be a tax and it would be difficult to define with sufficient precision the conditions under which it would be imposed.) In some industries a single firm might be selected to concentrate largely on export and in return receive preferential allocations of foreign exchange for machinery, materials, foreign travel, etc.; such a firm could achieve economies of scale in foreign marketing and could concentrate on types and qualities demanded abroad. In some industries, levies on home sales might be necessary to finance export subsidies despite the general measures; in others it might be sufficient for individual firms to finance any losses on exports by higher profits on home sales.

If, moreover, the general cost and price structure had been substantially shifted in favour of exports, expenditure on trade fairs and missions, more liberal allocation of foreign exchange to would-be exporters, and all the other paraphernalia of an export drive would be likely to yield much higher returns.

Selecting the New Manufactures

The proportion of India's total output of the new manufacturing industries that has to be exported by the Fifth Plan seems likely to be less than 10 per cent. But, since this ratio will not be uniform, some industries may have to export 20 per cent, 30 per cent, or even more of their output. Since these are substantial fractions, it is important to get some idea of what the industries are likely to be so that provision can be made for them in the Third as well as in the Fourth Plans. A number of promising candidates could already be selected with some confidence, and it is important that these be given every facility and encouragement to expand, especially where rapidly growing supplies are vital for the domestic market as well. Home demand cannot be significantly restrained without harm to the country's economic development as a whole; this will be true of a good many producers' goods (materials, components, and equipment) as well as of some consumer goods. (The corollary that less vital projects will have to be postponed has already been mentioned in a more general context, but it bears repetition.)

It is often difficult to forecast an industry's export possibilities, certainly much more difficult than forecasting demand for the home market; because so much depends on developments abroad and it is very hard to tell which infant industries will mature most quickly into adults capable of exporting. A great deal of flexibility will thus have to be maintained.

Marketing the New Manufactures

The provision of capacity to export will not, however, be enough. The exports have to be sold; and getting into foreign markets for manufactures can be a slow, difficult, and expensive business, quite different from that of selling primary products in highly organized world markets (although the marketing of some primary products admittedly requires a high degree of skill and experience). Markets for manufactures are imperfect. Success in selling depends not only on price, though this is very important, but also on quality, attention to local needs and preferences, quick delivery, effective advertising, employment of the right agents, facilities for after-sales service, the provision of spare parts, and so on. Moreover, since competitors will often fight hard to preserve their share of the market, exporting manufactures is a much more competitive business than producing for a highly protected home market where often there are few competitors.

It is thus necessary to start now an intensified export drive. Such a drive may well take five years to bear much fruit. This was, I believe, broadly the experience of Western Europe and Japan in their attempts to raise exports of manufactures to the United States after the war to help fill the dollar gap.

The export drives of most of the European countries hardly began until, say, 1949. (Previously they had few goods to export, and their currencies were often overvalued until the 1949 devaluations.) Many people were rather sceptical about the possibilities, just as some people are sceptical in India today. 'How,' they asked, 'can you possibly export large quantities of manufactures to the United States when her productivity is so high, when she always has the latest things, and when her industry is so flexible? Moreover, whenever you start doing well, the American government will impose protective measures or American industry will find other ways of driving you out of the market.'

Despite these forebodings, European governments embarked on export drives and European businessmen went to the United States to explore the market and begin selling. During the five years, 1950–54, progress was slow and often frustrating, but the ground was being well prepared. And during the following five years, 1955–

59, the harvest was reaped. Exports of manufactures to the United States were trebled; and the success was achieved by a wide variety of industries. It was not simply a matter of small cars, as is sometimes thought; these accounted for only about one-quarter of the increase.

As I see it, the Third Plan period should correspond to the European experience of 1950–54 and the Fourth Plan to that of 1955–59. Hand in hand with the development of capacity during the Third Plan should go preparations for a massive expansion of exports all over the world in the Fourth; and one of the best ways of preparing to export in larger quantities is to start off in a small way. The 'infant industry' argument can be applied not only to exports as well as to import-replacement but also to selling as well as to producing.

In deciding whether to grant licences to schemes involving the collaboration of foreign firms, it is important to remember the advantages that could accrue to India's export trade through the use of their selling organizations abroad. Any attempt to impose restrictive agreements limiting the right to export from India would naturally have to be resisted. Where such agreements already exist and exports seem possible, foreign firms may be prepared to waive them if they are shown that, unless foreign exchange can be earned by exporting, it will be difficult to grant them import licences for components, machinery, etc.

Investment in Selling

The selling of vast additional amounts of exports is bound to be an expensive business in terms both of rupees and, more particularly, of foreign currencies. Such expenditure must be regarded as essential investment designed to earn foreign exchange and must not be skimped any more than investment in, say, steel works to save foreign exchange. Expenditure of foreign currency, both public and private, that can properly be attributed to export promotion probably does not exceed a very few crores. Even a large proportionate increase in this amount, say a doubling, though apparently difficult to afford in present circumstances, would be small in relation to the extra exports it might yield.

More government money will have to be spent on, for example, trade fairs and missions; on trade representatives abroad (who will have to supply much more detailed and expert market information than has hitherto been available, for use both by government and by business); and perhaps on export credit guarantees (the terms must be fully competitive with those offered by competitors abroad, which may require government subsidization of the Export Risks Insurance Corporation).

Foreign exchange must also be granted quite liberally to business firms, including those not yet well established, and to government agencies engaged in export trade, not only for travel abroad but also for advertising, for building up stocks abroad, and for the other needs of marketing. Some firms or industries may need offices, showrooms, or even foreign subsidiaries. Nor can India afford not to grant credits as long as those offered by other exporting nations even if this sometimes involves waiting several years for the foreign exchange; this will still be a well worthwhile investment.

IV. IMPORT ECONOMY

Until recently there has been much more emphasis on import-saving than on export promotion in the strategy of India's economic development. This has quite rightly led to large investments in the production of goods that were previously imported, and the process will continue; without it India's economic development could not proceed very far. However, it is necessary to ensure that the imports required to maintain this rapidly growing production are forthcoming; and to pay for them there must be far higher exports. The greater emphasis on investment in exports must not be at the expense of import-saving. It must be at the expense of activities that are not essential and that would neither earn nor save substantial quantities of foreign exchange, and especially those that would involve a continuing expenditure of foreign exchange.

Since, however successful the export drive, foreign exchange will remain scarce for many years and must be husbanded with great care, it may be worth mentioning some ways in which import economies might be made.

I doubt, for example, whether imported capital equipment is always used as sparingly as it should be. There is often a good deal more flexibility than is sometimes realized in the extent to which capital may be substituted for labour, and *vice versa*, in the large number of processes of production, handling, and so on, involved in a modern enterprise. Licensing authorities cannot possibly check up

O

on every detail in a proposed investment, and a private business naturally tends to choose the methods that are cheapest at ruling prices. But ruling prices substantially understate the scarcity and cost to the nation of imported equipment (and indeed of capital equipment generally, but that is a problem in itself).

An increase in taxes on such equipment even above the levels to which they were raised in the last budget, which was a step in the right direction, would induce more economy and lead to some substitution of India's plentiful labour. Such taxes should also apply to equipment used by public enterprises. Ideally they could be told to use high shadow prices for equipment when choosing their methods of production, but I am doubtful whether this would be effective in practice. Although such taxes might lead to higher prices for the finished product, any increase would usually be rather small. Where the product was exportable, a rather larger export subsidy could be given if necessary.

The planned increases of production could also be achieved with smaller imports of capital equipment if more industries worked double or even treble shifts. Table 1 illustrates the surprising lack of multiple-shift working in India. It may even be less common than in an advanced country like the United States, an extraordinary state of affairs in a country so short of capital as India. The extension of multiple-shift working in an industry could greatly reduce the marginal capital-output ratio, especially while shift working was being increased, but also later when it was fully in operation. It would also help to spread the electricity load throughout the twenty-four hours of the day and so alleviate the power shortage.

Single-shift working may often appear more economical, but the advantage may be more apparent than real, at least from a national point of view. It would probably pay some firms to introduce multiple shifts if the prices of capital equipment and power were brought nearer to their cost to the nation, say by a tax on equipment as suggested above, and if electricity charges for industry were made higher during the day than at night. Multiple shifts would be further encouraged if, for example, firms that work them were given preferential allocation of materials and higher income tax allowances for depreciation. Shift working could be enforced by stricter policies towards the licensing of new capacity in industries until double- or treble-shift working was in operation, even at the risk of limiting competition.

V. DEVALUATION

It may be argued that the measures proposed in this paper, and particularly the taxes on imports and subsidies to exports, are rather similar in their effect to devaluation and that devaluation would be a much simpler and more straightforward alternative. I have no space to discuss this complicated matter in any detail, but a few brief comments may be made.

The import taxes would apply to only a fraction of imports and the export subsidies to only a fraction of exports. Devaluation would have much more widespread effects. It may prove necessary at some later date if detailed controls become unworkable and ineffective because the gains from evasion become so great; but this time has not yet arrived, and it may never come. It may eventually prove possible to achieve a balance, at existing rates of exchange and without too many controls or special taxes and subsidies, when infant export and import-saving industries have grown up and when sufficient investment has been made in export and import-saving activities generally.

If this is so, there is a strong case against a drastic measure that would have inflationary tendencies, reduce confidence in the currency, weaken a powerful argument for cost reduction, and be fraught with other dangers and uncertainties. It might well, moreover, actually worsen the balance of payments, at least in the short run, because the foreign exchange earnings from exports might well be reduced while the foreign exchange cost of imports, which are severely restricted, would not fall.

VI. CONCLUSIONS

The balance of payments may well be the most important factor limiting India's economic development.

Shortage of imported materials, components, fertilizers, etc., is at present seriously holding up production and preventing anything like the full use of the nation's industrial capacity, labour, and land, and thus also limiting savings and investment. More imports could make possible an increase in production several times as great in value.

There is a real danger that shortage of foreign exchange will prevent the achievement of the output targets of the Third Plan—for import needs were substantially underestimated in the *Draft Outline*

—unless more aid is obtained than has yet been asked for, including aid for maintenance imports, and exports can be rapidly increased during the next five years.

Such an increase is also necessary to provide a base for a further massive expansion during the Fourth Plan; for, if India is to achieve substantial independence of foreign aid by the Fifth Plan, and yet maintain rapid growth, exports will have to be around Rs. 1,500 crores per annum, more than double the present Rs. 650 crores. (Exports two-thirds higher are needed merely to pay for present imports; more imports will be needed in ten years, despite massive import-saving, to maintain much higher levels of activity; heavy debt repayments will fall due.)

Even if it is thought that substantial aid will continue to be available, this will not change the export target that should be aimed at.

The task is a tremendous one for a country whose exports have been stagnant for a decade and depend heavily on products where world trade is relatively stagnant. But it is not impossible. Even the three staples—tea, jute, and cotton textiles—can contribute to the expansion, and some of the other items, such as iron ore, coffee, fish, vegetable oils, and tourism, look very promising. Exports of the newer manufactures can be multiplied many times over and must play a major role, at least in the Fourth Plan; if India could carve out a share in world markets for these equal to that of Sweden or Switzerland, much of her problem would be solved.

Conditions for success:

1. Though most of the actual exporting will have to be done by private business, the role of government is crucial. Exports must have very high priority. Some difficult decisions must first be made on general policy, involving much more drastic measures than have hitherto been taken. But these will be fruitless without really effective machinery which can cut through conflicting departmental interests to translate them rapidly into concrete measures, including schemes for each product, and to take quick decisions on their day-to-day implementation.

If Indian products are to compete abroad without prohibitive subsidies, it is essential to go all out for maximum economic efficiency and large-scale plants even if this means less regional dispersion of industry, more concentration of economic power, and some apparent loss of employment opportunities. (Even when large plants provide fewer jobs directly than smaller ones, they may, by earning foreign exchange which can be spent on scarce materials, make possible more employment in industry as a whole.)

3. Adequate supplies must be made available for export:

(a) The public must be persuaded that restraints on consumption of exportable goods (such as vegetable oils, tea, the better grades of coffee, leather, and a fairly wide range of manufactures) are as vital for the balance of payments as those on imports, and a much less serious matter than the general slowing down of expansion that would result from inadequate exports.

(b) Since the scope for restraining home demand, especially for essentials, is limited, output of exportable goods must be adequately expanded; it must not lag behind home demand, as has happened too often in the past. Since resources are scarce, an essential corollary is that investment in other production that is not absolutely essential must be severely limited.

4. Even if sufficient supplies are made available for export, they cannot be sold unless prices are competitive. Since reductions in costs will take time, a good many exports—especially of the newer manufactures but also of a few other items—will, for a time at least, have to be sold below the domestic price and sometimes below cost of production. There will be some antagonism abroad, but India can make a good case for indulging in such practices.

5. The selling of vastly increased exports is bound to cost foreign exchange. More will have to be spent by the government on trade promotion abroad, and it must be granted liberally to businesses embarking on exports. This must be regarded as essential investment to earn foreign exchange and must not be skimped any more than investment in, say, steel works to save foreign exchange.

6. The advanced, aid-giving nations must be persuaded not only to refrain from restricting imports of manufactures made with 'cheap' labour in underdeveloped countries but also actively to encourage them, as the United States did with European goods as part of the Marshall Plan.

India, with potentially cheap steel and low wages, should in time be able to compete abroad over a wide range of manufactured products.

Already the range is significant but not yet wide enough. Moreover, even where Indian products are competitive, the pull of the sellers' market at home, with its strong demand and good prices, seriously weakens any incentive to export. Powerful measures are thus necessary to make the home market less profitable and the export market more so, probably by as much as would result from a devaluation of around 25 per cent.

This can be done by a combination of measures such as drawbacks of customs and excise duties; lower prices for steel used to make exports; additional excises on home sales; remission of taxes on exporters' profits, as in Germany, Japan and Ireland; currency retention schemes, as in Pakistan.

Against a background of such general measures, specific measures —which are also essential—to increase exports to individual industries, export houses, etc., will have much more chance of success.

Getting into foreign markets for manufactures can be a slow and difficult business. It is thus vital to get producers in many fields to make a start now. Judging by the attempts of Western Europe and Japan to raise sales of manufactures to the United States after the war, an export drive may well take five years to bear much fruit. Progress during 1950–54 was slow, but the ground was being prepared; many exporters were learning by experience and by making mistakes. In 1955 the harvest was reaped; exports trebled. The Third Plan should correspond to 1950–54 and the Fourth Plan to 1955–59. Hand in hand with the development of capacity and reduction of costs during the Third Plan should go preparations for a massive expansion of exports in the Fourth.

However successful the export drive, foreign exchange will remain scarce for many years and must be husbanded with great care.

The greater emphasis now required on investment in exports must be at the expense, not of import saving but of less essential production that will neither earn nor save foreign exchange.

A given expansion of output could be obtained with less expenditure on imported equipment if (a) there were higher taxes on such equipment, to induce more careful use; (b) more double or treble shifts were worked in industry.

TABLE 1

UTILIZATION OF MANUFACTURING CAPACITY

PRODUCTION DURING 1959–60 AS PER CENT OF INSTALLED CAPACITY
AT THE BEGINNING OF YEAR IN 121 INDUSTRIES

Production as per cent of capacity*	Basis of capacity figures		Total
	2 or 3 shifts†	1 shift	
		Number of industries	
Over 150	1	4	5
Over 100, not over 150	7	16	23
Over 90, not over 100	4	7	11
Over 80, not over 90	7	10	17
Over 70, not over 80	4	6	10
Over 60, not over 70	—	15	15
Over 50, not over 60	—	10	10
Over 40, not over 50	2	15	17
Over 0, not over 40	2	11	13
Total	27	94	121

* It is assumed that plants work 300 days in the year, or 330 in some of the three-shift industries.

† Including some industries on continuous operations, with allowance for shut-downs for normal repairs and maintenance.

Source: *Monthly Statistics of the Production of Selected Industries of India.*

TABLE 2

EXPLANATION OF SOME OF THE FIGURES IN THE TEXT

	1960–61 estimated	1971–72 assumed	Increase	Per cent per annum
National income, Rs. crores	13,700	24,700	11,000	5·5
Imports, Rs. crores	1,080	1,400	320	2·4
Imports, per cent of 1	7·9	5·7	2·9	—
Exports, Rs. crores	640	1,500	860	8
Exports, per cent of 1	4·7	6·1	7·8	—

Year	National income (current price) Rs. crores	† Imports c.i.f. Rs. crores	Per cent of National income	† Exports f.o.b. Rs. crores	Per cent of National income
1951–52	9,970	962·9	9·7	730·1	7·3
1952–53	9,820	633·0	6·4	601·9	6·1
1953–54	10,480	591·8	5·6	539·7	5·1
1954–55	9,610	683·8	7·1	596·6	6·2
1955–56	9,980	761·4	7·6	640·2	6·4
Average 1st Plan	9,972	726·6	7·3	621·7	6·2
1956–57	11,310	1099·5	9·7	635·2	5·6
1957–58	11,400	1233·6	10·8	594·1	5·2
1958–59	12,470	1029·6	8·25	575·9	4·6
1959–60	13,000*	923·7	7·1*	623·3	4·8
1960–61	13,700*	1080*	7·9*	640*	4·7*
Average 2nd Plan	12,376*	1073·3*	8·7*	613·7*	5·0*

* Estimated.
† Balance of Payments basis (E.D.).

TABLE 3

FAIR EX-WORKS PRICE AS PER CENT OF C.I.F. IMPORT PRICE EXCLUDING DUTY, FOR 63 MANUFACTURES*

	No. of items	Per cent of Total	Per cent Cumulative
60 per cent and under 70 per cent	1	2	2
70 per cent and under 80 per cent	7	11	13
80 per cent and under 90 per cent	8	13	26
90 per cent and under 100 per cent	7	11	37
100 per cent and under 110 per cent	5	8	45
110 per cent and under 120 per cent	7	11	56
120 per cent and under 130 per cent	6	10	66
130 per cent and under 140 per cent	5	8	74
140 per cent and under 150 per cent	3	5	79
150 per cent and under 200 per cent	8	13	92
200 per cent and over	5	8	100
	63	100	

* See Table 4 for details.

TABLE 4

FAIR EX-WORKS PRICE AS PER CENT OF C.I.F. IMPORT PRICE EXCLUDING DUTY*

(BASED ON REPORTS OF TARIFF COMMISSION)

		Year of Tariff Commission's Report
Under 70 per cent	Cotton belting	1957
70 per cent and under 80 per cent	Diesel fuel injection equipment— pump Kirlosker	1959
	Transformers 750 kVA.	1960
	Fluted rollers	1960
	Sewing machines	1954
	Oil pressure lamps	1957
	Plastic shirt buttons	1959
	Sodium bichromate	1958
80 per cent and under 90 per cent	Automobile leaf springs	1959
	Piston rings	1960
	Automobile hand tyre inflator (pump)	1960
	Wood screws	1960
	Machine screws ¼ in. × 2 in.†	1959
	Aluminium circles	1960
	Phenol formaldehyde moulding powder‡	1959
	Potassium bichromate	1958
90 per cent and under 100 per cent	Hair belting	1959
	Aluminium sheets	1960
	Brass sheets	1959
	Bare copper conductors	1960
	Bleaching powder	1958
	Calcium lactate	1960
	Plastic bush coat buttons	1959
100 per cent and under 110 per cent	Electric motors (squirrel cage) 3 and 10 h.p.	1958
	ACSR conductors 30/7/0·083 in.	1960
	Oleic acid	1959
	Tea-chest plywood	1960
	Pears in syrup	1957
110 per cent and under 120 per cent	Transformers 3,000 kVA.	1960
	Aluminium ingots	1960
	Copper sheets	1959
	ACSR conductors 6/1/0·83 in.	1960
	Hydroquinone	1959
	Plastic pant buttons	1959
	Dry cells§	1953

TABLE 4
(CONTINUED)

		Year of Tariff Commission's Report
120 per cent and under 130 per cent	Piston assembly (Fiat)	1960
	Electric motors (squirrel cage) 50 h.p.	1958
	Transformers 25 kVA.	1960
	Automatic looms	1960
	Grinding wheels	1959
	Stearic acid	1959
130 per cent and under 140 per cent	Spinning ring frames	1960
	Copper tubes	1959
	Brass tubes	1959
	ACSR conductors 7/0·1379 in.	1960
	Caustic soda	1958
140 per cent and under 150 per cent	Acid dyes	1954
	Commercial plywood	1960
	Raspberry jam	1957
150 per cent and under 200 per cent	Diesel fuel injection equipment— Nozzle holders Kirlosker	1959
	Automobile sparking plugs	1960
	Bicycles‖	1960
	Machine screws $\frac{3}{16}$ in. × $\frac{1}{2}$ in.†	1959
	Zinc sheets	1959
	Calcium carbide	1958
	Direct dyes	1954
	Sheet glass	1960
200 per cent and over	Ball bearings	1960
	Ball bearing adapter	1960
	Soda ash	1958
	Congo red dyes	1954
	Sulphur black dyes	1954

* The 'fair ex-works price' is a slightly smaller percentage of the landed cost, ex duty.

† Compared with imports from Japan. If a comparison is made with imports from Sweden, the fair ex-works price is less than 80 per cent of the c.i.f. price for machine screws of $\frac{1}{4}$ in. × 2 in., and less than 110 per cent for screws of $\frac{3}{16}$ in. × $\frac{1}{2}$ in..

‡ Exclusive of duty on phenol formaldehyde and hexamine.

§ Compared with imports from Hong Kong. If comparison is made with imports from the US, the fair ex-works price is less than 10 per cent of the c.i.f.

‖ Lowest Indian price compared with prices of imports from Japan. British bicycles are more expensive.

INDEX

213